T0191320

DB2 9
for Developers

DB2 9
for Developers

Philip K. Gunning

MC Press Online, LP
Lewisville, TX 75077

DB2 9 for Developers
Philip K. Gunning

First Edition

First Printing—January 2008

© 2008 Philip K. Gunning. All rights reserved.

Every attempt has been made to provide correct information. However, the publisher and the author do not guarantee the accuracy of the book and do not assume responsibility for information included in or omitted from it.

The following terms are trademarks or registered trademarks of International Business Machines Corporation in the United States, other countries, or both: DB2, Lotus, Tivoli, WebSphere, Rational, IBM, the IBM logo, and IBM Press. Java and all Java-based trademarks are trademarks of Sun Microsystems, Inc. in the United States, other countries, or both. Microsoft, Windows, Windows NT, and the Windows logo are trademarks of the Microsoft Corporation in the United States, other countries, or both. Linux is a registered trademark of Linus Torvalds. Intel, Intel Inside (logo), MMX, and Pentium are trademarks of Intel Corporation in the United States, other countries, or both. OSF/1 and UNIX are registered trademarks and The Open Group is a trademark of the The Open Group in the United States and other countries. Other company, product, or service names mentioned herein may be trademarks or service marks their respective owners.

Printed in Canada. All rights reserved. This publication is protected by copyright, and permission mut be obtained from the publisher prior to any prohibited reproduction, storage in a retrieval system, or transmission in any form or by any means, electronic, mechanical, photocopying, recording, or likewise.

MC Press offers excellent discounts on this book when ordered in quantity for bulk purchases or special sales, which may include custom covers and content particular to your business, training goals, marketing focus, and branding interest.

For information regarding permissions or special orders, please contact:
    MC Press
    Corporate Offices
    125 N. Woodland Trail
    Lewisville, TX 75077 USA

For information regarding sales and/or customer service, please contact:
    MC Press
    P.O. Box 4300
    Big Sandy, TX 75755-4300 USA

ISBN: 978-158347-071-9

This book is dedicated to my wife Cindy
and daughters Paula and Katie,
and I can't forget Sandy.

Acknowledgments

This is my fourth book on DB2, and just when I thought I had learned just about everything about DB2, the IBM Toronto Lab came up with a bunch of power-packed new features in DB2 9. You will learn about these great new features, such as compression, table partitioning, self-tuning memory manager and more in this book. IBM has done a great job in providing features that enable DB2 to achieve high levels of continuous up-time. In fact, many of my clients have kept instances up for months without a restart.

Just as continuous process improvement is so dear to me, I hope this book helps you to learn just one more thing about DB2 in your continuous journey to learn as much as you can about DB2. And as you know, there is much more to come in DB2 9 Viper II and subsequent releases.

As I write these acknowledgments, I will soon be heading out for 5 continuous weeks of DB2 consulting. To all you road warriors out there, I hope this book finds a spot in your laptop bag.

I would like to thank Susan Visser from the IBM Toronto Lab for her support and assistance in getting this book done and published. Thanks to John Hornibrook, IBM Toronto Lab for reviewing Chapter 9. And thanks to all my former colleagues, from whom I have always learned as much as I can, and then some!

And finally, I deeply appreciate the support from the following book reviewers who hung in there through thick and thin:

Denis Vasconcelos, IBM Brazil

Al Shazly, IBM

Stay tuned,

Philip K. Gunning
Sinking Spring, Pennsylvania

Contents

Foreword

DB2, formally called DATABASE 2, was born on MVS in 1983. In 1987, DB2 arrived on the Personal Computer as the Database Manager in OS/2 1.3 Extended Edition; a year later, it emerged as SQL/400 for IBM's new AS/400 server. By 1992, DB2 had become a standalone product on OS/2 (it now had the name DB2/2), and in 1993, DB2 appeared on AIX. This debut prompted another name change, and DB2/2 became DB2 for Common Servers. New editions of DB2 were introduced on HP-UX and Solaris in 1994, on Windows in 1995, and on Linux in 1999. Along the way, the name changed again, and DB2 for Common Servers became DB2 Universal Database.

DB2 9 is the latest release of IBM's popular data management software for distributed systems (and with this release comes yet another name change.) Like previous versions, DB2 runs on a wide variety of platforms (AIX, HP-UX, Linux, Solaris, Windows, i5/OS, and z/OS), and several editions are available—each of which has been designed to meet a specific business need. Unlike previous versions, which were built solely on Dr. E. F. Codd's relational model and presented data in a simple tabular form that could be accessed through the powerful Structured Query Language (SQL), DB2 9 is the first truly hybrid database system that allows Extensible Markup Language (XML) data to coexist in its hierarchical format alongside other relational data. But learning to deploy DB2 9 databases that take advantage of this new technology can be challenging. And learning to use XQuery—a new query language designed to work uniquely with XML data—can be a daunting task.

This comprehensive text by Phil Gunning does an excellent job of covering the new technology delivered with DB2 9. The book gives the user an in-depth, "under the covers" look at DB2 9's XML data management capabilities. And because the material is presented by one of the industry's leading independent DB2 consultants, it contains practical advice that both DB2 application developers and database administrators will benefit from. In addition to covering everything from XML essentials to tuning and problem determination, Phil shares his experience implementing pureXML-enabled databases and provides tips on tuning a DB2 9 XML hybrid database so it will deliver optimum performance. I'm sure you'll find this book both a joy to read and a tool you can't afford to be without in your quest to become a developer or DBA who is comfortable working with both relational and XML data stored in a DB2 database.

Roger E. Sanders
Certified Advanced Database Administrator, DB2 9 for Linux, UNIX, and Windows
Author of 14 books on DB2 and a regular columnist for DB2 Magazine

December 2007

1

DB2 9 Product Overview

DB2 9 for Linux, UNIX, and Windows (LUW) comes in several *editions*, or product offerings. IBM developed these different editions to meet the needs of small, medium, and large businesses. There are offerings for developers, workgroups/departments, and enterprises, as well as for embedded applications and very large databases.

Foremost among the enhancements in DB2 9 is the introduction of native support for XML data across the entire DB2 product line. Performance and scalability enhancements are also integrated into all editions, giving developers, database administrators (DBAs), and companies added flexibility in choosing the right DB2 solution.

In this chapter, we review the key features and benefits of each edition. A familiarity with the different offerings will help you choose or recommend the DB2 product that best meets your business objectives. In Chapter 2, we'll look more closely at the new features and enhancements available in DB2 9.

DB2 Express-C

DB2 Express-C is a no-charge, entry-level, hybrid data server available via Web download or on the DB2 Discovery Kit CD. This DB2 product is especially suited for application developers and can be used with the Starter Toolkit for DB2 Ruby on Rails and the enhanced DB2 PHP Data Object (PDO) for PHP5. DB2 Express-C is available for the following platforms.

Operating system	Platforms
Microsoft Windows 32-bit	AMD and Intel (x86), Windows Vista
	AMD and Intel (x86), Windows XP Home
Microsoft Windows 64-bit	AMD and Intel EM64T systems (x86-64)
Linux 32-bit	32-bit AMD and Intel (x86), 2.6 kernel
Linux 64-bit	AMD and Intel EM64T systems (x86-64), 2.6 kernel; Power (IBM System i and System p) systems

You can download DB2 Express-C at *http://www-306.ibm.com/software/data/ db2/express/download.html*. The download page also provides a link to the DB2 Express-C online community.

DB2 Express

IBM designed the DB2 Express Edition to be embedded in applications that require a relational database. By packaging the database with the application, independent software vendors (ISVs) can make it easier for their customers to install vendor software packages that contain an integrated DB2 database. DB2 Express 9 contains all core DB2 capabilities and is easy to install and use. It provides all the data integrity, backup, and recovery capabilities usually found in an industrial-strength database.

DB2 Express makes maximum use of DB2 autonomics (self-management) and workload management. It provides tight integration with application development tools and enables developers to construct enterprise applications quickly. All these capabilities make DB2 Express ideal for ISVs and for small and medium businesses (SMBs).

DB2 Express Edition does not include some advanced features of DB2 9:

- DB2 High Availability Feature
  - » High Availability Disaster Recovery (HADR)
  - » Online Reorganization
  - » IBM Tivoli System Automation for Multiplatforms (SAMP)
- DB2 Performance Optimization Feature
  - » Multidimensional Clustering (MDC)
  - » Query Parallelism
- DB2 pureXML Feature
- DB2 Storage Optimization Feature
  - » Backup Compression
  - » Row Compression
- DB2 Workload Management Feature
  - » Connection Concentrator
  - » Query Patroller (QP)
  - » DB2 Governor
- IBM Homogeneous Federation Feature

Other than the Storage Optimization Feature, all these features are available as additional priced options for DB2 Express.

DB2 Workgroup Server Edition

DB2 Workgroup Server Edition (WSE) is designed for small- to medium-volume online transaction processing (OLTP) and Web-based databases. This widely used edition helps companies minimize software license costs, keeping them in line with business and data requirements. IBM offers DB2 WSE on a per-processor or a per-authorized-user model. You can use this edition on servers with up to four processors and 16 GB of memory.

Many of my clients have started out using WSE for medium-volume OLTP and Web databases. This edition is an excellent entry point for companies that are getting started with DB2 or are porting to DB2 from other databases. Some of my clients have stayed on WSE for several years; others have moved to DB2 Enterprise Server Edition (ESE, described later) as they required additional capability.

When the time comes, moving from WSE to ESE is easy. Best of all, you can purchase many enterprise features for WSE as your processing requirements evolve. The following features are available as additional priced options for DB2 WSE (as well as for DB2 Express):

- DB2 High Availability Feature
- DB2 Performance Optimization Feature
- DB2 pureXML Feature
- DB2 Workload Management Feature
- IBM Homogeneous Federation Feature

DB2 Personal Edition

DB2 Personal Edition (PE) is available for single-user environments. This fully functional DB2 product features built-in replication and is ideal for desktop deployments and occasionally connected laptop users. DB2 PE can be managed remotely, providing an advantage for companies that need to support a database at a remote location. A typical deployment of DB2 PE might be as part of a sales force automation application or a customized insurance agent solution.

The following features and capabilities are not included in DB2 PE:

- HADR
- Online Reorganization
- DB2 Performance Optimization Feature

- DB2 pureXML Feature
- DB2 Workload Management Feature
- Row Compression
- IBM Homogeneous Federation Feature

DB2 Enterprise Server Edition

DB2 Enterprise Server Edition (ESE) is a high-performance, scalable, complete database solution for medium to large businesses. In use today by Fortune 500 companies worldwide, DB2 ESE can be deployed on servers containing from one to hundreds of processors. It is ideal for data warehouses, OLTP systems, and Web applications and for enterprise-wide database solutions such as customer relationship management (CRM), enterprise resource planning (ERP), business intelligence (BI), and supply chain management (SCM). If you know that your business requirements are going to demand more than four CPUs or will need access to more that 16 GB of memory, ESE is the entry point for you.

In a typical deployment, DB2 ESE might function as the back-end database to an e-commerce site, as an OLTP database in support of teller or branch operations, as a mixed hybrid database in an OLTP or complex query environment, or as a large data warehouse using the Database Partitioning Feature (DPF) option. DB2 ESE serves business-critical applications that require top performance and high availability in continuous-operation environments.

DB2 ESE is available on a per-user or a per-processor pricing model and includes the following capabilities:

- Connection Concentrator
- DB2 Governor
- HADR
- IBM Tivoli SAMP

- Materialized Query Tables
- Multidimensional Clustering
- Online Reorganization
- Query Parallelism
- Table Partitioning (new in DB2 9)
- DB2 Advanced Access Control Feature
- DB2 Database Partitioning Feature
- DB2 Geodetic Management Feature
- DB2 pureXML Feature
- DB2 Storage Optimization Feature
- Row Compression
- Real-Time Insight

Database Enterprise Developer Edition

Database Enterprise Developer Edition is a low-cost DB2 solution that developers can use to prototype and construct applications for deployment on a wide variety of IBM Information Management platforms. This edition includes all the DB2 9 features, enabling developers to develop applications using the full breadth of new DB2 capabilities, and comes with the following software:

- DB2 WSE
- DB2 ESE
- Informix Dynamic Server (IDS) Enterprise Edition
- Cloudscape
- DB2 Connect Unlimited Edition for zSeries

Note: All DB2 9 products include the DB2 Net Search Extender and the DB2 Spatial Extender.

DB2 Developer Workbench

A key component of every edition of DB2 for LUW is DB2 Developer Workbench, a feature-rich application development tool that replaces the former DB2 Development Center. Based on the Eclipse framework, Developer Workbench is shipped in the same media pack as DB2 9 but requires a separate install. As with most IBM development software, you can also download Developer Workbench from the Web.

The workbench is the primary interface for developing applications for DB2 9, and it serves as a common interface for working with DB2 on System i and z/OS systems. You can also use the workbench with Apache Derby and IBM Cloudscape.

Developer Workbench contains many features that increase developer productivity. Using the workbench, you can

- browse, create, and edit database objects
- edit tables and columns
- migrate previous Development Center projects
- collaborate with other developers
- copy, move, and extract data
- build SQL and XQuery statements
- develop SQL, SQLJ, and XML applications
- develop and deploy stored procedures and user-defined functions

IBM provides extensive information and tutorials to help developers learn and use Developer Workbench so they can easily build and deploy DB2 applications.

Information Management Products

Although not part of DB2, three WebSphere products provide information integration, replication, and event publishing support for DB2 9 databases:

WebSphere Federation Server, WebSphere Replication Server, and
WebSphere Data Event Publisher.

WebSphere Federation Server

WebSphere Federation Server V9.1 provides seamless access to enterprise
information, making it appear as though the data originates from a single
source. This offering provides the following capabilities:

- Federated two-phase commit (which enables the updating of multiple
  distributed data sources simultaneously)
- A common view of data
- The ability to use federated stored procedures in a federated query

WebSphere Replication Server

WebSphere Replication Server V9.1 provides high-volume DB2 SQL and
queue-based replication (Q-Replication) for the DB2 9 WSE and ESE offerings.
Version 9.1 offers increased scalability and performance over previous releases.
Administration has been improved, and the replication server features additional
auditing and monitoring capability. Supported replication sources and targets
include DB2, Informix Dynamic Server, Microsoft SQL Server, Oracle, Sybase
Adaptive Server Enterprises, and Sybase SQL Server. Informix Extended
Parallel Server and Teradata are supported as replication targets.

WebSphere Data Event Publisher

WebSphere Data Event Publisher V9.1 enables business integration by
publishing changed data events that can feed updated data into critical
applications such as master data management and data warehousing.

Summary

DB2 9's unparalleled support for XML data, and its integration of this support into the entire DB2 product line, enables companies to reach new levels of information integration. This chapter highlighted the benefits and features of each DB2 9 edition, giving you the background you need to choose the right solution for your business.

2

DB2 9 Enhancements

DB2 9 is a hybrid relational and XML data server that provides the
ability to store both relational and XML data. DB2 is the first database
to provide integrated support for a native XML data type, and it supports
both SQL and XQuery using the same optimizer and database engine. Many
in the database industry are comparing the significance of this fundamental
change with the invention of the relational database.

XML has become the interchange and document format of choice across
a broad range of industries. Until now, however, XML hasn't been tightly
integrated into relational databases. DB2 9 introduces a new native XML
data store that is fully integrated in the DB2 database engine, letting you
access and manage XML data by leveraging DB2 functionality. DB2 9 lets
you use SQL and XQuery in the same query, and it supports the indexing
of XML data to enable rapid retrieval of XML documents.

> **Note:** Starting with DB2 9, IBM uses the term "data server" to describe its database product. A data server provides software services for the secure and efficient management of structured information. DB2 9 is a hybrid relational and XML data server.

This chapter highlights the new features in DB2 9. Subsequent chapters provide additional implementation details and examples. Our discussion here breaks down the enhancements into the following categories:

- Native XML data store support
- Application development enhancements
    - » Enhanced .NET integration
    - » Developer Workbench
    - » Java Database Connectivity (JDBC)
- Performance and scalability enhancements
    - » Row compression
    - » Table partitioning
    - » Materialized query tables (MQTs)
    - » Large record identifiers
    - » Statistical views
    - » Faster data loading capabilities
- Manageability enhancements
    - » ALTER TABLE statement
    - » Improved maintenance policies
    - » Database administration
- Installation and fix pack enhancements
- Backup and recovery enhancements
- Security enhancements
- Problem determination and troubleshooting enhancements

Native XML Data Store Support

IBM has created a "paradigm shift" with the invention of the native XML data store. While other relational databases require XML data to be shredded or parsed to enable storage in a single column or over multiple columns, DB2 9 is unique in that it stores XML data using a native XML data type. This native type lets you store well-formed XML documents in their hierarchical forms within columns of a table.

The native XML data type also enables DB2 to store and retrieve XML data without any of the overhead associated with shredding. DB2 9 stores XML data in a hierarchical format using the XPath Data Model (XDM), and new DB2 9 XML index structures enable rapid retrieval of XML data. The native XML data type also preserves digital signatures.

IBM has integrated support for the XQuery language tightly into the hybrid engine. In DB2 9, you can invoke XQuery directly by calling XML functions or invoke it indirectly from inside an SQL query.

New tools can help you develop XML/SQL queries without having to be an expert on XQuery syntax. DB2 9 Developer Workbench (which I introduced in the previous chapter) is a new development environment based on the Eclipse framework. It contains support for building XML functions using the XML data type and for registering XML schema. XQuery Builder, part of Developer Workbench, is a graphical interface that enables you to create and test XML queries without the need to understand the XQuery language.

IBM has enhanced the DB2 Control Center in DB2 9 to support the new DB2 9 XML data types, letting you administer both relational and XML data from the Control Center. Enhanced DB2 Explain and Visual Explain facilities support SQL/XML functions and XQuery statements and enable rapid development and tuning of SQL/XML queries.

Application Development Enhancements

DB2 9 adds support for BINARY, VARBINARY, and DECFLOAT data types, providing increased application support and flexibility. The DB2 Call Level Interface (CLI) and DB2 .NET Data Provider now support these types as well.

In keeping with the tight integration within the DB2 family of products, the DB2 9 CLI, IBM DB2 Driver for JDBC, and SQLJ now support making trusted connections to DB2 V9.1 for z/OS. A trusted connection can acquire a special set of privileges that are unavailable to it outside the trusted context.

The DB2 Command Line Processor (CLP)'s 64 K limit for SQL statements has been removed. The new limit of 2 MB provides CLP compatibility with other DB2 tools.

Also new in DB2 9 is support for the TRIM scalar function, which lets you remove blanks or occurrences of a specified character from the end or beginning of a string expression.

Enhanced .NET Integration

The DB2 9 .NET Data Provider supports the Microsoft .NET Framework V2.0. Additional new features enable you to develop powerful .NET applications. With support for the System.Data.Common base classes, you can develop a generic .NET database application without referencing any data-provider-specific classes. This support enables use of the generic DB2Connection class from the DB2 .NET Data Provider. The provider supports use of the common base classes declared in the System.Data. Common namespace.

New DB2Types classes provide a way to represent DB2 database column values as individual nullable objects. You can also use these classes as parameters for Common Language Routine (CLR) stored procedures or user-defined functions. The new classes belong to the IBM.Data.DB2Types namespace.

The new DB2 9 .NET Data Provider contains a DB2ResultSet class that supports scrollable and updatable result sets. Also included is a new data paging capability that provides a method to fetch a specific set of rows and a bulk data copy facility that uses the DB2BulkCopy, DB2CopyColumnMapping, and DB2CopyColumnMappingCollection classes.

Last, a new DB2DataAdapter property, UpdateBatchSize, enables applications to determine the number of SQL statements to collect before issuing the statements as a batch to the DB2 9 database.

DB2 Developer Workbench

In DB2 9, the new DB2 Developer Workbench replaces the former DB2 Development Center. An integrated development environment (IDE) based on the Eclipse framework, Developer Workbench enables you to rapidly develop, test, and deploy SQL and XQuery applications, user-defined functions, and stored procedures. Developer Workbench provides the following new abilities:

- Compare and make changes between routines
- Deploy and create routines for DB2 for Linux, UNIX, and Windows databases and for DB2 for z/OS
- Perform a binary deploy of SQL or Java stored procedures to DB2 for z/OS 8 or later
- Launch DB2 Visual Explain for DB2 9 and DB2 for z/OS platforms
- Export data to a file that can then be used to load a table

In addition to these capabilities, Developer Workbench includes the following:

- Complete XML support for building and deploying XML functions and XQueries, plus an integrated XQuery builder
- Enhanced support for DB2 V9.1 for z/OS
- Support for developing SQLJ applications
- A built-in table editor

- An integrated stored procedure debugger for SQL and Java stored procedures
- Support for Derby Java stored procedures
- Support for migrating existing Development Center projects

Chapter 5 covers Developer Workbench in detail.

JDBC Enhancements

The IBM DB2 Driver for JDBC has been significantly enhanced in DB2 9 and is fully compliant with the JDBC 3.0 specification. Highlights of the JDBC enhancements are as follows:

- Full support for the new DB2 9 XML data type
- New DB2-only methods for performing XML schema registration and trusted connections to DB2 V9.1 for z/OS
- New RETURN DATA UNTIL clause enhancements with tolerance for +100 SQLCODEs
- Support for heterogeneous connection pooling and connection reuse
- Secure Sockets Layer (SSL) support that enables applications with the JDBC driver SSLCONNECTION property set to obtain a connection using an SSL socket
- A new sendDataAsIs property that does not require the conversion of application data types to column data types
- Enhanced support for connection to DB2 for z/OS
- Support for using progressive streaming for retrieval of large objects (LOBs) and XML data
- Support for the new DB2 for z/OS data types BINARY, VARBINARY, and DECFLOAT

Performance and Scalability Enhancements

Several IBM labs have put significant time and effort into improving the already stellar performance of DB2 products. As a result, DB2 9 is packed with feature-rich performance enhancements, which the following paragraphs summarize.

Row Compression

Row compression uses a variation of the Lempel-Ziv compression algorithm. By enabling more rows to fit on a page, row compression can allow more efficient use of buffer pools and save substantial disk space. In addition, it reduces disk and log I/O (because rows remain compressed in the log and buffer pool).

Table Partitioning

Table partitioning is similar in concept to range partitioning, a feature previously available on DB2 for z/OS. By enabling tables to be divided across multiple table objects, table partitioning permits increased table sizes, a capability that is paramount in today's "information as a server" age. In addition, the DB2 optimizer can limit table access to the partition of interest, thereby improving performance. Partitions can be rolled in or rolled out as needed, and maintenance can be performed at the partition level.

Materialized Query Table Enhancements

Explain output has been enhanced in DB2 9 and now indicates when the optimizer considered but did not choose a materialized query table. The explain output includes a description as to why the MQT wasn't chosen (whether due to cost or no match). Performance is improved for queries that insert, update, or delete data in a Database Partitioning Feature (DPF) environment and for those that have expressions that are equivalent, but not identical, to those in the MQT definition.

Better refresh times are possible through improved maintenance when a logical hierarchy of MQTs is involved. In this case, DB2 refreshes MQTs at the base of the hierarchy first and then applies those results to higher MQTs in the hierarchy.

Larger Record Identifiers

Large record identifiers (RIDs) permit more data pages per object and more records per page in DB2 9. This enhancement can reduce disk I/O and improve the performance of join operations.

Statistical Views

Statistical views provide the capability to collect statistics about views. With this information, access plans can be improved for queries that overlap the view definition. Statistical views also give the optimizer accurate statistics for estimating cardinality.

Faster Data Loading Capabilities

A new user exit option, SOURCEUSEREXIT, lets DBAs input data into the LOAD utility using a customized script or executable. In addition, index keys have been expanded to support up to 64 columns and a size up to 8 K.

Manageability Enhancements

DB2 9 contains many new features that make managing the data server easier for DBAs and application developers alike. These features also help to improve the availability of DB2 9 in a robust 24x7 environment.

Alter Table Statement

DB2 9 offers an enhanced ability to alter tables without requiring a drop and re-create. This capability will significantly add to the availability of DB2 9 databases.

Improved Maintenance Policies

New maintenance policies for automatic table and index reorganization options have been incorporated into the Control Center.

Database Administration

A new capability to copy database schemas between instances and databases enables enhanced database administration. SQL routines and convenience views provide an easy way to monitor and administer DB2 9 databases.

New autonomic database configuration parameters are enabled by default. Simplified database memory management is provided via the new Self Tuning Memory Manager (STMM), which is enabled by default for newly created DB2 databases. Internal IBM tests have shown that the STMM can do in a few hours what it would take a DBA weeks or months to accomplish.

Installation and Fix Pack Enhancements

Autonomic database configuration and maintenance parameters are now enabled by default for databases newly created in DB2 9. Automatic statistics and table maintenance are enabled by default. Automatic database storage is now the default, and support has been extended to DPF databases.

DB2 9 lifts the longstanding restriction against installing more than one copy of DB2 on Windows. You can now install multiple DB2 versions and fix packs on the same server. Additional enhancements include the following:

- More flexible and efficient management of product licenses
- New response-file keywords that let IT staff install and set up DB2 products without involving end users
- The ability, using the Windows elevated privilege feature, to install DB2 9 on Windows without having to be an administrator

Backup and Recovery Enhancements

DB2 9 lets you restart interrupted recovery operations, saving time during database recovery. The ability to generate redirected restore scripts from backup images is provided, as is the ability to rebuild databases from tablespace-level backups. The latter capability, a longstanding user requirement, enables more flexible recovery in environments where either time or resources make full or incremental database backups infeasible. With very large database environments now the norm, the ability to restore from tablespace-level backups offers improved availability and business flexibility.

Security Enhancements

DB2 9 offers fine granularity for access control at the row and column level via label-based access control (LBAC). A new security administrator authority level (SECADM) enables centralized security administration of DB2 9 database objects. (A similar capability has been available on DB2 for z/OS for quite some time.)

The CREATE DATABASE command provides a new RESTRICT option that permits greater control over the granting of database permissions.

Problem Determination and Troubleshooting Enhancements

DB2 9 provides increased control over the set of diagnostic information produced when the database manager encounters a fatal or severe error. The db2cos script now is run automatically when fatal or severe errors occur. This script contains db2pd commands that collect information. DBAs or IBM support personnel can use the file created by the script to troubleshoot the cause of the problems.

The db2trc (trace) command now includes the ability to set trace masks, letting you limit the operations traced by the trace facility. Trace masks are provided by DB2 Support to help customers resolve problems.

Summary

This chapter introduced the key new features and enhancements in DB2 9, including the XML data type and other DB2 9 data server enhancements. You can use this information to determine which features apply to your company and be cognizant of how they can help your company better meet business objectives.

3

XML Evolution and Revolution

This chapter describes the origin and evolution of Extensible Markup Language (XML) and discusses the reasoning behind the need for a hybrid DB2 data server and native XML data type. We'll review some fundamental XML terminology that is essential for understanding, implementing, and supporting DB2 9 XML implementations. You'll also get an overview of the basic XML components and learn how XML, XPath, XQuery, and the native DB2 XML data type are integrated into DB2 9.

XML Introduction and Historical Perspective

I first became interested in XML in 1998. I learned of the language by reading journals and associated literature. Through that and my own experiences, I realized XML had huge capabilities for improving and streamlining data interchange.

My interest in data interchange goes back to my days as a project leader at a large mutual fund company. There, I was responsible for obtaining a daily feed from NASDAQ and other sources and reformatting the data into a CICS/DB2/VSAM application for further processing. Later, as a project leader for DB2 Database Administration, I led a team of DBAs responsible for supporting an electronic data interchange (EDI) application for suppliers to a large department-store chain. We often had problems with the standard EDI formats. I always thought there should be an easier way to do data interchange. You'll see from a DB2 9 perspective that XML is the way!

SGML, HTML, and XML

The Worldwide Web Consortium (W3C) published the XML 1.0 specification in 1996. Started by Tim Berners-Lee while he was a researcher at the Organisation Européenne pour la Recherche Nucléaire (CERN) laboratory in Switzerland, the W3C is an Internet standards organization with hundreds of member organizations representing many of the top software companies in the world. The W3C's purpose is to promulgate Web specifications and standards. Other standards handled by this organization include XQuery and XPath, which we'll discuss in later chapters.

Key to the enablement of the World Wide Web were two additional specifications upon which XML is based: Hypertext Markup Language (HTML) and its predecessor, Standard Generalized Markup Language (SGML). (Of course, we owe most of the impetus for HTML and XML to Vint Cerf and Bob Kahn, co-inventors of the Internet—without which we'd have no need for XML.)

SGML, which IBM invented in 1969, became an International Standards Organization (ISO) standard in 1986. Used primarily as a document markup language in pre-Internet days, SGML was the natural choice upon which Internet pioneers chose to build a markup language for the Web.

HTML, a markup language understood by Web browsers and Web servers, was initially the de facto language of the Web and Web sites. Used to display information via a Web browser, the HTML language is based on the use of *tags* that describe the attributes of the data (e.g., fields, images) to be displayed in a Web page.

For example, using HTML, I could highlight the name of my company on my home page as follows:

```
Welcome to <b> Gunning Technology Solutions, LLC </b>
```

In this example, the specified text would appear like this in a Web page:

```
Welcome to Gunning Technwology Solutions, LLC
```

The <b> tag causes the company name to appear in bold.

HTML is good for describing how data or fields should be formatted and displayed, but you can't use it to give meaning to an individual field, and the format applies only to the specific Web page that contains the field. In addition—and most important—you can't use HTML pages to exchange data between applications. That's because there is no way to link HTML fields or documents together and no industry standard to support such linking. If I wanted to change the name of my company, for example, I'd need to change every Web page where that name appears. With XML, in addition to being able to describe the layout, I can make the change in one location and have it applied to all documents. The XML specification provides for a way to know about *all* company names, not just one specific one. And XML doesn't just format the data for display; it supplies syntax and specifications not only to describe but also to give meaning to a particular field or piece of data. These capabilities make XML much more powerful than HTML.

XML builds on HTML and is well-structured based on specifications published by the W3C organization. The language provides mechanisms for giving meaning to a specific instance of a data field or piece of data. Returning to our HTML example, we humans must decode (interpret) the company name displayed in bold font; we have no other way to understand the definition of the company name. With XML, developers can use XML Document Type Definitions (DTDs) or XML Schemas to give meaning to the data.

XML was originally implemented to support business-to-business (B2B) applications using relational databases. XML is a subset of SGML, but you can really think of it as a superset because XML enables widespread adoption and use through the use of user-defined markup tags.

DTDs, a construct that XML inherits from SGML, provide meaning to instances of XML elements and attributes. You can think of DTDs as similar to the record definitions and structures used in COBOL or to variables in C or Java. They provide for meaning and define the data type.

> **Note:**   DTDs provide a way to develop XML documents for just about any application because the author of the document defines markup tags.

A DTD is a document that describes XML instances, elements, attributes, and text and provides a way to validate XML documents. DTDs define how individual XML instances are constructed. They describe which XML elements are allowed, the attributes of those elements, and how the different elements fit together to form a valid piece of XML. XML applications can use DTDs to validate individual XML instances. An instance is usually the same as an instance of an XML document, but it can be a single XML document made up of several concatenated XML documents. Developers can develop their own markup tags and DTDs and are no longer dependent on proprietary formats.

DTDs can be self-contained in the XML to be validated, or they can be registered with an XML Schema Repository (XSR). You'll see in Chapter 4 that DB2 9 provides a built-in XSR.

Components of XML

Before delving into the details of DB2 9 native XML integration, let's take a closer look at just what XML is and how it differs from relational data.

XML is *hierarchical* in nature and is best represented as a tree data structure. This point is important because the relational database model requires data to be stored in tables, as rows consisting of columns or attributes.

A table is, for the most part, a flat structure (not considering relationships between tables or foreign keys). In contrast, XML documents are stored as trees, with a *root* node and *child* nodes. All child nodes are derived from the root. This tree structure preserves the structure of documents because documents contain a sequence of *elements*. Elements are similar to columns in a relational table, but they don't have all the rules associated with relational data.

However, there are rules for XML documents. These rules are defined by the W3C and the XML 1.0 specification, as previously indicated. Specifically, an XML document (also known as an XML *instance* because each document is an instance of the XPath Data Model, or XDM) can consist of elements, attributes, and text.

Listing 3.1 shows a sample XML document that describes an XML book instance.

```
<book>
<title>DB2 9 for Developers</title>
<identifier isbn="123456"></identifier>
<chapter>XML Evolution and Revolution
<para>The Beginning</para>
<para>The Evolution</para>
</chapter>
</book>
```

Listing 3.1: Sample XML document

As the figure shows, book is the root element. The elements title, identifier, and chapter are child elements of book, and book is the parent element of these elements. The title, identifier, and chapter elements are siblings because they have the same parent.

The following rules apply to elements:

- Elements have content.
- Elements can have different content types.
- An XML element is everything from (and including) the element's start tag to (and including) the element's end tag.
- Element names can contain letters, numbers, and other characters.
- Element names cannot start with a number or a punctuation character.
- Element names cannot start with "xml," "XML," or "Xml."
- Element names cannot contain spaces.

An element can have element content, mixed content, simple content, or empty content. An element can also have attributes. In the sample code, the book element has element content because it contains other elements. The chapter element has mixed content because it contains both text and other elements. The para element has simple (or text) content because it contains only text. The identifier element has empty content because it carries no information. Last, only the identifier element has attributes; in the example, the attribute identifier isbn has the value "123456".

XML Namespaces

Within an XML document, an *XML namespace* provides a way to uniquely identify an instantiation of an element. In simple terms, declaring an XML namespace is similar to identifying unique fields in a program or specific columns in a database table.

To use unique fields in a program, you must define the fields in the file definition or structure section of an application program. When you reference a particular column in an SQL query, you prefix the column name with the schema or qualifier of the table. Although you might have many tables with the same columns and attributes, the tables have separate schemas and are thus unique, preventing ambiguity or, even worse, incorrect results.

XML namespaces do the same thing for XML that schemas and qualifiers do for relational tables: they tell the XML parser that the elements and attributes are unique within the named or default namespace, which you can specify in an XQuery or in a DTD.

XSLT

Extensible Stylesheet Language Transformations (XSLT) is an XML-based W3C specification that defines the rules for transforming source trees into result trees. A transformation in the XSLT language is expressed as a well-formed XML document. The XPath language uses XSLT when transforming and reordering XML instances. We'll explore XPath in more detail in Chapter 4.

XML-Only Databases

Early adopters in the XML database arena offered databases that worked exclusively with XML. These XML-only databases had no built-in support for SQL or relational databases. They targeted document-centric companies, such as newspaper, book, and magazine publishers. Such organizations typically dealt with large amounts of document-like data that was (and still is) suited for XML use and representation.

The problem with XML-only databases is their inability to interface with other sources of data, such as relational databases, IBM's Information Management System (IMS) hierarchical database, or the massive amount of data still stored on a plethora of proprietary file systems across multiple software and hardware vendors. Of course, the most important data store to interface with is the relational database, which stores the bulk of all data in most companies around the world. The shortcoming is evidenced by the fact that many early XML-only database companies are no longer in business. Some of the prominent XML-only databases available today are Berkeley DB XML (which sits on top of the relational Berkeley DB), MarkLogic Server, Sedna, Timber (University of Michigan), and Xindice (part of the

Apache project and formerly dbXML Core, which was donated to the Apache Software Foundation in 2001).

Although niches exist for XML-only databases, my experience has been that people spend an inordinate amount of time writing feeds to and from disparate systems. You might need an XML-only database if all you want to do is process and store XML data, but this situation is probably the exception rather than the norm.

XML's Emergence As a Data-Interchange Mechanism

Because of the qualities we've discussed thus far, XML has gradually taken over as the data-interchange language of choice. Even though an EDI standard data-interchange format existed, it was still possible for retailers, wholesalers, and suppliers to get out of synchronization—for example, if one company changed formats without coordinating with another or some other change occurred that caused the two to become out of synch. Because of the self-describing nature of the XML markup tags, the XML language takes care of this synchronization problem. Instead of using a separate, often proprietary structure to define the format of the data to be exchanged (with the associated difficulties in keeping the sender (client or supplier) in synch), the XML specification guarantees that the data stream is compliant if it has been validated. This characteristic enhances the exchange of data within and between businesses and enables more efficiencies to be gained.

The exchange of XML data is also enhanced by the hundreds of XML industry schemas now available, such as the Financial Information eXchange XML (FIXML) standard in the financial services industry (*http://www.fixprotocol. org*) and other XML schemas being developed by the OASIS Consortium (*http://www.oasis-open.org*) in association with government and industry organizations. We'll discuss XML schemas, XML namespaces, and XML document validation in more detail in Chapter 4.

Initial XML Relational Database Implementations

Soon after publication of the XML specifications, database vendors quickly recognized XML's importance to data interchange and the management of all kinds of documents. Early support for XML in relational database management systems (RDBMSs) consisted of extensions or enhancements to make XML work with existing database architectures. This support was accomplished primarily through the use of non-native methods, via shredding or storing entire XML documents as character large object (CLOB) data. Shredding, parsing, or decomposing XML documents required significant overhead because the database engine didn't handle XML support natively, relying instead on extensions to the existing relational capability. Although this approach worked adequately for storing and manipulating a small amount of XML data (as compared to relational data), non-native access was unlikely to meet the ever-increasing need to process XML data in medium- to high-volume mixed OLTP environments.

Early XML Support in DB2

First introduced in DB2 Universal Database (UDB) V7.1, DB2 XML support was originally provided via the DB2 XML Extender. The extender provided a way to either store whole XML documents or decompose them using user-defined functions. The extender also permitted users to compose XML documents from existing relational data.

Early DB2 XML support required a Data Access Definition (DAD) file to define how XML documents were mapped to and from a DB2 database (node mapping). DAD files supported two types of node mapping: SQL node mapping and relational database (RDB) node mapping.

SQL node mapping provided mapping instructions in the form of an SQL statement. This type of mapping could be used only to compose new XML documents from existing relational data; you couldn't use it to decompose an XML document into its elements and insert those elements into DB2 tables.

RDB node mapping was based on the XML Path Language (XPath) W3C standard and supported composition and decomposition of XML documents. It used XPath to identify elements, attributes, and text contained inside an XML document, assigning each element, attribute, and text to a column in a DB2 table. You could use XPath to search XML documents that weren't decomposed into table columns.

DB2 XML columns defined as XMLVARCHAR, XMLCLOB, or XMLFILE data types were used to store entire XML documents inside DB2 columns. For frequently accessed XML elements and attributes, DB2 "side" tables could be used. Side tables provided faster access to this frequently accessed data.

Last, the XML Extender provided a set of user-defined functions and stored procedures to manipulate XML columns and to compose and decompose XML documents.

Although the XML Extender provided good support for XML, this non-native method did not supply the full-fledged XML support needed in today's XML-centric computing environment. Based on the convoluted nature of non-native access to relational databases and subsequent inefficiencies, it became evident that a "native" method for storing, processing, and retrieving XML data was required.

DB2 9: The Revolution

Non-native methods are inefficient because with them you can't use indexes to search or retrieve XML data without incurring cost-prohibitive overhead. In addition, because earlier versions of DB2 lacked a native hierarchical storage method, decomposing XML documents tended to cause the documents to lose context as well as the relationships between elements and attributes. But with years of extensive research, development, and improvements in RDBMSs, it made sense to IBM researchers to try to improve the existing RDBMS architecture to support a native XML data type in order to reduce overhead costs and realize all the benefits of an underlying RDBMS architecture. It also made sense to have a central storage access method or layer for storing and retrieving both types of data.

Why have separate storage and access methods for relational and XML data when they are both necessary for accessing, returning, or exchanging business information? After all, part of the problem with EDI was that each and every store or vendor had its own implementation. We want to avoid that with XML, and integrating the storage of both types of data into a single storage engine is a way to accomplish this goal. Remember the old adage, "Let's not reinvent the wheel"? Well, IBM didn't want to reinvent the relational database. Instead, IBM researchers decided take advantage of what IBM did with DB2 and improve on it via XML native integration. And that's what you see in DB2 9. DB2 9 revolutionizes relational database support of XML by providing a combined relational and hybrid data server.

Relational and XML Integration

IBM researchers arrived at the hybrid data server solution in DB2 9 after extensive research and review of empirical data collected over 25 years of relational database experience. Specifically, the scientists based their case for a hybrid DB2 9 data server on the following key factors:

- XML and relational data coexist and complement each other in enterprise solutions.
- A successful XML repository requires much of the same infrastructure that already exists in a relational database management system.
- XML query languages have considerable conceptual and functional overlap with SQL.

New DB2 9 Architecture

The new DB2 9 hybrid data server supports XML via a new DB2 XML native data type. The XML data type provides a first-class data type for tight integration with the DB2 9 databases engine. Figure 3.1 provides an overview of the new DB2 9 XML architecture.

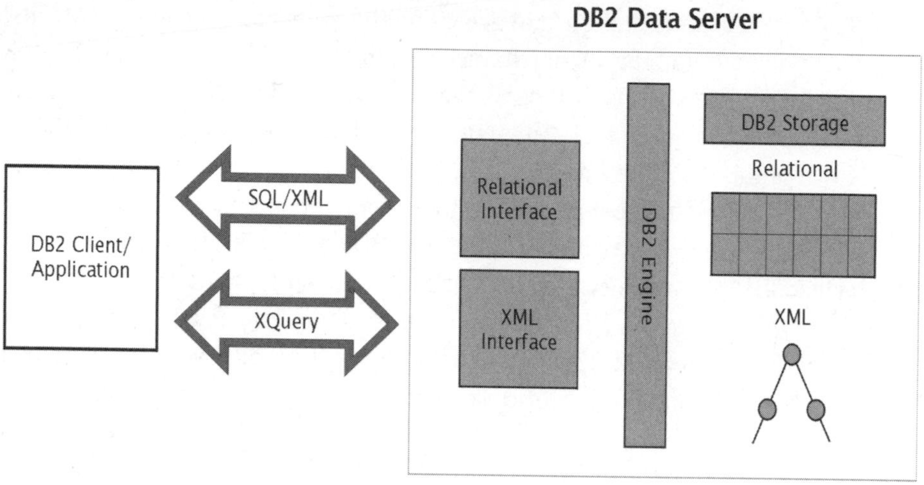

DB2 Data Server

Figure 3.1: Overview of DB2 9 XML architecture

DB2 9 treats both XQuery and SQL as primary query languages. An XML application can use the XML interface via an XQuery expression or can access both XML and relational data via a combination of SQL statements and XQueries, which can be used to combine XML and relational data. DB2 unifies new XML native storage, indexing, and query processing with existing relational storage, indexing, and query processing.

Existing DB2 9 database architecture is used to the maximum extent possible. Because both relational and XML data are accessed and used together fairly often, mechanisms are provided to integrate both. However, because relational and XML data use different storage schemes, two types of data storage are provided.

> **Note:** XML data is hierarchical (tree structure) and consists of structured and semi-structured data, whereas relational data is well-structured data stored in relational tables.

DB2 9 implements XML nodes as annotated trees. Annotated tress provide for direct node lookup, which is essential to providing excellent performance for relational operations (joins) and subdocument lookups (direct-node lookups). We'll discuss direct node lookups further in Chapter 4. There is no change in the way relational data is processed and stored. Figure 3.2 provides an overview of native XML storage in DB2 9.

The combination of native XML storage and traditional relational-database storage provides improved application flexibility and eliminates the high number of person-hours required to integrate disparate data sources. You can look at this as the best of both worlds: XML storage, processing, and retrieval is optimized right along with the time-proven DB2 relational optimization and storage architectures. The bottom line is more efficient and timely development timelines and reduced cost.

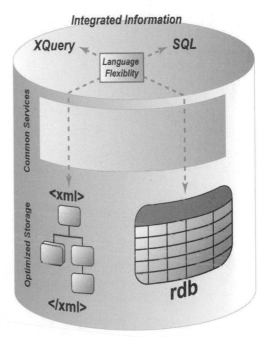

Figure courtesy of IBM, used with permission.

Figure 3.2: Hybrid data server storage

Summary

This chapter summarized the evolution of XML and presented the case for a hybrid solution that combines the flexibility of XML with the power of SQL. Key XML concepts and specifications were covered, and an overview of DB2 9 XML capabilities was presented. With this background, you should have a good understanding of where XML has come from and where it is going, both within the industry in general and specifically as implemented in DB2 9.

4

The Path to DB2 9 XML Capabilities

In this chapter, you'll learn more about XQuery, XPath, and the XPath Data Model and receive an introduction to DB2 9's XML components and native XML support. The chapter continues to build on XML as the foundation for effective understanding and use of XML in DB2 9 and introduces the DB2 9 XML components and architecture.

XQuery and XPath

Just as SQL provides a query language for relational databases, a native query language for XML was needed due to the synchronization problem between XML and relational data that we discussed in Chapter 3. To address this need, the W3C organization developed XQuery, the query language for XML, defining the language in the XQuery 1.0 specification. As of the writing of this book, the XQuery 2.0 draft is in the works.

XQuery is the main entry point for accessing and processing XML data in DB2 9. It is a domain-specific language designed to work with XML data that is highly variable, unstructured, and unpredictable. XQuery provides the flexibility to work with this kind of data. For example, you can use XML queries to perform the following operations:

- Return results that have mixed types
- Search XML data for objects that are at unknown levels of the hierarchy
- Perform structured transformations on the data (e.g., invert a hierarchy)

Note: DB2 supports storing and retrieving well-formed XML data in a column of a table. XML instances (documents) consisting of XML that conforms to XML's syntax rules are legal and are considered to be well-formed.

XQuery queries use expressions written in the XML Path (XPath) language to navigate through XML trees and extract XML fragments as well as to create, sort, aggregate, combine, and iterate over sequences (examine or manipulate each item in a sequence) and construct new XML data. At the heart of the XPath language is the *path expression*, which provides for the hierarchical addressing of nodes in an XML tree.

The following excerpt from the *XML Path Language (XPath) 2.0* W3C recommendation describes the XPath language in detail.

"XPath 2.0 is an expression language that allows the processing of values conforming to the data model defined in [the] XQuery/XPath Data Model (XDM) [specification]. The data model provides a tree representation of XML documents as well as atomic values such as integers, strings, and booleans, and sequences that may contain both references to nodes in an XML document and atomic values. The result of an XPath expression may be a selection of nodes from the input documents, or an atomic value, or more generally, any sequence allowed by the data model."

> **Note:** XPath is an expression language that allows the processing of values conforming to the data model defined in the XQuery/ XPath Data Model W3C specifications. DB2 9 supports these specifications.

An XQuery 1.0 expression takes one or more XDM instances as input and returns an XDM instance as a result. The current XQuery 1.0 specification does not support updating instances of the XDM. However, DB2 9 provides facilities to accomplish this; you'll learn how to do this in Chapter 5.

> **Note:** The XQuery 1.0 and XPath 2.0 Data Model does not allow for updating of nodes. As of the writing of this book, extensions to XQuery 1.0 are being considered that would provide for an XQuery update facility.

Like most data models, XDM defines the format of the data but not the application programming interfaces (APIs) to access the data. That is where specific implementations such as DB2 9 come into play. In a nutshell, the XQuery language is the fundamental query language for querying XML data, and it is guided by the XDM for data format rules.

Because XQuery is a reference-based language, subsequent expressions on the result of a path expression may traverse the document in both forward and reverse direction. With XQuery and XPath, you can store, compose, and decompose XML documents.

Creating Queries in XQuery

You form queries in XQuery by making declarations in the form of expressions. Queries consist of an optional *prolog* and a *query body*. Figure 4.1 shows a sample DB2 9 XQuery structure.

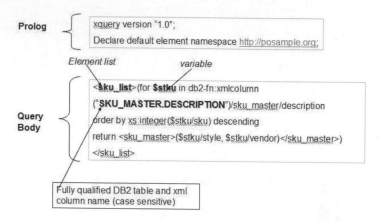

Figure 4.1: Basic XQuery structure

The prolog defines the processing environment for the query. It is followed by the query body, which consists of one or more expressions that define the query results.

Expressions can consist of multiple XQuery expressions that are combined using various XQuery operators or keywords. In the example, the prolog contains two declarations: a version declaration, which specifies the version of the XQuery syntax to apply to the query, and a default namespace declaration, which specifies the namespace Uniform Resource Identifier (URI) to use for unprefixed element and type names.

The sample query body contains an expression that constructs a sku_list element. The content of the sku_list element is a list of sku_master elements. The sample query uses the for expression along with the $stku variable to iterate through the description subelements of the sku_master elements contained in the SKU_MASTER.DESCRIPTION column. The /sku_master/description path expression iterates through every node in the expression on the left (the *context*) and for each such node performs the selection on the right (the *step*). Last, the return expression indicates that for each iteration, the value of $stku is returned. The constructed sku_list element is a list of sku_master elements sorted in descending order.

> **Note:** An XML sequence returned by the db2-fn:xmlcolumn or db2-fn:
> sqlquery function can contain any XML values, including atomic
> values and nodes.

DB2 9 supports queries written in SQL, XQuery, or a combination of SQL and XQuery. Both languages are supported as primary query languages, and each provides functions for invoking the other language.

Before we delve into specific aspects of DB2 9 support for XML, it will be helpful to take a closer look at details of the XPath Data Model.

XPath Data Model

The *XQuery 1.0 and XPath 2.0 Data Model (XDM)* W3C recommendation (23 January 2007) defines the data model used by XQuery 1.0, XPath 2.0, and Extensible Stylesheet Language Transformations (XSLT) 2.0. as follows:

"The XQuery 1.0 and XPath 2.0 Data Model . . . serves two purposes. First, it defines the information contained in the input to an XSLT or XQuery processor. Second, it defines all permissible values of expressions in the XSLT, XQuery, and XPath languages."

XDM provides support for XML Schema types and extends the Infoset model by providing precise type information and supporting the representation of collections of documents and complex values.

Every value in the XDM is the *sequence* of zero or more *items*. An item may be a node or an atomic value. A sequence may contain nodes, atomic values, or any mixture of nodes and atomic values. A *node* is one of the seven kinds of nodes defined by the XPath 2.0 specification:

- *Document nodes* encapsulate XML documents and have the following properties, which can be empty:
  - » base-uri
  - » children
  - » unparsed-entities
  - » document-uri
- *Element nodes* encapsulate elements and have the following properties:
  - » base-uri
  - » node-name
  - » parent (can be empty)
  - » type
  - » children (can be empty)
  - » attributes (can be empty)
  - » namespaces (can be empty)
  - » nilled
- *Attribute nodes* represent XML attributes and have the following properties:
  - » node-name
  - » string value
  - » parent (can be empty)
  - » type
- *Text nodes* contain XML character content and have the following properties:
  - » content
  - » parent
- *Namespace nodes* contain information about XML namespaces:
  - » prefix (can be empty)
  - » uri
  - » parent (can be empty)

- *Processing instruction nodes* contain XML processing instructions and have the following properties:
  - » target
  - » content
  - » base-uri (can be empty)
  - » parent (can be empty)
- *Comment nodes* contain XML comments and have the following properties:
  - » content
  - » parent

Although namespace nodes are part of the XPath 2.0 specification, support for them by applications (in this case, by DB2 9) is application-dependent. In DB2 9, namespace nodes are not supported; instead, IBM has chosen to represent namespaces in an internal format that complies with the specification. However, I've included namespace nodes in this section to give you an overall understanding of node types.

Table 4.1 provides a complete list of the rules defined by the W3C for the seven types of nodes.

Table 4.1: Rules for XPath Data Model node types
Document nodes
1. Every document must have a unique identity, distinct from all other nodes.
2. The children must consist exclusively of element, processing instruction, comment, and text nodes if the property is not empty. Attribute, namespace, and document nodes can never appear as children.
3. The sequence of nodes in the children is ordered and must be in document order.
4. The children property must not contain two consecutive text nodes.
5. If node N is a child of a document node D, the parent of N must be D.
6. If N has a parent document node D, N must be among the children of D.
7. The children property must not contain two nodes with the same identity.

Table 4.1: Rules for XPath Data Model node types (contiuned)

Element nodes

1. Every element node must have a unique identity, distinct from all other nodes.

2. The children must consist exclusively of element, processing instruction, comment, and text nodes if the property is not empty. Attribute, namespace, and document nodes can never appear as children.

3. The sequence of nodes in the children property is ordered and must be in document order.

4. The children property must not contain two consecutive text nodes.

5. The children property must not contain two consecutive nodes with the same identity.

6. The attributes of an element must have distinct xs:QNames.

7. The namespace nodes of an element must have distinct names. At most one of the namespace nodes of an element has no name (this is the default namespace).

8. If node N is a child of element E, the parent of N must be E.

9. Exclusive of attribute and namespace nodes, if a node N has a parent element E, N must be among the children of E. (Attribute and namespace nodes have a parent, but they do not appear among the children of their parent.)

10. If an attribute node A has a parent element E, A must be among the attributes of E.

11. If a namespace node has a parent element E, N must be among the namespaces of E.

Attribute nodes

1. Every attribute node must have a unique identity, distinct from all other nodes.

2. If an attribute node A has a parent element E, A must be among the attributes of E. Attribute nodes are permitted without parents, but such attributes must not appear among the attributes of any element node.

Text nodes

1. A text node must not contain the empty string as its content. Two consecutive text nodes cannot appear as adjacent siblings.

Namespace nodes

1. Every namespace node must have a unique identity, distinct from all other nodes.

2. If a namespace node N has a parent element E, N must be among the namespaces of E. Namespace nodes without parents are permitted in special cases.

Processing instruction nodes

1. Every processing instruction node must have a unique identity, distinct from all other nodes.

2. The target must be an NCName.

Comment nodes

1. Every comment node must have a unique identity, distinct from all other nodes.

2. The string "--" must not occur within the content.

Figure 4.2 shows how you can browse XML documents, elements, and attributes using the DB2 9 Control Center. You can also use the Control Center to drill down to each node type and to view entire documents.

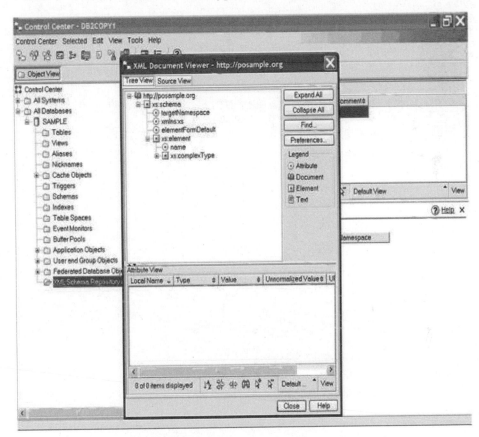

Figure 4.2: Browsing XML documents with the DB2 Control Center

DB2 9 Hybrid Architecture

Key to DB2 9's hybrid architecture is the integration of the native DB2 XML data type into the existing relational engine. This integration enables a company to store both relational and XML data in the DB2 9 hybrid data server. This integration of XML data in the DB2 9 database engine and seamless XML support is packaged as IBM's *pureXML* technology.

Although DB2 9 provides complete XML support, this support is offered as an option and does not come with the base DB2 9 product. This approach is in keeping with today's flexible software configuration and pricing movement. With this flexibility, you can customize your DB2 installations to use just the features you need. This capability can help to reduce annual database licensing costs. So, even though pureXML is tightly integrated into DB2 9, the feature is optional.

Components of DB2 9 XML Support

Figure 4.3 provides an overview of the DB2 9 pureXML architecture.

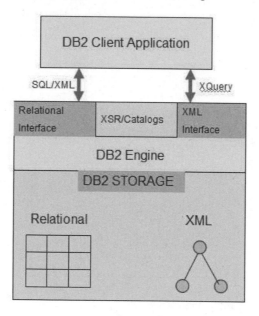

Figure 4.3: DB2 hybrid data server architecture

As the diagram depicts, DB2 9's XML support can be broken down into several areas. DB2 9 supports the XQuery language through the XML interface and supports SQL through existing relational interfaces. The hybrid architecture supports combinations of SQL, SQL/XML, and XQuery. The DB2 9 architecture supports the W3C XQuery 1.0 and XPath 2.0 specifications.

DB2 9 Optimizer Extensions

Chapter 3 outlined how IBM integrated DB2 9 native XML support using the existing DB2 architecture. Key to this integration was the fact that the optimizer component of DB2 was designed from the beginning in a modular fashion. Thanks to this modularity, DB2 9 developers were able to "extend" the optimizer components to support XML expressions. In DB2 9, XQuery is represented with an internal query graph model. The optimizer Query Graph Model (QGMX) has been modified to incorporate the internal data flow model, with native constructs that are specific to XML and represent complex navigation of XQuery and XPath.

Figure 4.4 provides an overview of the hybrid query compiler.

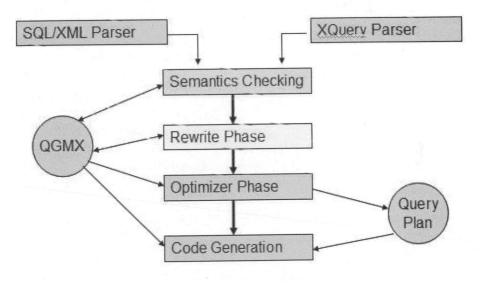

Figure 4.4: Hybrid SQL/XQuery compiler

The XQuery parser is new in DB2 9; all other components were extended to support the XQuery language and the XPath Data Model. As the figure illustrates, an SQL statement or XQuery expression is compiled into an internal data flow graph. In the next step, rewrite transformations are applied to optimize the data flow. The optimizer then uses the data flow graph to generate a physical query plan, which the code-generation step translates into executable code.

XML Schema Repository

The XML Schema Repository (XSR) is a DB2 9 repository for all XML artifacts used to validate and process XML instance documents stored in XML columns. The XSR is unique to DB2 9 and is based on the W3C XML Schema specification.

DB2 9 uses the XSR to validate XML instance documents pointed to by a URI associated with an XML schema, DTD, or other external entity. The XSR enables DB2 9 well-formed documents to be validated without requiring external resources that could be unavailable when needed. For example, if an XML instance document contained a reference to an external URI and that external URI wasn't available to complete the validation, the situation would cause validations to fail and would adversely impact DB2 9 processing and be beyond the control of the DB2 9 database system. For this reason, the XSR is internal to DB2, and there is an XSR for each database.

Each DB2 9 database contains an XSR that is composed of catalog tables, five catalog views, and system-provided stored procedures to enable schemas to be defined to the XSR. Each XML schema, DTD, or external entity registered with the XSR is represented as an XSR object. The XSR object is used to validate and process DB2 XML instance documents stored in XML columns.

You can register an XSR object using any of the following methods:

- DB2 9–provided stored procedures
- A Java application
- The DB2 command line processor

Using stored procedures, XSR object registration is a three-step process:

1. Register the primary XML schema document by calling the SYSPROC. XSR_REGISTER stored procedure.

2. Add any additional XML schema documents to be included with the primary XML schema by using the SYSPROC.XSR_ADDSCHEMADOC stored procedure.

3. Complete the registration by calling the SYSPROC.XSR_COMPLETE stored procedure.

Using the DB2 command line processor involves a similar three-step process:

1. Register the primary XML schema document using the REGISTER XMLSCHEMA command.

2. Optionally add any additional XML schema documents to be included with the primary XML schema using the ADD XMLSCHEMA DOCUMENT command.

3. Complete the registration by issuing the COMPLETE XMLSCHEMA command.

To register using a Java application, call the previously mentioned stored procedures. In addition, the following methods let you perform the same operations from a Java application program.

- DB2Connection.registerDB2XMLSchema registers an XML schema using one or more XML schema documents.

- DB2Connection.deregisterDB2XMLObject removes an XML schema definition from DB2.

Note that by default the XSR samples aren't installed in DB2 9; to create them, run the db2sample_XML command line processor script contained in the DB2 9 samples subdirectory. You'll see a complete example of the XML Schema registration process using the Developer Workbench (DWB) in Chapter 5.

DB2 9 Native XML Storage Architecture

Together, native XML data-type integration into the database engine and integration of XML support into the DB2 Storage Model form the pillars of the XML support provided by the DB2 9 hybrid data server. Figure 4.5 gives a high-level overview of the DB2 9 native XML storage architecture. The diagram illustrates how both relational and XML storage are integrated into the DB2 Storage Model.

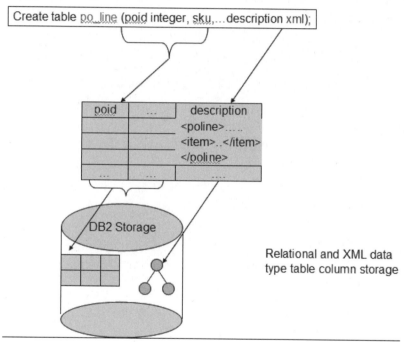

Figure 4.5: DB2 9 integrated storage architecture

Although DB2 9 stores the two types of data differently, it uses the same DB2 storage "subsystem" to manage both types of storage, providing seamless integration for applications accessing both relational and XML data. This powerful solution increases productivity because developers don't have to spend time writing interfaces to access XML documents stored elsewhere.

DB2 stores XML instance documents in columns of type XML, and their hierarchical structure and meaning are preserved. The amount and nature of XML data can vary widely, from small XML documents to large XML documents that can be many gigabytes in length. Retrieval and update frequency can also vary widely. In such an environment, documents must be able to span disk pages because a single text node could be larger than a page.

The DB2 9 solution to this problem is to implement a storage model that stores XML documents as instances of the XDM in a structured, type-annotated tree. DB2 9 stores the binary representation of type-annotated XML trees, which avoids the repeated parsing and validation of documents. This approach also enables digital signatures to be preserved, a capability that is increasingly important in the financial sector, where digital signatures are used to provide proof of authorization for sensitive financial transactions, such as buy and sell orders.

In most cases, you won't want to concern yourself with how DB2 9 internally manages XML storage; however, to help you understand what DB2 9 is doing under the covers, I'll briefly discuss how XML data is managed internally using the sample document shown in Figure 4.6 as an example.

```
<customerinfo xmlns="http://posample.org" Cid="9000">
    <name>Phil Gunning</name>
    <addr country="USA">
      <street>1 Whitetail Drive</street>
      <city>Bucktown</city>
        <prov-state>Pa</prov-state>
        <pcode-zip>19608</pcode-zip>
    </addr>
    <phone type="work">888-241-1070</phone>
  </customerinfo>
```

Figure 4.6: Customerinfo document

As the figure shows, the customerinfo document contains multiple elements represented in a hierarchy. The customerinfo root element contains subelements and attributes such as name, address, city, and state. Figure 4.7 is a representation of the customerinfo document in hierarchical form.

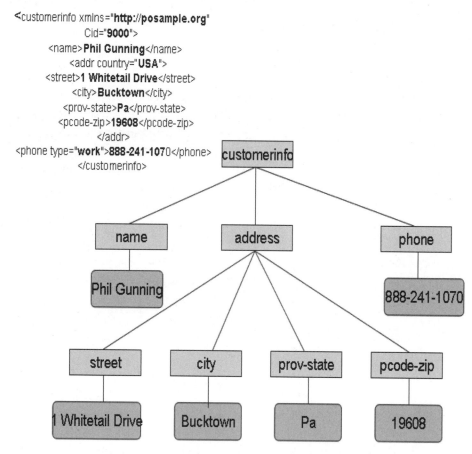

```
<customerinfo xmlns="http://posample.org"
              Cid="9000">
  <name>Phil Gunning</name>
    <addr country="USA">
  <street>1 Whitetail Drive</street>
      <city>Bucktown</city>
    <prov-state>Pa</prov-state>
    <pcode-zip>19608</pcode-zip>
            </addr>
  <phone type="work">888-241-1070</phone>
            </customerinfo>
```

Figure 4.7: Hierarchical representation of the customerinfo document

When this document is stored, DB2 preserves its internal structure and converts its tag names and other information into integer values. Figure 4.8 shows how DB2 assigns *StringIDs* internally to nodes.

String Table

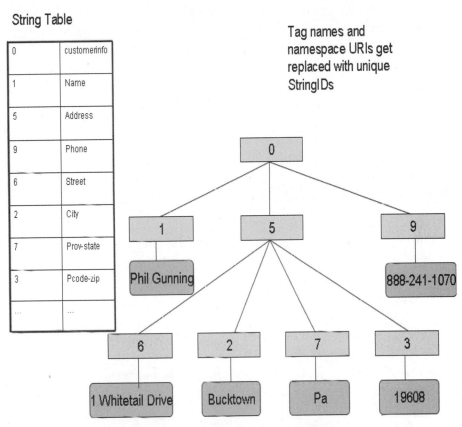

0	customerinfo
1	Name
5	Address
9	Phone
6	Street
2	City
7	Prov-state
3	Pcode-zip
...	...

Tag names and namespace URIs get replaced with unique StringIDs

Figure 4.8: Hierarchical representation of customerinfo document with StringIDs

Replacing tags with StringIDs enables DB2 to provide excellent query performance. StringIDs let DB2 perform node comparisons using integers instead of strings. DB2 9 also stores extra information with each node. Child slots are associated with element nodes and have hints within them to provide information about what the child represents, enabling non-qualifying children to be skipped. This mechanism helps reduce I/O by allowing navigation across child nodes.

A unique identifier is assigned to each node and provides for logical and physical addressability that may be used for indexing and query optimization. If a document tree doesn't fit on one page, DB2 9 will split it into *regions* containing subtrees of nodes. Regions are connected by a *region index*, which is created automatically for every table that contains one or more XML columns. Region indexes enable DB2 9 to use efficient prefetching techniques. Finally, because logical node identifiers are independent of physical node locations, it's much easier to insert, update, and delete nodes or subtrees. Similarly, documents or page reorganization is facilitated.

Querying DB2 9 XML Data

DB2 9 contains two XQuery functions for obtaining input XML data from DB2 9 databases. The db2-fn:xmlcolumn function (which you saw used in a sample query earlier in the chapter) retrieves an entire XML column. The db2-fn:sqlquery function retrieves XML values based on an SQL fullselect.

The db2-fn:xmlcolumn function takes as input a string literal that identifies an XML column (defined as a DB2 XML data type) and returns a sequence consisting of all document nodes in the specified column. The following example shows how you use this function.

```
for $c in db2-fn:xmlcolumn ("ORDERS.PO_ORDER")
where $c/order/customer/custid = 4388
return $c/tot_qty
```

You can use db2-fn:xmlcolumn multiple times in a single XQuery to reference different XML columns in the same or separate tables or to reference the same XML column several times.

The db2-fn:sqlquery function lets you restrict the input to an XQuery based on conditions placed on relational columns in the same or related tables. This function accepts any select statement that returns a single XML column. The following example filters the set of input documents to XQuery by using a predicate and a join on another relational table.

```
for $c in db2_fn:sqlquery ('select po_order from purchases, ship-
ping where purchases.cust_id = shipping.SORDER and purchases.sku
="12345"')/order/
customer
where $c/cust_ID =4388
return $C/tot_qty
```

DB2 9 Methods of Querying XML Data

DB2 9 provides four ways to query and/or manipulate DB2 XML data:

- XQuery-only
- XQuery that invokes SQL
- SQL-only
- SQL/XML functions that execute XQuery expressions

The preceding examples demonstrated retrieving XML data via the XQuery-only method. Which method you choose depends on the type of data to be accessed and the processing to be performed, whether by the DB2 application or an application (e.g., a Web service) downstream.

XQuery-Only

A query that invokes XQuery directly in DB2 9 must begin with the keyword XQUERY. By specifying this keyword, you indicate to DB2 that XQuery is being used and that the query must be processed in accordance with the case-sensitivity rules that apply to the XQuery language.

XQuery-only is the perfect method to use when you'll be accessing only XML data and there is no need to access non-XML relational data. This method is also a good choice when migrating queries previously written in XQuery, when returning query results to be used as values for constructing XML documents, and when the person writing the query has more experience with XQuery than SQL.

XQuery That Invokes SQL

XQuery that invokes SQL can be a good choice for all the aforementioned uses of XQuery-only, as well as in the following cases:

- For queries that use both relational and XML data when SQL predicates on relational data can be used
- When applying XQuery expressions to the results of user-defined function (UDF) calls (because you can't invoke UDFs directly from XQuery)
- When constructing XML from relational data using SQL/XML publishing functions
- For queries that use the DB2 Net Search Extender V9.1, which requires the use of SQL

SQL-Only

The SQL-only method is a good fit when you want to retrieve an entire XML document in an SQL query that accesses or joins only relational data and you have no need to query based on values in an XML document.

SQL/XML Functions That Execute XQuery Expressions

SQL/XML is an American National Standards Institute (ANSI) and ISO standard that provides for the new XML data type that DB2 9 supports. DB2 9 provides SQL/XML functions using the following query elements.

- XMLQUERY (scalar function)
- XMLTABLE (table function)
- XMLEXISTS (predicate)

The XMLQUERY and XMLTABLE functions, along with the XMLEXISTS predicate, enable you to execute XQuery expressions from within the SQL context. Executing XQuery within SQL might be a good choice under the following conditions:

- When existing applications need to query within XML
- When you need to pass parameter markers to an XQuery expression
- When you need to return both relational and XML data in a single query
- For joining XML and relational data
- To group or aggregate XML data
- When you're more familiar with SQL than XQuery

Summary

This chapter covered essential XML specifications and provided a foundation for understanding XML and its integration into DB2 9. DB2 9's native XML data type database engine integration and DB2 Storage Model integration are the foundation of the XML support provided by the DB2 9 hybrid data server.

5

Developer Workbench: Developing Applications

The new DB2 9 Developer Workbench (DWB) is based on the Eclipse framework and replaces the former DB2 Development Center, which was based on Swing. (You can use DWB to migrate objects developed with the former Development Center.) The DWB is an integrated development environment designed to let you develop everything you need to from a single interface.

DWB is a flexible environment that supports developing applications for DB2 for Linux, UNIX, and Windows; DB2 for i5/OS; DB2 for z/OS; and IBM Derby databases. Because DWB is based on Eclipse, you can even develop your own DWB plug-ins. In addition to being a useful tool for developing applications, DWB provides good administration and application deployment capabilities, so developers and DBAs alike can use it.

With DWB, you can develop, test, and explain SQL statements, user-defined functions, stored procedures, and XQuery and SQL/XML applications. The environment provides support for creating and validating XML schemas and XML documents. The table editor has also been integrated into DWB.

Getting Started with DWB

DWB doesn't come with the base DB2 product, but you can download it from the DB2 Express-C download page at *http://www-306.ibm.com/software/data/db2/express/download.html*. Getting started with DWB involves several steps:

1. Launch the workbench.
2. Connect to a database.
3. Set up the data perspective.
4. Create a project.
5. Switch workspaces (optional).

To launch DWB on Windows, navigate to **Start > All Programs > DB2 Developer Workbench 9.1 > Developer Workbench** as shown in Figure 5.1.

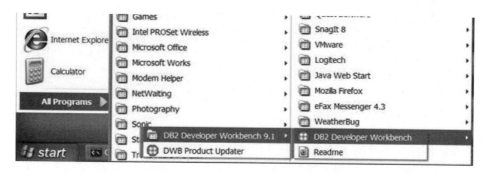

Figure 5.1: Launching DWB

The first time you start DWB, you need to set up a *workspace*, where your projects and definitions will be stored. You can accept the default workspace displayed by the Workspace Launcher (shown in Figure 5.2) or specify your own location.

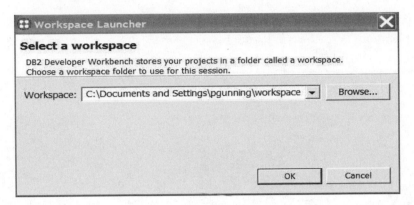

Figure 5.2: Selecting a DWB workspace

The next time you launch DWB, the Workspace Launcher defaults to the last workspace you used. You can select the launcher's check box option to make the current selection your default workspace. In that case, you'll no longer be presented with a workspace choice after launching DWB; however, you can still create or select a different workspace later.

After selecting a workspace for the first time, you're presented with the DB2 DWB First Steps Welcome tab. From here, you can view DWB tutorials, consult DWB help, or choose to get started working with your own data and applications.

To get started with DWB, choose "Start working with your own data and applications" as shown in Figure 5.3.

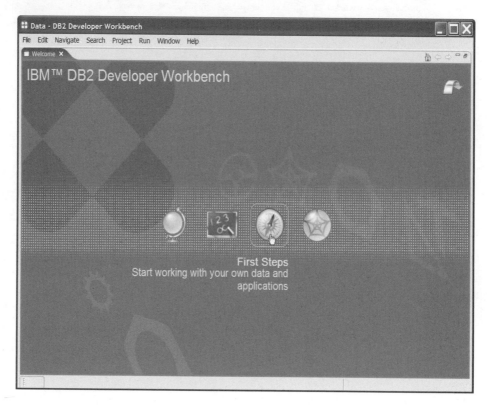

Figure 5.3: Getting started with First Steps

You'll see the tab shown in Figure 5.4. If you're just starting out with DWB, you'll need to connect to a database. To obtain help on how to do this, you can select the "Connecting to a database" option shown in the figure.

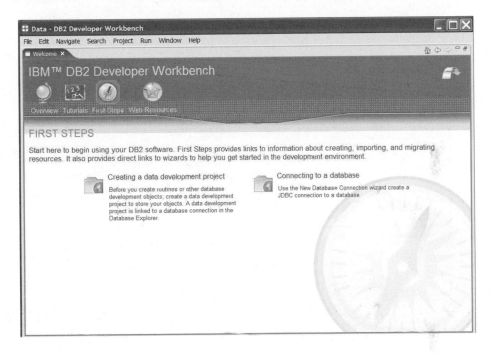

Figure 5.4: More First Steps

Figure 5.5 shows the DWB help that's displayed if you select this option.

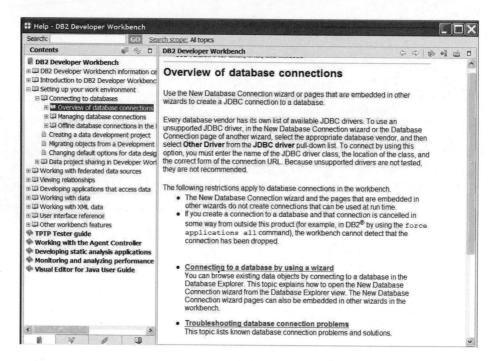

Figure 5.5: DWB help

The DWB help facility offers tips and pointers for just about anything you need to do with DWB. You can use this reference to familiarize yourself with DWB wizards and capabilities.

To open the workbench from the First Steps tab, click the workbench icon, which is located in the upper-right corner of the tab as shown in Figure 5.6.

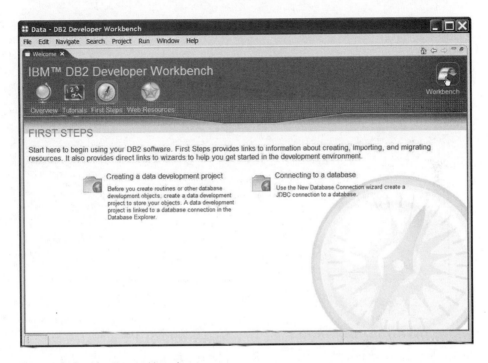

Figure 5.6: Opening the workbench

Opening the workbench places you in the Data perspective view of the DWB. Figure 5.7 shows this view; you can tell this by the word "Data" in the window's title bar and by the focus of the **Data** icon in the upper-right corner of the view.

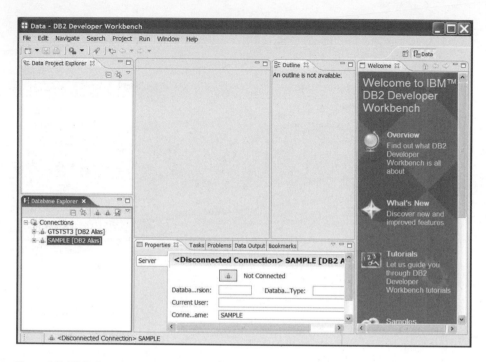

Figure 5.7: DWB Data perspective

As you can see in the figure, the **Database Explorer** tab is highlighted, and a list of cataloged databases is displayed. To set up a connection, right-click on the database of interest to display the **Connection Properties** box (Figure 5.8). Here, you can accept the defaults or customize the values to fit your needs.

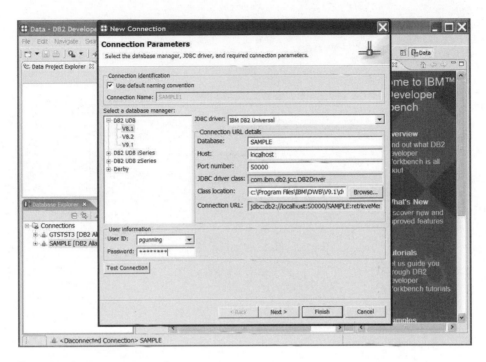

Figure 5.8: Setting up a connection

To test a connection to a database, you first need to select the version and server type from the list in the tree. For this example, I selected V8.1. However, the actual database server I was connecting to was at V9.1; as a result, I received the error message shown in Figure 5.9.

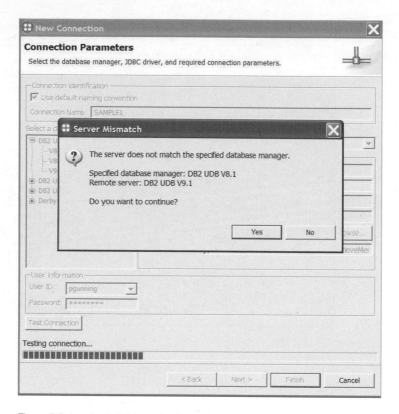

Figure 5.9: Incorrect database level specified

If you specify the target database DB2 version improperly, you'll receive this
error when trying to connect. To correct the problem, select the correct DB2
version of the target database, and retry the connection.

The next step is to test the connection by specifying a user ID and password.
Figure 5.10 shows the notification displayed upon successful connection to
the specified database.

Figure 5.10: Successful connection

Following a successful test, the new connection is added to the Database
Explorer, as shown in Figure 5.11.

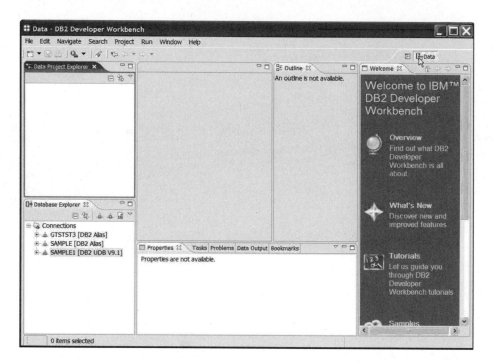

Figure 5.11: Updated Data perspective

Creating a Project

At the heart of a DWB development effort is the *project*. A project contains
all the objects related to a project, such as connections, authorizations,
and user-created objects (SQL queries, stored procedures, and so on). A
Data Development Project is linked to one database connection in the Data
Explorer. To create a project, right-click in a whitespace area of the Data
Project Explorer, and select **New > Project** as shown in Figure 5.12.

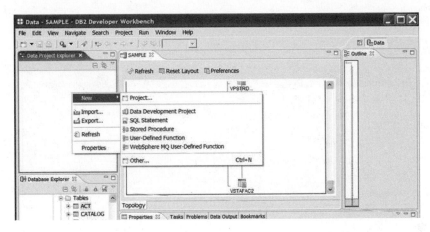

Figure 5.12: Creating a project

Select the Data Development Project wizard as shown in Figure 5.13 to perform the steps necessary to create the new project.

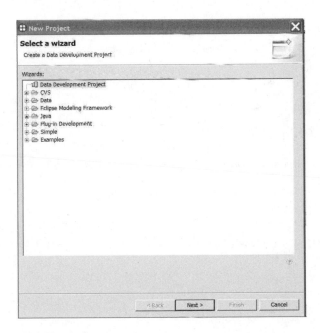

Figure 5.13: Data Development Project

The first step is to name the project. As shown in Figure 5.14, we've named ours **Project1**.

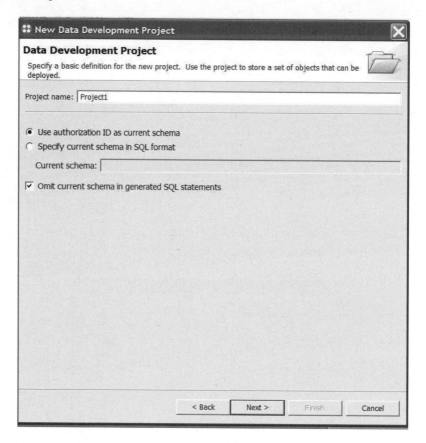

Figure 5.14: Specifying a new Data Development Project

Each Data Development Project is linked to one database connection in the Data Explorer. As shown in Figure 5.15, our project will use an existing connection.

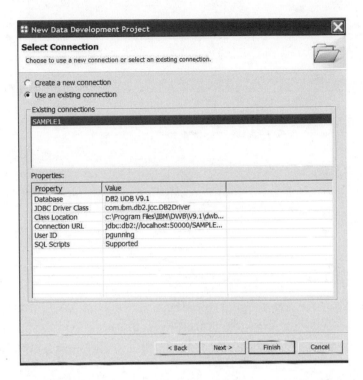

Figure 5.15: Specifying use of an existing connection

The last step is to specify the path for the Java Development Kit (JDK). You can use the default indicated in Figure 5.16 or specify your unique directory.

New Data Development Project

Specify routine parameters

Specify the JDK home directory.

JDK home: C:\Program Files\IBM\SQLLIB\java\jdk   Browse...

Figure 5.16: Specify routine parameters

Click **Finish** to create the new project. Figure 5.17 shows project Project1 as it appears in the Data Project Explorer.

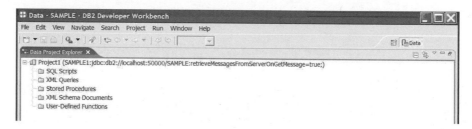

Figure 5.17: New Project1 created

Creating an SQL Procedure

Now, let's look at how to build stored procedures using DWB. To create a new procedure, right-click the **Stored Procedure** folder in the Data Project Explorer, and select **New > Stored Procedure** as shown in Figure 5.18.

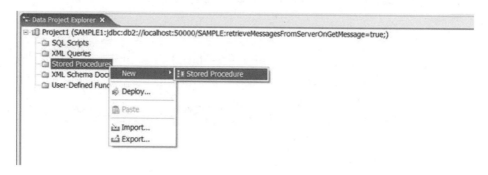

Figure 5.18: Creating a stored procedure

You'll be prompted to provide a project name (Figure 5.19).

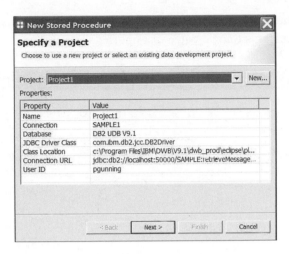

Figure 5.19: Use existing project

For this example, we'll specify **Project1** to match the new project we've already created. Then click **Next**.

On the resulting **Name and Language** window (Figure 5.20), name the procedure (**getproduct** in this example) and specify **SQL** as the language. Click **Next**.

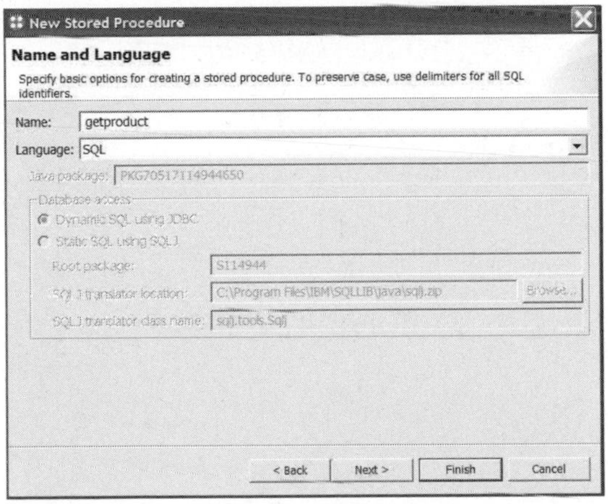

Figure 5.20: Name the procedure and language

The **SQL Statements** window (Figure 5.21) appears next. Here, you specify the SQL statements to be created or imported.

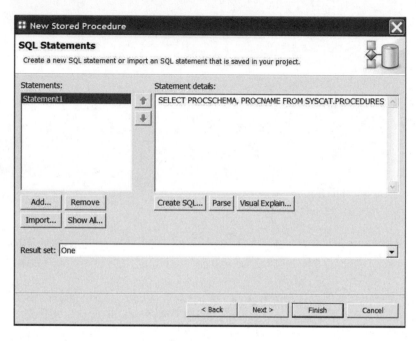

Figure 5.21: Specifying SQL statements

In this case, we'll click the **Create SQL** button to display the window shown in Figure 5.22.

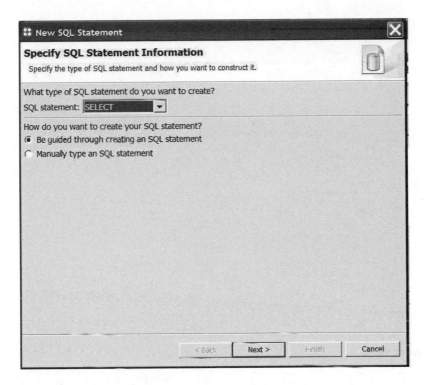

Figure 5.22: Creating a Select statement

As shown in this figure, we choose the option to "Be guided through creating an SQL statement." Click **Next** to display the **Construct an SQL Statement** window (Figure 5.23).

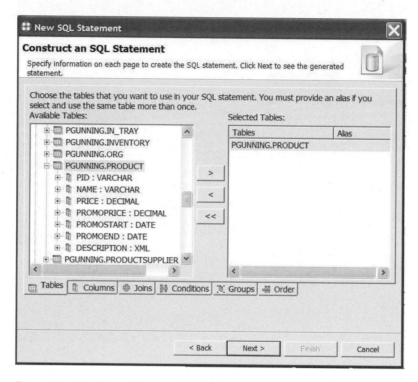

Figure 5.23: Selecting a table to work with

For this example, select the PRODUCT table. Then, move to the **Columns** tab and specify the columns to be used in the query as shown in Figure 5.24.

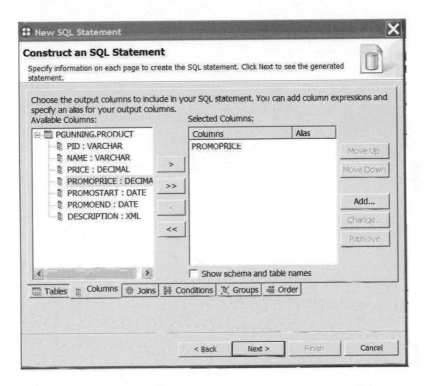

Figure 5.24: Select desired columns

After selecting columns, the next step is to choose the conditions for the query. Click **Next**, and then define the conditions as shown in Figure 5.25.

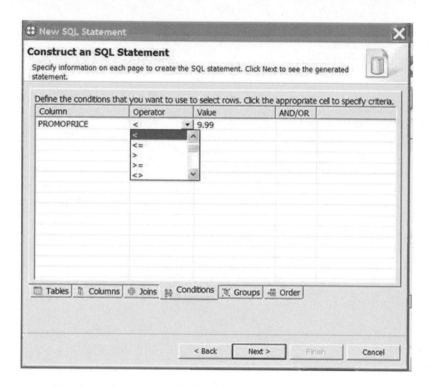

Figure 5.25: Select the conditions for the query

Click **Next** after selecting the conditions for the query. Then click **Run** in the **Run SQL Statement** window to run the query. The results shown in Figure 5.26 indicate that the query was successful, with one row returned.

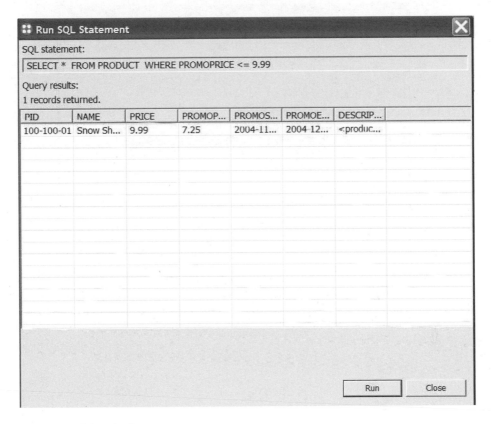

Figure 5.26: Query results

Now, you can add an input parameter for the stored procedure as shown in Figure 5.27.

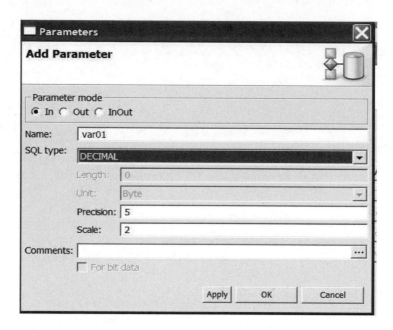

Figure 5.27: Adding an input parameter

Deploying a Stored Procedure

After specifying an input parameter, click **OK** to move on to the **Deploy Options** window (Figure 5.28).

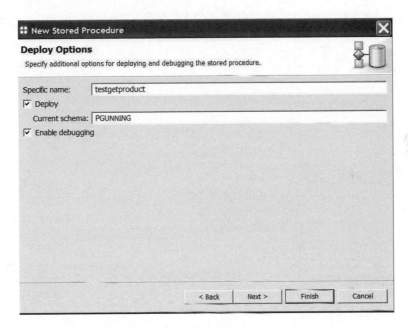

Figure 5.28 Specifying deploy and debug options

Click **Finish**, and then check the Data perspective (Figure 5.29) for a successful deploy. The **Status** column of the **Data Output** tab (bottom center of the window) should indicate a successful deploy.

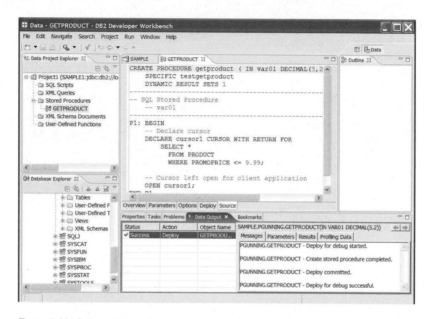

Figure 5.29: Successful create and deploy

Debugging a Stored Procedure

To add breakpoints to the procedure for debugging purposes, position the cursor anywhere in the left vertical margin where you want to add a breakpoint, and then right-click and select **Add Breakpoint** from the shortcut menu, as shown in Figure 5.30.

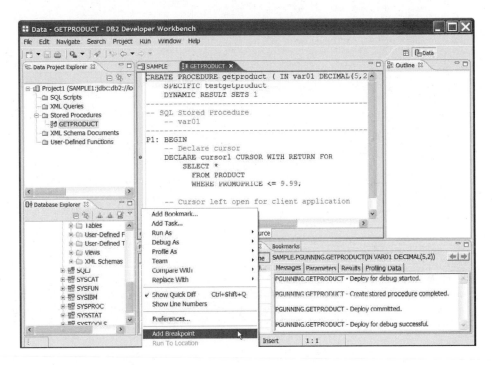

Figure 5.30: Adding a breakpoint

Next, move to the **Database Explorer** tab, right-click stored procedure
GETPRODUCT, and select **Debug** as shown in Figure 5.31.

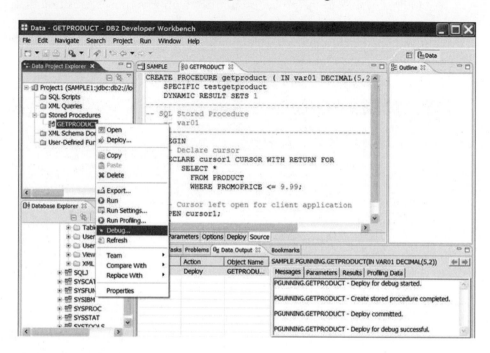

Figure 5.31: Debugging

You use the resulting window (Figure 5.32) to specify input variables for running or debugging the stored procedure.

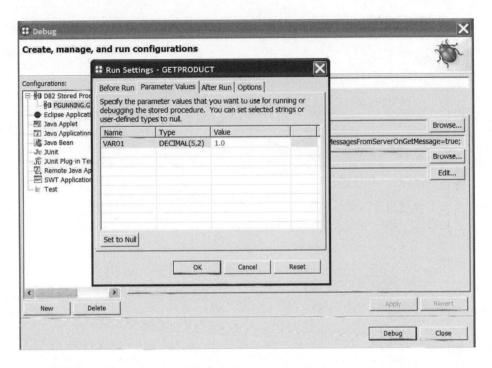

Figure 5.32: Specifying an input variable for debug

After specifying an input variable, click **OK** and then click **Debug** to start the debugger. Figure 5.33 shows the debugger running.

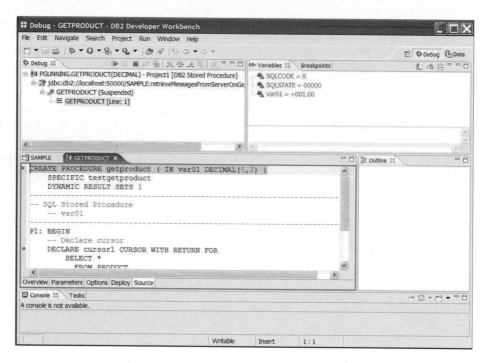

Figure 5.33: Breakpoints and debug

The debugger highlights the current code line (breakpoint) in green. You can step into the procedure by using the cursor to select the Step-into icon on the Debug window's task bar as shown in Figure 5.34.

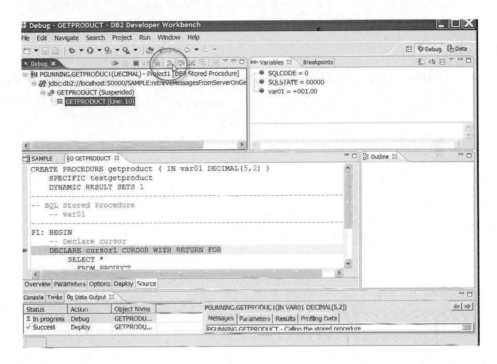

Figure 5.34: Step-into

Again, the debugger highlights the current code line in green. In this case, we've stepped to the DECLARE cursor1 breakpoint. To continue stepping through the code, click the Step-into icon again. You can then finish debugging or rerun the procedure as necessary.

Exporting a Stored Procedure

Now that you've seen how to create, deploy, and debug a stored procedure, you need to learn how to export one. You can export a stored procedure by right-clicking on the procedure you want to export in the Data Project Explorer and selecting **Export** as shown in Figure 5.35.

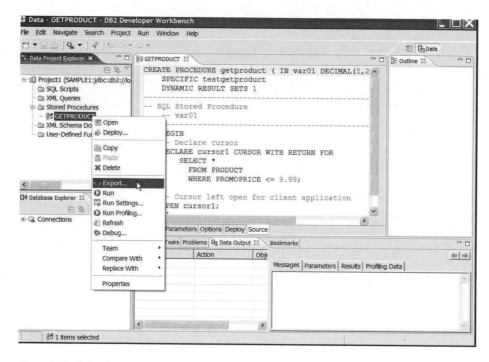

Figure 5.35: Exporting a stored procedure

The **Target and Options** window (Figure 5.36) is displayed. Enter **getproduct** as the file name and **c:\temp\out** as the directory. If the directory doesn't exist, DWB will prompt you and create it if necessary.

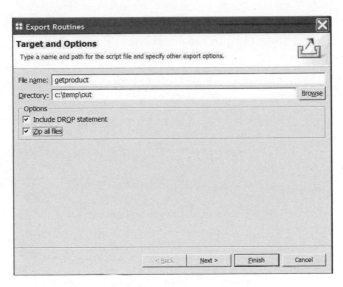

Figure 5.36: Specifying export options

Select the **Include DROP statement** and **Zip all files** options. Then click
Next to display the **Summary** window (Figure 5.37).

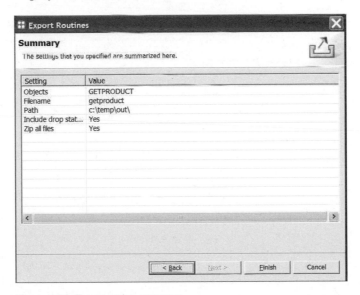

Figure 5.37: Export action summary

Click **Finish** here to export the stored procedure. Then review the status of the export in the **Data Output** tab as shown in Figure 5.38.

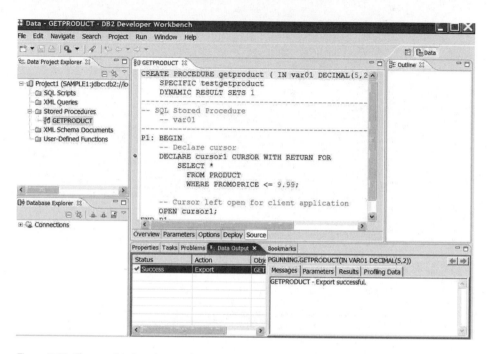

Figure 5.38: Successful stored procedure export

The created script is saved in the specified directory. There, you'll find a file called DeployInstructions.txt that contains instructions (shown in Figure 5.39) that describe how to deploy the script.

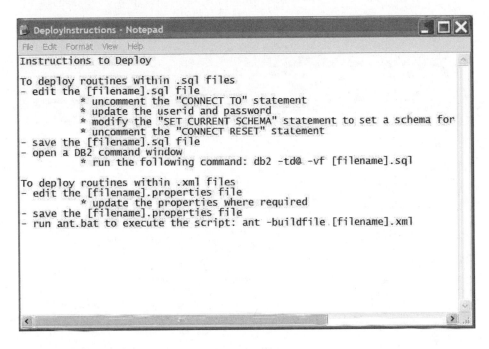

Figure 5.39: Export script instructions

Switching Workspaces

While we're at it, I'll show you how to switch between workspaces. From the **File** menu, select **Switch Workspace** (Figure 5.40).

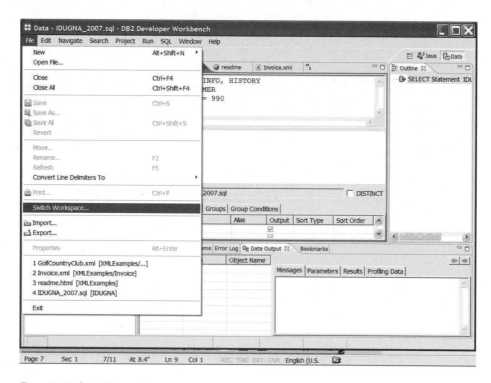

Figure 5.40: Switching workspaces

The Workspace Launcher (Figure 5.41) will be displayed. You can specify a path to the workspace you want to switch to or click the **Browse** button to browse a file system and select the workspace that way. Switching workspaces is useful if you work on multiple projects and need to move between them, as is often the case.

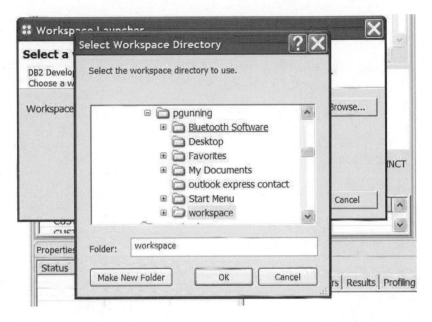

Figure 5.41: Switching workspaces

Topology View

The Data Perspective's topology view provides good way to see the list of objects you're working with and how they're related. The view presents this information in a pictorial manner, making it easy for you to see what you're working with and the relationships involved. By selecting any object in the hierarchy, you can drill down into lower-level objects.

You launch the topology view by right-clicking on a database in the Database Explorer. Choose **Visualize Topology Diagram** from the resulting shortcut menu to display the **Topology** tab, shown in Figure 5.42.

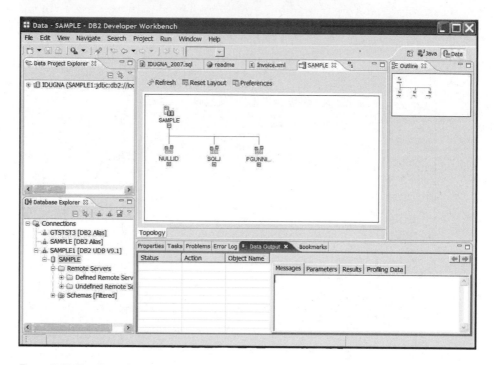

Figure 5.42: Topology view

Working with XML and DWB

To get started with XML, you need to have a schema or DTD definition created. As you may recall from Chapter 3, a schema or DTD describes the content and format of the XML document.

Building XML Schema

You can use DWB's XML Schema Editor to create an XML schema. The editor has two views: the Source view and the Graph view. In the Source view, you can see the source as text; the Graph view presents a pictorial image. You can drill down on elements in the Graph view by double-clicking on an element. To switch between views, select the tab for the view you want to use.

You can create an XML schema from the Database Explorer by right-clicking the **XML Schema Documents** node. Select **New** from the menu to launch the Create XML Schema wizard (Figure 5.43). For our example, select the **Project1** folder, and name the file **xmltabschema.xsd**. Then click **Finish**.

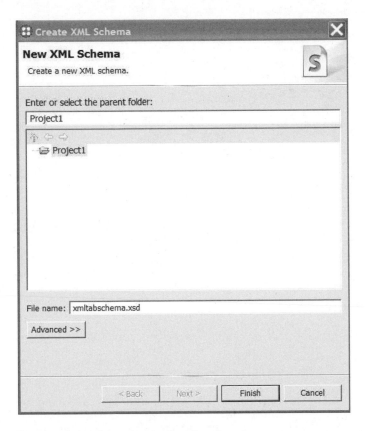

Figure 5.43: Naming and saving the new schema

The schema is created, and the XML Schema Editor, shown in Figure 5.44, is launched.

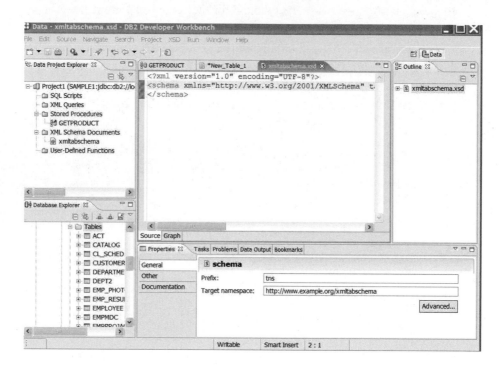

Figure 5.44: XML Schema Editor

Now that we've created a schema, the next step is to add an element. An element is the basic building block in XML, similar to a column in a relational schema. To add an element, move to the **Graph** tab in the XML editor, right-click anywhere in the resulting **Elements** pane where there is white space, and select **Add Element** from the resulting shortcut menu (Figure 5.45).

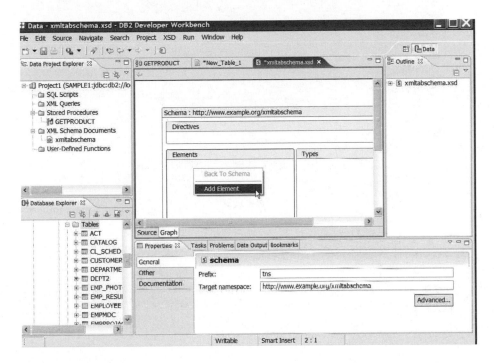

Figure 5.45: Adding an element

You'll be prompted to enter an element name and type as shown in Figures 5.46 and 5.47.

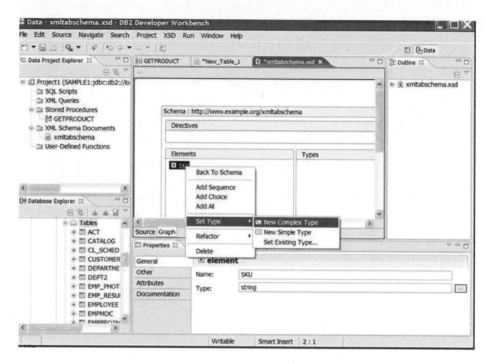

Figure 5.46: Adding an element

To add an element, double-click the sku element, which creates an element hierarchy. Right-click the resulting sequence box, and add the Vendor element as shown in Figure 5.47.

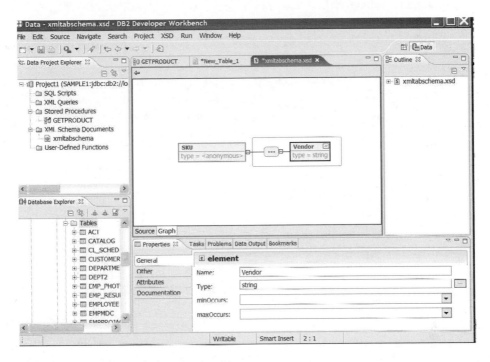

Figure 5.47: Providing an element name and type

You can add additional elements in the same manner. For demonstration purposes, I added the Color and Style elements and then confirmed that they were added by viewing them in the Source and Graph views (Figures 5.48 and 5.49, respectively).

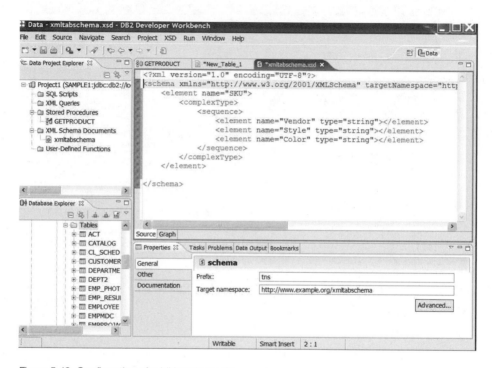

Figure 5.48: Confirmation of additions in the Source view

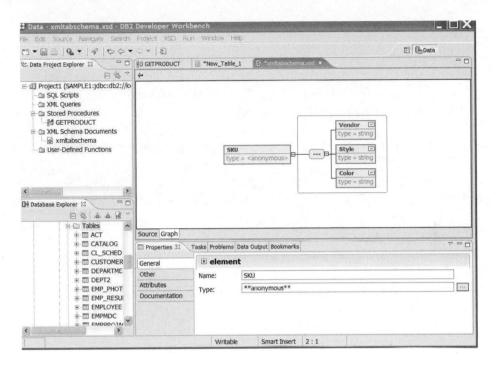

Figure 5.49: Confirmation of additions in the Graph view

Registering XML Schemas

Once you've created an XML schema, you need to register it so it can be used to validate instances of the schema. You use the Register an XML Schema wizard to accomplish this task. Figure 5.50 shows an example of launching the Register XML Schema wizard.

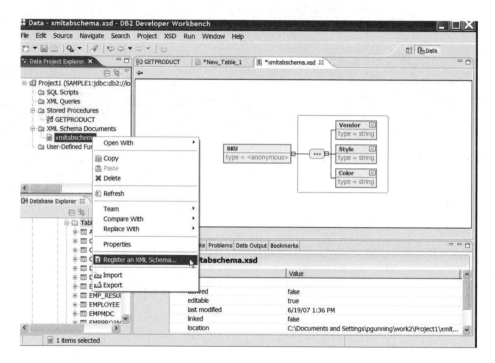

Figure 5.50: Launching the Register XML Schema wizard

> **Note:** To register an XML schema, you must have all the documents in your project.

The wizard (Figure 5.51) prompts you to select an XML schema name from the list. After making your selection (**PRODUCT** in this case), click **Next** to continue the schema registration process.

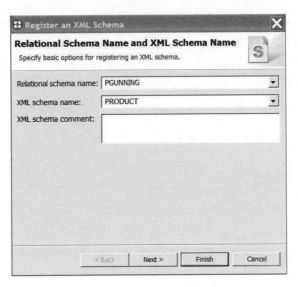

Figure 5.51: XML schema registration wizard

On the final window of the wizard (Figure 5.52), select the **xmltabschema.xsd** XML schema document, and click **Finish**.

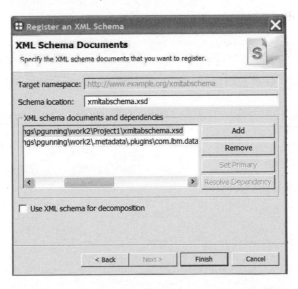

Figure 5.52: Concluding the schema registration process

Then check the **Data Output** tab to make sure the registration was completed successfully (Figure 5.53).

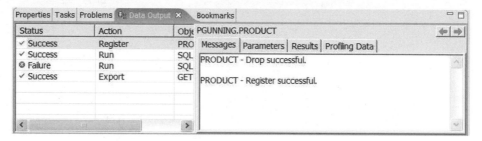

Figure 5.53: Confirm successful XML schema registration

With the XML schema registered, your next step is to generate documents from it.

Generating XML Documents from an XML Schema

From the DWB **Window** menu, select **Menu > Show View > Navigator** as shown in Figure 5.54 to generate an XML document.

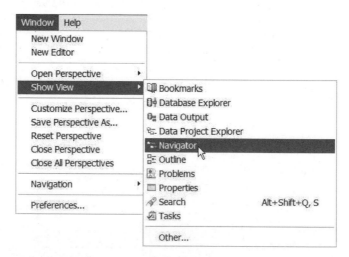

Figure 5.54 Launching the Navigator view

In the Navigator view, expand the **Project1** project tree, right-click
xmltabschema.xsd, and select **Generate > XML File** (Figure 5.55)
to launch the **Create XML File** dialog.

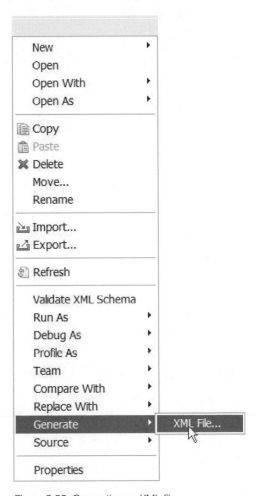

Figure 5.55: Generating an XML file

Figure 5.56 shows the Create XML File window. Select the root element and
click **Finish** to have an xmltabschema.xml document generated from the
xmltabschema.xsd file.

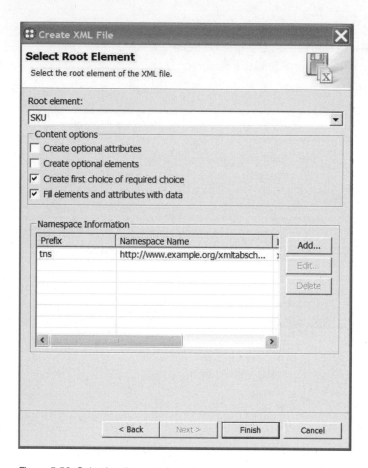

Figure 5.56: Selecting the root element

The newly generated xmltabschema.xml document opens in the XML Editor, as shown in Figure 5.57.

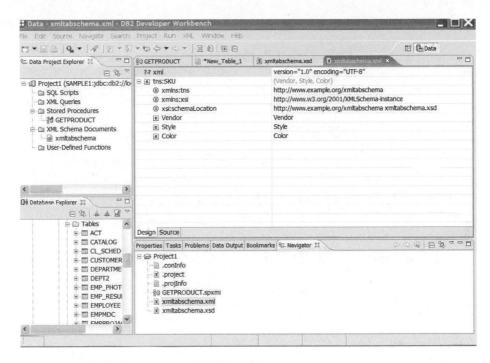

Figure 5.57: XML Editor Design view of XML document

Having generated an XML document from an XML schema, your next step is to edit an XML document using the XML Editor. Using the Design view, you can assign values to Vendor, Style, and Color elements by selecting these elements in the view and then assigning values to them.

Inserting an XML Document into an XML Column

You use the XML Cell Editor to insert documents into XML columns. To insert the xmltabschema.xml document into the DOC column of the PRODUCT table, go to the Database Explorer, expand the SAMPLE database schema tree, and right-click the product table node. Select **Data > Edit** as shown in Figure 5.58 to launch the table editor.

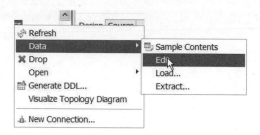

Figure 5.58: Launching the table editor

Figure 5.59 shows the table editor. Note that the last column in the table, DOC, is selected. Click on the ellipsis (...) to launch the XML Cell Editor.

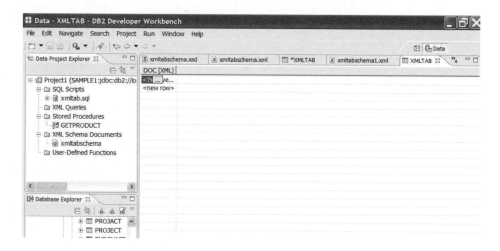

Figure 5.59: Table editor

Figure 5.60 shows the cell editor. Click **Import** here to import the XML document from the file system. Then click **Next**.

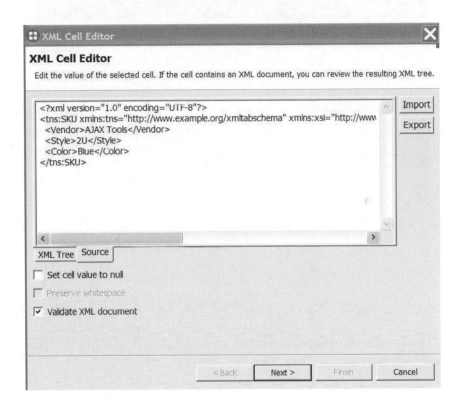

Figure 5.60: XML Cell Editor

The **XML document validation** window (Figure 5.61) is displayed.

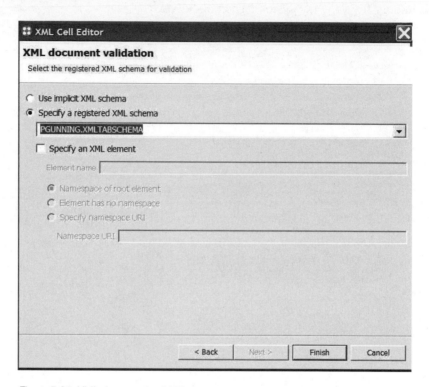

Figure 5.61: XML document validation

Click **Finish** to validate the new row and insert it into the sample XMLTAB table as shown in Figure 5.62.

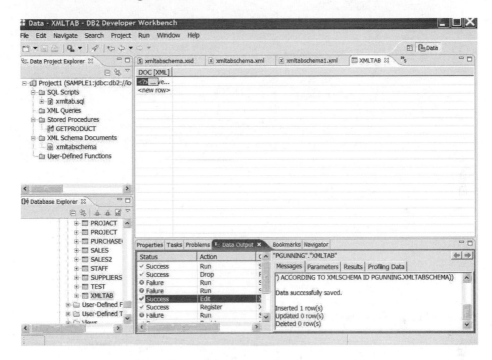

Figure 5.62: New row (document inserted)

To save the new row and cause validation to occur, click the Save icon in the menu bar. Then review the results as shown in Figure 5.63.

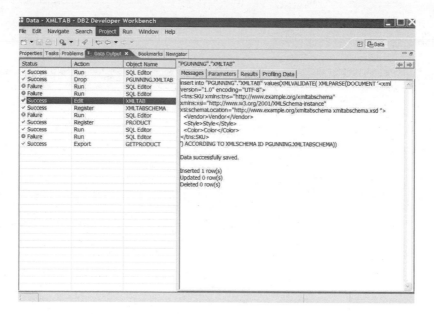

Figure 5.63: One row inserted and validated against the xmltabschema.xsd

Building an XQuery

You use the DWB XQuery Builder to build an XQuery. To launch the XQuery Builder, right-click the **XML Queries** folder in the Data Project Explorer and select **New XML Query** (Figure 5.64).

Figure 5.64: Launching XQuery Builder

Enter a name for the query (Figure 5.65). In this case, we name the query **samplequery**.

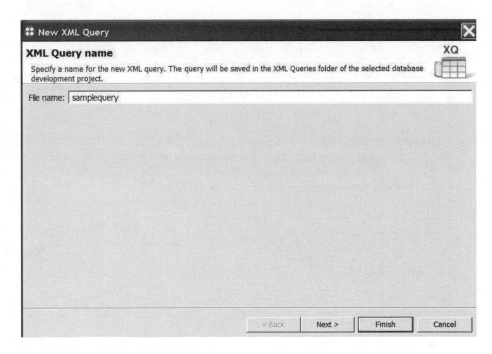

Figure 5.65: Naming an XQuery

Click **Next** to reach the **Add Representative XML Documents** window (Figure 5.66). In this case, we specify that the location of the documents is from the database.

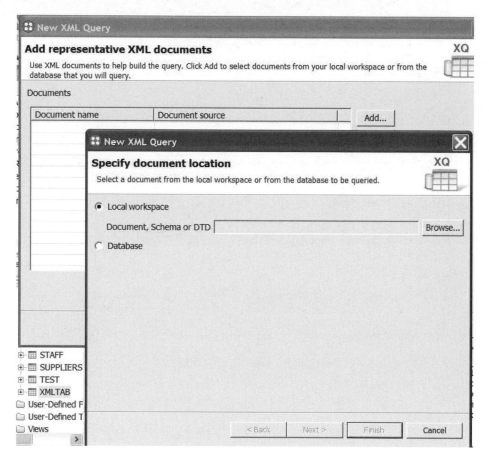

Figure 5.66: Adding representative documents

Next, we choose the table and column we want to work with (Figure 5.67).

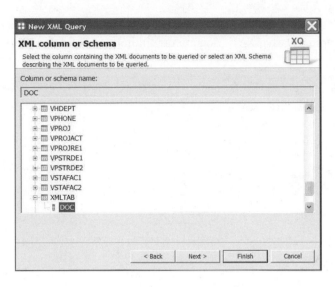

Figure 5.67: Specify the table and column to work with

Now, we need to select a document to use that will help us build the query. In Figure 5.68, we've selected the **PGUNNING_XMLTAB_DOC.xml** document.

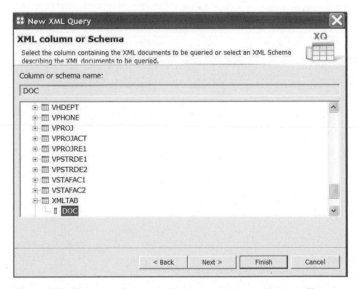

Figure 5.68: Choose a document that best represents those you'll query

After choosing a document to work with, the next step is to add it (Figure 5.69). Adding a representative XML document will help us build the query later.

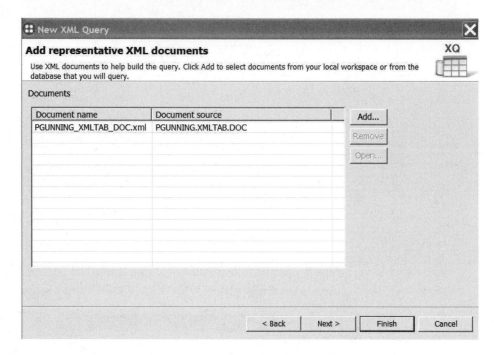

Figure 5.69: Adding representative XML documents

Click **Finish**, and the XQuery Builder is displayed (Figure 5.70).

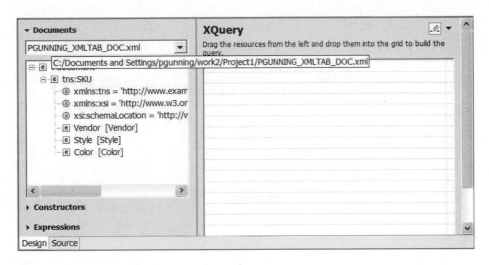

Figure 5.70: Building a query

Drag and drop the SKU node from the tree on the left into the grid on the right to build the query as shown in Figure 5.71.

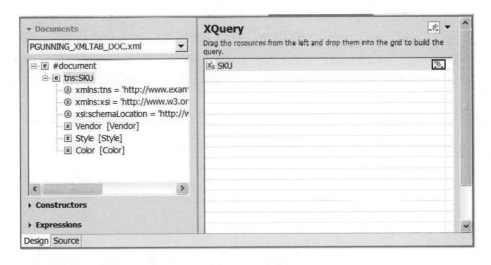

Figure 5.71: Dragging and dropping the SKU node to the grid

Next, click the Step-into icon in the upper-right corner of the grid to display
the **For Logic (FLWOR)** grid, shown in Figure 5.72.

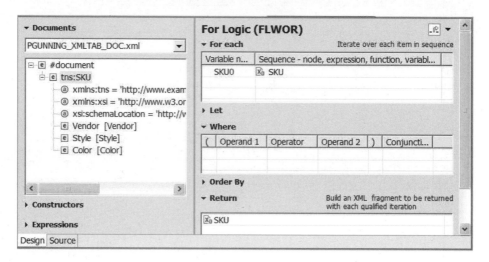

Figure 5.72: FLWOR grid

Add a WHERE predicate to the FOR logic. To do so, drag and drop the Vendor
element to the **Operand 1** column in the **WHERE** grid. Select the = operator
from the **Operator** column in the grid. Enter **Ajax** in the **Operand 2** column
of the **WHERE** grid. Then click the task bar's Save icon. Figure 5.73 shows
the data after it is entered.

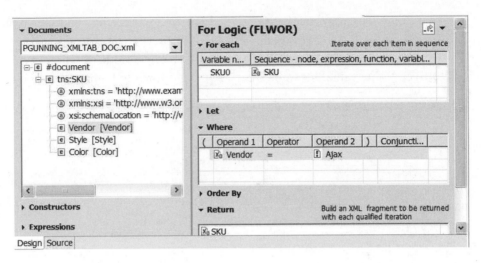

Figure 5.73: Building XQuery operators

Next, view the query in the **Source** tab (Figure 5.74).

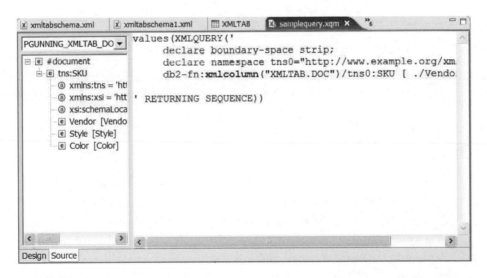

Figure 5.74: Source tab view

To execute the query, select **XQuery** > **Run** on the menu bar, and then click **Finish**. In the **Data Output** tab, verify that the query was run successfully. You should see a **Status** value of **Success**, an **Action** value of **Run**, and an **Object Name** value of **samplequery.xqm**, as shown in Figure 5.75.

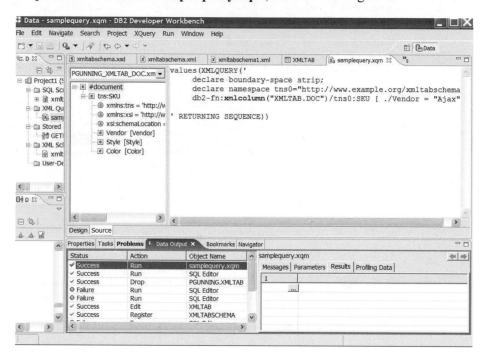

Figure 5.75: Reviewing query results

Summary

In this chapter, we covered the new DB2 9 Developer Workbench. You learned how to download, launch, and get started with DWB and worked through examples of how to set up and use DWB to develop applications. You saw how to navigate within DWB using Database and Data Explorer, explored other functionality, and learned how to create and deploy a stored procedure. With the information in this chapter, you should be able to leverage the power and flexibility of Developer Workbench to build, test, and debug your DB2 applications.

6

DB2 9 and Service Oriented Architecture

This chapter provides an overview of the Service Oriented Architecture (SOA) and how DB2 9's pureXML architecture exploits the SOA framework. You'll learn about the various components of SOA and some associated concepts and protocols, and we'll look at some examples.

Where does one begin to define SOA? A Google search on the term "SOA" (performed as I prepared to write this chapter) found 9,450,000 English-language pages. A search on "Service Oriented Architecture" yielded 1,600,000 results. When challenged by a new term, I find an encyclopedia can be a good place to start. But as the Wikipedia article that I consulted for a definition pointed out, "There is no widely agreed upon definition of SOA. . . ." Not an easy beginning. The article continued: "Service-orientation describes an architecture that uses loosely coupled services to support the requirements of business processes and users. . . ." Let me try to paint a clearer picture for you of what SOA is all about.

Service Oriented Architecture

SOA is an architecture that can be implemented using protocols. The protocols associated with SOA include Remote Procedure Call (RPC), Distributed Component Object Module (DCOM), and Web Services. The W3C defines its Web Services Architecture in terms of four models: policy, resource, service, and message. According to the W3C definition, a Web service is a software system based on this architectural model. The system interface is described using a format defined by Web Services Description Language (WSDL), and it interacts with other systems using Service Oriented Architecture Protocol (SOAP) messages.

To paraphrase, a *Web service* is reusable, self-contained software that performs a specific business task. Services have well-defined interfaces, and they are used independently of the applications or the computing platforms on which they run. Figures 6.1 and 6.2 provide an overview of the W3C's Web Services Architecture and Simplified Service Oriented Model.

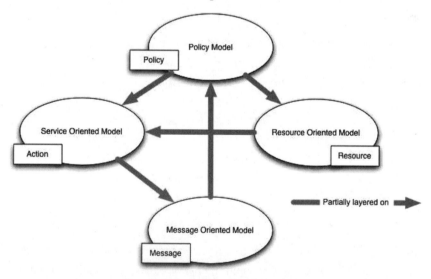

Copyright © 2004 W3C® (MIT, ERCIM, Keio), All Rights Reserved.
http://www.w3.org/TR/ws-arch/#gmm.

Figure 6.1: W3C Web Services Architecture

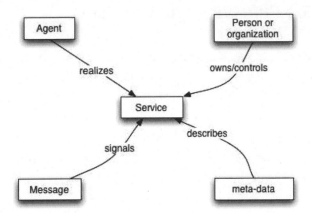

Copyright © 2004 W3C® (MIT, ERCIM, Keio), All Rights Reserved.
http://www.w3.org/TR/ws-arch/#gmm.

Figure 6.2: W3C Simplified Service Oriented Model

To the DBA, a Web service is simply a program that provides realtime access to business information. A simple example is an internal Web service application that provides the department name and number for an employee. The requester could be a payroll application or a task-scheduling module. Or, a Web service might provide a product description, image, and price as an XML document to a retailer's Web application. In each case, the requester knows neither the location of the data nor its internal format. What the requester does know is who to ask, what information to send, and the format of the returned information.

Providing information as a service can ensure verification, transformation, appropriate access, and consistency. Information as a service equals delivery on demand. It's about getting the right information to the right place at the right time.

SOA combines WSDL with XML Schema and SOAP to provide Web services. An application using a Web service reads the WSDL to determine available functions and any special data types used. Then it uses SOAP to call one of the listed functions. The WSDL specification provides the XML document format for this purpose.

Web Service Functions and Protocols

Web services involve a family of related protocols that can be subdivided based on common functions, such as interface description (WSDL), addressing (UDDI), messaging (XML), and delivery (HTTP or HTTPS). The most well-known of these functions is accomplished using the messaging protocol known as SOAP.

SOAP

SOAP is a protocol for exchanging XML-based messages. SOAP uses an Internet application layer protocol as its transport protocol. Both Simple Mail Transfer Protocol (SMTP) and Hypertext Transfer Protocol (HTTP) are valid application layer protocols used as transport for SOAP, but HTTP has gained wider acceptance because it works well with today's Internet infrastructure. SOAP can also be used over secure HTTP, or HTTPS (because HTTPS is the same protocol as HTTP at the application level), in either simple or mutual authentication.

WSDL

Web Services Description Language provides the interface definition function for Web services using a series of XML statements that constitute the definition for the interfaces of each service. WSDL contains four major elements: <portType>, <message>, <types>, and <binding>. A WSDL document can contain additional elements, such as extension elements and a service element that makes it possible to group the definitions of several Web services into a single WSDL document.

WSDL's <portType> element describes the Web service, the operation that can be performed, and the messaging elements. The <message> element defines the operational data. One or more parts of a message can be compared with the parameters of a function. The <types> element defines the data types used by the Web service, and the <binding> element defines the message format and protocol details for each port type.

Listing 6.1 shows a simplified portion of a WSDL document.

```
<message name="getDeptRequest">
   <part name="emp_no" type="xs:string"/>
</message>
<message name="getDeptResponse">
   <part name="deptname" type="xs:string"/>
</message>
<portType name="EmpInfo">
   <operation name="getDept">
      <input message="getDeptRequest"/>
      <output message="getDeptResponse"/>
   </operation>
</portType>
```

Listing 6.1: Simplified excerpt of a WSDL document

In this example, the <portType> element defines the port name as EmpInfo. The operation name is getDept. Operation getDept has an input message called getDeptRequest and an output message called getDeptResponse. In traditional programming terms, EmpInfo is a function library, and the getDept operation is a function that has getDeptRequest as its input and getDeptResponse as its output.

Listing 6.2 shows the <binding> element for our example.

```
<binding type="EmpInfo" name="b1">
  <soap:binding style="document"
      transport="http://schemas.xmlsoap.org/soap/http"/>
  <operation>
    <soap:operation
    soapAction="http://www.mycompany.com/services/getTerm"/>
    <input>
      <soap:body use="literal"/>
    </input>
    <output>
      <soap:body use="literal"/>
    </output>
  </operation>
</binding>
```

Listing 6.2: WSDL <binding> element

The <binding> element has two attributes: name and type. The name attribute specifies the name of the binding, and the type attribute points to the port for the binding—EmpInfo in this case. The <soap:binding> element also has two attributes: style (with value "rpc" or "document") and transport. The transport attribute defines the SOAP protocol to use—in this case, HTTP. The <operation> element specifies each operation that the port exposes. A corresponding SOAP action is defined for each operation, along with how the input and output are encoded.

UDDI

The next subdivision of the Web services family defines how Web services advertise themselves and find a service on the network. The Universal Description, Discovery, and Integration (UDDI) protocol defines a registry and associated protocols that services use to locate each other and access other services.

UDDI is an open industry initiative sponsored by the Organization for the Advancement of Structured Information Standards (OASIS), a global consortium that drives the development, convergence, and adoption of e-business and Web service standards. The UDDI protocol enables businesses to publish service listings, discover each other, and define how their services or software applications interact over the Internet. Figure 6.3 depicts the UDDI model.

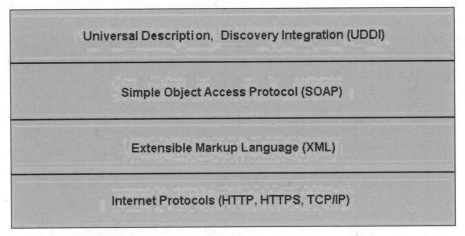

Figure courtesy of IBM, used with permission.

Figure 6.3: UDDI model

UDDI is based on W3C and Internet Engineering Task Force (IETF) standard protocols such as Domain Name Service (DNS), HTTP, and XML. UDDI uses WSDL to describe the interfaces to a Web service. UDDI benefits Web service providers and consumers in the following ways:

- By making it possible to discover the right business from the millions currently online
- By defining how to enable commerce once the preferred business is discovered
- By enabling businesses to reach new customers and increase access to current customers
- By expanding offerings and extending market reach

- By solving the customer-driven need to remove barriers to enable rapid participation in the global Internet economy
- By describing services and business processes programmatically in a single, open, and secure environment

Figure 6.4 depicts UDDI's high-level, distributed, Web service discovery architecture.

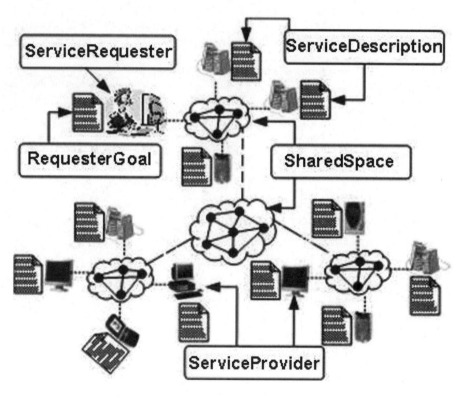

Figure courtesy of IBM, used with permission.

Figure 6.4: Web service discovery architecture

Table 6.1 describes the three components of a UDDI business registration: white pages, yellow pages, and green pages.

Table 6.1: UDDI components

Information	Operations	Detailed information
White pages: Information such as the name, address, telephone number, and other contact information of a given business.	**Publish**: How the provider of a Web service registers itself.	**Business information**: Contained in a BusinessEntity object, which in turn contains information about services, categories, contacts, URLs, and other things necessary to interact with a given business.
Yellow pages: Information that categorizes businesses.	**Find**: How an application finds a Web service.	**Service information**: Describes a group of Web services contained in a BusinessService object.
Green pages: Technical information about the Web services provided by a given business.	**Bind**: How an application connects to and interacts with a Web service after it's been found.	**Binding information**: The technical details necessary to invoke a Web service, including URLs, information about method names, argument types, and so on. The BindingTemplate object represents this data. **Service specification detail**: Metadata about the various specifications implemented by a given Web service.

UDDI is layered over SOAP and assumes that requests and responses are UDDI objects sent as SOAP messages. As an example, the query shown in Listing 6.3, when placed inside the body of a SOAP message, returns details about Microsoft.

```
<find_business generic="1.0" xmlns="urn:uddi-org:api">
<name>Microsoft</name>
</find_business>
```

Listing 6.3: UDDI SOAP message

Listing 6.4 shows the results of this query, which include information about the UDDI service itself.

```
<businessList generic="1.0"
  operator="Microsoft Corporation"
  truncated="false"
  xmlns="urn:uddi-org:api">
```

Listing 6.4: UDDI service description (part 1 of 2)

```
<businessInfos>
 <businessInfo
     businessKey="0076B468-EB27-42E5-AC09-9955CFF462A3">
  <name>Microsoft Corporation</name>
   <description xml:lang="en">
           Empowering people through great software -
           any time, any place and on any device is Microsoft's
           vision. As the worldwide leader in software for personal
           and business computing, we strive to produce innovative
           products and services that meet our customer's
   </description>
    <serviceInfos>
     <serviceInfo
        businessKey="0076B468-EB27-42E5-AC09-9955CFF462A3"
        serviceKey="1FFE1F71-2AF3-45FB-B788-09AF7FF151A4">
      <name>Web services for smart searching</name>
     </serviceInfo>
     <serviceInfo
        businessKey="0076B468-EB27-42E5-AC09-9955CFF462A3"
        serviceKey="8BF2F51F-8ED4-43FE-B665-38D8205D1333">
      <name>Electronic Business Integration Services</name>
     </serviceInfo>
     <serviceInfo
        businessKey="0076B468-EB27-42E5-AC09-9955CFF462A3"
        serviceKey="611C5867-384E-4FFD-B49C-28F93A7B4F9B">
       <name>Volume Licensing Select Program</name>
     </serviceInfo>
      <serviceInfo
        businessKey="0076B468-EB27-42E5-AC09-9955CFF462A3"
        serviceKey="A8E4999A-21A3-47FA-802E-EE50A88B266F">
       <name>UDDI Web Sites</name>
     </serviceInfo>
     </serviceInfos>
   </businessInfo>
 </businessInfos>
</businessList>
```

Listing 6.4: UDDI service description (part 2 of 2)

SOA and DB2 9

In Chapter 5, you learned about DB2 9's integrated development environment, DB2 Developer Workbench. In addition to creating DB2 stored procedures, user-defined functions, and SQLJ applications, Developer Workbench supports XML functions, the XML data type, and the creation of XQueries using the XQuery Builder.

When DB2 is a provider, a Web services client application can access a DB2 9 database through a WSDL interface. WSDL provides the interface to DB2 data using the capabilities of the Web Object Runtime Framework (WORF). Each operation can consist of DB2 stored procedure invocations, XML document storage or retrieval, or CREATE, SELECT, UPDATE, and DELETE tasks using SQL statements.

Services *consume*, or invoke, Web services by using SQL statements. Accessing Web services data directly from DB2 SQL statements does not require a Java application server or the DB2 Web service provider. A DB2 database administrator or database developer creates these SQL extensions. During SQL statement execution, a connection with the Web service provider is established, and the response document is returned as a relation table or a scalar value.

Figure 6.5 depicts DB2 functioning as a Web service provider and also as a Web service consumer and shows how other Web services components come into play.

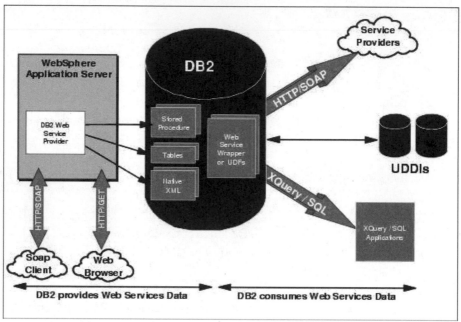

Figure courtesy of IBM, used with permission.
Figure 6.5: DB2 Web service components (provider and consumer)

The DB2 Web services runtime environment includes various database management tools and WORF. The WORF runtime environment provides a simple mapping of XML schema to SQL data types. If you don't use the WORF runtime environment, you must handle the details of creating the Web service, such as developing your own WSDL. Among the functions WORF provides are the following:

- Analyzing the Web service request
- Connecting to the database
- Executing the SQL request
- Encoding the output message from the SQL results
- Returning the message to the client WORF uses an XML data format called Document Access Definition Extension (DADX) to simplify access to DB2 data. A DADX file specifies how to create a Web service. Web services specified in a DADX file are called *DADX Web*

services or *DB2 Web services*. WORF provides the runtime support for invoking DADX documents as Web services. Figure 6.6 provides an overview of the WORF architecture.

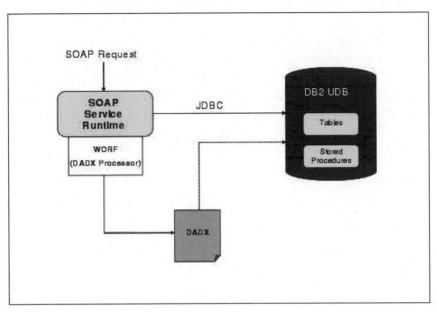

Figure courtesy of IBM, used with permission.

Figure 6.6: WORF architecture

The DADX file defines a Web service by specifying a set of available operations. The operation definition contains a list of parameters and the actions to be performed. A Web service developer creates the DADX by using SQL statements, a list of parameters, and, optionally, a Document Access Definition (DAD) file. A *DADX file* makes one Web service—meaning there is one WSDL document for each DADX file. A *DADX group* is a grouping of one or more DADX files. A DADX group contains connection (e.g., JDBC, JNDI) and other information that is shared among DADX files within the group.

DADX files support three kinds of operations: non dynamic SQL, dynamic SQL, and XML collection (from the DB2 XML Extender). A non dynamic

DADX file defines a set of predetermined SQL operations and contains information used to create the Web service. If the DADX file contains a dynamic query services tag (<DQS/>), you can specify the SQL operations from a browser or embed them in an application.

With dynamic query services, you can dynamically build and submit queries at runtime to select, insert, update, and delete application data, and you can call stored procedures rather than run queries that are predefined at deployment time. By using the dynamic query services of the Web services provider, Web applications can be more flexible.

Figure 6.7 depicts the relationship between DB2 and the DADX components.

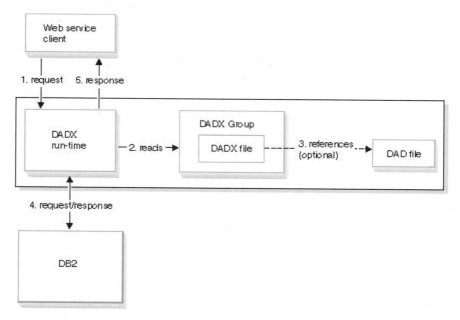

Figure courtesy of IBM, used with permission.

Figure 6.7: DB2, DADX runtime, DADX group, and DADX file relationships

DB2 Example

Let's put the concepts into action now by looking at an example. Imagine we have a business function that we'd like to publish: a Web service that provides the department name for a specific employee identifier. The first step to making this service available is to define a DADX file that describes how to create the Web service. You can create this file using a simple text editor or a tool such as DB2 Developer Workbench. The DADX file defines the database interface, which can be dynamic or static SQL, XQuery, or a stored procedure call. Listing 6.5 shows the DADX document for our example.

```xml
<?xml version="1.0" encoding="UTF-8"?>
<DADX   xmlns="http://schemas.ibm.com/db2/dxx/dadx">
  <documentation>
    Simple DADX example that accesses the SAMPLE database.
  </documentation>
  <operation name="getDept">
    <documentation>
      Returns an employee's department.
    </documentation>
    <query>
      <SQL_query>SELECT DEPT.DEPTNAME
                 FROM EMPLOYEE AS EMP
                 INNER JOIN DEPARTMENT AS DEPT
                 ON EMP.WORKDEPT = DEPT.DEPTNO
                 WHERE EMP.EMPNO = :emp_no
      </SQL_query>
      <parameter name="emp_no" type="xsd:string"/>
    </query>
  </operation>
</DADX>
```

Listing 6.5: Sample DADX file EmpInfo.DADX

By using the <update> element instead of the <query> element, the DADX can specify SQL INSERT, UPDATE, or DELETE statements. Similarly, it can invoke a stored procedure by using the <call> element. A DADX can contain multiple <operation> elements. The queries can also include the DB2 9 XQuery function. XQuery provides a way to extract and manipulate data from XML documents or any data source that can be viewed as XML, such as DB2 9 XML table columns. XQuery uses the XPath expression syntax to address specific parts of an XML document, supplementing this syntax with an SQL-like *FLWOR expression* for performing joins. A FLWOR expression is constructed from the five clauses after which it is named: FOR, LET, WHERE, ORDER BY, and RETURN.

To deploy the Web service defined in the DADX file, you copy it to the application server in the appropriate group directory. A group is a container for Web services that share common configuration options, such as database configuration, namespace setup, and message encoding setup. WORF and a DADX file generate a documentation page, a test page, the WSDL documents, and an XML schema.

If we deploy this Web service on the host www.mycompany.com, the following URL would invoke the service:

```
http://www.mycompany.com/services/EmpInfo.dadx/GetDept?
emp_no=000010
```

Summary

This chapter presented an overview of SOA and various SOA-related architectures. We looked at the protocols involved in providing and accessing Web services and discussed DB2 9's support for SOA functionality. With SOA, you can provide information as a service to ensure verification, transformation, appropriate access, and consistency.

7

Logical and Physical Design

In this chapter, we examine the concepts and tasks involved in designing a database. The process begins with the development of a logical design, which is documented in a logical model. The logical model in turn serves as the primary input to the physical database design.

Logical design is the most important step in designing a database. If you don't do it in the beginning (and do it right), the implementation will likely fail, requiring serious changes to the application and database structure in production. Such changes usually are made at the expense of business lost when the new system doesn't work or provides only limited functionality or performance. I've never worked on a project that skipped the logical design and was successful; I doubt that you have, or ever will, either.

Data governance and compliance represent additional areas where logical design has implications. The Enron fiasco and the passing of the Sarbanes-Oxley (SOX) and Healthcare Insurance Portability and Accountability (HIPAA) acts have sparked renewed interested in these issues. A solid business model and associated logical model are critical to making sure your company is in compliance and protected.

Logical Design

Logical design is the process of identifying business entities and the relationships between those entities. The process begins with the business model, which is transitioned to a logical model. All new database projects, as well as changes and improvements to existing applications, require a logical design.

You use a logical model to document the logical design. Several data modeling tools on the market facilitate this task, including ER/Studio from Embarcadero Technologies, ERwin from Computer Associates, PowerDesigner from Sybase, and Rational Application Developer from IBM, to name a few.

The logical design process and the availability and upkeep of the logical model are key ingredients to a successful project and database implementation. You can customize the logical design process or tailor it for enhancements or maintenance projects, but don't skip it.

Business Model

The *business model* describes business entities, functions, and relationships and the business rules associated with them. The business model is essential to logical design and serves as the primary input to the logical design process. Business architects and analysts are responsible for developing and maintaining the business model. Figure 7.1 shows an example.

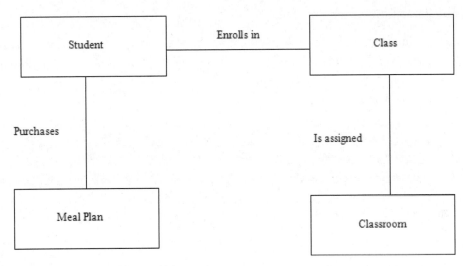

Figure 7.1: Sample business model

The business model in the figure identifies several business entities and the basic relationships among them. In addition to such a diagram, a complete business model includes data flow diagrams, state diagrams, business rule documentation, and other documents that help to further define the functions of the business. The business model reflects the business practices of an organization independently of any requirements for the underlying structure of an RDBMS.

The following rules guide the development and definition of business models:

- Each entity should have a *self-describing name* that is understood and acceptable throughout the organization.
- Each entity should have a *complete definition* that specifies what is included and excluded in the entity.
- Each entity should have an *identifier* to distinguish it from other entities or from multiple occurrences of the entity type.

Business Entities

Business architects are responsible for identifying and documenting business entities, relationships, and business rules. They often do so using a tabular form. Table 7.1 shows an example that documents a group of business entities in this way.

Entity name	Abbreviation	Identifier	Description
STUDENT	STUDENT	Unique Student ID	A registered student
CLASS	CLASS	Unique Class Number	Class offered
INSTRUCTOR	INST	Unique Instructor ID	Instructor ID

Table 7.1: Business entities documentation

Conceptual Model

Once you've identified and documented the business entities, you refine the business model into a *conceptual model* that further describes the entities and relationships represented. An *entity-relationship (ER) diagram* is one form of conceptual model. Figure 7.2 shows the ER diagram for our example.

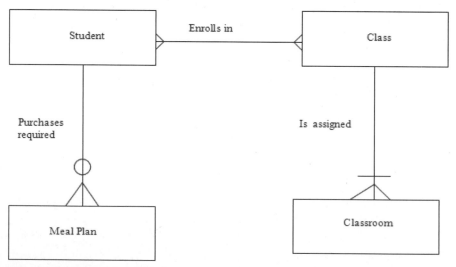

Figure 7.2: Entity-relationship diagram

Logical Model

After constructing the ER diagram, the next step is to convert it to a *logical model* using the following steps:

1. Convert business entities to data entities.
2. Represent the cardinality, or degree, of the relationships between entities.
3. Identify conditional relationships.
4. Convert many-to-many relationships.
5. Convert repeating groups to characteristic entities.

Figure 7.3 shows the logical model produced after converting the conceptual model in Figure 7.2 to a logical model using these steps.

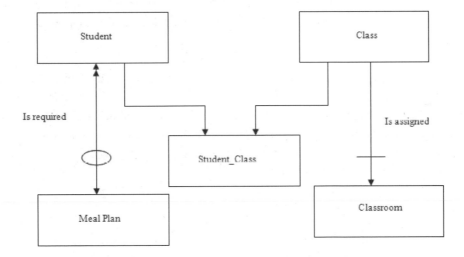

Figure 7.3: ER diagram converted to logical model

This diagram defines the cardinality of the relationships between the entities and creates the Student_Class associative entity to eliminate the many-to-many relationship between Student and Class. (You'll see the reasoning behind this step later in the chapter.) Notice the oval near the Meal Plan entity. This symbol denotes an *optional relationship* between Student and Meal Plan. A student can exist without having a meal plan, as is sometimes the case with students who commute. The short horizontal line across the vertical line connecting Class and Classroom identifies a *mandatory relationship*. A Class cannot exist unless it is assigned to a Classroom.

Business Rules

Optional and mandatory relationships are useful for documenting and enforcing business rules, which define how a business operates. For example, a business rule might state that a customer can have only one charge account, that an invoice can't be paid unless associated with a valid purchase order, or that a valid Social Security number must be associated with each customer charge account. These types of business rules are known as *constraints*. Business rules also define the cardinality of the relationship between business entities.

Business rules are unique to each business and can vary widely from one organization to another. However, with the advent of XML schemas, industry-standard schemas are becoming quite common, and associated business rules are being adopted along with them, facilitating the rapid exchange of information via XML among companies.

Entities and Relationships

Once you've identified the business entities, relationships, and rules, entity-relationship diagrams let you document these elements as part of the logical design process. The conceptual model represented using an ER diagram is as close to a real-world view of an organization's data as possible. P. P. Chen invented this method of diagramming in 1976.

Before you can develop ER diagrams and conduct the normalization process to identify and eliminate redundant data elements, it's helpful to understand some important terms, a few of which have come up already. Let's review some definitions.

Entity

An *entity* is a person, place, thing, concept, or event. You can think of an entity as a noun.

Relationship

A *relationship* describes the association between entities. You can think of a relationship as a verb. We define relationships in terms of action words. A relationship can be optional or mandatory, as previously described.

Relation

A *relation* is a two-dimensional table consisting of attributes (columns) and tuples (rows).

Functional Dependencies

A *functional dependency* is a relationship between or among attributes. An example would be that if we are given the value of one attribute, we can obtain the value of another attribute. For example, if we know the value of STUDENT_ID, we can find the value of GRADE_LEVEL. We can restate this relationship using the notation:

STUDENT_ID ➔ GRADE_LEVEL

which can be read as, "The attribute STUDENT_ID determines the attribute GRADE_LEVEL" (or, "GRADE_LEVEL is determined by STUDENT_ID"). The attributes on the left side of the arrow (→) are called *determinants*. Later, you'll see how functional dependencies can be used to normalize relations.

Key

A *key* is a group of one or more attributes that uniquely identifies a row. Every relation must contain a primary key. Note that keys and functional dependencies are determined not by some arbitrary set of rules but by the business rules of the organization.

Primary Key

A *primary key* is a candidate key that is selected as the unique identifier of a row.

Candidate Key

A *candidate key* is an attribute, or combination of attributes, that uniquely identifies an instance of a relation.

Foreign Key

You use a *foreign key* to record the relationships between entities. When you define a foreign key, you place the primary key of the entity that is on the "one" side of a one-to-one or one-to-many relationship into the entity on the corresponding one or many side. Foreign keys are used to implement referential integrity, and they can have additional rules associated with them. For example, a rule might state that if the parent entry in a parent-child relationship is deleted, the associated entries in the child entity will be deleted. (This type of delete is known as *cascade delete*.)

Cardinality

Cardinality is the degree of the relationship between entities. For our purposes, three cardinalities will be sufficient:

- One-to-one
- One-to-many
- Many-to-many

The following definitions use the functional dependency (FD) notation described earlier to indicate the relationships identified by each of these cardinalities.

One-to-One Relationship (A → B and B → A)

In a one-to-one relationship, a single instance of one type is related to a single entity of the other type. For example, in Figure 7.4, the EMPLOYEE-CUBICLE relationship associates a single employee with a single cubicle. According to this relationship, no employee has more than one cubicle, and one cubicle cannot be assigned to more than one employee.

Figure 7.4: One-to-one relationship

One-to-Many Relationship (A → B but B not → A)

In a one-to-many relationship, a single instance of one type is related to many instances of the other type. In Figure 7.5, the DEPARTMENT-EMPLOYEE relationship shows that an employee is assigned to one department and that a department has many employees.

Figure 7.5: One-to-many relationship

Many-to-Many Relationship (A Not → B and B Not → A)

In a many-to-many relationship, many instances of one type are related to many instances of the other type. In Figure 7.6, the STUDENT-ORGANIZATION relationship associates many instances of Student to many instances of Organization. A student can join more than one organization, and an organization can have many students as members.

Figure 7.6: Many-to-many relationship

Special Entity Relationships

Two special entity types can be used to resolve problems that arise under certain conditions in the logical model with repeating groups and many-to-many relationships that violate Codd's rules for relational databases: characteristic entities and associative entities.

Characteristic Entity

Repeating groups present a problem to relational databases. The trouble is caused by the storing of redundant data and the loss of flexibility if additional elements have to be added. To address this issue, you can define a *characteristic entity*, which essentially involves creating another entity using the primary key from the original entity and then adding columns to the primary key to ensure uniqueness.

For example, in the following relation, a manager can receive more than one bonus. Thus, we have a repeating group, the attribute MGR_BONUS.

MANAGER (MGR_ID, MGR_NAME, MGR_BRANCH, MGR_HIRE_DATE, MGR_BONUS1, MGR_BONUS2, ... , MGR_BONUS5)

As the MANAGER relation depicts, a finance company manager can receive up to five bonuses in a year. The relation defines five columns to store this BONUS information. However, if the company decides to give a manager a sixth bonus (BONUS6), it won't be able to. To solve this problem, we can create a new characteristic entity as follows:

BONUS (MGR_ID, BON_DATE, BON_AMOUNT)

With MGR_ID and BON_DATE together serving as the primary key, this relation resolves the repeating group problem and is much more flexible, enabling a manager to receive any number of bonuses without necessitating any changes to the underlying table. However, the business rule in this case allows just one bonus to be issued per day. That certainly is a reasonable business rule!

Associative Entity

You use an *associative entity* to resolve many-to-many relationships, which are difficult to support in an RDBMS and are subject to modification anomalies. In the following example, a many-to-many relationship exists between STUDENT and CLASS:

STUDENT (ID, NAME, ADDRESS, PHONE_NMR, EMERG_CONTACT)
CLASS (CLASS_NAME, NBR_CREDITS, PREREQUISITES, CLASS_NBR)

149

We can resolve the many-to-many relationship by creating an associative entity, STU_CLASS, that serves as a "go-between" between the two related identities:

STU_CLASS (<u>ID</u>, <u>CLASS_NBR</u>, NAME)

The new entity contains the primary keys from STUDENT and CLASS (ID and CLASS_NBR) as the new primary key. These columns are also foreign keys, which point to the parent table. The new relationship contains two one-to-many relationships, which are much easier to understand and more accurately reflect how the data is used.

Normalization

After identifying business entities and converting them to a logical model, you need to normalize the logical model. *Normalization* is the process of identifying and eliminating redundant data elements in the logical design to avoid update and delete anomalies.

The normalization process evolves through a series of forms (defined by the computer scientist E. F. Codd in 1970) that have defined rules that you apply to each entity in an iterative approach. For our purposes, we'll discuss five types of normal forms:

- First normal form (1NF)
- Second normal form (2NF)
- Third normal form (3NF)
- Boyce-Codd normal form (BCNF)
- Domain/key normal form (DK/NF)

DBAs should also be familiar with elementary key normal form (EKNF) and project-join normal form (PJNF), but these forms are beyond the scope of this chapter.

First Normal Form (1NF)

A relation is in *first normal form* if it contains no repeating groups. In other words, each attribute (or column) must have only one value; neither arrays nor repeating groups are allowed. Let's take a look at the CUSTOMER_ACCOUNT relation, defined as

CUSTOMER_ACCOUNT (CUST_ID, ACCT_NBR, CUST_NM, ADDRESS, TYPE, DESCRIPTION, BRANCH_NBR, BRANCH_ADDR)

where:

- CUST_ID = Customer identifier
- ACCT_NBR = Account number
- CUST_NM = Customer name
- ADDRESS = Customer address
- TYPE = Account type
- DESCRIPTION = Account description
- BRANCH_NBR = Branch number
- BRANCH_ADDR = Branch address

This relation is in 1NF because it has no repeating groups. However, it has some inherent modification anomalies. What happens if a customer closes his or her account? All data regarding that customer, such as customer identification, account number, and customer address, will be lost. Also, inserting new data is a problem. The account type, account description, and branch address cannot be inserted until a customer opens an account.

The problem with the CUSTOMER_ACCOUNT relation is that non-key attributes are dependent on parts of the primary key, but not the entire key. We can see this by identifying the functional dependencies involved:

- CUST_ID → CUST_NM but ACCT_NBR → CUST_NM
- CUST_ID → ADDRESS but ACCT_NBR → ADDRESS
- CUST_ID → TYPE but ACCT_NBR → TYPE
- ACCT_NBR → DESCRIPTION but CUST_ID → DESCRIPTION
- ACCT_NBR → BRANCH_NBR but CUST_ID → BRANCH_NBR
- ACCT_NBR → BRANCH_ADDR but CUST_ID → BRANCH_ADDR

To eliminate modification anomalies, relations in 1NF must be normalized to 2NF and 3NF. These steps will result in more entities being created throughout the normalization process.

Second Normal Form (2NF)

A relation is in *second normal form* if it is in 1NF and all of its non-key attributes are dependent on all of the key. Therefore, if the key has only one attribute, the relation must be in 2NF.

We can decompose the CUSTOMER_ACCOUNT relation into four new relations as follows:

CUST_MSTR (<u>CUST ID</u>, CUST_NM, ADDRESS)
BRANCH_LOC (<u>BRANCH NBR</u>, BRANCH_ADDR)
ACCT_TYPE (<u>TYPE</u>, DESCRIPTION)
CUST_ACCT (<u>CUST ID</u>, <u>ACCT NBR</u>)

These new relations are in 2NF. The CUST_MSTR, BRANCH_LOC, and ACCT_TYPE relation have primary keys with just one attribute. And the CUST_ACCT relation contains no non-key attributes. Customer information can be inserted into the CUST_MSTR relation before an account is opened. Deletion of all customers assigned to a certain branch will not result in branch information being deleted. Deletion of all accounts for a customer will not result in loss of customer data.

Relations that are in 2NF can still have modification anomalies. For example, the relation

BANK_FEES (<u>ACCT NBR</u>, TRAN_TYPE, FEE)

is in 2NF because the primary key, ACCT_NBR, has only one attribute, but there is a dependency involving a non-key attribute (TRAN_TYPE) on another non-key attribute (FEE). By identifying functional dependencies, we can identify the anomalies as follows:

ACCT NBR ➔ TRAN_TYPE
ACCT_NBR ➔ TRAN_TYPE ➔ FEE

We have dependencies between non-key attributes: the TRAN_TYPE and FEE.

TRAN_TYPE ➔ FEE

The fee charged is determined by the transaction type. What happens if we delete an account number from the BANK_FEES relation? We lose the fact that a certain transaction type is associated with a specific fee.

Another method you can use to normalize relations is the concept of *themes*. In general, if there are multiple themes in a relation, the relation can be decomposed further into relations with single themes to eliminate modification anomalies. Consider the following relation, which has two

themes, one containing student activity information and one containing
activity cost information.

STUD_ACTIVITY (STU ID, ACTIVITY, FEE)

We can decompose these relations into additional single-theme relations:

STU_ACT (STU ID, ACTIVITY)
ACTIVITY_COST (ACTIVITY, FEE)

You can use whichever technique you're more comfortable with.

Third Normal Form (3NF)

A relation is in *third normal form* if it is in 2NF and has no transitive
dependencies. Another well-known definition for 3NF is a situation in
which an attribute is "a function of the key, the whole key, and nothing
but the key."

The BANK_FEES relation illustrated the transitive dependency between
TRAN_TYPE and FEE. To resolve this dependency, the relation can be
decomposed into two new relations as follows:

BANK_FEES (TRAN TYPE, FEE)
ACTIVITY (ACCT NBR, TRAN_TYPE)

Boyce-Codd Normal Form (BCNF)

Relations in 3NF can still have modification anomalies. Hence, we can
continue to normalize relations in our search to eliminate modification
anomalies. A relation is in *Boyce-Codd normal form* if every determinant
is a candidate key. Consider the following relation:

ADVISER (SID, MAJOR, FAC_NAM)

In this relation, a student can have more than one major (MAJOR). A major can have several faculty members (FAC_NAM) as advisers, and a faculty member (FAC_NAM) advises in only one major area. The (SID, MAJOR) combination determines FAC_NAM, and the (SID, FAC_NAM) combination determines the major. Hence, both of these combinations are candidate keys. In addition, FAC_NAM determines MAJOR (any faculty member advises in only one major; therefore, given the FAC_NAM, we can determine MAJOR). So, FAC_NAM is a determinant. But ADVISER is in 3NF because it is in 2NF and there are no transitive dependencies.

However, ADVISER still has modification anomalies. Suppose a student drops out of school? If we delete the row with the SID of 500, we lose the fact that the assigned adviser advises in psychology. This is a *deletion anomaly*. Similarly, we cannot store the fact that an adviser advises in history until a student majors in history. This is an *insertion anomaly*. As with previous examples, we can decompose ADVISER into two relations to resolve the anomalies. The two new relations are:

STUDENT_ADVISER (STU_ID, FAC_NAM)
ADV_SUBJ (FAC_NAM, SUBJECT)

These two new relations are now in BCNF normal form and have no anomalies in regard to functional dependencies.

Domain/Key Normal Form (DK/NF)

The *domain/key normal form* was defined in 1981 by R. Fagin. A relation is in DK/NF if every constraint on the relation is a logical consequence of the definition of keys and domains. To understand DK/NF form, you need to understand a couple of additional definitions.

A *constraint* is any rule governing the static values of attributes that is precise enough to enable us to determine whether the constraint is true. (Note that time-dependent constraints are excluded from this definition.) Valid constraints are edit rules, functional, and multi-value dependencies and inter- and intra-relational constraints.

A *domain* is a description of the allowed values of an attribute. Check constraints are an example of this in DB2. A domain has two parts: a physical description, which defines the set of values the attribute can have, and a logical description, which defines the meaning of the attribute.

A relation is in DK/NF if enforcing key and domain restrictions causes all the constraints to be met. DK/NF is especially important to RDBMSs because they can prohibit modification anomalies by enforcing key and domain restrictions.

A straightforward approach for converting relations to DK/NF has not been defined. However, most RDBMSs provide the facilities for accomplishing this task. If the database can't implement the constraints, they can be coded into the application logic.

Consider the CUSTOMER relation:

CUSTOMER (CUST_ID, ACCT_LEVEL, ACCT_TYPE, FEE)

---

where

- CUST_ID = Customer identifier
- ACCT_TYPE = Account type
- FEE = Fee charged based on type of account

In this relation, CUST_ID functionally determines ACCT_LEVEL, ACCT_TYPE, and FEE, so CUST_ID is the key. Our business rules in this relation place domain constraints on each of the attributes, and we know that ACCT-TYPE ➔ FEE. In accordance with the rules for DK/NF, we need to make the functional dependency ACCT_TYPE ➔ FEE a logical consequence of keys. If ACCT_TYPE were a key attribute, ACCT_TYPE ➔ FEE would be a logical consequence of the key.

ACCT_TYPE cannot be a key in CUSTOMER because more than one customer can have the same account type. But it can be a key of its own relation. So, we define the following domain definition, relations, and attributes.

- Domain definitions:
  - » CUST_ID in *DDDDDD*, where *D* is a decimal digit 0–999999
  - » ACCT_LEVEL in ("PERS", "CML", "INTB")
  - » ACCT_TYPE in CHAR (3)
  - » FEE in DEC (4)
- Relation and key definitions:
  - » CUSTOMER (CUST_ID, ACCT_LEVEL, ACCT_TYPE)
  - » ACCT_FEE (ACCT_TYPE, FEE)

We know that by converting the relation to DK/NF, the relations have no modification anomalies whatsoever. We could have arrived at this result by converting form 2NF to 3NF to remove transitive dependencies. However, using DK/NF, we just need to make all the constraints logical consequences of domain and key definitions.

Unified Modeling Language

The Object Management Group (OMG) adopted the *Unified Modeling Language (UML)* in November 1997 as a language for object-oriented analysis and design. The OMG received input on the UML specification from industry leaders such as IBM, Microsoft, and Oracle. In addition to being used to design object-oriented programs, UML has made inroads into logical database design. This evolution is a natural one because UML-capable tools are widely used to model, construct, and deploy enterprise applications.

UML class diagrams are similar to entities in ER diagrams and can be used for conceptual and logical design. Many UML-capable tools can input and convert ER diagrams to object class diagrams. In practice, I find that the Information Engineering (IE) notation presented earlier in this chapter is still the most prevalent modeling language in use, but you need to become familiar with UML so that you can understand and support application development efforts that are based on UML.

A Word About Modeling Tool Support for XML

As of the writing of this book, most of the leading data-modeling tool vendors have not yet integrated XML modeling into their tools. However, IBM's Rational Software Architect (RSA) provides support for transforming UML into XML schemas (XSDs) as well as support for Web Service Definition Language (WSDL) artifacts. You can find additional open-source software for generating application code from XML schemas and DTDs at *http://www.rpbourret.com/xml/XMLDataBinding.htm*.

Logical Design Outputs

The primary output of the logical design process is a logical model that identifies the entities, relationships, and attributes for the data being modeled. The logical design is complete with primary and foreign keys and constraints defined on the data, and it should contain data normalized to at least 3NF, or to DK/NF if possible. The logical model is the primary input to physical design, to which we now turn our attention.

Physical Design

Once the logical design has been completed, physical design can begin. *Physical design* consists of the following five steps:

1. Denormalization
2. Creation of indexes
3. Creation of table spaces and tables
    » Container layout
    » Disk strategy
4. Table space breakout strategy
5. Buffer pool strategy

Denormalization

Normalized relations eliminate or reduce modification anomalies. However, the process also results in many more relations, which subsequently will be converted (in most cases) to DB2 tables. Sometimes the costs (query runtime and complexity) outweigh the benefits of normalization.

With continued enhancements to the DB2 optimizer, cost is not as much a factor as it used to be (in terms of processing many table joins and so on), but it still can be a factor to consider when trying to optimize the physical design. *Denormalization* is the process of combining relations, or attributes from relations, to reduce the number of relations to be processed and lessen the complexity of queries. Denormalization is sometimes referred to as "controlled redundancy." It is primarily done for performance gains, to provide read-only tables for decision reports, or for ad hoc reporting. But, like "Caveat emptor," the data administrator or DBA must be aware of the subsequent modification anomalies that such redundancy can produce. You can perform denormalization using just the logical model, but the results are much better if you have access to the SQL as well so you can be aware of the relationships and joins involved.

Reverse Engineering

Reverse engineering is useful when a logical or physical model isn't available and there is a need to document the design. It is also helpful when a packaged application has been purchased but the requisite data model is not available. With a model of the data, you can develop customized interfaces, fill gaps in data, develop interfaces, or just generally better understand the entities and relationships involved.

Reverse engineering tells you what you have, but it doesn't tell how the design was developed. Reverse engineering is a good start when you have nothing, but it does not replace logical design. It is not a substitute for business process modeling and logical design. Most modeling tools include a reverse-engineering option.

Forward Engineering

Forward engineering is concerned with applying knowledge gained from lessons learned from current business processes, designs, and models and using such knowledge to improve business processes and logical and physical models. Forward engineering is often thought of as being just the capability to generate database objects (Data Definition Language, or DDL) from existing models, but it is more than that. You can apply forward engineering during logical design to improve existing designs, create new designs, or develop modifications to existing designs. You can obtain forward-engineering data from former systems, business process models, and ongoing monitoring of existing systems.

> **Note:** Many logical-modeling tools can generate DDL to create the physical objects. Use this generated SQL (you can modify it, if necessary) to save time and increase productivity.

Creation of Indexes

Unique (primary key) indexes and indexes on foreign keys should be created based on the logical model. Secondary indexes to support SQL queries, join operations, and business reports should be created as part of the physical design. For this to occur, the SQL must be provided to the DBA staff at this time. Too often, though, this is not the case and the SQL is not available, making it difficult to identify all the required secondary indexes. What usually happens in this case is that the application doesn't meet performance expectations in production, and significant modification to programs and indexes is required.

If the SQL is available at the initial physical design, the DBA can create indexes to meet the needs of the business. Follow these guidelines when creating secondary indexes:

- Create indexes to eliminate sorts required by ORDER BY, GROUP BY, and DISTINCT SQL statements.
- Create indexes on joined columns. (Failure to do so could result in a Cartesian product, which is not always desirable.)
- Create indexes on local predicates to achieve index-only access.
- Consider using INCLUDE columns to obtain index-only access.
- Create indexes including the ALLOW REVERSE SCANS clause to eliminate sorts.
- Create indexes on foreign keys.
- Create a clustering index on every table.
- Consider use of APPEND ON for highly inserted tables.

- Use multidimensional clustering (MDC) indexes for data warehousing environments, and consider MDC for OLTP environments.

- Consider purge or archive requirements (use of partitioned tables for archives).

For more information about indexes, see Chapter 9.

Creation of Table Spaces and Tables

You also need to develop a table space and table strategy as part of the physical design process, resolving issues such as the type of space that will be used (system-managed or database-managed) as well as the size and number of tables per table space and the number of containers to be used.

> **Note:** By default the DB2_PARALLEL_IO environmental variable assumes that table spaces are defined on RAID devices with a default of six physical disks. If you're using a different configuration, change this setting to reflect the correct number of disks.

File systems must be built or drive assignments verified and logical volumes requested from network or storage administrators. Coordination with system, storage, and possibly network administrators goes a long way in developing an efficient physical design. Develop your storage space estimates in conjunction with developers and business architects. When evaluating your disk space requirements, the overriding factor to consider is the number of physical disks required to provide the requisite database performance. *Don't let space requirements alone dictate the number of physical disks required.* As a DBA or developer, you must be concerned with identifying the number of physical disks required to meet design requirements, not just space!

With disk densities ever-increasing, never has it been more important to identify the number of physical disks required to provide requisite database performance. Use the following best practices to guide you:

- For OLTP and Web applications: 10 to 20 physical disks per CPU
- For DW/BI applications, 6 to 10 physical disks per CPU

In nearly every consulting engagement I've ever been involved in, when all was said and done the lack of physical disks was a major performance bottleneck. So the message is worth repeating: Follow the guidelines above!

Table Space Breakout Strategy

A table space breakout strategy consists of the following:

- Assigning high-priority tables to a single table space
- Placing high-priority table spaces in dedicated buffer pools and/or on separate physical disks or disk arrays
- Creating separate table space for indexes and/or assigning indexes to separate buffer pools

Buffer Pool Strategy

The physical design should assign objects to buffer pools based on business priorities and access type. Business priorities are contained in or derived from business needs. Access type pertains to whether the access is sequential or random. Place objects with different access types into different buffer pools. That way, an object with lots of sequential prefetch against it won't compete for buffer pool space with randomly accessed objects. Refer to Chapter 8 for more information about tuning buffer pools.

Summary

As you've learned, logical design is the single most important step in database design. During this process, business architects identify business entities and business rules and develop the conceptual model. Data administrators or DBAs then develop the logical design and normalize it to meet business objectives, typically to 3NF or DK/NF.

The logical model is the key input to the physical design process. Most modeling tools can generate DDL for use in building the physical design. Table space design, as well as container strategy and disk layout, need to be planned and coordinated with system, SAN and network administrators. The need to identify the number of physical disks as part of physical design is critical. Last, use business priorities in developing a table space breakout and buffer pool strategy.

8

Tuning Buffer Pools

DB2 uses areas of computer memory called *buffer pools* to minimize disk I/O to the computer's disk storage devices. When DB2 executes SQL statements, the DB2 optimizer controls access to certain index and data pages. Often, especially in OLTP systems, indexes are accessed first to locate actual table data (using the RID, or row ID); then, the table space data pages are accessed to retrieve the data. DB2 first tries to locate the required index and data pages in its buffer pool memory by performing *logical reads*. If the required data isn't found to be already present in buffer pool memory, DB2 issues a *physical read* to obtain the required data from disk storage.

Accessing memory is extremely fast because most commercially available memory chips deliver performance that is measured in nanoseconds—often 70 ns or faster. Contrast this performance with the time typically required to access disk storage devices, a rate we commonly measure in milliseconds. Good disk performance typically is measured in the 3 ms to 4 ms range, suggesting that accessing memory for data is about 900 to 1,000 times faster than accessing disk storage. It follows logically, then, that the more data we can store in DB2 buffer pool memory, the faster the database will perform because it can avoid physical reads of disk storage devices.

Be cautioned, however, that you cannot successfully use extremely large buffer pools to offset the poor performance of an application that has an improper physical design. If indexes are missing, or are suboptimally defined, DB2 will have to perform hundreds, if not thousands, of logical reads (which may require physical reads) to search memory and find appropriate results for SQL statements. Large memory scans consume a great deal of CPU resources, and this is why so many of today's business applications are CPU-constrained and fail to scale as new users and data are added. Large memory scans and subsequent high CPU burn are manifested even more with large buffer pools and the advent of 64-bit addressability.

This chapter introduces you to buffer pools, describing how to create, alter, drop, and monitor them. You'll also read how to monitor tables and table spaces and learn several important formulas for evaluating table space and buffer pool performance. We'll discuss tuning in detail later in the chapter.

Creating Buffer Pools

You can define buffer pools in 4K, 8K, 16K, or 32K page sizes. The page size to use depends on the page size (or sizes) of the table space (or spaces) assigned to the buffer pool. You'll use larger page sizes when table row widths (number of bytes) exceed the capacity of the smaller page sizes. It is good and common practice to limit any given database to using either one or two different page sizes, with larger page sizes becoming more prevalent.

The amount of memory allocated to buffer pools will be limited primarily to the amount of real memory installed in the machine, less reserves for operating system functions, application programs, and other DB2 memory heaps and caches. As a rule of thumb, shops often dedicate 50 percent to 75 percent of real memory to DB2 buffer pools on a DB2 server machine. However, you should base the ultimate amount of memory used for buffer pools on an amount that meets the business requirements. My consulting experience has shown that in almost all cases, buffer pools are significantly under-allocated.

Buffer pools should have an intended I/O purpose or strategy. If the I/O performed within a buffer pool will be predominately asynchronous prefetch I/O, this fact will dictate the use of certain buffer pool features that optimize prefetch I/O. If I/O will be predominantly synchronous (random), other attributes will be important to a buffer pool's definition.

To create a buffer pool with an 8K page size that is intended for random I/O in an OLTP database, you could use the following SQL CREATE BUFFERPOOL statement:

```
CREATE BUFFERPOOL randombuffpool IMMEDIATE SIZE 61440
NUMBLOCKPAGES 0 PAGESIZE 8192;
```

The size of this buffer pool would be

61,440 x 8,192 / 1,048,576 = 480 MB

with zero pages reserved for prefetch block I/O.

To create a buffer pool with a 4K page size that is intended for sequential I/O in a business intelligence or data warehousing (BI/DW) database, you could use this command:

```
CREATE BUFFERPOOL seqbuffpool IMMEDIATE SIZE 81920 NUMBLOCK-
PAGES 80256 BLOCKSIZE 64 PAGESIZE 4K;
```

The size of this buffer pool would be

81,920 x 4,096 / 1,048,576 = 320 MB

with 80,256 pages reserved for prefetch block I/O.

The NUMBLOCKPAGES value cannot exceed 98 percent of the buffer pool size, and it should be a multiple of the BLOCKSIZE (which by default is 32). Ideally, the BLOCKSIZE should match the EXTENTSIZE of the table space(s) assigned to the buffer pool. To find the largest possible NUMBLOCKPAGES value, use this formula:

NUMBLOCKPAGES = (Floor (Floor (*Num_buffpool_pages* x 98 / 100) / *Num_blocksize_pages*)) x *Num_blocksize_pages*

Because not all I/O in a BI/DW database is sequential (some random I/O may occur via nested loop joins or other DB2 data accesses), consider reserving 60 percent of the buffer pool size for sequential I/O with this formula:

NUMBLOCKPAGES = (Floor (Floor (*Num_buffpool_pages* x 60 / 100) / *Num_blocksize_pages*)) x *Num_blocksize_pages*

We'll discuss tuning buffer pools for OLTP versus BI/DW databases in greater detail later in the chapter.

Altering Buffer Pools

You can use an ALTER command to change the definition of a buffer pool. Use ALTER BUFFERPOOL to change the SIZE of a buffer pool, the NUMBLOCKPAGES value, or the BLOCKSIZE. A change to the size of the buffer pool takes effect immediately unless you specify the DEFERRED option. (We'll return to the topic of NUMBLOCKPAGES and BLOCKSIZE in depth later in the chapter.)

The following ALTER BUFFERPOOL command updates the number of pages for the buffer pool to use to 81920.

```
ALTER BUFFERPOOL bufferpoolname SIZE 81920;
```

> **Note:** DB2 9 uses internal hidden buffer pools at DB2 start-up if memory can't be obtained in the requested amount. This feature enables DB2 to start, and you can then alter the affected buffer pool to the appropriate size. To make sure an appropriate buffer pool is available in all circumstances, DB2 creates small buffer pools, one for each page size. The size of these buffer pools is 16 pages.

As of Version 8, DB2 stores the buffer pool descriptor pages in database shared memory, so the DBHEAP (database heap) size is no longer a concern with respect to buffer pool sizes.

Dropping Buffer Pools

You can remove buffer pools from a database by dropping them with the DROP BUFFERPOOL command. Before a buffer pool can be dropped, the DBA must ensure that no table spaces are currently assigned to it; otherwise, the drop will fail. Once you drop a buffer pool, the real memory used by the buffer pool becomes immediately available to the operating system for other purposes, including allocation or assignment to other DB2 caches, heaps, or buffer pools.

The DROP BUFFERPOOL command takes the following form:

```
DROP BUFFERPOOL bufferpoolname;
```

Monitoring Buffer Pool Performance

DB2 provides several tools and methods for monitoring the performance of buffer pools. This next part of the chapter describes how to collect and evaluate performance data associated with buffer pools.

Monitor Switches

Before you can obtain DB2 buffer pool performance data, the BUFFERPOOL monitor switch must be turned ON. To check the status of the DB2 monitor switches, use the following command:

```
GET MONITOR SWITCHES;
```

(Chapter 11 covers DB2 monitoring, including the use of monitor switches, in detail.)

To turn on the buffer pool monitor switch, use this command:

```
UPDATE MONITOR SWITCHES USING BUFFERPOOL ON;
```

This update command turns on the buffer pool monitor switch for the current connection to DB2. To make performance information from the buffer pool monitor available for all connections at all times, update the database manager configuration and set the default monitor switch to ON using this command:

```
UPDATE DBM CFG USING DFT_MON_BUFPOOL ON;
```

Snapshot Commands

Once you've turned on the buffer pool monitor switch, you can obtain buffer pool performance information by issuing DB2 *snapshot commands*. Snapshots for DATABASE, BUFFERPOOLS, and TABLESPACES each provide buffer pool performance information that is aggregated to the named object level, with DATABASE snapshots providing summaries of all buffer pools, BUFFERPOOLS snapshots providing summaries for each buffer pool, and TABLESPACES snapshots providing the greatest level of detail for I/O performance at the table space level. You can also use DB2 9 administrative SQL routines to take a snapshot, compute the results, and/or store the results in DB2 tables. You can then use SQL to query this snapshot repository.

To obtain buffer pool performance summarized at the overall database level, issue the following GET SNAPSHOT command:

GET SNAPSHOT FOR DATABASE ON *dbname*;

To obtain buffer pool performance for each buffer pool individually, issue this command:

GET SNAPSHOT FOR BUFFERPOOLS ON *dbname*;

To obtain buffer pool performance I/O details for each table space individually, issue this command:

GET SNAPSHOT FOR TABLESPACES ON *dbname*;

Later, we'll look at some sample output from a BUFFERPOOLS snapshot command and a TABLESPACES snapshot command. We'll discuss the interpretation of the various numbers, along with additional formulas.

DB2 Event Monitors

You can also obtain buffer pool performance information from DB2 *event monitors*. Database, buffer pool, table space, and connection events all provide detailed buffer pool I/O numbers, similar to the DB2 snapshot commands. Again, the performance metrics are aggregated at the corresponding DB2 object level, with database events summarizing buffer pool performance across all buffer pools for the entire database, buffer pool events detailing performance for each individual buffer pool, table space events detailing buffer pool I/O performance at the individual table space level, and connection events detailing buffer pool I/O performance for each individual connection to the database.

DB2 writes database, buffer pool, and table space event records only when the database is stopped or you issue the FLUSH command. For purposes of evaluating buffer pool performance, the DB2 snapshot commands are usually the best choice because their data is easy to obtain and interpret. Connection event records, however, are interesting to analyze because this data can help the DBA answer questions such as the following:

- Which users or applications experience the best I/O performance? The worst?

- Which users or applications perform the most physical read or write I/O? The most direct I/O?

- Do certain applications or users experience I/O times substantially better or worse than the norm (i.e., than the overall average for the database)?

Some companies may choose to implement cost-center charge-back systems based on the CPU times and buffer pool I/O counts reported by the connection event monitor.

Event monitors can write their data to raw binary-format files, to pipes, and directly to DB2 tables. Because a pipe is merely a memory address, this output method uses the least overhead, but it carries with it the burden of needing a program or process that continuously reads and processes the piped data. Writing event data directly to files usually uses very little disk space (the flat files have an efficient, compact, internal binary format) and captures the information at very low overhead cost to the database. Raw event files must be subsequently processed and formatted for human interpretation; most DBAs may want to use the IBM-supplied sample program db2evmon to format raw event data. Writing event data directly to tables provides the most convenient way to interpret the data, but this method carries a higher monitoring cost because DB2 must insert the event records into a table that is local to the monitored database.

Determining Buffer Pool Efficiency and Effectiveness

The next several paragraphs describe formulas that are applicable to both table spaces and buffer pools. After I describe the formulas, we'll explore how to use them to make effective buffer pool assignments.

Listing 8.1 presents information from a sample buffer pool snapshot, and Listing 8.2 presents information from a sample table space snapshot. Notice that the performance variables provided by both snapshots are essentially the same. The formulas we discuss will use sample data taken from this output (shown in bold in the listings).

```
Bufferpool name                              = IBMDEFAULTBP
Database name                                = GOLIATH
Database path                                = C:\DB2\NODE0000\
                                               SQL00002\
Input database alias                         = TRIUMPH
Snapshot timestamp                           = 04/29/2007
                                               15:14:41.689980


Buffer pool data logical reads               = 8472982250
Buffer pool data physical reads              = 34156334
Buffer pool temporary data logical reads     = 0
Buffer pool temporary data physical reads    = 0
Buffer pool data writes                      = 2071702
Buffer pool index logical reads              = 6765416198
Buffer pool index physical reads             = 3909527
Buffer pool temporary index logical reads    = 0
Buffer pool temporary index physical reads   = 0
Total buffer pool read time (milliseconds)   = 56113793
Total buffer pool write time (milliseconds)  = 3192311
Asynchronous pool data page reads            = 28565114
Asynchronous pool data page writes           = 2066603
Buffer pool index writes                     = 2946722
Asynchronous pool index page reads           = 1000308
Asynchronous pool index page writes          = 2941733
Total elapsed asynchronous read time         = 12915740
Total elapsed asynchronous write time        = 3134116
Asynchronous data read requests              = 1264256
Asynchronous index read requests             = 58393
Unread prefetch pages                        = 161416
Vectored IOs                                 = 206783
```

Listing 8.1: Buffer pool snapshot (part 1 of 2)

```
Pages from vectored IOs                = 806920
Block IOs                              = 883453
Pages from block IOs                   = 27247581
Physical page maps                     = 0
Tablespaces using bufferpool           = 100
Alter bufferpool information:
 Pages left to remove                  = 0
 Current size                          = 1280000
 Post-alter size                       = 1280000
```

Listing 8.1: Buffer pool snapshot (part 2 of 2)

```
Tablespace name                        = TSD_TRANS
  Tablespace ID                        = 29
  Tablespace Type                      = Database managed
                                         space
  Tablespace Content Type              = Any data
  Tablespace Page size (bytes)         = 4096
  Tablespace Extent size (pages)       = 64
  Automatic Prefetch size enabled      = No
  Tablespace Prefetch size (pages)     = 192
  Buffer pool ID currently in use      = 1
  Buffer pool ID next startup          = 1
  Using automatic storage              = No
  Auto-resize enabled                  = No
  File system caching                  = No
  Tablespace State                     = 0x'00000000'
   Detailed explanation:
      Normal
  (Container information has been removed here. . . )

  Buffer pool data logical reads       = 5887566
  Buffer pool data physical reads      = 1331378
  Buffer pool temporary data logical reads = 0
  Buffer pool temporary data physical reads = 0
  Asynchronous pool data page reads    = 1178492
```

Listing 8.2: Table space snapshot (part 1 of 2)

174

```
Buffer pool data writes                        = 1120
Asynchronous pool data page writes             = 1072
Buffer pool index logical reads                = 0
Buffer pool index physical reads               = 0
Buffer pool temporary index logical reads = 0
Buffer pool temporary index physical reads = 0
Asynchronous pool index page reads             = 0
Buffer pool index writes                       = 0
Asynchronous pool index page writes            = 0
Total buffer pool read time (millisec)     = 1382521
Total buffer pool write time (millisec)    = 1265
Total elapsed asynchronous read time       = 337093
Total elapsed asynchronous write time      = 866
Asynchronous data read requests            = 38182
Asynchronous index read requests           = 0
No victim buffers available                = 138714
Direct reads                               = 4340224
Direct writes                              = 0
Direct read requests                       = 10565
Direct write requests                      = 0
Direct reads elapsed time (ms)             = 225867
Direct write elapsed time (ms)             = 0
Number of files closed                     = 0
```

Listing 8.2: Table space snapshot (part 2 of 2)

Index Hit Ratio

The following formula calculates the Index Hit Ratio (IHR):

IHR = (1 − (*Buffer pool index physical reads / Buffer pool index logical reads*)) * 100

Substituting the buffer pool snapshot values reported in Listing 8.1 yields the following result:

IHR = (1 − (3909527 / 6765416198)) * 100 = 94 percent

In this case, a page that was already in the buffer pool satisfied, on average, 94 out of 100 logical read requests.

The higher the index hit ratio, the less frequently DB2 needs to access disk devices to bring pages into the buffer pool. A high IHR is especially important to transactional OLTP applications and Web-based databases.

Overall Hit Ratio

The following formula calculates the Overall Hit Ratio (OHR):

OHR = (1 − ((*Buffer pool data physical reads* + *Buffer pool index physical reads*) / (*Buffer pool data logical reads* + *Buffer pool index logical reads*))) * 100

Listing 8.1's values produce the following result:

OHR = (1 − ((34156334 + 3909527) / (8472982250 + 6765416198))) * 100 = 99.75 percent

Again, the higher the hit ratio, the less frequently DB2 needs to access disk devices to bring pages into buffer pools. Because you usually have many times more data pages than index pages, the OHR is often less than the IHR for most applications. You may see high OHR numbers when tables are small or when an application performs application joins.

Physical Pages Read per Minute

The following formula calculates the Physical Pages Read per Minute (PRPM):

PRPM = (*Buffer pool data physical reads* + *Buffer pool index physical reads*) / *Number of elapsed minutes since monitor switches activated or reset*

Given a reasonably steady workload, PRPM provides a measure of buffer pool effectiveness. As buffer pool hit ratios increase, physical I/O rates should conversely decrease, yielding quicker elapsed times for SQL statements.

By computing PRPM for each table space and then ranking the table spaces by this value, the DBA can quickly determine which table spaces have the heaviest physical I/O workloads. For the table spaces with the highest PRPM rates, you can optimize performance by ensuring that table spaces have their containers distributed across as many disk devices as possible. This practice increases the number of disk arms and improves opportunities to do parallel I/O, thus generally lowering disk read times.

Asynchronous Pages Read per Request

The following formula calculates the Asynchronous Pages Read per Request (APPR):

APPR = (*Asynchronous pool data page reads* + *Asynchronous pool index page reads*) / (*Asynchronous data read requests* + *Asynchronous index read requests*)

Listing 8.1's values produce the following result:

APPR = (28565114 + 1000308) / (1264256 + 58393) = 22.35

The APPR value gives the DBA a measure of *prefetch effectiveness*. Each table space has a PREFETCHSIZE assigned to it. The PREFETCHSIZE is supposed to determine how many pages are asynchronously delivered to the buffer pool in anticipation of the application SQL statement's requirement for large quantities of data.

By way of example, consider the following scenario. Along comes an SQL statement with an access strategy of TBSCAN (table scan). DB2 issues prefetch requests using prefetchers (defined by the NUM_IOSERVERS database configuration parameter), and these prefetchers prefetch data measuring approximately one PREFETCHSIZE worth of data. The NUM_IOSERVERS agents go out to disk, retrieve the PREFETCHSIZE number of pages, and return them to the buffer pool manager. One of two things now happens:

- The buffer pool manager accepts the pages and places them into the designated buffer pool. (This is good.) APPR is equal, or nearly equal to, the EXTENTSIZE(s) of the table space(s) assigned to the buffer pool.

- The buffer pool manager assesses the current state of activity within the target destination buffer pool and decides that there just isn't enough room in the buffer pool for all those PREFETCHed pages. This happens when pages that have just been placed in the buffer pool by another agent to be used have not yet been used. In this case, the buffer pool manager may accept only a few pages. The prefetchers go and prefetch another significant number of pages, and again the buffer pool manager can accept only a fraction of them. This process continues for some period of time. (This is not good.) This situation is a sign of an overheated buffer pool, and in this case APPR will be less than the EXTENTSIZE(s) of the table space(s) assigned to the buffer pool. This discussion brings us to the golden rule of sizing buffer pools:

Asynchronous buffer pools should be sized at least large enough to accommodate the prefetch demands placed on them. APPR should be at least 90 percent to 95 percent of the average EXTENTSIZE of table spaces assigned to a given buffer pool.

Asynchronous and Synchronous Read Percentages

The following formulas calculate the Asynchronous and Synchronous Read Percentages (ARP and SRP):

ARP = ((*Asynchronous pool data page reads + Asynchronous pool index page reads*) * 100) / (*Buffer pool data physical reads + Buffer pool index physical reads*)

SRP = 100 – ARP

Substituting the table space snapshot values reported in Listing 8.2 for table space TSD_TRANS yields the following ARP result:

ARP = ((1178492 + 0) * 100) / (1331378 + 0)) = 88.5 percent

The ARP, together with the SRP, indicates whether an object (buffer pool or table space) is predominantly randomly read or asynchronously read (prefetched). Simply stated, the ARP and SRP percentages effectively help you assign table space objects to appropriate buffer pool "clubs." You should assign table spaces that are randomly read (high SRP) to buffer pools with random objectives. Assign table spaces that are asynchronously read (high ARP) to buffer pools with asynchronous objectives.

I/O Performance Measurements: ORMS, ARMS, and SRMS

The following formula calculates the Overall Read Milliseconds (ORMS):

ORMS = (*Total buffer pool read time (ms)*) / (*Buffer pool data physical reads + Buffer pool index physical reads*)

Listing 8.2's values yield the following result:

ORMS = 1382521 / (1331378 + 0) = 1.04 ms

For each table space, compute the ORMS time and then create a list of table spaces ordered by this value. Is there a table space with a much higher than average ORMS? If so, find out why. Table spaces with higher ORMS numbers (slower I/O) may have containers of unequal size, multiple containers accidentally placed on the same physical devices, and/or one supersized container on a single disk. It's also possible that table spaces with slower physical I/O performance may be placed on disk devices or controllers with above-average activity rates. Improving I/O response time by a few milliseconds may seem trivial, but the gain becomes significant when millions of physical I/Os are involved.

The following formula calculates the Asynchronous Read Milliseconds (ARMS):

ARMS = *(Total elapsed asynchronous read time (ms))* / *(Asynchronous pool data page reads* + *Asynchronous pool index page reads)*

Listing 8.2's values yield the following result:

ARMS = 337093 / (1178492 + 0) = 0.29 ms

Average asynchronous read time (calculated in milliseconds) gives the DBA the average time required to complete an asynchronous I/O. Like ORMS, ARMS values can be computed for and compared against all table spaces to discover table spaces with slower response times.

The following formula calculates the Synchronous Read Milliseconds (SRMS):

SRMS = *(Total buffer pool read time (ms)* – *Total elapsed asynchronous read time)* / *((Buffer pool data physical reads* + *Buffer pool index physical reads)*— *(Asynchronous pool data page reads* + *Asynchronous pool index page reads))*

Listing 8.2's values yield the following result:

SRMS = (1382521 – 337093) / ((1331378 + 0) – (1178492 + 0)) = 6.84 ms

The snapshot examples in Figures 8.1 and 8.2 were taken on a moderately sized Windows 2003 server with four Xeon CPUs and 16 GB of RAM. We commonly see ARMS values of 1 to 3 ms and SRMS values of 3 to 10 ms.

Of course, actual results will depend on many factors, including the number and types of devices in use, the number of containers on devices, processor speeds, and more.

> **Note:** The Metrics.txt script, which uses DB2 9 snapshot SQL administrative routines, provides all the formulas given in this chapter. You can download this script file at www.mcpresson-line.com/mc/forums/reviews/5086

Monitoring and Tuning Tables, Buffer Pools, and Table Spaces

Buffer pools (and memory allocations in general) can profoundly impact DB2 performance regardless of platform. Ever since multiple buffer pools became available in DB2/MVS V3.1, strategies for configuring multiple buffer pools have been a widely discussed and frequently written-about topic. Today, you can find many articles on the subject on the Internet. Although opinions and circumstances vary, most experts seem to agree that between six and 10 buffer pools provide optimized performance.

Table Activity

Begin your buffer pool analysis by determining which tables in your database are the most frequently read, for there is little value in dedicating buffer pool memory to tables that are rarely referenced. The DB2 Control Center can provide this information, or you can use the command line interface:

```
db2 "get snapshot for tables on DBNAME"
```

Sort the results of the snapshot in descending sequence by ROWS READ to come up with your list of "heavy hitters," or the tables that could benefit most from focused buffer pool tuning. Of course, this list could also include tables that are victims of excessive table scans due to missing or suboptimal indexes.

> **Note:** Use the db2pd command with the–tcbstats option to identify high-activity tables. Save the command output to a file, and then import it to a spreadsheet for additional analysis. Put the db2pd command into your toolbox, and use it often!

The trouble, however, with the table snapshot is that it doesn't provide the low-level I/O numbers as found in the table space or buffer pool snapshots. So, even though determining the most heavily read tables is relatively easy, it's difficult, if not impossible, to know whether the reads are random (synchronous) or prefetch (asynchronous). Therefore, once you have your list of the "Top 10 Most Frequently Read Tables," you need to take steps to ensure that these tables are placed into their own table spaces so you can accurately determine the type of I/O. As a rule of thumb, each frequently read table should be assigned to its own table space.

Speaking of private table placements, if you're using materialized query tables, be sure to define each MQT in its own table space as well. Doing so will let you effectively measure whether the MQT is being used in a way that is consistent with its objectives. You could also assign your MQT table to an MQT table space if the frequency of access warrants dedicated resources.

Table Space Activity

Once you have the database's "important" tables isolated into their own table spaces, you should compute performance metrics for each table space on a regular basis and save the results of your calculations in a table space performance history table or spreadsheet. Of particular importance are the I/O performance times (ORMS, ARMS, SRMS), Asynchronous Pages

Read per Request (APPR), Physical Pages Read per Minute (PRPM), and Asynchronous and Synchronous Read Percentages (ARP and SRP). If you also track and save Used Pages on a periodic basis, you may be able to infer a growth rate, or Pages Added per Day (PPD).

Assigning Table Spaces to Buffer Pools: General Concepts

In one sense, buffer pools are like a private club. They work best when the majority of the members share the same beliefs, principles, and behaviors. The DBA should try to organize a number of buffer pool "clubs" within his or her database to make the buffer pools more effective.

In society, there are certain clubs or organizations whose objectives and behaviors clash. In DB2, the central controversy lies between random and sequential I/O. When you assign objects to DB2 buffer pools, it's critical, first and foremost, to keep objects with random I/O patterns (high SRP values) separated from objects with sequential I/O patterns (low SRP values). Within these two broad groupings, it can also be beneficial to create special-purpose buffer pools that have very specific and well-defined objectives.

Given these premises, I suggest the following general guidelines for buffer pools to define in an OLTP database (individual circumstances and results may vary):

- TEMPBP: A buffer pool dedicated to TEMPSPACE table space I/O, which tends to be predominantly sequential (low SRP value) and can be substantial when occasional decision support queries are executed.
- RANDOMBP: A buffer pool for objects whose access patterns are highly random in nature; that is, they rarely exhibit prefetch or asynchronous I/O behaviors (high SRP value).
- ASYNCBP: A buffer pool for objects whose access patterns are predominantly asynchronous; that is, prefetch I/O occurs more often than not (low SRP value). Allocate at least 35 percent of this buffer pool to block-based usage.

- HOTINDEXBP: A buffer pool for indexes of tables that are very frequently read via index access. Access should be predominantly random (high SRP value).

- HOTDATABP: A buffer pool for tables that are very frequently read, especially those at the heart of an OLTP system (high SRP value).

- MQTBP: A buffer pool for table spaces containing MQTs.

- SYSCATBP_R: A randomly read buffer pool for the SYSCATSPACE table space.

The first three of these buffer pools can have broad object membership. The latter four are buffer pools with special causes and specific agendas.

> **Note:** First introduced in DB2 V8.1, block-based buffer pools improve the performance of table spaces that are primarily asynchronous in nature. It is a myth that OLTP databases use primarily synchronous reads, so be sure to compute ARP for table spaces and configure a significant amount of block-based buffer pools based on the ARP value. If ARP is over 50 percent, configure a block-based buffer pool to use at least 35 percent for block-based pages.

For a BI/DW database, fewer buffer pools are better. I suggest using four to six, with one per temporary table space page size, one for indexes, and one for table spaces. Further isolation may be necessary.

Optimum Buffer Pool Assignments

Armed with the knowledge of the asynchronous and synchronous read percentages for each table space, you'll be able to prudently assign table spaces that are predominantly read asynchronously to buffer pools designed for asynchronous (sequential) I/O and assign table spaces that are mostly randomly read to buffer pools designed for random I/O. If the SRP for a table space is greater than 80 percent, assign the table space to a random I/O buffer pool. If the SRP for a table space is less than or equal to 80 percent, assign the table space to a sequential I/O (prefetch) buffer pool. Tables with very high random read activity may have their table spaces assigned to special "hot" buffer pools. Table spaces assigned to an asynchronous (highly sequential/prefetch) buffer pool should have their APPR carefully monitored. In addition, it is strongly recommended that a significant portion of the buffer pool be block-based. Asynchronous buffer pools should be large enough to accommodate the prefetch demand that is placed on them and, in today's 64-bit environment, should be sized so as to reduce or eliminate physical reads. The key point is to remove prefetch I/O from your random table space so that the random buffer pool memory can be effectively used toward reducing physical I/O rates.

In OLTP and DW/BI databases, assign the TEMPSPACE table spaces their own buffer pool. Access in these environments tends to be highly asynchronous, although some synchronous access may also be observed, especially when nested loop joins are performed. Use System Managed Space (SMS) for temporary table spaces.

Sizing Buffer Pools

In a BI/DW database environment, using four to six buffer pools is ideal. Because I/O will be predominantly asynchronous sequential, the primary objective is to ensure that prefetching is effective. Compute and monitor the APPR value for each table space, and verify that it is not less than 80 percent of the table space's EXTENTSIZE. If the APPR is less than 80 percent of the EXTENTSIZE value, the buffer pool is too small to accommodate prefetch I/O demands (requests) placed on it. As a rule of thumb, a 1 GB buffer pool is a good start.

In an OLTP database environment, use a multiple-buffer-pool strategy that separates random I/O from sequential I/O (as we've discussed). Again, the sequential I/O buffer pools should be large enough to satisfy the prefetch request demands placed on them, and you should measure and verify this fact by computing the APPR for each table space assigned to a sequential I/O buffer pool. If the APPR is less than 80 percent of the table space's EXTENTSIZE, you need to increase the size of the sequential I/O buffer pool. For table spaces with mostly random I/O, the DBA should determine the optimum buffer pool size as the size that is neither too small (which results in unnecessary physical I/O and slows transactions) nor too large (which may cause operating system paging and consumes excessive CPU to manage all the pages in the pool). The size that is "just right" lies at the point of diminishing returns—the point where a larger buffer pool size does not provide improved performance results (as measured by the IHR, OHR, and PRPM) and where a smaller buffer pool size results in measurably poorer performance (as measured by IHR, OHR, and PRPM). Often, you can determine the optimum size by sampling performance at varying buffer pool sizes until you discover the point of diminishing returns.

Block Prefetch I/O: Special Considerations

As we've discussed, block-based buffer pools provide the ability to reserve portions of a buffer pool's pages for sequential I/O. This new capability makes optimum use of memory for block prefetch I/O and should result in faster query times for SQL that performs table scans. To reserve a portion of DB2 buffer pool memory for prefetch I/O, use the new NUMBLOCKPAGES parameter with the CREATE BUFFERPOOL or ALTER BUFFERPOOL statement.

My experience has shown that even though block-based buffer pools have been available since V8.1, people are not using them. I've been able to improve performance by more than 30 percent and reduce CPU consumption by 10 to 15 percent for clients by implementing block-based buffer pools.

Summary

Most database administrators are handed an application or a database and instructed to make it go faster. They receive no documentation, no SQL activity rates, nothing. To discover the tuning opportunities, the DBA needs to use the monitoring facilities available in DB2. Find out which tables are most frequently read, and assign those tables to their own table spaces. Pair synchronously read table spaces with buffer pools that are intended for random access, and pair table spaces that are heavily asynchronously read with buffer pools that are intended for prefetch access. Prefetch buffer pools need to be large enough to accommodate the demand, while random buffer pools should seek to minimize physical I/O rates via size increases until either system paging occurs or the point of diminishing returns is reached.

9

The Way to DB2: The Optimizer

In this chapter, you'll learn how the DB2 optimizer works. An understanding of the optimizer and associated built-in facilities and tools will help you to write SQL/XML applications that perform well. Key to effective optimization is the availability of current statistics about database objects and adequate indexes. We'll look at the DB2 9 RUNSTATS statistics utility and review some recommendations for attaining and achieving consistent, efficient SQL/XML applications.

The DB2 Optimizer

At the heart of the DB2 engine is the DB2 optimizer component of the SQL/XML compiler. New in DB2 9 is the optimizer's ability to optimize access plans for SQL/XML and XQuery. (An *access plan* is what the DB2 engine executes to return results to the program or user interface that submitted the SQL/XML.) As a result of the modular design of the optimizer code, IBM optimizer developers were able to extend the existing optimizer component to support and optimize XML. This capability greatly enhances the ease with which IBM can support XML in DB2 9, and it positions DB2 9 to take advantage of the rapid changes in the XML area.

The SQL/XML compiler is a sophisticated program that converts static and dynamic SQL/XML into code that the DB2 engine can execute. The optimizer code analyzes SQL and determines the best access plan with the lowest cost. In developing the lowest-cost access plan, the optimizer generally considers CPU and I/O costs. The output of the optimization process is an access plan generated in an internal, executable, DB2 format.

The methods and procedures that the optimizer converts to executable code consist of various join operations and list-processing techniques that the optimizer uses to process the request and return the result(s) to the requesting application. Among these techniques are the following:

- Join techniques: Nested loop join, merge scan join, hash join
- Access methods: List prefetch, table scan, index ANDing/ORing, index scan (including block index scan)

For static SQL, the optimizer stores the access plan in DB2's SYSCAT.SYSPACKAGES catalog view. For dynamic SQL, the access plan is cached in the package cache. (Note that static SQL is also cached in the package cache to avoid physical disk I/O to the SYSCAT.SYSPACKAGES view.) The package cache management algorithms ensure that the most recently executed dynamic and static SQL access plans are stored in the cache. This mechanism improves performance by reducing physical I/O to the catalog tables.

Program Preparation

When you use static SQL, the SQL is contained in a source file of one of the supported high-level programming languages. The DB2 kernel doesn't understand high-level programming language constructs, so programs containing static SQL must be "bound" to the database ahead of time. You use the DB2 SQL/XML compiler component to bind static SQL and to prepare dynamic SQL. When you use dynamic SQL, the program-preparation process takes place at run time. Figure 9.1 provides an overview of the DB2 9 SQL/XML compiler.

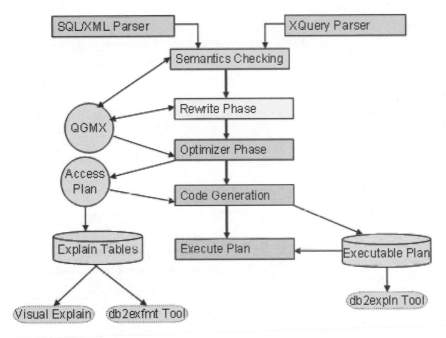

Figure 9.1: SQL/XML compiler

The query compiler generates an executable plan for static SQL that is stored in the form of a package in the DB2 catalog tables. Again, for dynamic SQL this process occurs at runtime, and the executable plan is stored in the package cache.

For dynamic SQL, DB2 verifies authorities and objects at runtime using object descriptors stored in the catalog cache. If the required object descriptors aren't present in the catalog cache, DB2 reads them into the cache from the DB2 catalog using a direct read. After a PREPARE is done for dynamic SQL, the section is cached in the package cache. If the exact dynamic SQL statement is run again, DB2 will find a match for the SQL in the cache for the SQL section, and another won't be required. This approach reduces CPU consumption and provides better overall response to the application. The use of parameter markers in SQL statements can improve package cache hit rates by eliminating subsequent PREPAREs. This technique is widely used in third-party vendor applications.

At bind or prepare time, the SQL compiler uses information contained in the database manager (DBM) or database (DB) configuration and DB2 catalog tables to develop the lowest-cost access plan. Table 9.1 lists the inputs to the optimization process.

Table 9.1: Optimization process inputs	
Input	**Purpose**
Buffer pool size (number of pages)	Used to determine how much of the buffer pool may be available for the involved tables/indexes.
SORTHEAP DB CFG parameter	Used to determine whether a piped sort can be used, as well as the cost of spilling to disk.
LOCKLIST	Used to determine the amount of memory available for storing locks for this access plan and type of lock mode.
CPU speed	Specifies the speed of CPUs available.
PREFETCHSIZE	Used to determine I/O costs.
Value of INTRA_PARALLEL DBM CFG parameter	Used to determine whether parallelism may be used.
Type of table space and number of containers	Used to determine I/O costs and degree of I/O parallelism.
Disk speed	Used to estimate I/O costs.
Degree of clustering	Used to determine the effectiveness of prefetching and to determine how clustered data is.
Indexes available	Used to determine index access cost
DFT_DEGREE	Provides the default for the CURRENT DEGREE special register or the DEGREE bind option, which specify the degree of intra-partition parallelism.
AVG_APPLS	Used to determine the amount of buffer pool space available for a query.

Table 9.1: Optimization process inputs (continued)	
Input	**Purpose**
MAXLOCKS	Indicates the percent of LOCKLIST used by a single application before lock escalation occurs.
DFT_QUERYOPT	Specifies the default optimization class to be used.
STMTHEAP	Used as a work space by the SQL compiler during compilation of an SQL statement. The statement heap size can affect the amount of optimization conducted.
COMM_BANDWIDTH	Indicates the communications speed between physical database partitions in a Database Partitioning Feature (DPF) environment. This value is used by the cost model to estimate the cost of transferring rows between database partitions in a DPF environment.

If enabled, several DB2 registry variables also affect optimization.
(For information about DB2 registry and environmental variables, go to
*http://publib.boulder.ibm.com/infocenter/db2luw/v9/index.jsp?topic=/com.ibm.
db2.udb.admin.doc/doc/c0007340.htm*. Appendix B provides descriptions of five
environment variables that are new in DB2 9.) The optimizer also uses statistics
stored in DB2 catalog tables that contain important information about tables,
columns, indexes, and other DB2 objects. The following SYSSTAT catalog views
provide input to the DB2 optimization process:

- SYSSTAT.COLDIST
- SYSSTAT.COLGROUPS
- SYSSTAT.COLUMNS
- SYSSTAT.INDEXES
- SYSSTAT.ROUTINES
- SYSSTAT.TABLES

These views are updatable for the purpose of modeling production statistics in a test environment or for updating statistics without using the RUNSTATS utility.

Keep in mind that if you change any of the configuration parameters listed in Table 9.1, you should rebind your static SQL, and the changes may cause dynamic SQL to use a new access plan. You can use the FLUSH PACKAGE CACHE DYNAMIC command to flush the package cache so that the next execution of dynamic SQL will cause a PREPARE to occur and a new access plan to be developed.

> **Note:** Running RUNSTATS or a manual statistics update automatically invalidates cached dynamic statements that depend on the target table.

DFT_QUERYOPT Parameter

The database configuration parameter DFT_QUERYOPT (default query optimization class) controls the level of optimization. By default, DFT_QUERYOPT has a value of 5. This parameter provides the default for the CURRENT QUERY OPTIMIZATION special register and the QUERYOPT bind option. There are seven query optimization classes.

Optimization Class 0

Optimization class 0 restricts the amount of optimization that the optimizer performs as follows:

- The optimizer does not consider non-uniform distribution statistics.
- Only basic query rewrite rules are applied.

- Greedy join enumeration occurs. (The greedy join algorithm selects a join method in only one direction, which means that the join method selected won't be changed during further optimization.)
- Only nested loop join and index scan access methods are enabled.
- List prefetch and index ANDing are not used in generated access methods.
- The star-join strategy is not considered.

Optimization class 0 is appropriate only when you want the lowest possible query compilation overhead and when simple, dynamic SQL statements access well-indexed tables.

Optimization Class 1

Optimization class 1 is similar to class 0, except additional join methods are available as follows:

- The optimizer does not consider non-uniform distribution statistics.
- Only a subset of the query rewrite rules are applied.
- Greedy join enumeration occurs.
- List prefetch and index ANDing are not used in generated access methods, although index ANDing is issued when working with the semijoins used in star joins.

Optimization Class 2

Optimization class 2 causes the optimizer to use optimization significantly higher than class 1 while keeping the compilation cost significantly lower than class 3 and above for complex queries as follows:

- All available statistics, including both frequency and quantile non-uniform distribution statistics, are used.

- All query rewrite rules are applied, including routing queries to materialized query tables, except computationally intensive rules that apply only in very rare cases.

- Greedy join enumeration occurs.

- A wide range of access methods is considered, including list prefetch and MQT routing.

- The star-join strategy is considered, if applicable.

Optimization class 2 has the most optimization of all classes that use the greedy join enumeration algorithm.

Consider using class 2 for business intelligence and online analytical queries (OLAP). In these environments, the same SQL statement is seldom repeated; thus, the access plan is unlikely to remain in package cache, so recompilation will be required each time the SQL is executed. Class 2 results in good access paths for the previously identified queries, and because they will require recompilation each time they are executed, the compilation cost is significantly lower for complex queries that use higher optimization classes. Use this optimization class only after confirming, through a trial-and-error process, that it is the best setting for your environment. Greedy join enumeration may miss a good plan that a higher optimization class might find, and the resulting access plan could be suboptimal.

Optimization Class 3

Optimization class 3 uses a moderate amount of optimization. It is the closest match to the query optimization characteristics of DB2 for z/OS. Optimization class 3 has the following characteristics:

- Non-uniform distribution statistics are used if available.
- Most query rewrite rules are used, including subquery-to-join transformation.
- Dynamic programming join enumeration is used, including limited use of Cartesian products for star schemas involving lookup tables.
- A wide range of join techniques is considered, including list prefetch, index ANDing, and star joins.

Optimization class 3 improves access plans for queries containing four or more joins. In practice, however, class 3 is rarely used.

Optimization Class 5

Optimization class 5 is the default DFT_QUERYOPT setting. This class directs the optimizer to use a significant amount of optimization to generate an access plan. The optimizer uses all available statistics and applies all query rewrite rules, including dynamic programming join enumeration and a wide range of access methods.

If the optimizer detects that additional resources and processing time are not warranted for complex dynamic SQL queries, it reduces optimization. The extent or size of the reduction depends on the size of the machine and number of predicates. When the query optimizer reduces the amount of optimization, it continues to apply all the query rewrite rules that normally would be applied. However, it uses the greedy join enumeration method and reduces the number of access plan combinations considered.

Use class 5 as the default, and, if necessary, use a trial-and-error process to determine whether a different class is better for your environment. You can use the db2batch and DB2 explain tools to see whether you can obtain better prepare time and good access plans using a lower optimization class. In my experience, class 5 works very well in mixed OLTP/ERP/CRM environments. In practice, this class is widely used, and it is adequate for most environments.

Optimization Class 7

Optimization class 7 is similar to class 5, but it uses a few more query rewrite rules and does not reduce the amount of optimization done for complex dynamic SQL queries. Consider using class 7 in a DW environment if it helps you obtain better, more consistent access plans.

Optimization Class 9

Optimization class 9 directs the optimizer to use all available optimization techniques:

- All available statistics
- All query rewrite rules
- All possibilities for join enumeration, including Cartesian products and unlimited composite inners
- All access methods

Class 9 can greatly expand the number of access plans the optimizer considers. My experience has been that class 9 in most cases does not improve access plans over and above what was obtained with class 7. In practice, class 9 is used only in conjunction with DB2 Support.

You can use the SET CURRENT QUERY OPTIMIZATION command to set the special register to a different optimization class for dynamic SQL statements for which you want to use a value different from the parameter setting. In addition, you can use the QUERYOPT bind option to set the optimization level for static SQL.

Optimization Class Recommendations

The following general recommendations provide some guidance regarding the optimization class:

- Use the DFT_QUERYOPT class of 5 initially, and investigate changing it to a lower value if you're experiencing high prepare times or access path problems.

- Use a trial-and-error process with your applications *during application development* to determine the appropriate DFT_QUERYOPT setting.

- *Don't* suddenly change the DFT_QUERYOPT setting in a production environment without extensive testing!

- For OLTP and Web applications, consider setting DFT_QUERYOPT to 1 or 2 (keeping restrictions in mind).

- For mixed environments, use the DFT_QUERYOPT default setting of 5. Such environments are usually a mixture of simple and complex SQL. Most ERP, CRM, and SCM packaged applications fall into this category.

- For BI/DW environments, consider setting DFT_QUERYOPT to 7. You can evaluate differences between optimization class 7 and 9 in your environment through a trial-and-error process with your applications.

- Set DFT_QUERYOPT to 9 only when directed by DB2 Support.

Note that many environments don't fit nicely into standard OLTP and BI/DW categories (e.g., OLTP returning only a row or two, BI/DW using complex SQL and large table scans). ERP/CRM/SCM environments fall somewhere in between these categories, and many environments are a mixture of the two.

SQL/XML Predicate Coding Best Practices

SQL/XML and XQuery are languages used for communicating with DB2. Because DB2 does work on behalf of applications using SQL/XML, SQL/XML is the number one place to concentrate your initial tuning efforts. Therefore, it is best if your SQL/XML is written with the following best practices in mind.

- Limit the amount of data returned.
- Avoid use of SELECT *.
- Use predicates with good selectivity.

- Use range delimiting predicates first, and then use index sargable predicates wherever possible.
- When joining tables, specify join predicates and make sure they are indexed.
- Analyze local and join predicates and ORDER BY clause columns, and ensure that indexes are created on the columns being joined first, then on the columns to support the ORDER BY clause, and then on local predicates for index access (index-only access).
- Consider use of INCLUDE columns to achieve index-only access for important queries.
- Use the DB2 Design Advisor (covered later) to evaluate all access plans.

Note: New in DB2 9, indexes are created by default using the ALLOW REVERSE SCANS clause. This change lets DB2 use the index for both forward and backward scans, which can improve performance and eliminate sorts.

Table 9.2 summarizes the predicate types.

Table 9.2: Predicate table				
Characteristic	*Predicate type*			
	Range delimiting	**Index sargable**	**Data sargable**	**Residual**
Reduce index I/O	Yes	No	No	No
Reduce data page I/O	Yes	Yes	No	No
Reduce number of rows copied from data pages	Yes	Yes	Yes	No
Reduce number of qualifying rows	Yes	Yes	Yes	Yes

You use range delimiting (Index Manager) predicates to bracket an index scan or provide start and stop keys for the index search. Such predicates are the best kind of predicates to use.

The next best type of predicate is an index sargable predicate, which is evaluated from the index via a scan of the index. Columns involved in index sargablepredicates are part of the index and are evaluated by the Index Manager.

Data sargable predicates cannot be evaluated by the Index Manager; instead, they are evaluated by Data Management Services (DMS). They require data access. DMS retrieves the columns to evaluate the predicate as well as any columns in the select list that could not be obtained via an index.

Residual predicates require I/O beyond just accessing the base table, such as the following examples:

- Quantified subqueries: ANY, ALL, IN, SOME
- Data types: LONG VARCHAR, LOBs

Residual predicates are evaluated by Relational Data Services (RDS) and are the most costly of the four categories of predicates.

Partition Elimination

When you use table partitioning, a feature new in DB2 9, the optimizer can limit the data access to the table partition containing only the data of interest. Table partitioning can significantly improve query performance; for this reason, I expect to see widespread use of this feature.

Table partitioning also lets you roll data partitions in and out on the fly. With this capability, you can roll stale partitions out to a separate table for archiving and roll in new partitions.

To enable table partitioning, you select a partitioning column using the PARTITION BY RANGE clause in the CREATE TABLE statement, as shown in Listing 9.1.

```
CONNECT TO SAMPLE;
CREATE TABLE PGUNNING.SALES(SKU BIGINT NOT NULL,
                           "MONTH" DATE NOT NULL,
                           SALES_TOT DECIMAL(8,0) NOT NULL)
  PARTITION BY RANGE("MONTH" NULLS LAST)
  (STARTING FROM('2007-01-01') INCLUSIVE
```

Listing 9.1: Creating a table partition

```
    ENDING AT ('2007-12-31') EXCLUSIVE EVERY (1 MONTHS))
IN USERSPACE1 CYCLE;
CONNECT RESET;
```

Listing 9.1: Creating a table partition

This SQL creates a table with 12 data partitions, each containing a month's worth of sales data. Using a capability called *partition elimination*, the DB2 optimizer can then determine which data partitions contain the data of interest and can limit data access and retrieval to the partitions that qualify.

> **Note:** Partition elimination can improve performance significantly by eliminating unnecessary access to unqualified data.

Figure 9.2 provides an overview of how table partitioning works.

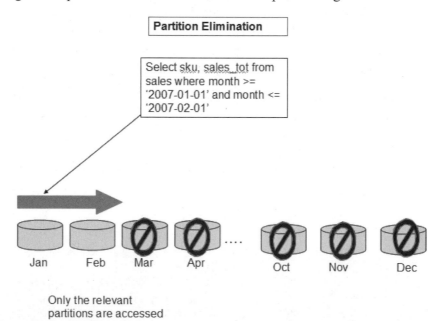

Figure 9.2: Partition elimination

The optimizer uses statistics stored in the catalog tables to develop the access plan and to limit access to only the partitions that qualify based on the query being optimized.

IBM has enhanced Visual Explain in DB2 9 to support table partitioning. Figure 9.3 shows sample Visual Explain statistics for a partitioned table, including the number of partitions (the NUM_DATA_PARTS statistic).

Statistics	Explained	Current
CREATE_TIME	06/03/2007 2:08:15 PM	06/03/2007 2:08:15 PM
STATS_TIME	Statistics not updated	Statistics not updated
CARD	1745(default)	-1
NPAGES	12(default)	-1
FPAGES	12(default)	-1
COLCOUNT	3(default)	3
OVERFLOW	0(default)	-1
TABLESPACE	<VARIOUS>	
INDEX_TABLESPACE		
LONG_TABLESPACE		
VOLATILE	No(default)	No
NUM_COLGROUPS	0(default)	
NUM_DATA_PARTS	12(default)	
ACTIVE_BLOCKS	-1(default)	

Figure 9.3: Visual Explain against partitioned table

Visual Explain also reports the actual number of partitions accessed, as shown in Figure 9.4.

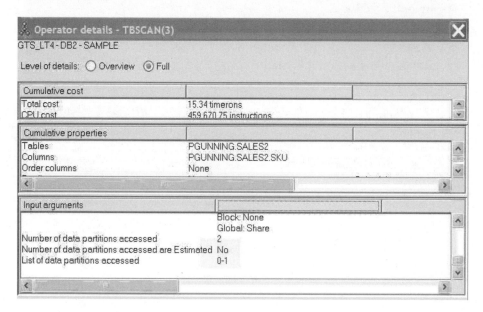

Figure 9.4: List of data partitions accessed

You should use Visual Explain to verify that you're getting the partition elimination and access plans you expect.

Creating Indexes over XML Data

DB2 9 supports indexes over XML data. XML indexes aren't like traditional row ID (RID) or block-based indexes, where index keys are composed of one or more table columns. Instead, XML indexes over XML data use a specific XML pattern expression to index paths and values in XML documents of type XML.

XML index entries provide access to nodes within an XML document via index keys on XML pattern expressions.

> **Note:** XML index entries don't provide access to the beginning of a
> document but provide access to nodes within the document.

You can create XML indexes using the CREATE INDEX statement;
however, not all keywords are supported for indexes over XML data.
Let's consider the example of a Candidate table that has an XML
column named resume that contains XML document fragments
such as those shown in Listing 9.2.

```
< resume name = "Jones"/>
 <candidate_id = "1234" occupation = "DBA">
   <Full_name>
    <first> DB2 </first>
    <last> Jones </last>
   </Full_name>
 <phone type="Mobile">610-451-5801</phone>
</resume>

< resume name = "Smith">
 <candidate_id = "4567" occupation = "Consultant">
   <Full_name>
    <first> Smythe </first>
    <last> Smith </last>
   </Full_name>
 <phone type="Office">888-241-1070</phone>
</resume>
```

Listing 9.2: XML document fragments

Users of the Candidate table often retrieve candidate information using the
candidate_id. An index on candidate_id would speed up this retrieval because
the entire document wouldn't have to be searched. You could create the index
with the following statement:

```
CREATE INDEX cand_idx1 on Candidate(resume)
 GENERATE KEY USING XML PATTERN
 'resume/candidate_id/@id' AS SQL DOUBLE
```

This statement creates an index over XML data on the resume column of the Candidate table. The XML pattern clause indicates that you want to index the values of the id attribute of each candidate_id element. Specifying SQL DOUBLE directs that the indexed values be stored as DOUBLE values.

Only one index specification clause is allowed per CREATE INDEX statement.

Note that if you want to interpret the result of an XML expression as multiple data types, you must create an XML index for each data type. For example, the value 1234 has a character representation, but it could also be interpreted as the number 1234. To index the path /candidate/candidate_id/@id as both a character string and a numeric string, you must create two indexes, one for the VARCHAR data type and one for the DOUBLE data type. You can create indexes on the same XML pattern with different data types as follows:

```
CREATE INDEX cand_idx2 on Candidate(resume)
 GENERATE KEY USING XML PATTERN
 'resume/candidate_id/@id' AS SQL VARCHAR(12)
CREATE INDEX cand_idx3 on Candidate(resume)
 GENERATE KEY USING XML PATTERN
 'resume/candidate_id/@id' AS SQL DOUBLE
```

> **Note:** When using the VARCHAR HASHED data type, keep in mind that range scans cannot be performed and that only equality lookups can use the index.

Follow these general guidelines when creating indexes over XML data:

- Make sure the data type requested by the query matches the indexed data type.
- Follow the rules for indexing elements with complex schema types.
- If the XML pattern used to create the index is more restrictive than the query predicates, the query cannot use the index.

SQL and XML Explain Facilities

DB2 contains *explain* facilities that you can use to analyze and evaluate SQL/XML access plans. These facilities interact with the SQL/XML compiler and optimizer to show developers and DBAs the access plans and costs involved in processing queries. DB2 explain facilities use a cost element called *timerons*. Although there isn't a publicly available definition of the timeron cost formula, it is generally made up of CPU, I/O, and communications costs }(in a Database Partitioning Feature environment) summed together with regard to the query under review and on the hardware and configuration in use. In general, if you can reduce the timeron cost by rewriting the SQL or creating indexes, the query's overall performance will improve. DB2 reports timerons for each step of the access plan and also as a cumulative cost.

Explain is the primary tool for evaluating access plans developed by the DB2 optimizer. Application developers should use explain when developing SQL and periodically when evaluating the performance of SQL once it is in production. DBAs use explain in support of application development efforts (e.g., acceptance or regression testing, walkthroughs) and to troubleshoot performance problems in the production environment. Application developers should use explain throughout the application development life cycle.

DB2 offers three types of explains:

- DB2 Visual Explain produces a graphical explain and is launched from the DB2 Control Center, DB2 Developer Workbench, and other tools.

- The db2exfmt facility is a "complete explain." It produces information from explain tables in a text format.

- The db2expln facility does not use explain tables. It is based on the access section or executable plan and provides less information than the other two forms of explain.

> **Note:** To use DB2 Visual Explain or db2exfmt with static SQL, specify the EXPLAIN bind option and retain a history of explains in the explain tables.

Which explain facility you use is up to you. The decision really comes down to personal preference. Developers tend to like Visual Explain, while DBAs tend to use db2exfmt. It's easier to share the output from db2exfmt or db2expln because you can send it via e-mail as a text file. The following paragraphs describe Visual Explain and db2exfmt.

DB2 Visual Explain

DB2 Visual Explain is available with DB2 free of charge. You launch it from the Control Center by right-clicking on the database of interest and selecting **Explain Query** from the resulting shortcut menu (shown in Figure 9.5) to display the Explain Query Statement dialog box (Figure 9.6).

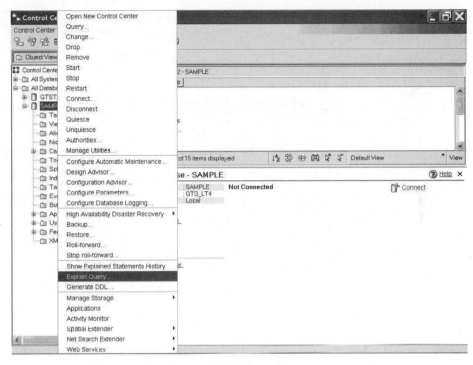

Figure 9.5: Launching Visual Explain from the DB2 Control Center

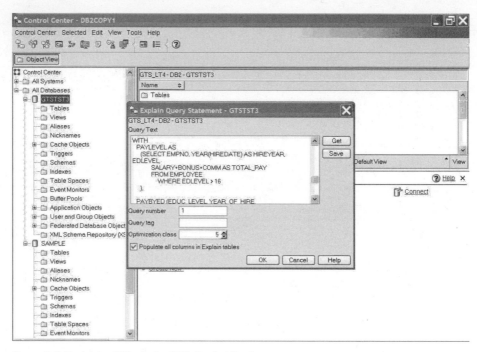

Figure 9.6: Explaining SQL via the DB2 Control Center

You can paste SQL into the dialog box or click the **Get** button to import SQL from a file. The Control Center will create the explain tables if they don't already exist for the user ID being used for the explain. Figure 9.7 shows an example of the Control Center creating explain tables automatically.

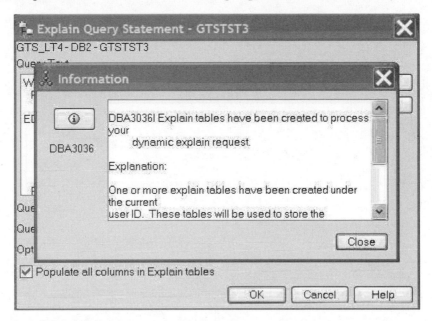

Figure 9.7: Automatic creation of explain tables

When you're ready to explain the SQL, click **OK**. The Control Center will display the access plan as shown in Figure 9.8.

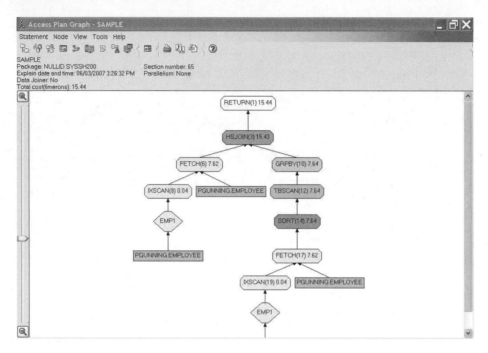

Figure 9.8: Access plan graph

DB2 Visual Explain does a good job of documenting the selectivity of predicates, as you can see in Figure 9.9.

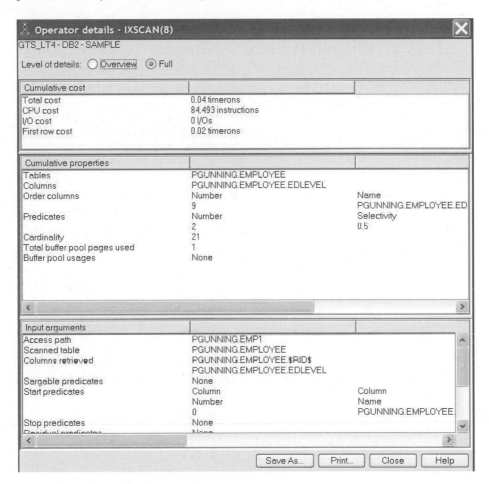

Figure 9.9: Operator drill-down

The selectivity reported (in the cumulative properties section) for the EDLEVEL column is 0.5, which means that 50 percent of the rows will be processed. Best practice suggests that you limit the number of rows processed. As a guideline, you should use predicates with a selectivity of 0.10 or less if possible.

This means that for a table of 50,000 rows, 5,000 rows would be returned by using a predicate with selectivity of 0.10.

Developers should take selectivity into consideration when writing SQL queries. The DB2 9 Visual Explain Tutorial available at *ftp://ftp.software.ibm.com/ps/products/db2/info/vr9/pdf/letter/en_US/db2tve90.pdf* provides a good way to get to know this facility. Visual Explain should be an integral part of your application development process.

db2exfmt

You use the db2exfmt facility to format the contents of SQL that has been explained and captured in explain tables. You invoke db2exfmt from the command line. You can use a series of commands to set the CURRENT EXPLAIN MODE special register to explain and explain SQL contained in an input file.

The following command sets the special register to explain and disables SQL execution:

```
db2 set current explain mode explain
```

This next statement directs db2exfmt to read in the SQL contained in the file query.txt:

```
db2 –tvf c:\query.txt
```

This statement runs db2exfmt and directs the output to file badsqlout.txt:

```
db2exfmt –d sample –g TIC –w –n % -s % -#0 –o c:\badsqlout.txt
```

This example uses the following db2exfmt options:

Option	Description
-g TIC	Specifies to graph the plan and include total cost under each operator in the graph (T), include I/O cost under each operator in the graph (I), and include the expected output cardinality of each operator in the graph (C)
-w	Specifies to use the current timestamp
-n %	Specifies the name of the source of the explain request; % indicates ALL
-s %	Specifies the schema of the source of the explain request
-#0	Specifies that all sections should be used
-o	Designates the output file for the results

The following statement resets the explain special register so that SQL can be executed:

```
db2 set current explain mode no
```

If necessary, db2exfmt will prompt you for additional information.

db2exfmt Output

Let's look at some examples of db2exfmt output. (Note that when you're working with DB2 Support, this is the preferred explain format.)

Figure 9.10 contains information from the EXPLAIN_INSTANCE table, such as database parameters and package information.

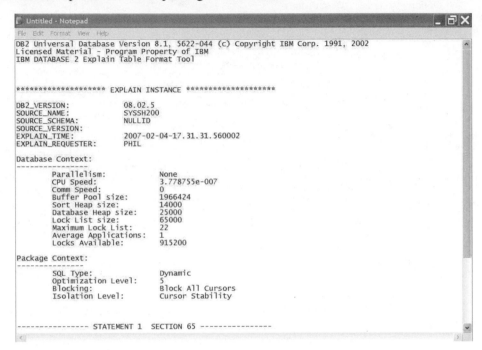

Figure 9.10: Sample db2exfmt output: Database parameters and package information

Figure 9.11 presents the access plan in a text-like format. Although I don't think this format is as helpful to developers as the graph provided by Visual Explain, it shows the same information, albeit in a text format. The format is easy to use and easy to share with or e-mail to others.

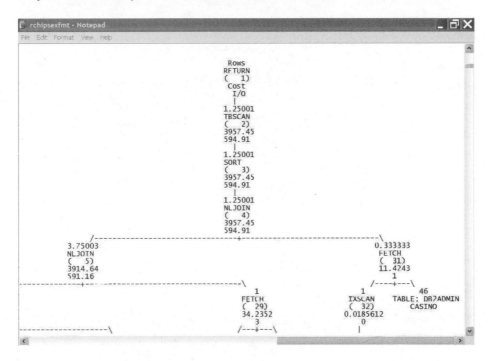

Figure 9.11: Sample db2exfmt output: Access plan

You can obtain explain operator details for each step in the access plan (Figure 9.12). These details help you to understand each step of the access plan and can aid in identifying tuning opportunities.

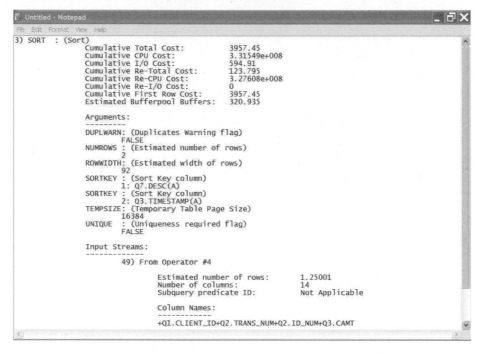

Figure 9.12: Sample db2exfmt output: Operator details

Creating Explain Tables for Use with db2exfmt

Both db2exfmt and Visual Explain require explain tables to be created in which to store the results of the explain. As you learned earlier, this creation takes place automatically if you use the Control Center. You can also create explain and Design Advisor tables from the command line (Design Advisor tables are required for Design Advisor to work properly). The DDL to create these tables is provided with DB2 and is stored in the EXPLAIN.DDL file. You can find this

DDL in the DB2 installation MISC subdirectory of the SQLLIB directory. To create explain tables, issue the following command from a command line:

```
db2 –tvf EXPLAIN.DDL
```

When you run the DDL, the explain and Design Advisor tables will be created. The explain tables will be created with a schema equal to the user ID of the person executing the command.

You'll need to create explain tables for various application development groups so that each group can have their own set to work with during the development process. Table 9.3 lists the DB2 explain and Design Advisor tables (these descriptions are adapted from Appendix C of IBM's *DB2 Performance Guide*). Familiarize yourself with the contents of these tables and use them to better understand the type of explain and Design Advisor information they capture. You can also extract the contents of these tables for use in building MQTs and other objects recommended by the Design Advisor.

Table 9.3: Explain and Design Advisor tables	
Table	**Description**
EXPLAIN_ARGUMENT	Contains information about the unique characteristics for each individual operator, if any.
EXPLAIN_DIAGNOSTIC	Contains an entry for each diagnostic message produced for a particular instance of an explained statement in the EXPLAIN_STATEMENT table.
EXPLAIN_DIAGNOSTIC_DATA	Contains message tokens for specific diagnostic messages that are recorded in the EXPLAIN_DIAGNOSTIC table.
EXPLAIN_INSTANCE	Serves as the main control table for all explain information. Each row of data in the explain tables is explicitly linked to one unique row in this table. This table stores basic information about the source of the SQL statements being explained and environment information.
EXPLAIN_OBJECT	Identifies the data objects required by the access plan generated to satisfy the SQL statement.
EXPLAIN_OPERATOR	Contains all the operators needed to satisfy the SQL statement by the SQL compiler.

Table 9.3: Explain and Design Advisor tables (continued)	
Table	**Description**
EXPLAIN_PREDICATE	Identifies the predicates that are applied by a specific operator.
EXPLAIN_STATEMENT	Contains the text of the SQL statement as it exists for the different levels of explain information. The original SQL statement as entered by the user is stored in this table along with the version used by the optimizer to choose an access plan. When an explain snapshot is requested, additional explain information is recorded here to describe the access plan selected by the SQL optimizer. This information is stored in the table's SNAPSHOT column in the format required by Visual Explain. This format is not usable by other applications.
EXPLAIN_STREAM	Represents the input and output data streams between individual operators and data objects. The data objects themselves are represented in the EXPLAIN_OBJECT table. The operators involved in a data stream are represented in the EXPLAIN_OPERATOR table.
ADVISE_INDEX	Stores information about recommended indexes. This table can be populated by the SQL compiler, the db2advis utility, or a user. The table is used in two ways: • To obtain recommended indexes • To evaluate indexes based on input about proposed indexes
ADVISE_INSTANCE	Contains information about the db2advis Design Advisor tool execution, such as workload compression and MQT runtime options.
ADVISE_MQT	Contains information about MQTs recommended by the Design Advisor, such as query text that defines the MQT.
ADVISE_PARTITION	Contains information about database partitions recommended by the Design Advisor.
ADVISE_TABLE	Stores DDL for table creation based on Design Advisor recommendations for MQTs, multidimensional clustering (MDC), and database partitioning.
ADVISE_WORKLOAD	Lets users describe a workload to the database. Each row in the table represents an SQL statement in the workload and is described by an associated frequency. The db2advis tool uses this table to collect and store work and information.

DB2 Design Advisor

The DB2 Design Advisor tool is used primarily by the DBA staff to evaluate SQL statements or workloads. The tool can help identify index solutions to improve CPU usage or reduce the cost of such statements or workloads. You can run the advisor on single SQL statements or on a workload, invoking it from the command line or from the Control Center. Thanks to enhancements made over the past few releases, the Design Advisor can now recommend the following objects to improve performance:

- MQTs
- Multidimensional clustering (MDC) tables
- Indexes
- Clustering indexes
- Include columns
- Database partitioning columns

The Design Advisor is an excellent tool that should be run on a regular basis to influence database design and improve the performance of existing databases.

RUNSTATS

You use the RUNSTATS utility to keep statistics about objects current (up-to-date) in the DB2 catalog. You can invoke RUNSTATS using the command line, a script, an administrative API, or other DB2 facilities.

The optimizer relies on information collected by RUNSTATS to enable it to develop an accurate access plan. Unless RUNSTATS has been run against an object, there won't be any statistics stored in the DB2 catalog about that object. In that case, the optimizer will use intelligent defaults.

The optimizer uses special catalog tables in the SYSSTAT schema as input into the access-plan development process. By default, the optimizer expects data to be distributed as a normal distribution. In cases involving non-uniform data, you can specify the following options on the RUNSTATS utility to collect additional statistics:

- DETAILED INDEXES STATISTICS: This option calculates extended index statistics, specifically the PAGE_FETCH_PAIRS and CLUSTERFACTOR statistics. With this information, the optimizer can better estimate the cost of accessing a table through an index. The optimizer considers both buffer pool size and degree of clustering when it estimates the cost of accessing a table through an index.
- WITH DISTRIBUTION: This option specifies that both basic statistics and distribution statistics are collected on columns. Distribution statistics are collected on all columns of the table.

Frequency statistics provide information about the columns and data values with the highest number of duplicates, the next-highest number of duplicate values, up to the number specified by the num_freqvalues database configuration parameter. Quantile statistics may also be collected. Distribution statistics should be collected for a table *when dynamic SQL is being used* and when static SQL is being used without host variables. Collect distribution statistics when at least one column in a table has a highly "non-uniform" distribution of data and the column occurs frequently in equality or range predicates as well as when duplicate data values occur often.

When you run RUNSTATS for a table or indexes, the following statistical information is stored in the DB2 catalog tables.

- For a table and index:
  - » Number of pages in use
  - » Number of pages that contain rows
  - » Number of rows that overflow
  - » Number of rows in the table (cardinality)

- For each column in the table and the first column in the index key:
  - » Cardinality of the column
  - » Average length of the column
  - » Second-highest and second-lowest values in the columns
  - » Number of NULLs in the column
- For indexes only:
  - » Number of leaf pages
  - » Number of index levels
  - » Degree of clustering of the table data to the index
  - » Ratio of leaf pages on disk in index key order to the number of pages in the range of pages occupied by the index
  - » Number of distinct values in the first column of the index
  - » Number of distinct values in the first two, three, and four columns of the index
  - » Number of distinct values in all columns of the index
  - » Number of leaf pages located on disk in index key order, with few or no large gaps between them
  - » Number of pages on which all RIDs are marked deleted
  - » Number of RIDs marked deleted on pages on which not all RIDs are marked deleted

It's important to run RUNSTATS on a regular basis. In static SQL environments, it is standard procedure to run RUNSTATS weekly, when indexes are added or changed, or when the amount of data changes significantly. Packages with static SQL must be rebound to use the latest statistics. In a dynamic SQL environment, it is standard procedure to run RUNSTATS weekly or nightly. This is due to the fact that each time a dynamic SQL statement is run (if a hit is not found in the package cache), the SQL statement is reoptimized or prepared and uses the latest statistics available. Note that this is the default behavior; you can use the REOPT bind option to change it.

> **Note:** Any statement in the package cache that depends on the table on which RUNSTATS has been performed will be soft-invalidated and reoptimized for subsequent executions.

If the statistics are current, DB2 may be able to use them to develop a better access plan. Proper execution frequency of RUNSTATS is critical to maintaining good overall database performance. Consider using automatic RUNSTATS to ensure that statistics are current.

Summary

This chapter introduced the DB2 optimizer and associated tools for analyzing and improving SQL/XML query performance. Index design and predicate coding tips and techniques also were presented. The partition elimination benefits of the new DB2 9 table partitioning feature were described, and you saw how to use Visual Explain to review table-partitioning explain information. The importance of RUNSTATS to proper database performance also was emphasized.

10

Utilities

This chapter focuses on utilities and commands that you, as an application developer or database administrator, should be familiar with to execute your normal duties in support of DB2 databases. Enhancements to several utilities enable DB2 9 to exploit the new XML data type and to provide the continuous availability demanded by today's businesses.

One of DB2 9's most exciting new utility features is the ability to restore a database from table space images and logs. Instead of having to back up an entire database (which can be costly in terms of processing power and time), you can now back up a subset of mission-critical table spaces and use this backup to restore those table spaces at a later date. At a time when increased data storage and retention requirements continue to fuel the rapid increase in database sizes, this capability goes a long way in providing added flexibility for customizing backup and restore operations to fit your requirements.

Another major enhancement in DB2 9 is row compression. With this feature, you create a compression dictionary that DB2 uses to compress data rows. You'll learn how to use the INSPECT utility to determine the compression benefits for an existing table. We'll also examine some other essential utilities that can help you to efficiently and reliably support and maintain databases. (For our purposes, this chapter uses the terms "utility" and "command" interchangeably.)

> **Note:** For utility and command information for partitioned databases and the data link feature, refer to IBM's DB2 9 Information Center, located at http://publib.boulder.ibm.com/infocenter/ db2luw/v9/index.jsp.

The XML Data Type and the IMPORT Command

With the introduction of an XML column type, DB2's import and export utilities gain support for XML data. XML data is not actually stored in a table but is represented by a data structure called an *XML Data Specifier (XDS)*. XML data involved in the import and export utilities must be stored in files separate from the main data file.

The IMPORT command provides three options for handling well-formed XML documents: XML FROM path, XMLVALIDATE, and XMLPARSE.

XML FROM path

Specifies the path (or paths) containing the XML documents. Use a comma to separate multiple path names.

XMLVALIDATE

Specifies whether a schema will be used to validate the XML document. Three parameters determine how IMPORT performs the validation.

- USING XDS: This parameter has three optional components:
  - » DEFAULT schema-id: The specified schema is used for validation when the XDS of an imported XML document contains no SCH attribute

identifying an XML schema (we'll talk more about the SCH attribute later, when we cover the XDS). The DEFAULT clause takes precedence over the IGNORE and MAP clauses, described next. If an XDS satisfies the DEFAULT clause, IMPORT ignores the IGNORE and MAP specifications.

» IGNORE (schema-id): This clause specifies a list of one or more schemas to ignore if they are identified by an SCH attribute. If an SCH attribute exists in the XDS for an imported XML document and the schema identified by the attribute is included in the list of schemas to IGNORE, no schema validation will occur for the imported XML document. If a schema is specified in the IGNORE clause, it cannot also be present on the left side of a schema pair in the MAP clause. A schema that is mapped by the MAP clause will not be subsequently ignored if specified by the IGNORE clause.

» MAP ((schema-id-1, schema-id-2)): Use the MAP clause to specify alternate schemas to use in place of those specified by the SCH attribute of an XDS for each imported XML document. This clause specifies a list of one or more schema pairs, where each pair represents a mapping of one schema to another. The first schema in the pair represents a schema referred to by an SCH attribute in an XDS. The second represents the schema that should be used to perform schema validation. If a schema is present on the left side of a schema pair in the MAP clause, it cannot also be specified in the IGNORE clause. Once a schema pair mapping is applied, the result is final. The mapping operation is non-transitive; therefore, the chosen schema won't subsequently be applied to another schema pair mapping. A schema cannot be mapped more than once, meaning that it cannot appear on the left side of more than one pair.

- USING SCHEMA schema-id: This XMLVALIDATE parameter specifies the schema to be used to validate the XML document. When you use this parameter, the SCH attribute in the XDS is ignored.

- USING SCHEMALOCATION HINTS: This XMLVALIDATE parameter causes the XML documents to be validated against the schemas identified by XML schema location hints in the source XML documents. If an XML document contains no schemaLocation attribute, no validation occurs. When you specify this parameter, IMPORT ignores the SCH attribute of the XDS. To define a schemaLocation attribute, you use an <xs:import> element. The following code defines a sample schemaLocation element:

```
<xs:import namespace=+http://www.w3.org/XML/1998/namespace"
schemaLocation="customer.xsd"/>
```

XMLPARSE

Defines how the XML documents are analyzed. There are two possible values:

- STRIP WHITESPACE: Removes all whitespace when the XML is parsed.
- PRESERVE WHITESPACE: Retains all whitespace when the XML is parsed.

If you omit this parameter, the IMPORT command uses the value of the CURRENT XMLPARSE OPTION special register, which determines the handling of whitespace when parsing XML without validation. Possible special register values are 'STRIP WHITESPACE' and 'PRESERVE WHITESPACE' (case insensitive), with no additional blank characters between the keywords. 'STRIP WHITESPACE' is the initial value. You can change the special register value by invoking the SET CURRENT IMPLICIT XMLPARSE OPTION statement:

```
SET CURRENT IMPLICIT XMLPARSE OPTION = 'PRESERVE WHITESPACE'
```

IMPORT Example

Here is a sample DB2 IMPORT command:

```
IMPORT FROM xmldata.del OF DEL
 XML FROM xmldatadir
 MODIFIED BY XMLCHAR
 XMLVALIDATE using XDS
  DEFAULT customer
  IGNORE (supplier)
  MAP((product,customer))
 INSERT INTO customer_xml;
```

The following Data Definition Language (DDL) creates the target table for this example.

```
CREATE TABLE customer_xml(Cid INT, Info XML);
```

XML Data Specifier (XDS)

An XML Data Specifier is an XML tag containing attributes that provide information about the actual XML data in the column, including the name of the file that contains the data and the offset and length of the data within that file. There are four XDS attributes:

- FIL: The name of the file that contains the XML data.
- OFF: The byte offset of the XML data in the file named by the FIL attribute, where the offset begins from 0 (zero).
- LEN: The length in bytes of the XML data in the file named by the FIL attribute.
- SCH: The fully qualified SQL identifier of the XML schema used to validate this XML document. The schema and name components of the SQL identifier are stored as the OBJECTSCHEMA and OBJECTNAME values, respectively, of the row in the SYSCAT.XSROBJECTS catalog table that corresponds to this XML schema.

In the following input file for the IMPORT example, the first line states that the XML data is stored in the file named xmlfiles.001.xml. Because the OFF and LEN attributes are not specified, the named file contains only one XML document. The schema identifier is named CUSTOMER.

```
1001,"<XDS FIL='xmlfiles.001.xml' SCH='CUSTOMER' />"
1002,"<XDS FIL='xmlfiles.001.xml' SCH='CUSTOMER' />"
1003,"<XDS FIL='xmlfiles.001.xml' SCH='PRODUCT' />"
1004,"<XDS FIL='xmlfiles.001.xml' SCH='SUPPLIER' />"
```

The XML Data Type and the EXPORT Command

Using DB2 9's export utility, you can export data from tables that include one or more columns with an XML data type. Exported XML data is stored in files separate from the main data file that contains the exported relational data. In the main exported data file, the XDS represents information about each exported XML document. Exported XML data is stored as XQuery Data Model (QDM) instances. An instance of the QDM is a well-formed XML document, a sequence of XML nodes, a sequence of atomic values, or any combination of nodes and atomic values.

The EXPORT command provides three options for handling well-formed XML documents: XML TO xml-path, XMLFILE filename, and XMLSAVESCHEMA. A fourth parameter, MODIFIED BY, lets you specify processing options based on the file type.

XML TO xml-path

Specifies one or more paths to directories where the XML files are to be stored. There will be at least one file per XML path, and each file will contain at least one QDM instance. If you specify more than one path, the QDM instances are distributed evenly among those paths.

XMLFILE filename

Names one or more base file names for the XML document files. When the name suffix is exhausted for the first name, EXPORT uses the second name, and so on. The utility constructs the XML file names by appending the current base name from this list to the current path (from xml-path) and adding a three-digit sequence number followed by the three-character identifier xml. For example, if the current XML path is the directory /u/pg/xml/path/ and the current XML file name is myfile, the first XML file created will be /u/pg/xml/path/myfile.001.xml. The second XML file created will be /u/pg/xml/path/myfile.002.xml.

XMLSAVESCHEMA

Saves the XML schema information for all XML columns. The option is not compatible with XQuery sequences that don't produce well-formed XML documents. If the exported XML document was validated when it was inserted, the fully qualified SQL identifier of that schema will be stored as an SCH attribute inside the corresponding XDS. The schema and name portions of the SQL identifier are stored as the OBJECTSCHEMA and OBJECTNAME values in the row of the SYSCAT.XSROBJECTS catalog table corresponding to the XML schema.

MODIFIED BY

Specifies file-type modifier options:

- xmlinsepfiles: Causes each QDM instance to be written to a separate file. By default, multiple values will be concatenated together in the same file.

- xmlnodeclaration: Causes the QDM instances to be written without XML declaration tags. By default, this tag is written at the beginning of each QDM instance. Here's an example of an XML declaration tag: <?xml version="1.0"?>.

- xmlchar: Lets you change the character code page. By default, QDM instances are written out in Unicode. The code page is determined by either the codepage file-type modifier or the application code page.

- xmlgraphic: Causes the exported XML document to be encoded in the UTF-16 code page regardless of the application code page or the codepage file-type modifier.

Exporting XML Data

XQuery is a query language, similar to SQL, designed to query XML data. You can execute XQuery expressions in DB2 either using SQL as the primary language (using the XMLQUERY SQL function) or using XQuery as the primary language. When you execute an XQuery expression using either method, an XML sequence is returned. How the resulting sequence appears in a result set, however, differs depending on whether SQL or XQuery is the primary language.

For example, given the command

```
EXPORT TO /mypath/t1export.del OF DEL
  XML TO /home/user/xmlpath XMLFILE xmldocs XMLSAVESCHEMA
  SELECT * FROM customer_xml
```

the exported DEL file /mypath/t1export.del contents will resemble the input file we used for the IMPORT example above. There will be only one exported XML file /home/user/xmlpath/xmldocs.001.xml. This one file will contain four sets of XML.

Here's another EXPORT example:

```
EXPORT TO /mypath/t1export.del OF DEL
  XML TO /home/user/xmlpath XMLFILE xmldocs
  SELECT
    xmlquery( '$m/addr/city/text()' passing by ref info as "m"
      returning sequence)
  FROM customer_xml
```

Here, the contents of the DEL file would be only an XDS element. The contents of the XML file would be the value of the city element within the <addr> element in the info column.

The db2look Command and XML Support

With DB2 9, IBM has updated the db2look command to allow the reproduction of the database objects required to validate and process XML documents. These database objects include the XML schemas, Document Type Definitions (DTDs), and external entities registered with the XML

Schema Repository (XSR). The db2look command can export all the XSR objects required to validate and process XML documents, along with the DDL statements needed to register them at the target database. The command has two new options:

- -xs: Exports all the files necessary to register the XML schemas and DTDs at the target database. The appropriate commands for registering them are also generated. The set of XSR objects that will be exported is controlled by the -u, -z, and -a options.

- -xdir pathname: Specifies the location for the exported XML-related files. If you don't specify this option, all XML-related files will be exported into the current directory.

The db2move Command and XML Support

The db2move command has four possible actions: EXPORT, IMPORT, LOAD, or COPY. The command does not support the LOAD option for tables containing XML columns. As a workaround, you can use the command's EXPORT and IMPORT options or the EXPORT and IMPORT utilities.

Reorganizing Indexes and Tables

Reorganizing data is one of the most important actions you can take to improve the performance of DB2. To reorganize the data in a table or an index, you use the REORG utility. The utility's table option reorganizes a table by reconstructing the rows to eliminate fragmented data and by compacting information. The index option reorganizes all indexes defined on a table by rebuilding the index data into unfragmented, physically contiguous pages. DB2 9 adds the ability to run REORG on just a single index of a DB2 9 data-partitioned table. This feature applies only to data-partitioned tables; for nonpartitioned tables, the utility still must process all the indexes on a table. You cannot use REORG against declared temporary tables and associated indexes.

You must have one of the following authorities to run the REORG command:

- SYSADM
- SYSCTRL
- SYSMAINT
- DBADM
- CONTROL privilege on the table

A connection to the database is also required.

The REORG utility contains many options that affect the objects being reorganized. Both offline and online reorganization of indexes and tables is supported. Which method you choose will depend on your business requirements. Most businesses today use online reorganization of tables and indexes because this method provides a high level of availability, with full read or write access. You can also throttle both offline and online utilities so that the utilities don't consume all available CPU but can run in the background while your applications continue processing.

Index Reorganization Options

The REORG command provides the following parameters for reorganizing indexes.

INDEXES ALL FOR TABLE table-name

Specifies the table whose indexes are to be reorganized. The table can be in a local or a remote database. You can specify additional options for REORG as follows:

- ALLOW NO ACCESS: Specifies that no other users can access the table while the indexes are being reorganized. This setting is the default.

- ALLOW READ ACCESS: Gives other users read-only access to the table while the indexes are being reorganized.

- ALLOW WRITE ACCESS: Lets other users read from and write to the table while the indexes are being reorganized.

- CLEANUP ONLY: Instructs REORG to perform a cleanup rather than a full reorganization. The indexes are not rebuilt, and any freed pages are available for reuse by indexes defined on this table only. You can qualify the cleanup operation further as follows.

  » CLEANUP ONLY PAGES: Instructs the utility to search for and free committed pseudo-empty pages—that is, pages for which the keys are all marked as deleted and for which these deletions are known to be committed. You can find the number of pseudo-empty pages in indexes by running the RUNSTATS utility and looking at the NUM_EMPTY_LEAFS column in SYSCAT.INDEXES. The CLEANUP ONLY PAGES setting will clean these leaf pages if they are determined to be committed.

  » CLEANUP ONLY ALL: Frees committed pseudo-empty pages and removes committed pseudo-deleted keys from pages that are not pseudo-empty. With this option, REORG also tries to merge adjacent leaf pages if doing so will result in a merged leaf page where PCTFREE is 10 percent. If two pages can be merged, one of the pages will be freed. To determine the number of pseudo-deleted keys in an index, excluding those on pseudo-empty pages, run RUNSTATS and check the NUMRIDS_DELETED column in SYSCAT.INDEXES. CLEANUP ONLY ALL will clean the NUMRIDS_DELETED and the NUM_EMPTY_ LEAFS if they are determined to be committed.

Table Reorganization Options

TABLE table-name

Indicates the table to reorganize. The table can be in a local or a remote database. You can specify the name or an alias in the form schema.

table-name, where schema is the user name under which the table was created.If you omit the schema name, the default schema is assumed.

> **Note:** You cannot specify an index for the reorganization of a multidimensional clustering (MDC) table.

> **Note:** You cannot use inplace reorganization of tables for MDC tables. A REORG of MDC tables is required only in exceptional circumstances.

INDEX index-name

Specifies the index to use when reorganizing the table. If you don't specify the fully qualified name in the form schema.index-name (where schema is the user name under which the index was created), the default schema is assumed. The database manager uses the index to physically reorder the records in the table it is reorganizing.

For an inplace table REORG, if a clustering index is defined on the table and an index is specified, the index must be clustering index. If you don't specify the INPLACE option (described next), any specified index will be used. If you don't specify an index, DB2 reorganizes the records without regard to order. If, however, the table has a clustering index defined and you've specified no index, the clustering index is used to cluster the table. You cannot specify an index if you're reorganizing an MDC table.

INPLACE

Reorganizes the table while permitting user access. Inplace table reorganization is permitted only on tables with type-2 indexes and without extended indexes.

- ALLOW READ ACCESS: Permits only read access to the table during reorganization.

- ALLOW WRITE ACCESS: Permits both read and write access to the table being reorganized.

- NOTRUNCATE TABLE: Instructs DB2 not to truncate the table after an inplace reorganization. During truncation, the table is S-locked.

- START: Starts the inplace REORG processing. Because this behavior is the default, specifying this keyword is optional.

- STOP: Stops the inplace REORG processing at its current point.

- PAUSE: Suspends or pauses inplace REORG for the time being.

- RESUME: Continues or resumes a previously paused inplace table reorganization.

USE tablespace-name

Specifies the name of a system temporary table space in which to store a temporary copy of the table being reorganized. If you don't provide a table space name, the database manager stores a working copy of the table in the table spaces that contain the table being reorganized.

For an 8K, 16K, or 32K table object, the page size of any system temporary table space you specify must match the page size of the table spaces in which the table data resides, including any LONG or LOB column data.

INDEXSCAN

For a clustering REORG, instructs DB2 to use an index scan to reorder table records, reorganizing table rows by accessing the table through an index. The default method is to scan the table and sort the result to reorganize the table, using temporary table spaces as necessary. Even though the index keys are in sort order, scanning and sorting is typically faster than fetching rows by first reading the row identifier from an index.

When an indexed table has been modified many times, the data in the indexes may become fragmented. If the table is clustered with respect to an index, the table and index can get out of cluster order. Both of these factors can adversely affect the performance of scans using the index and can reduce the effectiveness of index page prefetching. You can use the REORG INDEXES command to reorganize all the indexes on a table to remove any fragmentation and restore physical clustering to the leaf pages. To determine whether an index needs reorganizing, use the REORGCHK command.

> **Note:** The REORG TABLE command is not supported for declared temporary tables.

Additional REORG Information

Indexes may not be optimal following an inplace REORG TABLE operation because only the data object and not the indexes are reorganized. It is recommended that you perform a REORG INDEXES after an inplace REORG TABLE operation. Indexes are completely rebuilt during the last phase of a classic REORG TABLE, and as a result reorganizing indexes is not necessary.

Tables that have been modified so many times that data is fragmented and access performance is noticeably slow are candidates for the REORG TABLE command. You should also invoke this utility after altering the inline length of a structured type column to benefit from the altered inline length. Also, after making changes to data types, such as changing a CHAR column to VARCHAR, you must run REORG before the column can be accessed. Use the REORGCHK command to determine whether a table needs reorganizing. After reorganizing a table, use RUNSTATS to update the table statistics, and use REBIND to rebind the packages that use this table. The reorganize utility will implicitly close all the cursors.

If the table contains mixed row format because the table value compression has been activated or deactivated, an offline table reorganization can convert all the existing rows into the target row format.

> **Note:** If the reorganization is unsuccessful, temporary files should not be deleted. The database manager uses these files to recover the database.

If the name of an index is specified, the database manager reorganizes the data according to the order in the index.

> **Note:** To maximize performance, specify an index that is often used in SQL queries. If you don't specify the name of an index and a clustering index exists, the data will be ordered according to the clustering index.

The PCTFREE value of a table determines the amount of free space designated per page. If this value has not been set, REORG will fill as much space as possible on each page.

REORG Tips and Techniques

As noted, you should use the REORGCHK utility to identify tables and indexes in need of reorganization. Refer to the Reorgol.bat and Reorgol.txt scripts available at *www.mc-store.com/5086.html*.

DB2 writes information about the current progress of table reorganization to the recovery history file. This file contains a record for each reorganization event. To view the history file, run the command db2 list history for the database that contains the table you are reorganizing.

You can also use table snapshots and the db2pd tool to monitor the progress of table reorganization. DB2 records table reorganization monitoring data regardless of the Database Monitor Table monitoring switch setting. If an error occurs, an SQLCA dump is written to the history file. For an inplace table reorganization, the status is recorded as PAUSED.

You can monitor the status of an offline REORG using the db2 list utilities command. You can also obtain the status of an offline REORG using the following snapshot command:

```
GET SNAPSHOT FOR TABLES ON dbname
```

To monitor the status of an online REORG, use the db2pd command from the command line processor:

```
db2pd –db <dbname> -reorgs
```

This command returns the status of currently running online REORGs. Note that you can also use the table snapshot.

To pause an online REORG, use the following command:

```
db2 reorg table pgunning.sales inplace pause
```

To restart a paused online REORG:

```
db2 reorg table sales inplace resume
```

An online REORG that has been paused and resumed will restart from where you paused it and continue with the REORG. This feature enables you to pause and resume REORGs on large tables over time or run them during periods of lower system activity to accomplish a complete REORG.

To stop an online REORG, issue this command:

```
db2 reorg table pgunning.sales inplace stop
```

You cannot restart an online REORG that has been stopped. If another online REORG is subsequently done, it will start from the beginning. To enable a REORG to pick up where it left off, you need to pause, not stop, the REORG.

During normal operation, the online REORG command requires an S-lock to be taken at the end of the operation on the table involved to reclaim space. During periods of high activity, this step can cause the REORG to run for longer periods. In a high-activity database, you may want to use the NOTRUNCATE option to avoid this problem; with this option, however, the space is not reclaimed.

REORG Examples

To start, pause, and then resume an inplace REORG of the EVENT table with the default schema PGUNNING (specified explicitly in previous examples), enter the following commands:

```
db2 reorg table event Index empid inplace start
db2 reorg table event inplace pause
db2 reorg table event inplace allow read access notruncate table resume
```

Note that the command to resume the reorganization contains additional keywords to specify read access only and to skip the truncation step, which share-locks the table.

To reorganize a table online to reclaim space, enter this command:

```
db2 reorg table pgunning.sales inplace allow write access start
```

To clean up the pseudo-empty pages in all indexes on the ACCOUNTS table while allowing other transactions to read and update the table, use this command:

```
db2 reorg indexes all for table pgunning.accounts allow write access
cleanup only pages
```

To reorganize the PURCHASES table offline and use the system temporary table space TEMPSPACE1 as a work area, use this command:

```
db2 reorg table pgunning.purchases using tempspace1
```

Backup Database Utility

Backing up your company's data is one of the most important functions you perform as a database administrator. Companies entrust DBAs with enormous responsibility and rely on them to safeguard the corporate data. Some companies that have lost data due to inadequate or nonexistent database backups have lost sizable revenue, gone bankrupt, or even gone out of business completely.

As DBAs, we've all had our tense moments when we had difficulty restoring or recovering data due to inadequate backups, a lack of knowledge of the backup utility, or the absence of detailed backup and recovery procedures. Make sure your backup and recovery procedures are documented, tested, and practiced.

You use the BACKUP command to create a backup copy of a database or a table space. One of the following authorities is necessary to run this command:

- SYSADM
- SYSCTRL
- SYSMAINT

The BACKUP command automatically establishes a connection to the specified database. If a connection to the database already exists, that connection will be terminated and a new connection established specifically for the backup operation. At the completion of the backup operation, the connection is terminated.

This section's description of the BACKUP command and its parameters is adapted from IBM's *DB2 9 Command Reference* and is used with permission.

BACKUP Command Options

DATABASE database-alias

Specifies the alias of the database to back up.

TABLESPACE tablespace-name

Provides the names of the table spaces to back up.

- ONLINE: Specifies an online backup. (The default is offline.) Online backups are available only for databases configured with the LOGARCHMETH1 parameter.
- INCREMENTAL: Specifies a cumulative (incremental) backup image. An incremental backup image is a copy of all database data that has changed since the most recent successful full backup operation.
- DELTA: Specifies a non-cumulative (delta) backup image. A delta backup is a copy of all database data that has changed since the most recent successful backup operation of any type.

USE TSM

Instructs that the backup to use is Tivoli Storage Manager (TSM).

OPEN num-sessions SESSIONS

Indicates the number of I/O sessions to be created between DB2 and TSM or another vendor's backup product. Note that this parameter has no effect when backing up to tape, disk, or another local device.

TO dir/dev

Provides a list of target directory or tape device names. When specifying a directory, you must include the full path on which the directory resides. If you omit the USE TSM, TO, and LOAD keywords, the default target directory for the backup image is the current working directory of the client computer. This target directory or device must exist on the database server. You can repeat this parameter to specify the target directories and devices that the backup image will span.

If you list more than one target—target1, target2, and target3, for example—the first target is opened first. The media header and special files (including the configuration file, table space table, and history file) are placed in target1. All remaining targets are then opened and are used in parallel during the backup operation.

Because Windows operating systems provide no general tape support, each type of tape device requires a unique device driver. To back up to the FAT file system on Windows systems, users must conform to the 8.3 naming restriction. Use of tape devices may generate messages and prompts for user input. Valid response options are as follows:

- c (continue): Continue using the device that generated the warning message (e.g., when a new tape has been mounted).
- d (device terminate): Stop using only the device that generated the warning message (e.g., when there are no more tapes).
- t (terminate): Abort the backup operation.

If the tape system does not support the ability to uniquely reference a backup image, you're advised not to keep multiple backup copies of the same database on the same tape.

LOAD library-name

Names the shared library (DLL on Windows operating systems) that contains the vendor backup and restore I/O functions to be used.

WITH num-buffers BUFFERS

Specifies the number of buffers to be used. In DB2 9, if you don't specify a value, the BACKUP utility will choose an optimum value. When creating a backup to multiple locations, you can specify more buffers to improve performance.

BUFFER buffer-size

Indicates the size, in 4K pages, of the buffer to be used when building the backup image. The minimum setting for this parameter is eight pages; the default is 1,024 pages.

PARALLELISM n

Determines the number of table spaces that can be read in parallel by the backup utility. The default setting is 1.

UTIL_IMPACT_PRIORITY priority

Specifies the throttled priority (range 1–100) at which the BACKUP utility will run. For a backup to be throttled, the database manager configuration parameter

UTIL_IMPACT_LIM must be set to a value less than 100. The default value of 10 is a good starting point for an online backup so that the backup doesn't affect ongoing processing. Note that if you specify this keyword on the BACKUP command without a priority, the backup will be run with a default priority of 50 if a policy has been defined. If you don't specify the UTIL_IMPACT_PRIORITY parameter, the backup will be run unthrottled and will use as much CPU and I/O as is available. You can change the UTIL_IMPACT_PRIORITY setting once the utility is running by issuing the LIST UTILITIES command to obtain the utility ID and then issuing the SET UTIL_IMPACT_PRIORITY command to change the priority for that utility ID.

COMPRESS

Instructs that the backup image is to be compressed.

- COMPRLIB name: Specifies the name of the compression library to use. If no library is specified, the utility uses the default DB2 compression library.

- EXCLUDE: Specifies that the compression library is not to be stored in the backup image.

- COMPROPTS string: Describes a block of binary data that is passed to the compression library initialization routine.

EXCLUDE LOGS

Excludes logs from an online backup. For offline backups, logs are always excluded.

INCLUDE LOGS

Includes in an online backup image the logs required to restore the image to a consistent point in time.

WITHOUT PROMPTING

Specifies that the backup should be run unattended. Any actions that require user intervention will return an error message.

BACKUP Example

Here is a sample BACKUP command that uses throttling and TSM:

```
BACKUP DATABASE OW_PROD ONLINE USE TSM OPEN 1 SESSIONS WITH
2 BUFFERS BUFFER 1024 PARALLELISM 1 UTIL_IMPACT_PRIORITY 10
WITHOUT PROMPTING;
```

An actual customer used this BACKUP command to run an online nightly backup on a production JD Edwards ERP system. The backup ran in throttled mode and finished before the morning shift started, without impacting batch jobs than ran overnight. In this case, the need was to limit the impact of the backup on production work. However, in my experience, there are also times when companies want the backup to finish quickly; in those cases, the BACKUP command parameters are changed, and the throttled impact limit is higher. Set the amount of throttling you need to meet your business requirements.

Recover Database Command

You use the RECOVER command to restore a database and roll it forward, either to a particular point in time or to the end of the logs. You should practice using the RECOVER command (as well as the RESTORE and ROLLFORWARD commands) to recover databases and table spaces in your environment. Don't wait until an emergency to discover RECOVER.

To identify what needs to be recovered, the RECOVER command uses information stored in the history file, available backup images, and logs. To run the command, you need one of the following authorities.

- To recover an existing database: SYSADM, SYSCTRL, or SYSMAINT
- To recover to a new database: SYSADM or SYSCTRL

RECOVER Command Options

DATABASE database-alias

Specifies the alias of the database to recover.

TO isotime

Indicates the point in time to which all committed transactions are to be recovered (including the transaction committed precisely at that time as well as all transactions committed previously).

- USING LOCAL TIME: Specifies to use a point in time that is the server's local time rather than Coordinated Universal Time (UTC).
- USING UTC TIME: Specifies the UTC point in time to which to recover.

If you specify a local time for recovery, all messages returned will also be in local time. All times are converted on the server and, in partitioned database environments, on the catalog database partition.

The utility converts the timestamp string to UTC on the server, so the time is local to the server's time zone, not the client's. If the client is in one time zone and the server in another, use the server's local time. This local time differs from the local time option provided in the DB2 Control Center, which is local to the client.

If the timestamp string is close to the time change of the clock due to daylight savings time, it's important to know whether the stop time is before or after the clock change and to specify the time correctly.

END OF LOGS

Dictates that all committed transactions from all online archive log files listed in the database configuration parameter logpath are to be applied.

> **Note:** Before attempting any recovery operation, make a copy of all logs involved and save them to a safe location not involved in the recovery.

USING HISTORY FILE history-file

Lets you specify the history file to be used to drive the recovery. For example, you could use a previously saved history file if the recovery data is no longer available in the current history file.

OVERFLOW LOG PATH log-directory

Specifies an alternate log path to be searched for archived logs during recovery. Use this parameter if log files were moved to a location other than that specified by the logpath database configuration parameter. The OVERFLOW LOG PATH command parameter will overwrite the value (if any) of the database configuration parameter overflowlogpath.

COMPRLIB lib-name

Provides the name of the library to be used to perform the decompression. The name must be a fully qualified path referring to a file on the server. If you don't specify this parameter, DB2 tries to use the library stored in the image. If the backup was not compressed, the value of this parameter is ignored. If the specified library cannot be loaded, the restore operation will fail.

COMPROPTS options-string

Describes a block of binary data that is passed to the initialization routine in the decompression library.

RESTART

Restarts execution of the RECOVER command. You can use this keyword if a prior RECOVER operation was interrupted or otherwise was not completed. Starting in DB2 9, a subsequent RECOVER command will try to continue the previous RECOVER, if possible. Using the RESTART keyword forces RECOVER to start with a fresh restore and then roll forward to the specified point in time.

RECOVER Examples

The following example uses all default RECOVER command values to recover the GTSTST1 database using the latest backup image, rolling forward to the end of logs:

```
db2 recover database GTSTST1
```

To recover the GTSTST1 database to a point in time, use a command such as the following:

```
db2 recover database GTSTST1 to 2007-01-17-07.00.00
```

Restore Database Utility

You use the RESTORE utility to restore a database or table spaces from a database or table space backup image. The RESTORE utility operates on an image copy created by the BACKUP utility. The restored database is in the same state it was in when the backup copy was made. RESTORE can also restore to a database with a name different from the database name in the backup image (in addition to being able to restore to a new database).

> **Note:** Before attempting any RESTORE, make a copy of all logs involved and save them to a safe location.

You can also use RESTORE to restore backup images that were produced on DB2 UDB V8. If a migration is required, it will be invoked automatically at the end of the restore operation. However, certain database configuration parameters won't be set to new DB2 9 defaults. Review these in the DB2 9 migration guide available at IBM's DB2 9 for Linux, UNIX, and Windows Information Center (*http://publib.boulder.ibm.com/infocenter/db2luw/v9/index.jsp*), and make plans to update or enable them after migration.

If, at the time of the backup operation, the database was enabled for roll-forward recovery, you can return the database to the state it was in before the occurrence of the damage or corruption by invoking the ROLLFORWARD utility after successfully completing a restore operation. This utility can also restore from a table-space-level backup.

To restore a database that was backed up on a different workstation platform, use the db2move utility. You can restore databases created in one version of Windows from another version. Databases created on AIX, HP, and Sun platforms can also be restored from each other's system. If restoring to an existing database, RESTORE makes an implicit database connection; if restoring to a new database, an instance attachment is required.

You must have one of the following authorities to run the RESTORE command:

- SYSADM
- SYSCTRL
- SYSMAINT

Restoring to a new database requires one of the following authorities:

- SYSADM
- SYSCTRL

This section's description of the RESTORE command and its parameters is adapted from IBM's *DB2 9 Command Reference* and is used with permission.

RESTORE Command Options

DATABASE source-database-alias

Specifies the alias of the source database from which the backup was taken.

CONTINUE

Indicates that the containers have been redefined and that the final step in a redirected restore operation should be performed.

ABORT

This parameter:

- Stops a redirected restore operation. This action is useful when an error has occurred that requires one or more steps to be repeated. If you issue RESTORE DATABASE with the ABORT option, each step of a redirected restore operation must be repeated, including RESTORE DATABASE with the REDIRECT option (described later).
- Terminates an incremental restore operation before completion.

REBUILD WITH

Describes which table spaces the database will be restored with:

- ALL TABLESPACES IN DATABASE: Restores the database with all the table spaces known to the database at the time the image is restored. This restore overwrites a database if it already exists.
- ALL TABLESPACES IN DATABASE EXCEPT rebuild-tablespace-clause: Restores the database with all the table spaces known to the database at the time of the image being restored except for those specified in the list. This restore overwrites a database if it already exists.

- ALL TABLESPACES IN IMAGE: Restores the database with only the table spaces in the image being restored. This restore overwrites a database if it already exists.
- ALL TABLESPACES IN IMAGE EXCEPT rebuild-tablespace-clause: Restores the database with only the table spaces in the image being restored except for those specified in the list. This restore overwrites a database if it already exists.
- rebuild-tablespace-clause: Restores the database using a list of specified table spaces. This restore overwrites a database if it already exists.

TABLESPACE tablespace-name

Provides a list of names used to specify the table spaces that are to be restored.

ONLINE

Allows a backup image to be restored online. This means that other agents can connect to the database while the backup image is being restored and that the data in other table spaces will be available while the specified table spaces are being restored. This keyword is applicable only when performing a table-space-level restore operation.

HISTORY FILE

Restores only the history file from the backup image.

COMPRESSION LIBRARY

Restores only the compression library from the backup image. If the object exists in the backup image, it will be restored into the database directory. If the object does not exist in the backup image, the restore operation will fail.

LOGS

Restores only the set of log files contained in the backup image. If the backup image contains no log files, the restore operation will fail. If you specify this option, you must also specify the LOGTARGET option.

INCREMENTAL

Used without additional parameters, specifies a manual cumulative restore operation. During manual restore, the user must issue each restore command manually for each image involved in the restore, in the following order: last, first, second, third, and so on, up to and including the last image.

- **AUTOMATIC/AUTO**: Specifies an automatic cumulative restore operation
- **ABORT**: Specifies abortion of an in-progress manual cumulative restore operation

USE TSM

Says that the database is to be restored from TSM-managed output.

OPEN num-sessions SESSIONS

Dictates the number of I/O sessions to be used with TSM or the vendor product.

USE XBSA

Specifies that the Backup Services APIs (XBSA) interface is to be used.

FROM directory/device

Specifies the fully qualified path name of the directory or device on which the backup image resides. If you omit the USE TSM, FROM, and LOAD options, the default value is the current working directory of the client machine. This target directory or device must exist on the database server.

On Windows operating systems, the specified directory must not be a DB2-generated directory. For example, given the commands

```
db2 backup database sample to c:\backup
db2 restore database sample from c:\backup
```

DB2 generates subdirectories under the c:\backup directory that should be ignored. To specify precisely which backup image to restore, use the TAKEN AT parameter. There may be several backup images stored on the same path.

If several items are specified and the last item is a tape device, the user is prompted for another tape. Valid response options are as follows:

- c (continue): Continue using the device that generated the warning message (e.g., continue when a new tape has been mounted).
- d (device terminate): Stop using only the device that generated the warning message (e.g., terminate when there are no more tapes).
- t (terminate): Abort the restore operation after the user has failed to perform some action requested by the utility.

LOAD shared-library

The name of the shared library (DLL on Windows operating systems) containing the vendor backup and restore I/O functions to be used. The name can contain a full path. If the full path is not given, the value defaults to the path on which the user exit program resides.

TAKEN AT date-time

Provides the timestamp of the database backup image. The timestamp is displayed after successful completion of a backup operation and is part of the path name for the backup image, specified in the form *yyyymmddhhmmss*. You can also provide a partial timestamp. For example, if two different backup images with timestamps 20061001010101 and 20061002010101 exist, specifying 20061002 causes the image with timestamp 20061002010101 to be used. If you specify no value for this parameter, only one backup image can exist on the source media.

TO target-directory

Names the target database directory. RESTORE ignores this parameter when restoring to an existing database. The drive and directory you specify must be local. If the backup image contains a database that is enabled for automatic storage, only the database directory changes; the storage paths associated with the database remain the same.

DBPATH ON target-directory

Names the target database directory. RESTORE ignores this parameter when restoring to an existing database. The drive and directory you specify must be local. If the backup image contains a database that is enabled for automatic storage and you do not specify the ON parameter (covered next), this parameter is synonymous with the TO parameter, and only the database directory changes; the storage paths associated with the database remains unchanged.

> **Note:** In DB2 9, newly created databases use automatic storage by default.

ON path-list

Redefines the storage paths associated with an automatic storage database. Using this parameter with a database that is not enabled for automatic storage results in an error. The existing storage paths as defined within the backup image are no longer used, and automatic storage table spaces are automatically redirected to the new paths. If this parameter isn't specified for an automatic storage database, the storage paths remain as they are defined within the backup image.

You can specify one or more paths, separated by a comma. Each path must have an absolute path name, and it must exist locally. If the database does not already exist on disk and you don't specify the DBPATH ON parameter, RESTORE uses the first path as the target database directory.

> **Note:** Make sure enough physical disks are provided to each storage path you specify. Having enough physical disks is critical to DB2 performance. DB2 will try to balance table space containers across all available storage paths.

INTO target-database-alias

Specifies the target database alias. If the target database does not exist, it is created. When you restore a database backup to an existing database, the restored database inherits the alias and database name of the existing database. When you restore a database backup to a nonexistent database, the new database is created with the alias and database name you specify. This new database name must be unique on the system on which you restore it.

LOGTARGET directory

Provides the absolute path name of an existing directory to be used as the target directory for extracting log files from a backup image. If you specify this option, any log files contained in the backup image will be extracted into the target directory. Without this option, log files contained in a backup image will not be extracted. To extract only the log files from the backup image, specify the LOGS option.

NEWLOGPATH directory

Provides the absolute path name of a directory that will be used for active log files after the restore operation. This parameter has the same function as the newlogpath database configuration in which it is specified. You can use the parameter when the log path in the backup image is not suitable for use after the restore operations—for example, when the path is no longer valid or is being used by a different database.

WITH num-buffers Buffers

Indicates the number of buffers to be used. The default value is 2. However, you can use a larger number of buffers to improve performance when reading from multiple sources or if the value of PARALLELISM has been increased.

BUFFER buffer-size

Specifies the size, in pages, of the buffer used for the restore operation. The minimum setting for this parameter is eight pages; the default is 1,024 pages.

The restore buffer size must be a positive integer multiple of the backup buffer size specified during the backup operation. If you specify an incorrect buffer size, the buffers are allocated to be of the smallest acceptable size.

REPLACE HISTORY FILE

Specifies that the restore operation should replace the history file on disk with the history file from the backup image.

REPLACE EXISTING

Specifies that the restore utility is to replace the existing database with the restored database if a database with the same alias as the targeted database alias already exists. This option is useful for scripts that invoke the restore utility, because the command line processor won't prompt the user to verify deletion of an existing database. If you use the WITHOUT PROMPTING parameter, it's not necessary to specify REPLACE EXISTING, but in this case the operation will fail if events occur that normally require user intervention.

REDIRECT

Specifies a redirected restore operation. To complete such an operation, you should follow the RESTORE command with one or more SET TABLESPACE CONTAINERS commands and then by a RESTORE DATABASE command with the CONTINUE option. A redirected restore operation cannot be used against a table space that has automatic storage enabled.

GENERATE SCRIPT script

Specifies that a redirected restore script is to be generated with the specified file name. The script name can be relative or absolute, and the script will be generated on the client side. If the file cannot be created on the client side, an error message will be returned. If the file already exists, it will be overwritten.

WITHOUT ROLLING FORWARD

Specifies that the database is not to be put in rollforward-pending state after it has been successfully restored. If, following a successful restore operation, the database is in this state, you must run the ROLLFORWARD command before the database can be used again.

PARALLELISM n

Specifies the number of buffer manipulators that are to be spawned during the restore operation. The default value is 1.

COMPRLIB name

Specifies the name of the compression library to use. If you do not use this parameter, DB2 tries to use the library stored in the image. If the backup was not compressed, the parameter is ignored. If the specified library cannot be loaded, the restore operation will fail.

COMPROPTS string

Describes a block of binary data that is passed to the decompression library initialization routine.

WITHOUT PROMPTING

Specifies that the restore operation is to run unattended; actions that normally require user intervention will return an error message. When using a removable media device, such as a tape or diskette, the user is prompted when the device ends, even if the restore command does not include this option.

> **Note:** DB2 will automatically compute a value for the PARALLELISM, BUFFER, and WITH num_buffers BUFFERS parameters if they are not specified on the RESTORE command.

RESTORE Examples

For a sample backup and restore strategy, refer to the sample strategy in provided with the script files at *www.mc-store.com/5086.html*.

Here is a typical database restore command from a backup of a database on Windows 2003 Server with multiple targets to a new database on a new Windows 2003 Server:

```
db2 restore database goliath from "G:\offline\part1, G:\offline\part2",
"G:\offline\part3", "G:\offline\part4" with 10 buffers 256 parallelism 4
without prompting
```

To restore a database from incremental backup images using the automatic option:

```
db2 restore database gtstst1 incremental automatic
```

To create a backup image that includes logs for offsite recovery and subsequent restore:

```
db2 backup database gtstst1 online to /dev2/bkup include logs
```

Here is the subsequent restore and rollforward command:

```
db2 restore database gtstst1 from /dev2/bkup logtarget /prd/llogs
rollforward database gtstst1 to end of logs and stop overflow log path
/prd/llogs
```

For details about using table-space-level rebuild, consult the *DB2 9 Data Recovery and High Availability Guide and Reference.*

> **Note:** After the restore of an online backup, you must perform a roll forward recovery.

DB2 9 Data Compression and the INSPECT Utility

You can use DB2's INSPECT utility to check the database for architectural integrity. In DB2 9, INSPECT has been enhanced to support the new data compression feature.

You must have one of the following authorities to run the INSPECT command:

- SYSADM
- DBADM
- SYSCTRL
- SYSMAINT
- CONTROL privilege if single table

Although the INSPECT utility has many options, in this chapter we review only the use of the compression-related options.

> **Note:** You can enable a table for data compression by specifying COMPRESS YES on the CREATE TABLE or ALTER TABLE statement.

Compression-Related INSPECT Command Options

ROWCOMPESTIMATE

Estimates the effectiveness of row compression for a table. You can also specify the database partition (or partitions) on which to perform this operation.

The INSPECT tool is capable of taking a sample of the table data and building a dictionary from it. The utility can then use this dictionary to test compression against the records contained in the sample. From this test compression, INSPECT gathers data from which the following estimates are made:

- Percentage of bytes saved from compression
- Percentage of pages saved from compression
- Percentage of row ineligible for compression due to small data size
- Compression dictionary size
- Expansion dictionary size

The utility inserts the dictionary built for gathering these compression estimates if the COMPRESS YES attribute is set for this table and a dictionary doesn't already exist for the table. INSPECT tries to insert the dictionary concurrent to other applications accessing the table. Dictionary insert requires an Exclusive Table Alter lock and an Intent on Exclusive Table lock. INSPECT will insert a dictionary only into tables that support row compression. For partitioned tables, it builds a separate dictionary and inserts it on each partition.

TABLE NAME table-name

Names the table to be inspected.

SCHEMA schema-name

Specifies the schema name for the specified table name for a single-table operation.

TBSPACEID n OBJECTID n

Specifies the table to be inspected using a table space ID number and object ID number.

RESULTS

Specifies the result output file. The file will be written out to the diagnostic data directory path. If no error is found by the check processing, this result output file will be erased at the end of the INSPECT operation. If errors are found, the file will not be erased at the end of the INSPECT operation.

KEEP

Specifies that the result output file always be kept.

File-name

Specifies the name of the result output file.

INSPECT Example

The following example runs INSPECT against the ACT sample table and formats the results using the db2inspf tool:

```
db2 inspect rowcompestimate table name ACT results actcomp.txt
db2inspf actcomp.txt  c:\gun3.txt
```

Listing 10.1 shows the report output produced by db2inspf.

```
DATABASE: SAMPLE
VERSION : SQL09010
2007-06-13-17.22.23.953000

Action: ROWCOMPESTIMATE TABLE
Schema name: PGUNNING
Table name: ACT
Tablespace ID: 2  Object ID: 264
Result file name: gun3.txt

    Table phase start (ID Signed: 264, Unsigned: 264;
    Tablespace ID: 2) :
    PGUNNING.ACT

      Data phase start. Object: 264  Tablespace: 2
      Row compression estimate results:
      Percentage of pages saved from compression: 68
      Percentage of bytes saved from compression: 68
      Percentage of rows ineligible for compression due to small
      row size: 0
      Compression dictionary size: 6016 bytes.
      Expansion dictionary size: 3624 bytes.
      Data phase end.
    Table phase end.
Processing has completed. 2007-06-13-17.22.23.984000
```

Listing 10.1: Report output produced by db2inspf

Early user experiences of DB2 9 row compression have been good, with compression percentages reported as high as 85 percent data compression. This feature not only saves disk space; it also can improve performance by enabling more data to be placed into the buffer pool, and it can reduce log sizes as a result of logging smaller compressed rows.

> **Note:** After enabling data compression for a table, you must perform an offline REORG for the change to take effect.

Migrate Database Utility

Use the MIGRATE utility to convert previous versions of DB2 databases to current formats. Note that migration to DB2 9 is supported only from DB2 UDB V8.1 and later databases. Before running the utility, make certain you have a backup of the database being migrated. Also, be sure you've read the Information Center's DB2 9 Migration guide.

> **Note:** For migrated databases, several new features won't be enabled, and some database configuration parameters won't be set to the new DB2 9 defaults. Review these in the Information Center's DB2 migration guide, and make plans to update or enable them after migration. (This caution does not apply to newly created DB2 9 databases.)

You need SYSADM authority to run the MIGRATE utility. The utility establishes a database connection implicitly.

> **Note:** DB2 9 supports connectivity from DB2 clients at V8.1 and later and supports 32-bit operating systems on Windows and Linux x86.

You can execute the MIGRATE utility by specifying a single parameter. Simply use the DATABASE database-alias entry to provide the alias of the database to be migrated to the currently installed version of the database manager.

The following example migrates the database cataloged under the database alias GTSTST1:

```
db2 migrate database GTSTST1
```

Migration Tips and Techniques

The MIGRATE command migrates a database only to a newer DB2 version; you cannot use it to convert a migrated database to its previous version. Before migration, the database must be cataloged. If an error occurs during migration, you may need to issue the TERMINATE command before attempting the suggested user response. This is required for the CLP to refresh the database directory cache.

Before running MIGRATE, you should double the size of the database logs and make sure enough temporary space is available. MIGRATE uses additional log space as part of the migration process. Performing this step ahead of time will help to ensure a smooth migration.

> **Note:** If you migrate SQL procedures created in a 32-bit V8.1 instance to a 64-bit DB2 9 instance, you'll need to drop and re-create any SQL procedures.

The following migration checklist can assist you in migrating your databases to DB2 9:

1. Read the Information Center's DB2 9 migration guide.
2. Understand what is migrated and what settings remain unchanged.
3. Understand the new DB2 Developer Workbench, and brief developers.

4. Understand deprecated functions, and develop workarounds.

5. Install DB2 9 in a test environment, or convert a test database to DB2 9 and test *all* applications and new features.

6. Give management a "DB2 9 New Features" presentation, and decide which new features to exploit or defer.

7. Test and verify all applications with DB2 9 over a two-week period, and verify that DB2 UDB V8 clients work as expected.

8. Correct all issues or problems discovered during testing.

9. Develop a migration plan.

10. Have a fallback plan.

11. Conduct the migration.

12. Verify applications.

13. Exploit new DB2 features.

14. Post-migration: Migrate V8 clients to DB2 9.

Note: In DB2 9, newly created databases use automatic storage by default. This default does not apply to database that are migrated. To use automatic storage for a migrated database, you must drop and re-create the database under DB2 9.

LOAD Utility

The LOAD utility is the primary utility for loading data into DB2 tables. This tool loads multiple pages at a time, so it's much faster than SQL INSERTs or using the IMPORT utility. When possible, use LOAD to load large amounts of data into DB2 tables.

Unfortunately, it's been my experience that many Extract, Transform, and Load (ETL) tools and some applications try to insert large amounts of initial data into DB2 tables instead of using LOAD. In these cases, it's difficult, if not impossible, to meet user requirements. As a developer, be aware of the benefits of using LOAD, and incorporate its use to load large amounts of data.

This section's description of the LOAD command and its parameters is adapted from IBM's *DB2 9 Command Reference* and is used with permission.

The LOAD Command

Data residing on the server may be in the form of a file, tape, or named pipe. Data residing on a remotely connected client may be in the form of a fully qualified file or named pipe. You can also load data from a user-defined cursor. The LOAD utility supports the new data compression in DB2 9. If the table's COMPRESS attribute is set to YES, DB2 will compress the loaded data on every data and database partition for which a dictionary exists in the table.

You need one of the following authorities to run the LOAD utility:

- SYSADM
- DBADM
- Load authority on the database and
  » INSERT privilege on the table when invoking LOAD in INSERT mode, TERMINATE mode (to terminate a previous LOAD REPLACE operation), or RESTART mode (to restart a previous LOAD REPLACE operation)
  » INSERT and DELETE privilege on the table when invoking LOAD in REPLACE mode, TERMINATE mode (to terminate a previous LOAD REPLACE operation), or RESTART mode (to restart a previous LOAD REPLACE operation)
  » INSERT privilege on the exception table, if such a table is used as part of the load operation

In addition:

- To load data into a table that has protected columns, the session authorization ID requires LBAC credentials that permit write access to all protected columns in the table. Otherwise, the load will fail with an SQLSTATE 5U014 error.

- To load data into a table that has protected rows, the session authorization ID must hold a security label that

  » is part of the security policy protecting the table

  » was granted to the session authorization ID for write access or for all access

If the session authorization ID does not hold such a security label, the load will fail with an SQLSTATE 5U014 error.

- If the REPLACE option is specified, the session authorization ID must have the authority to drop the table.

Note: Because the instance owner owns all LOAD processes, the instance owner must have read access to input files.

Note: New in DB2 9, you can monitor the status of the LOAD utility by using the SNAPUTIL_PROGRESS administrative view and the SNAP_GET_UTIL_PROGRESS table function.

Load Command Options

CLIENT

Specifies that the data to be loaded resides on a remotely connected client. The utility ignores this option unless the load operation is being invoked from a remote client. The option is not supported in conjunction with the CURSOR file-type option.

FROM filename/pipename/device/cursorname

Specifies the file, pipe, device, or cursor referring to an SQL statement that contains the data being loaded. If the input source is a file, pipe, or device, it must reside on the database partition where the database resides unless you specify the CLIENT option. If you're loading data that resides on client machine, the data must be in the form of either a fully qualified file or a named pipe.

If you name multiple input sources, the utility will process them in sequence. If the last item is a tape device, LOAD will prompt the user for another tape. Valid responses are:

- c (continue): Continue using the device that generated the warning message (e.g., when a new tape has been mounted).
- d (device terminate): Stop using the device that generated the warning message (e.g., when there are no more tapes).
- t (terminate): Terminate all devices.

Note: Loading data from multiple integrated exchange format (IXF) files is supported if the files are physically separate but logically are one file. This function is not supported if the files are both logically and physically separate. (Multiple physical files would be considered logically one if they were all created with one invocation of the EXPORT command.)

OF filetype

Specifies the format of the data:

- ASC (non-delimited ASCII format)
- DEL (delimited ASCII format)
- IXF (PC version), exported from the same or another DB2 table
- CURSOR (a cursor declared against a SELECT or VALUES statement)

LOBS FROM lob-path

Provides the path to the data files containing LOB values to be loaded.
The path must end with a slash (/). If you specify LOAD's CLIENT option, you
must qualify the path. The names of the LOB data files are stored in the main
data file (ASC, DEL, or IXF), in the column that will be loaded into the LOB
column. You can specify multiple paths, up to a maximum of 999. Specifying
multiple paths implicitly activates the LOBSINFILE behavior.

LOAD ignores this option if you use it with the CURSOR file type.

MODIFIED BY filetype-mod

Specifies additional file-type modifier options.

METHOD

Describes how the columns to be loaded from the data file are to be selected:

- L: Specifies the start and end column numbers from which to load
  data. A column number is a byte offset from the beginning of a row
  of data. It is numbered starting from 1. This method works only
  with ASC (ascending) files, and it is the only valid method for that
  file type.
- NULL INDICATORS null-indicate-list: This option is available only when
  you specify the METHOD L option (i.e., when the input file is an ASC
  file). The null indicator list is a comma-separated list of positive
  integers that specify the column number of each null indicator field.
  The column number is the byte offset of the null indicator field from
  the beginning of a row of data. One entry must exist in the null
  indicator list for each data field defined in the METHOD L parameter.
  A column number of 0 (zero) indicates that the corresponding data
  field always contains data.

- A value of Y in the NULL indicator column specifies that the column data is NULL. Any character *other than* Y in the NULL indicator column specifies that the column data is not NULL and that column data specified by the METHOD L option will be loaded.

- You can change the NULL indicator character using the MODIFIED BY option.

- N: Specifies the names of the columns in the data file to be loaded. The case of these column names must match the case of the corresponding names in the system catalogs. Each table column that is not nullable should have a corresponding entry in the METHOD N list. For example, given data fields F1, F2, F3, F4, F5, and F6 and table columns C1 INT, C2 INT NOT NULL, C3 INT NOT NULL, and C4 INT, method N (F2, F1, F4, F3) is a valid request, while method N (F2, F1) is not valid. You can use METHOD N only with file types IXF and CURSOR.

- P: Specifies the field numbers (numbered from 1) of the input data fields to be loaded. Each table column that is not nullable requires a corresponding entry in the METHOD P list. For example, given data fields F1, F2, F3, F4, F5, and F6, and table columns C1 INT, C2 INT NOT NULL, C3 INT NOT NULL, and C4 INT, method P (2, 1, 4, 3) is a valid request, while method P (2, 1) is not valid. You can use METHOD P only with file types IXF, DEL, and CURSOR, and it is the only valid method for the DEL file type.

SAVECOUNT n

Specifies that the load utility is to establish consistency points after every *n* rows. This value is converted to a page count and rounded up to intervals of the extent size. Because DB2 issues a message at each consistency point, you should use this option if the load operation will be monitored using LOAD QUERY. If the value of *n* is not sufficiently high, the synchronization of the activities performed at each consistency point will impact performance.

The default is zero, meaning that no consistency points will be established, unless necessary.

The load utility ignores this option if it is used with the CURSOR file type.

ROWCOUNT n

Specifies the number of *n* physical records in the file to be loaded. This option lets you load only the first *n* rows in a file.

WARNINGCOUNT n

Stops the load operation after *n* warnings. Set this parameter if you expect no warnings but want to verify that the correct file and table are being used. If *n* is zero or this option is not specified, the load operation will continue regardless of the number of warnings issued. If the load is stopped because the threshold of warnings was encountered, you can start another load operation in RESTART mode; the load operation will automatically continue from the last consistency point. As an alternative, you can initiate another load operation in REPLACE mode, starting at the beginning of the input file.

MESSAGES message-file

Specifies the destination for warning and error messages that occur during the load operation. If you specify no message file, messages are written to standard output. If you don't provide the complete path to the file, LOAD uses the current directory and the default drive as the destination. If you specify the name of a file that already exists, the utility appends the information.

The message file is usually populated with messages at the end of the load operation and, as such, is not suitable for monitoring the progress of the operation.

TEMPFILES PATH temp-pathname

Specifies the name of the path to be used when creating temporary files during a load operation. The path name should be fully qualified according to the server database partition.

Temporary files take up file system space. Sometimes, this space requirement is quite substantial. Here is an estimate of how much file system space you should allocate for all temporary files:

- 136 bytes for each message that the load utility generates.
- 15 K overhead if the data file contains long field data or LOBs. This quantity can grow significantly if you specify the INSERT option and the table already contains a large number of long fields or much LOB data.

INSERT

One of four modes under which the load utility can execute. Adds the loaded data to the table without changing the existing table data. Insert is the default mode.

REPLACE

One of four modes under which the load utility can execute. Deletes all existing data from the table and inserts the loaded data. The table definition and index definitions are not changed.

RESTART

One of four modes under which the load utility can execute. Restarts a previously interrupted load operation. The load operation will automatically continue from the last consistency point in the load, build, or delete phase.

TERMINATE

One of four modes under which the load utility can execute. Terminates a previously interrupted load operation to the point in time at which it started, even if consistency points were passed. The states of any table spaces involved in the operation return to normal, and all table objects are made consistent (index objects may be marked as invalid, in which case index rebuild will automatically take place at next access).

If the load operation being terminated is a LOAD REPLACE, the table will be truncated to an empty table after the load TERMINATE operation. If the load operation being terminated is a LOAD INSERT, the table will retain all its original records after the LOAD TERMINATE operation. The LOAD TERMINATE option will not remove a backup-pending state from table spaces.

INTO table-name

Specifies the database table into which the data is to be loaded. This table cannot be a system table or a declared temporary table. An alias or the fully qualified or unqualified table name (in the form schema.tablename) can be specified. If you specify an unqualified table name, the table will be qualified with the CURRENT SCHEMA.

insert-column

Specifies the table column into which the data is to be inserted. The load utility cannot parse columns whose names contain one or more spaces.

NORANGEEXC

Indicates that if a row is rejected because of a range violation, the utility should not insert it into the exception table.

NOURNIQUEEXC

Indicates that if a row is rejected because it violates a unique constraint, the utility should not insert it into the exception table.

STATISTICS USE PROFILE

Instructs LOAD to collect statistics during the load according to the profile defined for this table. This profile must be created before you execute the utility. The profile is created by the RUNSTATS command. If the profile does not exist and you instruct LOAD to collect statistics according to the profile, a warning is returned and no statistics are collected.

STATISTICS NO

Specifies that no statistics are to be collected and that the statistics in the catalogs are not to be altered. This setting is the default.

COPY NO

Specifies that the table space in which the table resides will be placed in backup-pending state if forward recovery is enabled (i.e., if logretain or userexit is on). This option also puts the table space state into the Load in Progress table space state. This state is a transient one that will disappear when the load is completed or aborted. The data in any table in the table space cannot be updated or deleted until a table space backup or a full database backup is made. However, it's possible to access the data in any table by using the SELECT statement.

COPY YES

Specifies that a copy of the loaded data will be saved. This option is invalid if forward recovery is disabled (both logretain and userexit are off). The option is not supported for tables with DATALINK columns.

- USE TSM: Specifies that the copy will be stored using Tivoli Storage Manager.

- OPEN num-sess SESSIONS: Specifies the number of I/O sessions to be used with TSM or the vendor product. The default value is 1.

- TO device/directory: Specifies the device or directory on which the copy image will be created.

- LOAD lib-name: Specifies the name of the shared library (DLL on Windows operating systems) containing the vendor backup and restore I/O functions to be used. It may contain the full path. If the full path is not given, the option defaults to the path where the user exit programs reside.

NONRECOVERABLE

Specifies that the load transaction is to be marked as non-recoverable and that it will not be possible to recover it by subsequent roll forward action. The roll forward utility will skip the transaction and will mark the table into which data was being loaded as "invalid." The utility also will ignore any subsequent transactions against that table. After the roll forward operation is completed, such a table can be dropped or restored only from a backup (full or table space) taken after a commit point following the completion of the non-recoverable load operation. With this option, table spaces are not put in backup-pending state following the load operation, and a copy of the loaded data does not have to be made during the load operation.

WITHOUT PROMPTING

Specifies that the list of data files contains all the files that are to be loaded and that the devices or directories listed are sufficient for the entire load operation. If a continuation input file is not found, or if the copy targets are filled before the load operation finishes, the load operation will fail, and the table will remain in load-pending state.

If you don't specify this option and the tape device encounters an end-of-tape for the copy image or the last item listed is a tape device, the user is prompted for a new tape on that device.

You can monitor the status of a load operation by using the LOAD QUERY command.

DATA BUFFER buffer-size

Specifies the number of 4 K pages (regardless of the degree of parallelism) to use as buffered space for transferring data within the utility. If the specified value is less than the algorithmic minimum, the minimum required resource is used, and no warning is returned.

This memory is allocated directly from the utility heap, whose size can be modified through the util_heap_sz database configuration parameter.

If no value is specified, the utility calculates an intelligent default at run time based on a percentage of the free space available in the utility heap at the instantiation time of the loader, as well as some characteristics of the table.

SORT BUFFER buffer-size

Specifies a value that overrides the SORTHEAP database configuration parameter during a load operation. This option is relevant only when loading tables with indexes and only when the INDEXING MODE parameter is not specified as DEFERRED. The value you specify cannot exceed the value of SORTHEAP. This parameter is useful for throttling the sort memory that is used when loading tables with many indexes without changing the value of SORTHEAP, which would also affect general query processing.

CPU_PARALLELISM n

Specifies the number of processes or threads that the load utility will spawn for parsing, converting, and formatting records when building table objects. This parameter is designed to exploit intra-partition parallelism and is particularly useful when loading presorted data, because the option preserves record order in the source data. If the parameter's value is zero or has not been specified, the load utility uses an intelligent default value (usually based on the number of CPUs available) at run time.

Specifying a small value for the SAVECOUNT parameter causes the loader to perform many more I/O operations to flush both data and table metadata. When CPU_PARALLELISM is greater than 1, the flushing operations are asynchronous, permitting the loader to exploit the CPU. With a value of 1, the loader waits on I/O during consistency points. A load operation with CPU_PARALLELISM set to 2 and SAVECOUNT set to 10,000 is completed faster than the same operation with CPU_PARALLELISM set to 1, even though there is only one CPU.

DISK_PARALLELISM n

Specifies the number of processes or threads that the load utility will spawn for writing data to the table space containers. If no value is specified, the utility selects an intelligent default based on the number of table space containers and the table characteristics.

FETCH_PARALLELISM

When set to YES (the default), causes the load utility to try to parallelize fetching from the remote data source when performing a load from a cursor declared using the DATABASE keyword or when using the API sqlu_remotefetch_entry media entry. When set to NO, no parallel fetching is performed.

INDEXING MODE

Specifies whether LOAD should rebuild indexes or extend them incrementally. Valid values are:

- AUTOSELECT: The utility will automatically decide between REBUILD or INCREMENTAL mode.

- REBUILD: All indexes will be rebuilt. The utility must have sufficient resources to sort all index key parts for both old and appended table data.

- INCREMENTAL: Indexes will be extended with new data. This approach consumes index free space, requiring only enough sort space to append index keys for the inserted records. This mode is supported only in cases where the index object is valid and accessible at the start of a load operation (for example, it is not valid immediately after a load operation that specified the DEFERRED mode). If INCREMENTAL mode is specified but is not supported due to the index state, a warning is returned, and the load operation continues in REBUILD mode. Similarly, if a load restart operation is begun in the load build phase, INCREMENTAL mode is not supported.

Incremental indexing is not supported when all of the following conditions are true:

- The LOAD COPY option is specified.
- The table resides in a Data Management Services (DMS) table space.

- The index object resides in a table space that is shared by other table objects belonging to the table being loaded.

To bypass this restriction, place indexes in a separate table space.

DEFERRED

Instructs the load utility not to attempt index creation. Indexes will be marked as needing a refresh. The first access to such indexes that is unrelated to a load operation may force a rebuild, or indexes may be rebuilt when the database is restarted. This approach requires enough sort space for all key parts for the largest index. The total time subsequently taken for index construction is longer than that required in REBUILD mode. Therefore, when you're performing multiple load operations with deferred indexing, it's advisable (from a performance viewpoint) to let the last load operation in the sequence perform an index rebuild rather than allow indexes to be rebuilt at first non-load access.

Deferred indexing is supported only for tables with non-unique indexes, so that duplicate keys inserted during the load phase are not persistent after the load operation.

ALLOW NO ACCESS

Causes LOAD to lock the target table for exclusive access during the load. The table state will be set to LOAD IN PROGRESS during the load. ALLOW NO ACCESS is the default behavior and is the only valid option for LOAD REPLACE.

When constraints are defined on the table, the table state will be set to CHECK PENDING as well as LOAD IN PROGRESS. Use the SET INTEGRITY command to take the table out of CHECK PENDING status.

ALLOW READ ACCESS

Causes LOAD to lock the target table in a share mode. The table state will be set to both LOAD IN PROGRESS and READ ACCESS. Readers can access the non-delta portion of the data during the table load. In other words, data that existed before the start of the load is to be accessible by readers to the table, but data that is being loaded is not available until the load is completed. LOAD TERMINATE or LOAD RESTART of an ALLOW READ ACCESS load may use this option; LOAD TERMINATE or LOAD RESTART of an ALLOW NO ACCESS load may not use this option. Furthermore, the option is not valid if the indexes on the target table are marked as requiring a rebuild.

When constraints are defined on the table, the table state is set to CHECK PENDING as well as LOAD IN PROGRESS and READ ACCESS. At the end of the load, the LOAD IN PROGRESS table state will be removed, but the table states CHECK PENDING and READ ACCESS will remain. You must use the SET INTEGRITY command to take the table out of CHECK PENDING status. While the table is in CHECK PENDING and READ ACCESS, the non-delta portion of the data is still accessible to readers; the new (delta) portion of the data will remain inaccessible until execution of the SET INTEGRITY command is completed. A user may perform multiple loads on the same table without issuing a SET INTEGRITY command. Only the original (checked) data will remain visible, however, until the SET INTEGRITY command is issued.

ALLOW READ ACCESS also supports the following modifier:

- USE tablespace-name: If the indexes are being rebuilt, a shadow copy of the index is built in table space tablespace-name and is copied over to the original table space at the end of the load during an INDEX COPY PHASE. Only system temporary table spaces can be used with this option. If not specified, the shadow index will be created in the same table space as the index object. If the shadow copy is created in the same table space as the index object, the copy of the shadow index object over the old index object is instantaneous. If the shadow copy is in a different table space from the index object, a physical copy is performed. This operation could involve considerable I/O and time. The copy happens while the table is offline at the end of a load during the INDEX COPY PHASE.

Without this option, the shadow index is built in the same table space as the original. Because both the original index and the shadow index by default reside in the same table space simultaneously, there may be insufficient space to hold both indexes within one table space. Using this option ensures that you retain enough table space for the indexes.

The load utility ignores this option unless you specify INDEXING MODE REBUILD or INDEXING MODE AUTOSELECT. The option is also ignored if INDEXING MODE AUTOSELECT is specified and LOAD chooses to incrementally update the index.

SET INTEGRITY PENDING CASCADE

If LOAD puts the table into Set Integrity Pending state, specifies whether this state is immediately cascaded to all descendents (including descendent foreign key tables, descendent immediate materialized query tables, and descendent immediate staging tables).

- IMMEDIATE: Indicates that LOAD is to immediately extend Set Integrity Pending state to all descendent foreign key tables, descendent immediate materialized query tables, and descendent staging tables. For a LOAD INSERT operation, Set Integrity Pending state is not extended to descendent foreign key tables even if the you specify the IMMEDIATE option.

- DEFERRED: Indicates that only the loaded table will be placed in Set Integrity Pending state. The states of the descendent foreign key tables, descendent immediate materialized query tables, and descendent immediate staging tables will remain unchanged.

  Descendent foreign key tables might later be implicitly placed in Set Integrity Pending state when their parent tables are checked for constraint violations (using the IMMEDIATE CHECKED option of the SET

283

INTEGRITY statement). Descendent immediate materialized query tables and descendent immediate staging tables will be implicitly placed in Set Integrity Pending state when one of the underlying tables is checked for integrity violations. A warning (SQLSTATE 01586) is issued to indicate that dependent tables have been placed in Set Integrity Pending state. See the Notes section of the SET INTEGRITY statement description in the *SQL Reference* for when these descendent tables will be put into Set Integrity Pending state.

If you don't specify the SET INTEGRITY PENDING CASCADE option, only the loaded table will be placed in Set Integrity Pending state. The state of descendent foreign key tables, descendent immediate materialized query tables, and descendent immediate staging tables will remain unchanged and can later be implicitly put into Set Integrity Pending state when the loaded table is checked for constraint violations.

If LOAD does not put the target table into Set Integrity Pending state, the SET INTEGRITY PENDING CASCADE option is ignored.

LOCK WITH FORCE

Permits the load utility to force off other applications that hold conflicting locks (including table locks) rather than wait, and possibly timeout, when acquiring a lock. Forced applications will roll back and release the locks that LOAD needs so that utility execution can proceed. This option requires the same authority as the FORCE APPLICATIONS command (SYSADM or SYSCTRL).

ALLOW NO ACCESS loads may force applications holding conflicting locks at the start of the load operation. At that time, the utility may force applications that are trying to either query or modify the table.

ALLOW READ ACCESS loads may force applications holding conflicting locks at the start or end of the load operation. At the start of the load, the utility may force applications that are trying to modify the table. At the end of the load, it may force applications that are trying to either query or modify the table.

SOURCEUSEREXITexecutable

Specifies the name of an executable file that will be called to feed data into the utility. The following options can be specified with this parameter:

- REDIRECT INPUT FROM
  - » BUFFER input-buffer: The stream of bytes specified in input-buffer is passed into the STDIN file descriptor of the process executing the given executable.
  - » FILE input-file: The contents of this client-side file are passed into the STDIN file descriptor of the process executing the given executable.
- REDIRECT OUTPUT TO
  - » FILE output-file: The STDOUT and STDERR file descriptors are captured to the specified fully qualified server-side file.
- PARALLELIZE: Increases the throughput of data coming into the load utility by invoking multiple user exit processes simultaneously. This option applies only in multi-partition database environments and is ignored in single-partition database environments.

LOAD Command Examples

The following example loads and replaces the table data in the SALES table from a file containing data in IXF format:

```
db2 load table salestab.ixf of ixf messages sales.msgs tempfiles path
/db2inst1/work replace into pgunning.sales
```

The next example uses the NONRECOVERABLE option and inserts additional rows into the ORDERS table:

```
db2 load table orderstab.ixf of ixf messages orders.msgs insert into
pgunning.orders nonrecoverable
```

When you use the NONRECOVERABLE option, the table space isn't placed in backup-pending state, and a copy of the data is not required. It's best to use this option only when you can re-create the data that has been loaded.

Load from Cursor

Many times over the years, I've had to move tables out of 4 K table spaces when they were hitting the 64 GB table limit in DB2 UDB for Linux, UNIX, and Windows. This situation arose primarily at companies running large commercial enterprise resource planning (ERP) or materials resource planning (MRP) applications with many thousands of tables per table space.

Before the "load from cursor" capability became available in V8.1, the solution was either to export the data and then load it or to import the data into a new table space of a higher page size to provide relief from the 64 GB limit. Exporting and loading was time-consuming, usually required an outage, and could take several hours to complete.

You can get around these and other problems by using a six-step process to move tables to other table spaces and fix problems such as extent size, improper page size, and incorrect table space layouts on disks. In the following example, we'll move a table to a new table space because the old table space was not laid out correctly over the disk array and because the extent size was too large. The process is as follows:

1. Create the new table space:

```
create tablespace ts_misc_d
pagesize 4K
managed by database
using ( file 'd:\db2_space\TS_MISC_D' 433000,
file 'e:\db2_space\TS_MISC_D' 433000,
  file 'f:\db2_space\TS_MISC_D' 433000 )
```

```
extentsize 32
prefetchsize 96
bufferpool ibmdefaultbp
no file system caching;
```

2. Create the new target table from the table to clone.

```
create table db2admin.new_S_ACC_BALANCE like db2admin.
S_ACC_BALANCE in ts_misc_d;
```

3. Load from cursor.

```
declare c1 cursor for select * from db2admin.old_s_acc_balance;
open c1;
load from c1 of cursor insert into db2admin.s_acc_balance
nonrecoverable;
commit;
```

4. Rename the table to be moved to OLD and rename the copy to the OLD name.

```
rename table db2admin.S_ACC_BALANCE to OLD_S_ACC_BALANCE;
rename table db2admin.new_S_ACC_BALANCE to S_ACC_BALANCE;
```

5. Create the indexes and primary key constraint (obtained from db2look before beginning the work).

```
create unique index db2admin.pk_acc_balance on db2admin.
acc_balance ( timestamp, acc_num ) allow reverse scans;alter
table "db2admin"."acc_balance"
        add constraint "acc_balance_pk" primary key
            ("timestamp",
             "acc_num");
```

6. Run RUNSTATS on the newly loaded and created table and indexes.

```
runstats on table db2admin.S_ACC_BALANCE with distribution
and detailed indexes all allow write access;
```

Don't forget to drop the old table at the appropriate time. You can use this process to save time and to fix table and table space problems. It took me in less than 13 minutes on a midsized, eight-way server with 8 GB of RAM to perform all these steps for a 10-million row table in a table space that had reached the 64 GB limit. Your mileage may vary, but if you don't have the "load from cursor" load command in your toolbox, it's time to add it. In DB2 9, IBM has enhanced this tool to include remote fetch. With this feature, you can load data from one database into another by referencing a nickname within an SQL query.

Summary

In this chapter, you learned about DB2 utilities and commands that are important to you as a developer or DBA. I highlighted new DB2 9 features and provided utility and command implementation details. The tips and techniques included in this chapter have been provided to help you obtain maximum benefit from specific utilities. We discussed monitoring for both offline and online utilities using several methods. The use of LOAD FROM CURSOR was covered, as well as some techniques you can use in moving data between tables or table spaces.

11

Monitoring

I n this chapter, we cover DB2 monitoring, introducing the concepts of
online monitoring and exception-based monitoring and then addressing
in detail the DB2 9 facilities used to conduct these two essential activities:
snapshot monitoring, the DB2 Health Center and Health Monitor, Memory
Visualizer, Activity Monitor, Memory Tracker, the db2pd utility, and event
monitoring. We conclude the chapter with a summary of DB2 9 built-in
monitoring facilities and tools and look at some examples of how to use them
to monitor DB2 database performance.

Monitoring

There are basically two types of monitoring that we as DBAs need to use:
online (or real-time) monitoring and *exception-based* (24x7) monitoring. The
DB2 base product contains numerous built-in facilities to perform both types
of monitoring, and we'll look at those facilities in detail in this chapter. You
can use additional monitoring tools available from IBM and other independent
software vendors (ISVs) to augment the built-in DB2 monitoring facilities.

Online Monitoring

DBAs use online monitoring to identify and solve realtime problems—problems that are occurring currently and (usually) are adversely impacting the ability to conduct business. You can think of realtime problems as the kinds of problems one might refer to a help desk (if a DBA doesn't detect them first). An example would be a case where a currently executing query is taking minutes or hours to run versus the seconds it used to take. Lock-contention problems are another example. We typically use online monitoring to identify such issues, by taking DB2 snapshots and displaying the results in a graphical user interface (GUI) or inserting them into DB2 tables for analysis using predefined queries. Online monitoring enables DBAs to drill down and view current problem details to solve problems immediately.

Exception-Based Monitoring

Exception-based monitoring helps identify problems that occur when a predefined breach, or exception, occurs related to a user-defined threshold that has been defined for a database manager or database configuration parameter. The breaching of one of these predefined thresholds typically results in an e-mail or alert to an on-call DBA.

Exceptions are generally categorized as either *warnings* or *alarms*, with warning thresholds set somewhat below alarm thresholds. For example, the percent of the locklist memory heap in use may have an associated warning set at 70 percent and an associated alarm set at 80 percent. When the locklist memory heap reaches 70 percent full, a warning, which could be in the form of an e-mail or a message to a group of DBAs, is generated; when the locklist memory heap is 80 percent full, an alarm is generated via an e-mail or pager. You'll see later how warnings and alarms are associated with color-coded "health indicators" in the DB2 Control Center and the DB2 Health Center.

In today's demanding 24x7 environment, where data stored or managed by relational databases must be accessible from the Web at any time from any place, exception-based monitoring is the cornerstone type of monitoring required. With DBAs supporting hundreds or thousands of databases each, it's nearly impossible for them to do everything with online monitoring alone. In a typical exception-based monitoring environment, DBAs receive warnings and alarms via e-mail or pagers and then use online monitoring to drill down and analyze the problem. Depending on the parameter and severity of the problem, the affected parameter can be adjusted automatically via a script, or some other action may be taken based on the nature of the problem.

Snapshot Monitoring

Snapshot monitoring is DB2's primary realtime monitoring tool and should form the basis of your DB2 monitoring strategy. No other facility provides as much of the information necessary to record and track database performance in realtime and to store this information in a historical performance database for later analysis and trending purposes. DB2 provides two types of snapshots: those I refer to as "classic" and the new DB2 9 SQL administrative routines (formerly SQL snapshot functions) and convenience views.

You can generate classic snapshots using the DB2 Command Line Processor (CLP), a DB2 command window, a script, or an application, sending the output to the screen or to an application. Classic snapshots don't store their results in DB2 tables; they therefore provide no historical capability. As I've pointed out, it's important to have a historical capability so you can answer questions about what happened yesterday, how the database is performing this week versus last week, or why a query is suddenly taking hours versus seconds to run.

SQL administrative routines and convenience views return data in the form of a table, and you can insert this data directly into DB2 tables to create an immediate historical repository. You can select individual columns from the views instead of all the columns in the table. You'll see examples of this capability later in this chapter and in Chapter 12.

Monitor Switches

Before delving into the details of snapshot monitoring, you need to know how to review and set database manager *monitor switches*, which allow DB2 to collect snapshot data and enable the snapshot commands to return data. You can set DB2 monitor switches at the database manager (instance) level or at the database (application) level. To review the current settings of the database manager default monitor switches, issue the following command from the CLP:

```
db2 get dbm monitor switches
```

Listing 11.1 shows an example of the output produced by this command. (To conserve space, blank lines have been removed from the output that is shown in this and the following listings.)

```
            DBM System Monitor Information Collected

Switch list for db partition number 0

Buffer Pool Activity Information (BUFFERPOOL) = OFF
Lock Information                      (LOCK) = OFF
Sorting Information                   (SORT) = OFF
SQL Statement Information        (STATEMENT) = OFF
Table Activity Information           (TABLE) = OFF
Take Timestamp Information        (TIMESTAMP) = ON 11/03/2006
                                               11:44:34.000044
Unit of Work Information               (UOW) = OFF
```

Listing 11.1: Default database manager monitor switches

There are seven monitor switches that, when turned on, cause the DB2 database system monitor to collect monitor data. DB2 uses memory at the instance level out of the monitor heap (mon_heap_sz) to store this data for later analysis by DBAs. For monitoring data to be collected and made available to the snapshot commands, monitor switches must be enabled.

The command output shown in the listing reports the status of the seven monitor switches at the database manager level. By default, all switches other than the TIMESTAMP switch are turned off.

Instance-Level Switches

Enabling a monitoring switch at the database manager, or instance, level lets DB2 provide monitoring data to all applications. To enable a switch at this level, update the default database manager monitor switches by issuing the UPDATE DATABASE CONFIGURATION command (or the shorthand version, UPDATE DB CFG), specifying the desired switch:

```
db2 update dbm cfg using dft_mon_sort on
```

The default database manager configuration monitor switch parameters are as follows

- dft_mon_sort
- dft_mon_table
- dft_mon_bufpool
- dft_mon lock
- dft_mon_stmt
- dft_mon_uow

If you enable monitor switches at the database manager level, each monitoring application inherits the default database manager monitor switch settings. If the switches aren't enabled at this level, each application monitoring DB2 has its own logical view of monitor switches.

Application-Level Switches

If the default monitor switches aren't enabled and you don't want monitor data to be available to all applications, you can enable monitor switches at the database, or application, level for each monitoring application or third-party vendor tool. A DBA with the appropriate authority can turn on monitor switches by issuing the appropriate command from a command line, the Control Center, a third-party vendor tool, a program, or a scripted API.

To review the status of monitor switches at the database or application level, issue the following command from the CLP:

```
db2 get monitor switches
```

```
                 Monitor Recording Switches

Switch list for db partition number 0

Buffer Pool Activity Information   (BUFFERPOOL) = OFF
Lock Information                         (LOCK) = OFF
Sorting Information                      (SORT) = OFF
SQL Statement Information           (STATEMENT) = OFF
Table Activity Information              (TABLE) = OFF
Take Timestamp Information           (TIMESTAMP) = ON  11/07/2006
                                                      14:36:31.000046
Unit of Work Information                  (UOW) = OFF
```

Listing 11.2: Status of monitor switches

Listing 11.2 shows the status output provided by this command.

To enable a monitor switch, use the UPDATE MONITOR SWITCHES command:

```
db2 update monitor switches using sort on
```

This sample command turns on the sort monitoring switch for the application issuing the command. To enable additional snapshot monitor switches, issue the command with the appropriate monitor switch specified. The following is a list of the valid snapshot monitoring switches:

- sort
- lock
- uow
- timestamp
- table
- bufferpool
- statement

In summary, if you want to make monitoring data available to all applications, you can enable monitoring switches at the database manager level by turning on the default monitor switches. However, be aware that when you enable switches at this level, the system incurs additional overhead due to the continuous collection of snapshot data. Depending on your environment, you may decide to enable all switches or to enable switches only when you need snapshot data to troubleshoot problems. The problem with enabling monitor switches only when problems arise is that you usually never know when a problem will arise, and you may miss the problem you're trying to capture.

Depending on which switches you enable, snapshot monitoring adds approximately 3 to 10 percent overhead to the database manager. It's a best practice to enable the switches during periods of normal operation. However, in extremely CPU-intensive environments, snapshot monitoring may impose too much overhead. In this case, enable one switch at a time to collect the data of interest. You can use the db2pd command (covered later) to augment snapshot monitoring.

One more thing before we move on to taking snapshots: When determining time-sensitive metrics, such as the number of transactions per second or the average sort time, you need to reset the monitor switches at the start of the desired time interval. To reset monitor switches at the database level, use the RESET MONITOR command:

```
db2 reset monitor for database SAMPLE
```

To reset monitor switches at the instance level (which will affect all databases
in the instance), you can issue this command:

```
db2 reset monitor all
```

When you issue the reset command, DB2 records the last reset timestamp on
subsequent database snapshots. For an example of resetting monitor switches,
review the database snapshot excerpt shown in Listing 11.3.

```
                    Database Snapshot

Input database alias                      = SAMPLE
First database connect timestamp          = 11/09/2006
                                            12:58:53.173762

Last reset timestamp                      = 11/09/2006
                                            19:39:23.917544
```

Listing 11.3: Database snapshot excerpt resetting monitor switches

Classic Snapshots

Now, let's take a look at some actual output produced by the classic snapshot
commands. As you'll see, these commands provide a wealth of details about
what is happening on a DB2 system at a particular point in time. DB2 provides
commands for obtaining snapshot information about the database manager, the
database, buffer pools, tables, locks, applications, and dynamic SQL.

Database Manager Snapshot

The database manager snapshot records activity at the instance level. This
snapshot primarily provides overall information about instance-wide shared
sort memory usage and agent activity. Issue the following command to obtain
a database manager snapshot:

```
db2 get snapshot for database manager
```

Listing 11.4 shows sample (partial) output provided by this snapshot.

```
                Database Manager Snapshot

Node name                                   =
Node type                                   = Database Server
                                              with local
                                              and remote
                                              clients
Instance name                               = DB2
Number of database partitions in DB2 instance  = 1
Database manager status                     = Active

Private Sort heap allocated                 = 25
Private Sort heap high water mark           = 56527
Post threshold sorts                        = Not Collected
Piped sorts requested                       = 24337005
Piped sorts accepted                        = 24337005

Start Database Manager timestamp            = 11/23/2006
                                              04:17:21.750037
Last reset timestamp                        =
Snapshot timestamp                          = 11/24/2006
                                              08:36:50.713208

Remote connections to db manager            = 237
Remote connections executing in db manager  = 3
Local connections                           = 1
Local connections executing in db manager   = 0
Active local databases                      = 1

High water mark for agents registered       = 734
High water mark for agents waiting for a token = 0
Agents registered                           = 635
Agents waiting for a token                  = 0
Idle agents                                 = 134
```

Listing 11.4: Database manager snapshot (part 1 of 2)

```
Committed private Memory (Bytes)              = 798605312

Switch list for db partition number 0
Buffer Pool Activity Information  (BUFFERPOOL) = OFF
Lock Information                      (LOCK) = ON 11/23/2006
                                               04:18:06.113357
Sorting Information                   (SORT) = OFF
SQL Statement Information        (STATEMENT) = OFF
Table Activity Information           (TABLE) = OFF
Take Timestamp Information        (TIMESTAMP) = ON 11/23/2006
                                               04:17:21.750037
Unit of Work Information               (UOW) = OFF

Agents assigned from pool                    = 76758
Agents created from empty pool               = 754
Agents stolen from another application       = 0
High water mark for coordinating agents      = 734
Max agents overflow                          = 0
Hash joins after heap threshold exceeded     = 8

Total number of gateway connections          = 0
Current number of gateway connections        = 0
Gateway connections waiting for host reply   = 0
Gateway connections waiting for client request = 0
Gateway connection pool agents stolen        = 0

Memory usage for database manager:
    Memory Pool Type                         = Database
                                               Monitor Heap

        Current size (bytes)                 = 245760
        High water mark (bytes)              = 327680
        Configured size (bytes)              = 1196032
```

Listing 11.4: Database manager snapshot (part 2 of 2)

You should monitor and track the following key database manager snapshot elements on a regular basis:

- Post threshold sorts
- Piped sorts rejected
- High water mark for agents registered
- Joins after heap threshold exceeded
- Agents created from empty pool
- Agents stolen from another application

By taking database manager snapshots and tracking key monitoring elements over time, you should be able to determine whether shared sort memory and agent parameters are adequate for the workload and make adjustments as necessary.

Database Snapshot

The database snapshot records activity at the database level. This snapshot is the primary source of information about overall database performance. To obtain a database snapshot, issue this command:

```
db2 get snapshot for database on GOLIATH
```

Listing 11.5 shows sample output provided by this snapshot.

```
                Database Snapshot

Database name                              = GOLIATH
Database path                              = E:\DB2\NODE0000\
                                             SQL00001\
Input database alias                       = GOLIATH
Database status                            = Active
Catalog database partition number          = 0
Catalog network node name                  =
Operating system running at database server = NT 64BIT
Location of the database                   = Local
```

Listing 11.5: Database snapshot (part 1 of 6)

```
First database connect timestamp          = 12/16/2006
                                            18:51:44.452638
Last reset timestamp                      =
Last backup timestamp                     = 12/15/2006
                                            09:30:07.000000
Snapshot timestamp                        = 12/16/2006
                                            21:46:59.036790


Number of automatic storage paths         = 0

High water mark for connections           = 771
Application connects                      = 19902
Secondary connects total                  = 0
Applications connected currently          = 477
Appls. executing in db manager currently  = 14
Agents associated with applications       = 477
Maximum agents associated with applications = 771
Maximum coordinating agents               = 771

Locks held currently                      = 2636
Lock waits                                = 286813
Time database waited on locks (ms)        = Not Collected
Lock list memory in use (Bytes)           = 2215232
Deadlocks detected                        = 0
Lock escalations                          = 0
Exclusive lock escalations                = 0
Agents currently waiting on locks         = 0
Lock Timeouts                             = 5
Number of indoubt transactions            = 0

Total Private Sort heap allocated         = 358
Total Shared Sort heap allocated          = 0
Shared Sort heap high water mark          = 0
Total sorts                               = 6026564
Total sort time (ms)                      = Not Collected
Sort overflows                            = 2330108
Active sorts                              = 9
```

Listing 11.5: Database snapshot (part 2 of 6)

300

```
Buffer pool data logical reads              = 245775192
Buffer pool data physical reads             = 2801537
Buffer pool temporary data logical reads    = 15773560
Buffer pool temporary data physical reads   = 1265
Asynchronous pool data page reads           = 932995
Buffer pool data writes                     = 17908
Asynchronous pool data page writes          = 17772
Buffer pool index logical reads             = 31023345
Buffer pool index physical reads            = 554393
Buffer pool temporary index logical reads   = 0
Buffer pool temporary index physical reads  = 0
Asynchronous pool index page reads          = 18437
Buffer pool index writes                    = 4322
Asynchronous pool index page writes         = 4249
Total buffer pool read time (milliseconds)  = 285778
Total buffer pool write time (milliseconds) = 59962
Total elapsed asynchronous read time        = 20872
Total elapsed asynchronous write time       = 58616
Asynchronous data read requests             = 20651
Asynchronous index read requests            = 1519
No victim buffers available                 = 3357707
LSN Gap cleaner triggers                    = 1017
Dirty page steal cleaner triggers           = 170
Dirty page threshold cleaner triggers       = 0
Time waited for prefetch (ms)               = 10068
Unread prefetch pages                       = 73
Direct reads                                = 84
Direct writes                               = 0
Direct read requests                        = 18
Direct write requests                       = 0
Direct reads elapsed time (ms)              = 0
Direct write elapsed time (ms)              = 0
Database files closed                       = 0
Data pages copied to extended storage       = 0
Index pages copied to extended storage      = 0
Data pages copied from extended storage     = 0
```

Listing 11.5: Database snapshot (part 3 of 6)

```
Index pages copied from extended storage   = 0

Host execution elapsed time                = Not Collected

Commit statements attempted                = 10085776
Rollback statements attempted              = 65199
Dynamic statements attempted               = 34412690
Static statements attempted                = 10151656
Failed statement operations                = 396
Select SQL statements executed             = 12489917
Update/Insert/Delete statements executed   = 4897780
DDL statements executed                    = 9
Inactive stmt history memory usage (bytes) = 0

Internal automatic rebinds                 = 0
Internal rows deleted                      = 0
Internal rows inserted                     = 271
Internal rows updated                      = 0
Internal commits                           = 19902
Internal rollbacks                         = 5
Internal rollbacks due to deadlock         = 0

Rows deleted                               = 637506
Rows inserted                              = 1314903
Rows updated                               = 3200632
Rows selected                              = 29801888
Rows read                                  = 49551801061
Binds/precompiles attempted                = 0

Log space available to the database (Bytes) = 12211973271
Log space used by the database (Bytes)      = 28026729
Maximum secondary log space used (Bytes)    = 0
Maximum total log space used (Bytes)        = 412571830
Secondary logs allocated currently          = 0
Log pages read                              = 0
Log read time (sec.ns)                      = 0.000000004
Log pages written                           = 2919923
```

Listing 11.5: Database snapshot (part 4 of 6)

```
Log write time (sec.ns)                    = 6833.000000004
Number write log IOs                       = 2661599
Number read log IOs                        = 0
Number partial page log IOs                = 1173084
Number log buffer full                     = 0
Log data found in buffer                   = 0
Appl id holding the oldest transaction     = 16
Log to be redone for recovery (Bytes)      = 208599822
Log accounted for by dirty pages (Bytes)   = 206655649

File number of first active log            = 95790
File number of last active log             = 95819
File number of current active log          = 95791
File number of log being archived          = Not applicable

Package cache lookups                      = 17406522
Package cache inserts                       = 15385
Package cache overflows                    = 0
Package cache high water mark (Bytes)      = 16025855
Application section lookups                = 34413368
Application section inserts                = 436671

Catalog cache lookups                      = 147188
Catalog cache inserts                      = 253
Catalog cache overflows                    = 0
Catalog cache high water mark              = 0

Workspace Information
  Shared high water mark                   = 0
  Corresponding shared overflows           = 0
  Total shared section inserts             = 0
  Total shared section lookups             = 0
  Private high water mark                  = 5368172
  Corresponding private overflows          = 0
  Total private section inserts            = 436671
  Total private section lookups            = 17386690
```

Listing 11.5: Database snapshot (part 5 of 6)

```
Number of hash joins                    = 24454
Number of hash loops                    = 0
Number of hash join overflows           = 0
Number of small hash join overflows     = 0
```

Listing 11.5: Database snapshot (part 6 of 6)

Key database snapshot monitoring elements to monitor and track on a regular basis are as follows:

- Maximum coordinating agents
- Locks held currently
- Lock waits
- Time database waited on locks
- Deadlocks detected
- Lock escalations
- Exclusive lock escalations
- Agents currently waiting on locks
- Lock timeouts
- Total sort time
- Sort overflows
- Sort overflow percent (computed)
- Overall buffer pool hit ratio (computed)
- No victim buffers available
- Log sequence number (LSN) gap cleaner triggers
- Dirty page steal cleaner triggers
- Dirty page threshold cleaner triggers
- Unread prefetch pages
- Database files closed
- Secondary logs allocated currently

- Log pages read
- Log read time
- Log write time
- Number of write log I/Os
- Number of read log I/Os
- Number of partial page log I/Os
- Number log buffer full
- Log data found in buffer
- Package cache overflows
- Catalog cache overflows
- Package cache hit ratio (computed)
- Catalog cache hit ratio (computed)
- Shared high water mark
- Corresponding shared overflows
- Private high water mark
- Corresponding private overflows
- Number of hash loops
- Number of hash join overflows
- Number of small hash join overflows

It should be evident from the number of key monitoring elements that the database snapshot provides much of the data with which to monitor and tune at the database level. Several metrics, however, are not provided and must be separately computed, including buffer pool hit ratio, catalog and package cache hit ratios, asynchronous and synchronous read rates, and other key metrics. We'll look at these metrics in more detail in Chapter 12.

By taking database snapshots and tracking key monitoring elements over time, you should be able to determine whether the monitored database is meeting performance objectives and make any adjustments necessary.

Buffer Pool Snapshot

The buffer pool snapshot is the primary source of data about buffer pool performance. It records activity such as type of buffer pool access, data and index access, buffer pool read and write times, and monitoring elements from which to compute performance metrics such as buffer pool hit ratios, asynchronous and synchronous read and write rates, and other important metrics. Issue the following command to obtain a buffer pool snapshot:

```
db2 get snapshot for bufferpools on GOLIATH
```

Listing 11.6 shows sample output provided by this snapshot.

```
                Bufferpool Snapshot

Bufferpool name                           = IBMDEFAULTBP
Database name                             = GOLIATH
Database path                             = E:\DB2\NODE0000\
                                            SQL00001\
Input database alias                      = GOLIATH
Snapshot timestamp                        = 12/16/2006
                                            21:47:35.395868


Buffer pool data logical reads            = 250084200
Buffer pool data physical reads           = 2802458
Buffer pool temporary data logical reads  = 16979227
Buffer pool temporary data physical reads = 1265
Buffer pool data writes                   = 18562
Buffer pool index logical reads           = 32514094
Buffer pool index physical reads          = 554935
Buffer pool temporary index logical reads = 0
Buffer pool temporary index physical reads = 0
Total buffer pool read time (milliseconds) = 290236
Total buffer pool write time (milliseconds) = 60366
Asynchronous pool data page reads         = 932995
Asynchronous pool data page writes        = 18425
Buffer pool index writes                  = 4506
```

Listing 11.6: Buffer pool snapshot (part 1 of 2)

```
Asynchronous pool index page reads      = 18484
Asynchronous pool index page writes     = 4432
Total elapsed asynchronous read time    = 21056
Total elapsed asynchronous write time   = 59018
Asynchronous data read requests         = 20651
Asynchronous index read requests        = 1565
No victim buffers available             = 3359838
Direct reads                            = 86
Direct writes                           = 0
Direct read requests                    = 19
Direct write requests                   = 0
Direct reads elapsed time (ms)          = 0
Direct write elapsed time (ms)          = 0
Database files closed                   = 0
Data pages copied to extended storage   = 0
Index pages copied to extended storage  = 0
Data pages copied from extended storage = 0
Index pages copied from extended storage = 0
Unread prefetch pages                   = 73
Vectored IOs                            = 16681
Pages from vectored IOs                 = 846343
Block IOs                               = 0
Pages from block IOs                    = 0
Physical page maps                      = 0

Node number                             = 0
Tablespaces using bufferpool            = 119

Alter bufferpool information:
 Pages left to remove                   = 0
 Current size                           = 440000
Post-alter size                         = 440000
```

Listing 11.6: Buffer pool snapshot (part 2 of 2)

By taking buffer pool snapshots and tracking key monitoring elements over time, you should be able to assess the adequacy of buffer pool hit rates and buffer pool read and write times. With this data, you can determine whether your buffer pool settings are adequate for the workload and make adjustments as necessary.

Table Snapshot

The table snapshot records table activity, such as number of rows read and written. This snapshot is the primary source of information about table activity. To obtain a table snapshot, issue the following command:

```
db2 get snapshot for tables on GOLIATH
```

Listing 11.7 shows sample output provided by this snapshot.

```
                  Table Snapshot

First database connect timestamp      = 12/16/2006
                                        18:51:44.452638
Last reset timestamp                  =
Snapshot timestamp                    = 12/16/2006
                                        21:49:27.715521

Database name                         = GOLIATH
Database path                         = E:\DB2\NODE0000\SQL00001\
Input database alias                  = GOLIATH
Number of accessed tables             = 58

 Table Schema                         = DB2ADMIN
 Table Name                           = CLIENT
 Table Type                           = User
 Data Object Pages                    = 96982
 Index Object Pages                   = 8137
 Rows Read                            = 630189
 Rows Written                         = 25
 Overflows                            = 8621
 Page Reorgs                          = 3

 Table Schema                         = <1727><DB2ADMIN>
 Table Name                           = TEMP (00098,00016)
 Table Type                           = Temporary
 Data Object Pages                    = 62
 Rows Read                            = Not Collected
```

Listing 11.7: Table snapshot (part 1 of 2)

```
Rows Written                        = 3081
Overflows                           = 0
Page Reorgs                         = 0
```

Listing 11.7: Table snapshot (part 2 of 2)

By taking table snapshots and tracking table activity over time, you should be able to rank the 10 most active tables in the database. Use this information to monitor and identify the SQL running against these tables. The most active tables typically have SQL running against them that is in need of tuning. You can use this technique to quickly identify and then tune suboptimal SQL running against these tables. In addition, you can use the Overflows and Page Reorgs monitoring elements to identify tables requiring a reorganization and possible addition of page free space (pctfree table attribute). (Note that the db2pd –tcbstats option provides similar data with no overhead in the database manager.) With this information, you should be able to identify the most active tables in the database and target them for tuning activities.

Lock Snapshot

The lock snapshot is the lead source of information about database and application locking activity. It records activity such as lock type, lock mode, lock wait time, number of locks held on an object, the holder of the lock, and a list of all applications waiting for a lock on an object. Because locking is central to database operation, you should become very familiar with the data provided by the lock snapshot at the database and application levels. Lock information is available on three different snapshots:

- Database
- Application ID (APPLID)
- Application handle (AGENTID)

To obtain lock information at the database level, issue the following snapshot command:

```
db2 get snapshot for locks on SAMPLE
```

For lock information at the APPLID and AGENTID levels, issue the following snapshot commands:

```
db2 get snapshot for locks for application applid "AC100A4B.
L807.00B049161549"
db2 get snapshot for locks for application agentid 192
```

Listing 11.8 shows sample output provided by the lock snapshot at all three levels. (Note that there's no difference in the output between the APPLID and AGENTID options; only the snapshot syntax differs.)

```
                    Database Lock Snapshot

Database name                            = SAMPLE
Database path                            = C:\DB2\NODE0000\
                                           SQL00001\
Input database alias                     = SAMPLE
Locks held                               = 0
Applications currently connected         = 1
Agents currently waiting on locks        = 0
Snapshot timestamp                       = 11/08/2006
                                           21:56:55.609533


Application handle                       = 192
Application ID                           = *LOCAL.
                                           DB2.041109024734
Sequence number                          = 0001
Application name                         = db2bp.exe
CONNECT Authorization ID                 = PGUNNING
Application status                       = Connect Completed
Status change time                       = 11/08/2006
                                           21:47:33.921539
```

Listing 11.8: Lock snapshot (part 1 of 4)

```
Application code page                   = 1252
Locks held                              = 0
Total wait time (ms)                    = 0


Snapshot on APPLID/AGENTID:


            Application Lock Snapshot


Snapshot timestamp                      = 11-09-2006
                                          10:16:28.193629


Application handle                      = 609
Application ID                          = AC100A4B.
                                          L807.00B049161549

Sequence number                         = 0001
Application name                        = pgunning.exe
CONNECT Authorization ID                = PGUN1
Application status                      = UOW Executing
Status change time                      = 11-09-2006
                                          10:15:48.247644

Application code page                   = 1252
Locks held                              = 6
Total wait time (ms)                    = 0


List Of Locks
 Lock Name                              = 0x0800040001A6170D
                                          0000000052

 Lock Attributes                        = 0x00000000
 Release Flags                          = 0x00000001
 Lock Count                             = 1
 Hold Count                             = 0
 Lock Object Name                       = 219653633
 Object Type                            = Row
 Tablespace Name                        = TS_ACCOUNT
 Table Schema                           = PGUN
 Table Name                             = ACCOUNT1
 Mode                                   = NS
```

Listing 11.8: Lock snapshot (part 2 of 4)

```
Lock Name                        = 0x9B796A9F89AC92AC5
                                   558565241
Lock Attributes                  = 0x00000000
Release Flags                    = 0x40000000
Lock Count                       = 1
Hold Count                       = 0
Lock Object Name                 = 0
Object Type                      = Internal P Lock
Mode                             = S


Lock Name                        = 0x0C000000010000000
                                   100250056
Lock Attributes                  = 0x00000000
Release Flags                    = 0x40000000
Lock Count                       = 1
Hold Count                       = 0
Lock Object Name                 = 0
Object Type                      = Internal V Lock
Mode                             = S


Lock Name                        = 0xA6B2A69FA4A17C7D9
                                   175505041
Lock Attributes                  = 0x00000000
Release Flags                    = 0x40000000
Lock Count                       = 1
Hold Count                       = 0
Lock Object Name                 = 0
Object Type                      = Internal P Lock
Mode                             = S


Lock Name                        = 0x96A09A989DA09A7D8
                                   E8A6C7441
Lock Attributes                  = 0x00000000
Release Flags                    = 0x40000000
Lock Count                       = 1
Hold Count                       = 0
Lock Object Name                 = 0
```

Listing 11.8: Lock snapshot (part 3 of 4)

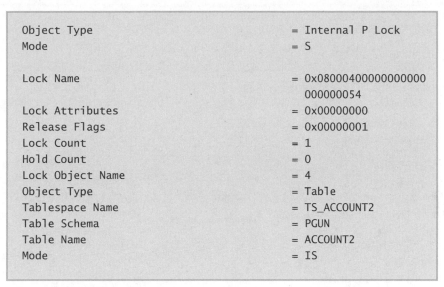

```
Object Type                              = Internal P Lock
Mode                                     = S

Lock Name                                = 0x08000400000000000
                                           000000054
Lock Attributes                          = 0x00000000
Release Flags                            = 0x00000001
Lock Count                               = 1
Hold Count                               = 0
Lock Object Name                         = 4
Object Type                              = Table
Tablespace Name                          = TS_ACCOUNT2
Table Schema                             = PGUN
Table Name                               = ACCOUNT2
Mode                                     = IS
```

Listing 11.8: Lock snapshot (part 4 of 4)

You can use the lock snapshot to identify lock-contention problems. The output includes a list of locks held, the type and duration of each lock, and list of applications waiting for locks. With the information provided by this snapshot, you can analyze current application locking activity and identify applications with potential concurrency problems. We'll review how to analyze lock chains using DB2's Activity Monitor in Chapter 12.

Application Snapshot

The application snapshot provides details about current application activity and serves as the primary information source for analyzing application performance. It records activity such as type of buffer pool access, data and index access, buffer pool read and write times, and monitoring elements from which to compute performance metrics such as buffer pool hit ratios, asynchronous and synchronous read and write rates, and other important metrics. Issue the following command to obtain an application snapshot:

db2 get snapshot for applications on GTSTSTP

Listing 11.9 shows sample output provided by this snapshot.

```
                    Application Snapshot

Application handle                          = 416
Application status                          = UOW Waiting
Status change time                          = 10-12-2006
                                              08:11:21.180560
Application code page                       = 1208
Application country/region code             = 0
DUOW correlation token                      = AC110318.
                                              B41E.0106E4C1E357
Application name                            = db2jccVBJ Thread-
                                              Pool
Application ID                              = AC110318.
                                              B41E.0106E4C1E357
Sequence number                             = 4938
TP Monitor client user ID                   =
TP Monitor client workstation name          =
TP Monitor client application name          =
TP Monitor client accounting string         =
Connection request start timestamp          = 10-12-2006
                                              07:15:43.465974
Connect request completion timestamp        = 10-12-2006
                                              07:15:43.466442
Application idle time                       = 187
CONNECT Authorization ID                    = DB2INST3
Client login ID                             = DB2INST3
Configuration NNAME of client               =
Client database manager product ID          = JCC01000
Process ID of client application            = 0
Platform of client application              = Unknown via DRDA
Communication protocol of client            = TCP/IP
Inbound communication address               = 172.17.3.24 46110
Snapshot timestamp                          = 10-12-2006
                                              08:14:28.217070
```

Listing 11.9: Application snapshot (part 1 of 3)

```
Coordinating database partition number    = 0
Current database partition number          = 0
Coordinator agent process or thread ID     = 101392
Agents stolen                              = 0
Agents waiting on locks                    = 0
Maximum associated agents                  = 1
Priority at which application agents work   = 0
Priority type                             = Dynamic
Locks held by application                  = 0
Lock waits since connect                   = 4
Time application waited on locks (ms)      = 73
Deadlocks detected                         = 0
Lock escalations                           = 0
Exclusive lock escalations                 = 0
Number of Lock Timeouts since connected    = 0
Total time UOW waited on locks (ms)        = 0
Total sorts                                = 247
Total sort time (ms)                       = 13828
Total sort overflows                       = 22
Data pages copied to extended storage      = 0
Index pages copied to extended storage     = 0
Data pages copied from extended storage    = 0
Index pages copied from extended storage   = 0
Buffer pool data logical reads             = 4353015
Buffer pool data physical reads            = 23902
Buffer pool data writes                    = 1
Buffer pool index logical reads            = 9800357
Buffer pool index physical reads           = 3182
Buffer pool index writes                   = 3
Total buffer pool read time (ms)           = 65792
Total buffer pool write time (ms)          = 17
Time waited for prefetch (ms)              = 1615
Unread prefetch pages                      = 0
Direct reads                               = 2934
Direct writes                              = 2
Direct read requests                       = 1467
Direct write requests                      = 1
```

Listing 11.9: Application snapshot (part 2 of 3)

315

```
Direct reads elapsed time (ms)           = 4503
Direct write elapsed time (ms)           = 11
Number of SQL requests since last commit = 0
Commit statements                        = 4937
Rollback statements                      = 0
Dynamic SQL statements attempted         = 10393
Static SQL statements attempted          = 4937
Failed statement operations              = 0
Select SQL statements executed           = 2805
Update/Insert/Delete statements executed = 37
DDL statements executed                  = 0
Internal automatic rebinds               = 0
Internal rows deleted                    = 0
Internal rows inserted                   = 0
Internal rows updated                    = 0
Internal commits                         = 1
Internal rollbacks                       = 0
Internal rollbacks due to deadlock       = 0
Binds/precompiles attempted              = 0
Rows deleted                             = 0
Rows inserted                            = 14
Rows updated                             = 13
Rows selected                            = 30800
Rows read                                = 6136856
Rows written                             = 724294
```

Listing 11.9: Application snapshot (part 3 of 3)

The application snapshot furnishes key monitoring elements with which to solve realtime performance problems and provides significant information to help you identify suboptimal applications.

Application Snapshot on AGENTID

As you've seen, the application snapshot provides a lot of information. Once you've narrowed down the problem to a specific AGENTID, you can take an application snapshot for that particular ID to discover details about application activity for the ID. Limiting a snapshot to the AGENTID of interest lets you quickly review the activity for only that AGENTID.

For example, assume we issued a snapshot for applications and obtained information such as that shown in the preceding listing for three applications. After determining that an application with an AGENTID of 424 requires detailed analysis, we can issue the application snapshot command for that ID:

```
db2 get snapshot for application agentid 424
```

Listing 11.10 shows sample output provided by this snapshot.

```
              Application Snapshot

Application handle                         = 424
Application status                         = UOW Executing
Status change time                         = 10-12-2006
                                             13:25:01.661747
Application code page                      = 1208
Application country/region code            = 0
DUOW correlation token                     = AC110318.
                                             B528.0106E5BDC8F6
Application name                           = db2jccVBJ Thread-
                                             Pool
Application ID                             = AC110318.
                                             B528.0106E5BDC8F6
Sequence number                            = 8035

Connection request start timestamp         = 10-12-2006
                                             11:50:51.774417
Connect request completion timestamp       = 10-12-2006
                                             11:50:51.774587
Application idle time                       = 0
CONNECT Authorization ID                    = DB2INST3
```

Listing 11.10: Application snapshot for a specific AGENTID (part 1 of 7)

317

```
Client login ID                               = DB2INST3
Configuration NNAME of client                 =
Client database manager product ID            = JCC01000
Process ID of client application              = 0

Database name                                 = GTSTSTB
Database path                                 = /GTSTSTB/db2inst3/
                                                NODE0000/
                                                SQL00001/
Client database alias                         =
Input database alias                          = GTSTSTB
Last reset timestamp                          =
Snapshot timestamp                            = 10-12-2006
                                                13:25:01.629231
Coordinating database partition number        = 0
Current database partition number             = 0
Coordinator agent process or thread ID        = 84126
Agents stolen                                 = 0
Agents waiting on locks                       = 0
Maximum associated agents                     = 1
Priority at which application agents work      = 0
Priority type                                 = Dynamic

Locks held by application                     = 5
Lock waits since connect                      = 0
Time application waited on locks (ms)          = 0
Deadlocks detected                            = 0
Lock escalations                              = 0
Exclusive lock escalations                    = 0
Number of Lock Timeouts since connected       = 0

Total time UOW waited on locks (ms)           = 0
Total sorts                                   = 925
Total sort time (ms)                          = 7400
Total sort overflows                          = 142
Data pages copied to extended storage          = 0
Index pages copied to extended storage         = 0
```

Listing 11.10: Application snapshot for a specific AGENTID (part 2 of 7)

```
Data pages copied from extended storage   = 0
Index pages copied from extended storage  = 0
Buffer pool data logical reads            = 17625564
Buffer pool data physical reads           = 46098
Buffer pool data writes                   = 624
Buffer pool index logical reads           = 26058526
Buffer pool index physical reads          = 6044
Buffer pool index writes                  = 1
Total buffer pool read time (ms)          = 102108
Total buffer pool write time (ms)         = 36925
Time waited for prefetch (ms)             = 6464
Unread prefetch pages                     = 0
Direct reads                              = 13568
Direct writes                             = 308
Direct read requests                      = 6784
Direct write requests                     = 154
Direct reads elapsed time (ms)            = 15789
Direct write elapsed time (ms)            = 231

Number of SQL requests since last commit  = 1
Commit statements                         = 28032
Rollback statements                       = 0
Dynamic SQL statements attempted          = 62047
Static SQL statements attempted           = 28032
Failed statement operations               = 0
Select SQL statements executed            = 15948
Update/Insert/Delete statements executed  = 277
DDL statements executed                   = 0
Internal automatic rebinds                = 0
Internal rows deleted                     = 0
Internal rows inserted                    = 0
Internal rows updated                     = 0
Internal commits                          = 1
Internal rollbacks                        = 0
Internal rollbacks due to deadlock        = 0
Binds/precompiles attempted               = 0
Rows deleted                              = 0
Rows inserted                             = 96
```

Listing 11.10: Application snapshot for a specific AGENTID (part 3 of 7)

```
Rows updated                                 = 86
Rows selected                                = 178849
Rows read                                    = 50732832
Rows written                                 = 5799097
Open remote cursors                          = 2
Open remote cursors with blocking            = 2
Rejected Block Remote Cursor requests        = 471
Accepted Block Remote Cursor requests        = 15477
Open local cursors                           = 0
Open local cursors with blocking             = 0
Total User CPU Time used by agent (s)        = 821.440000
Total System CPU Time used by agent (s)      = 23.090000
Host execution elapsed time                  = 0.000037

Package cache lookups                        = 16412
Package cache inserts                         = 4341
Application section lookups                   = 62047
Application section inserts                   = 5059
Catalog cache lookups                         = 21594
Catalog cache inserts                         = 0
Catalog cache overflows                       = 0
Catalog cache high water mark                 = 0

Workspace Information
 Shared high water mark                       = 29404265
 Total shared overflows                       = 0
 Total shared section inserts                 = 4782
 Total shared section lookups                 = 16135
 Private high water mark                       = 1880332
 Total private overflows                       = 0
 Total private section inserts                 = 277
 Total private section lookups                 = 277

Most recent operation                         = Fetch
Cursor name                                   = SQL_CURSH200C55
Most recent operation start timestamp         = 10-12-2006
                                                13:25:01.661749
```

Listing 11.10: Application snapshot for a specific AGENTID (part 4 of 7)

```
Most recent operation stop timestamp        =
Agents associated with the application      = 1
Number of hash joins                        = 3997665
Number of hash loops                        = 0
Number of hash join overflows               = 63
Number of small hash join overflows         = 0

Statement type                              = Dynamic SQL
                                              Statement
Statement                                   = Fetch
Section number                              = 55
Application creator                         = NULLID
Package name                                = SYSSH200
Consistency Token                           = SYSLVL01
Package Version ID                          =
Cursor name                                 = SQL_CURSH200C55
Statement database partition number         = 0
Statement start timestamp                   = 10-12-2005
                                              13:25:01.661749
Statement stop timestamp                    =
Elapsed time of last completed stmt(sec.ms) = 0.000037
Total user CPU time                         = 0.000000
Total system CPU time                       = 0.000000
SQL compiler cost estimate in timerons      = 5993
SQL compiler cardinality estimate           = 1
Degree of parallelism requested             = 1
Number of agents working on statement       = 1
Number of subagents created for statement   = 1
Statement sorts                             = 0
Total sort time                             = 0
Sort overflows                              = 0
Rows read                                   = 0
Rows written                                = 0
Rows deleted                                = 0
Rows updated                                = 0
Rows inserted                               = 0
Rows fetched                                = 0
```

Listing 11.10: Application snapshot for a specific AGENTID (part 5 of 7)

```
Blocking cursor                              = YES
Dynamic SQL statement text:
SELECT SUM(OrderReg_Draw) FROM tblOrderReg WHERE OrderReg_
FutureOrderIssueId                           =
 ? AND OrderReg_Status IN (1797, 1798) AND OrderReg_WholeId = 8992

    Agent process/thread ID                  = 84126
Statement type                               = Dynamic SQL
                                               Statement
Statement                                    = Fetch
Section number                               = 57
Application creator                          = NULLID
Package name                                 = SYSSH200
Consistency Token                            = SYSLVL01
Package Version ID                           =
Cursor name                                  = SQL_CURSH200C57
Statement database partition number          = 0
Statement start timestamp                    = 10-12-2006
                                               13:25:01.603785
Statement stop timestamp                     = 10-12-2006
                                               13:25:01.604368
Elapsed time of last completed stmt(sec.ms)  = 0.000556
Total user CPU time                          = 0.000000
Total system CPU time                        = 0.000000
SQL compiler cost estimate in timerons       = 191
SQL compiler cardinality estimate            = 1
Degree of parallelism requested              = 1
Number of agents working on statement        = 0
Number of subagents created for statement    = 1
Statement sorts                              = 0
Total sort time                              = 0
Sort overflows                               = 0
Rows read                                    = 81
Rows written                                 = 0
Rows deleted                                 = 0
Rows updated                                 = 0
```

Listing 11.10: Application snapshot for a specific AGENTID (part 6 of 7)

```
Rows inserted                              = 0
Rows fetched                               = 21
Blocking cursor                            = YES
Dynamic SQL statement text:
SELECT Issue_Id, Issue_Year, Issue_AddOn, Issue_OnsaleDate FROM
tblIssue WHERE
 Issue_DistributionDate > Current_Date AND Issue_TitleId = 4923
ORDER BY
 Issue_OnsaleDate
```

Listing 11.10: Application snapshot for a specific AGENTID (part 7 of 7)

Key application monitoring elements to monitor and review for indication of possible problems are as follows:

- Application status
- Application name
- Agents stolen
- Agents waiting on locks
- Locks held by application
- Lock waits since connect
- Time application waited on locks
- Deadlocks detected
- Lock escalations
- Exclusive lock escalations
- Number of lock timeouts since connected
- Total time UOW waited on locks
- Sort information
- Buffer pool data and index logical and physical reads (can be used to compute application buffer pool hit ratio)
- Unread prefetch pages
- Rows read/rows written
- Total user and system CPU time

- Number of hash loops
- Number of hash join overflows
- Number of small hash join overflows

By taking specific application snapshots and tracking key monitoring elements over time, you should be able to solve current application problems and, through regular monitoring, identify problem applications and take corrective action. A methodology I use when investigating application problems is to issue a db2 list applications show detail command, look for the executing application, and then issue a db2 snapshot for applications agentid <agentid of interest> command. I then focus in on the particular activity associated with this application. Later, you'll see how new SQL administrative routines and convenience views enable you to monitor and capture application performance history.

Dynamic SQL Snapshot

The dynamic SQL snapshot provides information about the performance of dynamic SQL. You can use this snapshot's data to quickly identify suboptimal SQL. Issue the following command to obtain a dynamic SQL snapshot:

```
db2 get snapshot for dynamic sql on GTSTSTB
```

Listing 11.11 shows sample output provided by this snapshot.

```
            Dynamic SQL Snapshot Result

Number of executions                    = 1
Number of compilations                  = 1
Worst preparation time (ms)             = 6
Best preparation time (ms)              = 6
Internal rows deleted                   = 0
Internal rows inserted                  = 0
```

Listing 11.11: Dynamic SQL snapshot (part 1 of 3)

```
Rows read                                 = 2129887
Internal rows updated                     = 0
Rows written                              = 0
Statement sorts                           = 0
Statement sort overflows                  = 0
Total sort time                           = 0
Buffer pool data logical reads            = 59937
Buffer pool data physical reads           = 0
Buffer pool temporary data logical reads  = 0
Buffer pool temporary data physical reads = 0
Buffer pool index logical reads           = 2
Buffer pool index physical reads          = 0
Buffer pool temporary index logical reads = 0
Buffer pool temporary index physical reads = 0
Total execution time (sec.ms)             = 24.196969
Total user cpu time (sec.ms)              = 3.140625
Total system cpu time (sec.ms)            = 0.031250


Statement text                            = SELECT
 PURCHASE_TO_DATE.ACC_NUM,PURCHASE_TO_DATE.AMOUNT as AMT,
 COALESCE(CLIENT_SEGMENT.SEGMENT_CODE,'') AS
 CODE,COALESCE(CLIENT_SEGMENT.LOCK,CURRENT TIMESTAMP) AS LOCK
FROM
 PURCHASE_TO_DATE LEFT OUTER JOIN CLIENT_SEGMENT ON PURCHASE_TO_
DATE.ACC_NUM =
 CLIENT_SEGMENT.ACC_NUM, CLIENT_ACC CA WHERE
 PURCHASE_TO_DATE.ACC_NUM=CA.ACC_NUM AND CA.CASINO_ID IN
 ('AM','BE','BM','HF','CI','CL','DG','EL','EM','ED','FN','GG','WS',
'MW','PT',
'PO','PH','RP','CM','UB','WP','XA') AND (CLIENT_SEGMENT.SET_TYPE
IS NULL OR
 CLIENT_SEGMENT.SET_TYPE = 'A') AND (CLIENT_SEGMENT.TYPE IS
NULL OR
 CLIENT_SEGMENT.TYPE = 'P') AND PURCHASE_TO_DATE.AMOUNT >=
(SELECT MIN_AMT FROM
 SEGMENT_CONF WHERE CODE = ? AND STATE = 'A' AND TYPE = 'P') AND
```

Listing 11.11: Dynamic SQL snapshot (part 2 of 3)

```
PURCHASE_TO_DATE.AMOUNT <= (SELECT MAX_AMT FROM SEGMENT_CONF
WHERE CODE = ?
 AND STATE = 'A' AND TYPE = 'P')
```

Listing 11.11: Dynamic SQL snapshot (part 3 of 3)

Key dynamic SQL snapshot monitor elements to review and analyze are as follows:

- Number of compilations
- Worst preparation time
- Rows read/rows written (indicator of activity)
- Statement sorts
- Statement sort overflows
- Total sort time
- Buffer pool logical and physical reads
- Total execution time
- Total user CPU time
- Total system CPU time
- SQL statement text

By reviewing these elements, you can identify SQL statements that are requiring more than one compilation and statements that are sorting and experiencing sort overflows, and you can compute the buffer pool hit ratio for an SQL statement. Of course, the most important element from this snapshot is the SQL statement itself. In conjunction with the table snapshot, you can search through a dynamic SQL snapshot looking for SQL that is running against the top 10 most active tables and target that SQL for review and tuning. Plus, you can use DB2's Design Advisor to review complex and costly SQL, as well as SQL that is performing sorts, and target these queries for tuning efforts.

SQL Administrative Routines and Convenience Views

Introduced in DB2 UDB V8.1, SQL snapshot functions have been deprecated in DB2 9. Table 11.1 lists the deprecated functions along with the replacement DB2 9 administrative routine or view.

Table 11.1: B2 9 SQL administrative routines and views		
DB2 UDB for Linux, UNIX, and Windows V8 deprecated function	**Equivalent DB2 9 routine or view**	**Purpose**
GET_DB_CONFIG	DBCFG administrative view	Retrieve database configuration parameter information
GET_DBM_CONFIG	DBMCFG administrative view	Retrieve database manager configuration parameter information
SNAP_GET_CONTAINER	SNAPCONTAINER administrative view and SNAP_GET_ CONTAINER_V91 table function	Retrieve tablespace_ container logical data group snapshot information
SNAP_GET_DB	SNAPDB administrative view and SNAP_GET_DB_V91 table function	Retrieve snapshot information from the dbase logical group
SNAP_GET_DETAILLOG	SNAPDETAILLOG administrative view and SNAP_GET_ DETAILLOG_V91 table function	Retrieve snapshot information from the detail_log logical data group
SNAP_GET_DYB_SQL	SNAPDYN_SQL administrative view and SNAP_GET_DYN_ SQL_V91 table function	Retrieve dynsql logical group snapshot information
SNAP_GET_STO_PATHS	SNAPSTORAGE_PATHS administrative view and SNAP_GET_ STORAGE_PATHS table function	Retrieve automatic storage path information
SNAPSHOT_BP	SNAPBP administrative view and SNAP_GET_BP table function	Retrieve information about buffer pools (specifically, the buffer pool logical data group) from a buffer pool snapshot
SNAPSHOT_LOCK	SNAPLOCK administrative view and SNAP_GET_LOCK table function	Retrieve lock logical data group snapshot information
SNAPSHOT_LOCKWAIT	SNAPLOCKWAIT administrative view and SNAP_GET_ LOCKWAIT table function	Retrieve lockwait logical data group snapshot information

Table 11.1: B2 9 SQL administrative routines and views (continued)		
DB2 UDB for Linux, UNIX, and Windows V8 deprecated function	**Equivalent DB2 9 routine or view**	**Purpose**
SNAPSHOT_QUIESCERS	SNAPTBSP_QUIESCER administrative view and SANP_GET_TBSP_QUIESCER table function	Retrieve quiescer table space snapshot information
SNAPSHOT_RANGES	SNAPTBSP_RANGE administrative view and SNAP_GET_TBSP_RANGE table function	Retrieve range snapshot information
SNAPSHOT_STATEMENT	SNAPSTMT administrative view and SNAP_GET_STMT table function	Retrieve statement snapshot information
SNAPSHOT_SUBSECT	SNAPSUBSECTION administrative view and SNAP_GET_SUBSECTION table function	Retrieve subsection logical monitor group snapshot information
SNAPSHOT_SWITCHES	SNAPSWITCHES administrative view and SNAP_GET_SWITCHES table function	Retrieve database snapshot switch state information
SNAPSHOT_TABLE	SNAPTAB administrative view and SNAP_GET_TAB_V91 table function	Retrieve table logical data group snapshot information
SNAPSHOT_TBREORG	SNAPTAB_REORG administrative view and SNAP_GET_TAB_REORG table function	Retrieve table reorganization snapshot information
SNAPSHOT_TBS	SNAPTBSP administrative view and SNAP_GET_TBSP_V91 table function	Retrieve tablespace logical data group snapshot information
SNAPSHOT_TBS_CFG	SNAPTBSP_PART administrative view and SNAP_GET_TBSP_PART_V91 table function	Retrieve tablespace_nodeinfo logical data group snapshot information
SNAPSHOT_UTIL	SNAPUTIL administrative view and SNAP_GET_UTIL table function	Retrieve utility_info logical data group snapshot information
SNAPSHOT_UTIL_PROG	SNAPTUTIL_PROGRESS administrative view and SNAP_GET_UTIL_PROGRESS table function	Retrieve progress logical data group snapshot information
SQLCACHE_SNAPSHOT	SNAPDYN_SQL administrative view and SNAP_GET_DYN_V91 table function	Retrieve dynsql logical group snapshot information

Table 11.1: B2 9 SQL administrative routines and views (continued)		
DB2 UDB for Linux, UNIX, and Windows V8 deprecated function	**Equivalent DB2 9 routine or view**	**Purpose**
SYSFUN.GROUPS*	*Deprecated in DB2 V9*	
SYSFUN.GROUPS_FOR _USER*	AUTH_LIST_GROUPS_ FOR_AUTHID table function	Retrieve group membership list for a given authorization ID
SYSFUN.USER_GROUPS*	*Deprecated in DB2 V9*	
SYSFUN.USERS*	*Deprecated in DB2 V9*	
SYSINSTALLROUTINES	*Deprecated in DB2 V9*	

* These functions were present in V8 but undocumented.

New in DB2 9, SQL administrative routines and convenience views have a schema of SYSIBMADM. The convenience views are new views containing precomputed values. For example, the SYSIBMADM.BP_HITRATIO view contains precomputed data such as the buffer pool hit ratio. This alternative represents an improvement in DB2 9 because in the past DBAs had to either compute the hit ratio manually or use a script or third-party vendor tool.

Unlike the classic snapshots presented earlier in the chapter, SQL administrative routines and views let you take snapshots and insert the resulting output into predefined DB2 tables in the same SQL statement. SQL snapshot functions, and now the administrative routines and views, provide the ability to establish a snapshot repository to use for online analysis of performance data. I've used these functions myself and usually leave a working snapshot repository with my clients so that they can accurately record and track database activity.

You can also use SQL administrative routines and views in a script that you can schedule to run as needed based on your database environment, snapshot frequency, and overall monitoring requirements. As a minimum, your snapshot repository should enable you to identify database activity for every 30 minutes of the day. In some environments, the interval may need to be every minute of the day. Thus, SQL administrative routines and views enable you to build a DB2 snapshot repository for use in analyzing current performance problems; over time, they also provide a repository that you can use for trending and historical analysis. Snapshot data stored in the repository can help you answer questions about what happened an hour ago, a week ago, or two days ago during a particular time period.

SQL administrative routines and views are included with the DB2 9 base product. In DB2 UDB 8.2.2, IBM started to provide release-specific views, using the SYSCAT schema with the "V82" suffix. IBM took this approach so that previous scripts and routines wouldn't need to be changed as the underlying tables were changed in a specific release. DB2 9 continues this convention, and SQL snapshot functions or routines that have changed are suffixed with "V91" (as shown in the table).

You can query the administrative routines and convenience views either directly or from the Control Center. As an example, Figures 11.1 and 11.2 show how to query the SYSIBMADM.SNAPSTMT view from the Control Center.

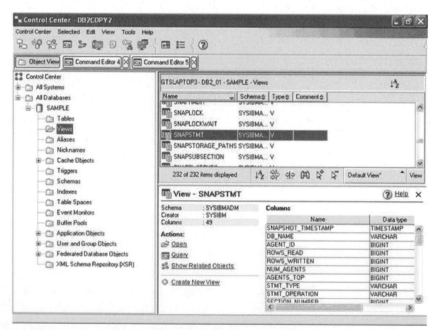

Figure 11.1: SNAPSTMT view in DB2 Control Center

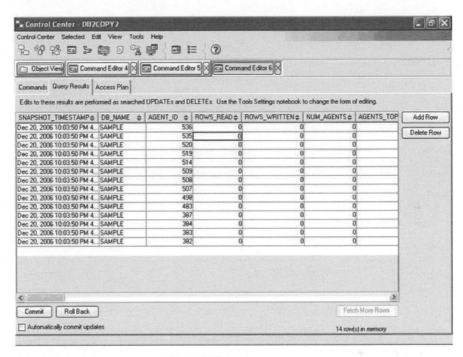

Figure 11.2: Query results from SNAPSTMT view

You can use the Control Center to query the administrative views or use the command editor or another ad hoc tool. Another option is to write a script to read administrative views and format the output for performance analysis.

Also new in DB2 9 is the ability to launch the list applications command from the Control Center. Previously, this function was available only via the command line or a third-party vendor tool. The enhancement lets DBAs easily identify problems from within the Control Center. Figure 11.3 demonstrates launching the command from the Control Center, and Figure 11.4 shows some sample output.

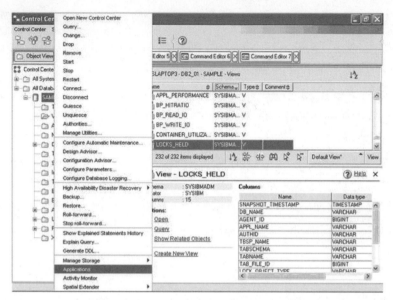

Figure 11.3: Launching the List Application command from the Control Center

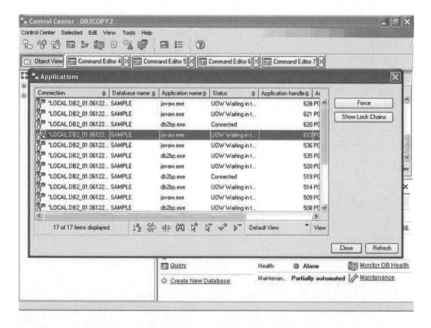

Figure 11.4: List Applications Show Detail command output in the Control Center

The SYSIBMADM snapshot views won't contain snapshot data unless you've enabled the default monitor switches for the monitoring elements of interest. When the views are launched from the Control Center, DB2 uses a separate instance attachment; as such, this requires the default instance level monitor switches to be enabled. If the switches are enabled at the database or application level, no data will be returned. Figure 11.5 shows the message you'll receive if you haven't enabled the correct level of monitor switches.

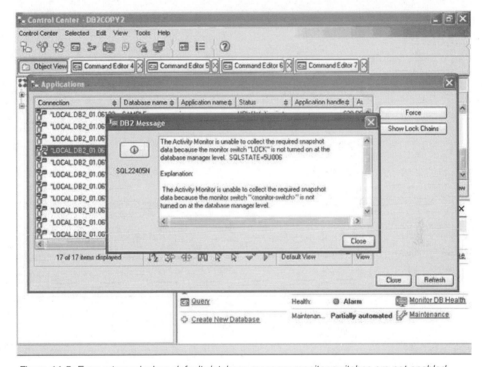

Figure 11.5: Error returned when default database manager monitor switches are not enabled

For more information about SQL administrative routines and convenience views, consult the DB2 Information Center, the *DB2 UDB System Monitor Guide*, the *DB2 UDB SQL Reference*, and the DB2 9 *SQL Administrative Routines and Views* manual.

DDL to create tables for use with the administrative routines and views is available from the DB2 Information Center or via the SQL DESCRIBE statement. Listing 11.12 shows the output that results from the following sample use of DESCRIBE:

```
db2 "describe select *
    from table (snap_get_container_v91('sample',-1) ) as t"
```

```
SQLDA Information

sqldaid : SQLDA      sqldabc: 896  sqln: 20  sqld: 14

Column Information

sqltype              sqllen   sqlname.data         sqlname.length
-------------------  -------  -------------------  --------------
393     TIMESTAMP       26    SNAPSHOT_TIMESTAMP               18
449     VARCHAR        128    TBSP_NAME                        9
493     BIGINT           8    TBSP_ID                          7
449     VARCHAR        256    CONTAINER_NAME                  14
493     BIGINT           8    CONTAINER_ID                    12
449     VARCHAR         16    CONTAINER_TYPE                  14
493     BIGINT           8    TOTAL_PAGES                     11
493     BIGINT           8    USABLE_PAGES                    12
501     SMALLINT         2    ACCESSIBLE                      10
493     BIGINT           8    STRIPE_SET                      10
501     SMALLINT         2    DBPARTITIONNUM                  14
449     VARCHAR         22    FS_ID                            5
493     BIGINT           8    FS_TOTAL_SIZE                   13
493     BIGINT           8    FS_USED_SIZE                    12
```

Listing 11.12: SQL describe statement

You can format the output from the DESCRIBE statement into a CREATE TABLE statement for use in capturing SQL snapshot function data to DB2 tables as shown in the following sample SQL statement.

```
INSERT INTO SNAPSHOT_CONTAINER
Select * from TABLE(SNAP_GET_CONTAINER_V91('SAMPLE',-1)) as T;
```

This SQL statement invokes the SQL snapshot function SNAP_GET_CONTAINER_V91 and stores the results in a previously defined table, SNAPSHOT_CONTAINER. The data stored in the table is then immediately available for analysis.

Inserting SQL snapshot function data directly into DB2 tables gives you the capability to immediately run canned or ad hoc queries against the snapshot data. Not only can you use the power of SQL to review critical performance-related snapshot data elements, but you can join, sort, and rank data to determine the top 10 tables, most costly applications, or most expensive SQL statements as well as to compute buffer pool hit ratios, asynchronous/synchronous read rates, sort overflow percentage, and other important performance-related metrics. You can do all this in realtime to solve realtime performance problems.

Health Center and Health Monitor

The DB2 Health Monitor is a lightweight, server-side agent (implemented in the DBA Administration Server). The DB2 Health Center is a graphical interface used to configure the Health Monitor and to present monitor data returned from the Health Monitor. Together, the Health Center and Health Monitor form the core of the DB2-provided 24x7 monitoring capability.

To launch the Health Center from the DB2 Control Center, simply click the Health Center toolbar icon, shown in Figure 11.6.

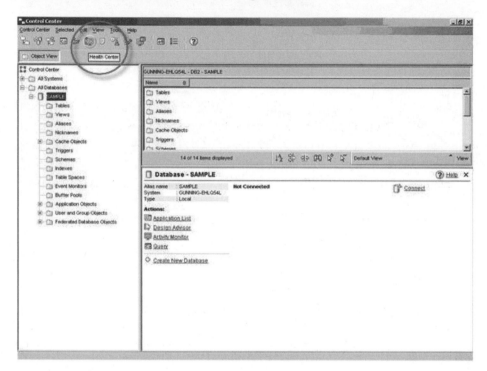

Figure 11.6: Launching the Health Center from the DB2 Control Center

The Health Center displays the current status of the monitored instance or database. You can also use it to make online changes to database configuration parameters and to set monitoring thresholds for configuration parameters. Figure 11.7 shows the Health Center home panel.

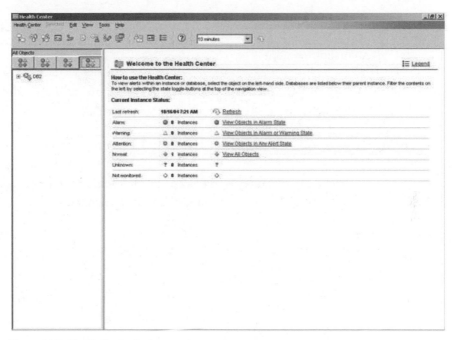

Figure 11.7: Health Center home panel

In conjunction with the Health Monitor, the Health Center reports on threshold violations via *health beacons*, which are also located on the toolbar of most of the DB2 monitoring tools. Using the Health Center, you can configure health indicators and record warnings and alerts generated by the Health Monitor.

The DB2 Health Monitor is a 24x7 application that monitors database manager and database configuration thresholds. Its warnings and alerts are recorded and reported via the Health Center through visual alerts and messages. The Health Center comes with default warning and alert settings for the DB2 configuration parameters. The Health Monitor is enabled by default, and the default settings enable the monitoring of health indicators. You can review the HEALTH_MON default database manager switch to determine whether health monitoring is enabled on your system.

To view the status of this switch, issue a database manager snapshot:

```
db2 get snapshot for dbm
```

The following line in the command output reports the status of the Health Monitor monitor switch:

```
Monitor health of instance and databases   (HEALTH_MON) = ON
```

To review or change the instance- or database-level default health indicator settings, launch the Health Indicator Configuration Launchpad by right-clicking on the instance or database icon as shown in Figure 11.8.

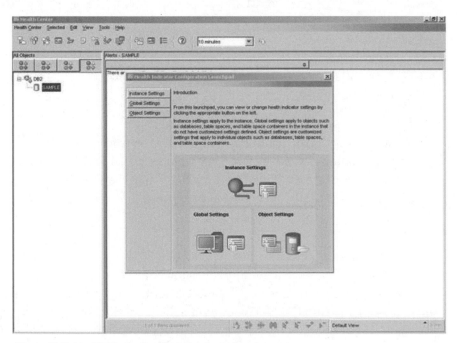

Figure 11.8: Health Center Configuration Launchpad

Click the **Instance Settings** button to display the current instance health indicator settings, shown in Figure 11.9.

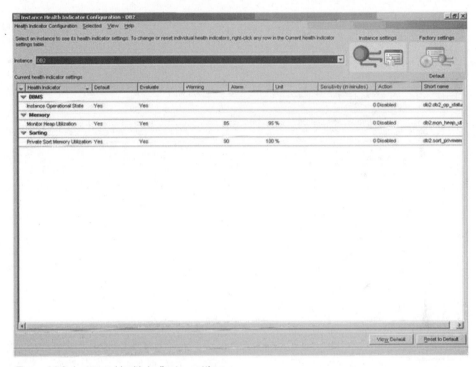

Figure 11.9: Instance Health Indicator settings

Right-click the health indicator you want to change, and select **Edit** to bring up the health indicator panel. From here, you can change the default thresholds (warning=90 percent, alarm=100 percent) and define a script or task to be executed when an alarm is triggered.

To launch Global Health Indicator Configuration, click the **Global Settings** button on the Health Indicator Configuration Launchpad. Figure 11.10 shows an example of the resulting configuration panel.

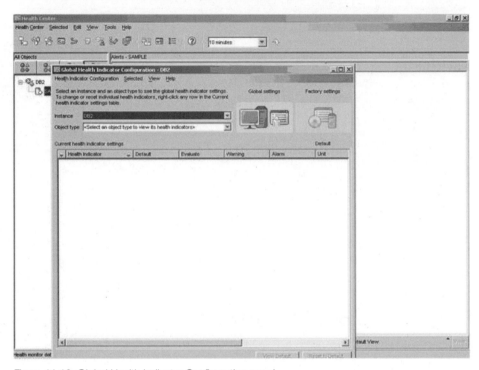

Figure 11.10: Global Health Indicator Configuration panel

As you can see in Figure 11.11, a drop-down list on this panel provides options for configuring three different object types: database, table space, and table space container. By right-clicking in the list, you can choose the object to be configured. In the figure, the database object is selected.

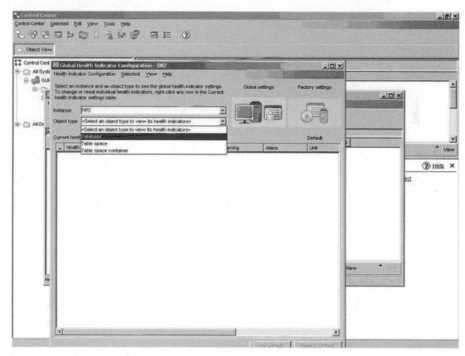

Figure 11.11: Selection of object types for configuration

Figure 11.12 shows the resulting database object health indicator configuration panel.

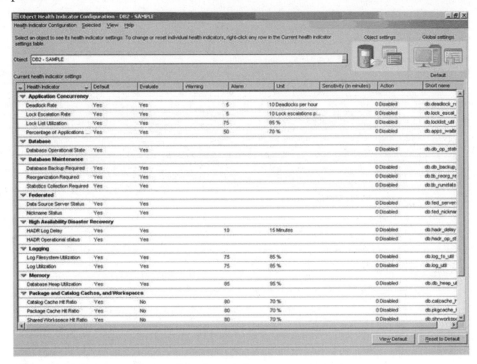

Figure 11.12: Database object configuration panel

You can change database health indicator settings and warning and alarm thresholds online via the Health Center or using one of the following DB2 commands:

```
db2 get alert configuration for database manager
```

```
db2 get alert configuration for databases
```

To update alert configurations, issue the following command with the desired options specified (note that the correct syntax depends on the object of the command):

```
db2 update alert configuration for <containers, databases, database
manager, table spaces> . . .
```

Clicking the **Object Settings** button on the Global Health Indicator Launch-pad lets you traverse down the object hierarchy and select the table space object to configure (Figure 11.13).

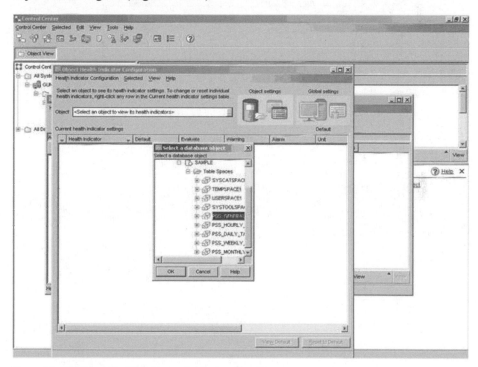

Figure 11.13: Object Health Indicator (table space) settings

After selecting a table space to configure, you can configure or change the associated storage thresholds as shown in Figure 11.14.

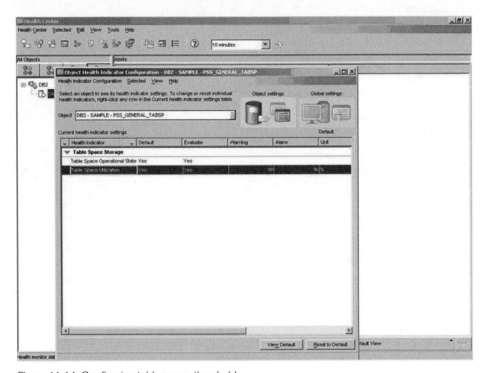

Figure 11.14: Configuring table space thresholds

Now that you've seen how to use and operate the Health Center, we'll look at a series of examples that were generated by sort overflows occurring in the SAMPLE database and review the alerts and recommendations that were produced. As Figure 11.15 shows, in this case the SAMPLE database icon contains an amber warning that indicates that 40 percent of sorts have overflowed during the monitored period.

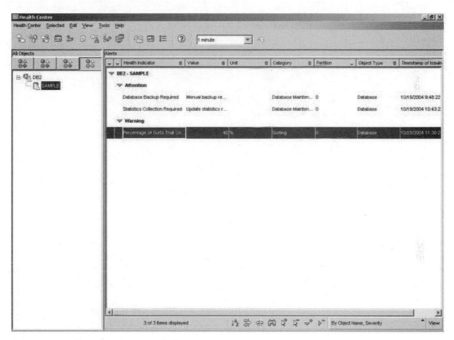

Figure 11.15: Sort overflow Health Center warning

By right-clicking the alarm entry and selecting the **History** tab, we can display and review the history associated with this health indicator, as shown in Figures 11.16 and 11.17.

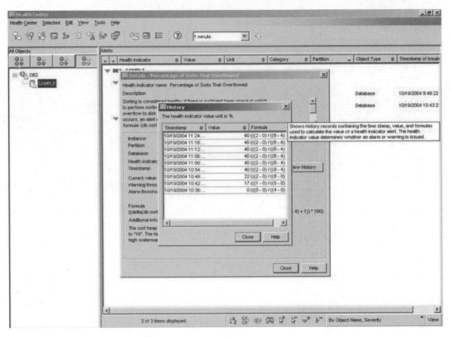

Figure 11.16: Sort overflow Health Center alert history

Right-click on an alert of interest to configure and accept the Health Center recommendations. If we select the **Requirements** tab of the Health Center's Recommendation Advisor, we can provide information that will help the advisor make recommendations about how to solve our problem. Figure 11.17 shows the health indicator recommendation generated by the advisor for our sort overflow problem.

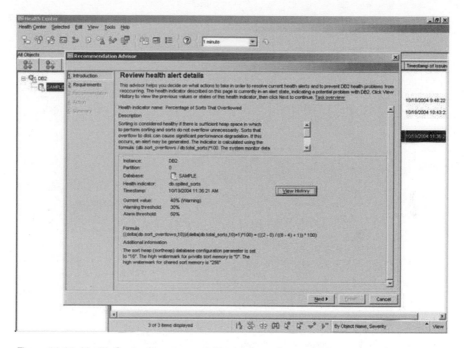

Figure 11.17: Health Center Recommendation Advisor – Sort overflows

To obtain this recommendation in text format, you can issue the following command from the CLP:

```
db2 get recommendations for health indicator "db.spilled_sorts"
```

As Figures 11.18 through 11.20 show, the Recommendation Advisor has three questions that you as a DBA can answer to help the advisor arrive at a final recommendation, shown in Figure 11.21.

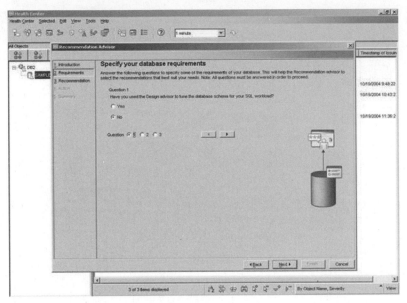

Figure 11.18: Sort overflow question #1

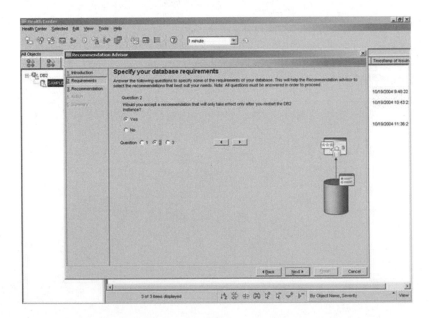

Figure 11.19: Sort overflow question #2

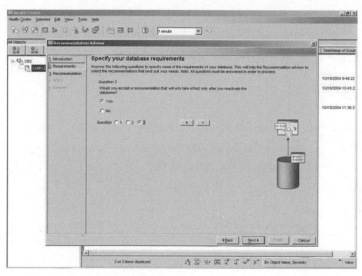

Figure 11.20: Sort overflow question #3

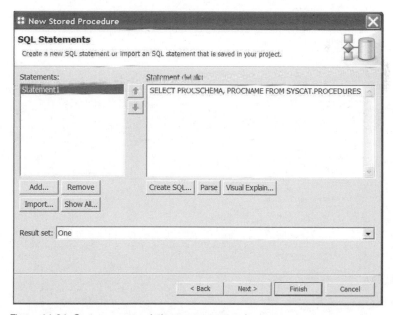

Figure 11.21: Sort recommendation summary panel

After reviewing the advisor's alarm and tuning recommendations, you can apply the recommendation by clicking **Finish**. Depending on the class of parameter recommended, the recommendation may not take effect until all applications have disconnected from the database or until a db2stop and db2start have been issued.

Note that you can also launch the Memory Visualizer (Figure 11.22) to observe how memory is being used over time. This tool lets you track memory usage over time, use the results to make memory heap parameter configuration changes, and then track the effects of those changes.

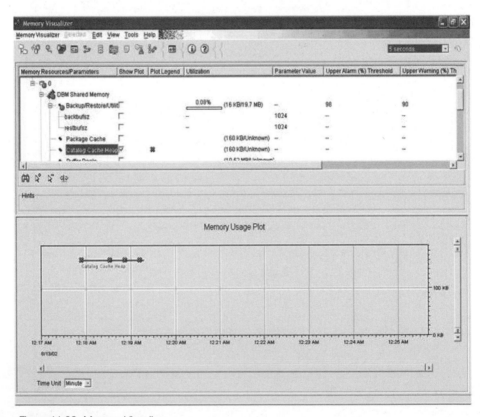

Figure 11.22: Memory Visualizer

One more feature of note is the ability to configure the Health Monitor to provide e-mail and pager notifications to a DBA or group of DBAs. This new capability goes a long way in enabling DB2 to provide 24x7x365 monitoring capability.

Activity Monitor

The Activity Monitor debuted in DB2 UDB V8.2. You can launch this useful monitoring tool from the Control Center by clicking the **Activity Monitor** link (shown in the lower panel of Figure 11.23) or by issuing the db2am command from the CLP.

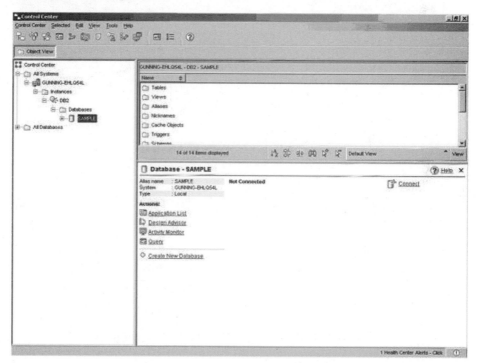

Figure 11.23: Launching the Activity Monitor from the Control Center

After launching the Activity Monitor, you're presented with the **Introduction** panel (Figure 11.24).

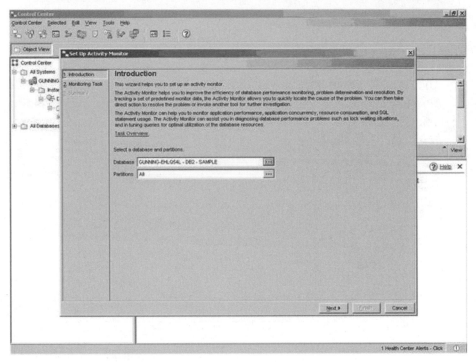

Figure 11.24: Activity Monitor setup panel

To set up the Activity Monitor, simply select a database and monitor task. Figure 11.25 shows the four monitoring tasks you can choose:

- Resolving a general database system slowdown
- Resolving the performance degradation of an application
- Resolving an application locking situation
- Tuning the dynamic SQL statement cache

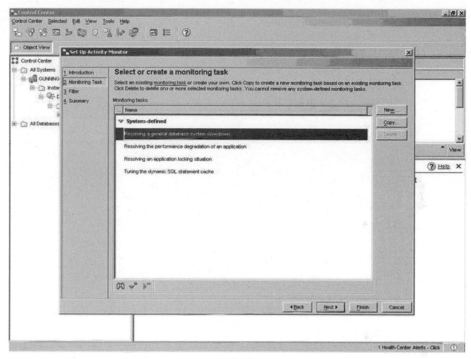

Figure 11.25: Creating a monitoring task

After selecting a monitoring task, you use the panel shown in Figure 11.26 to either apply the task to all applications or specify a filter by choosing from the following filter options:

- Authorization ID
- Application name
- Application handle

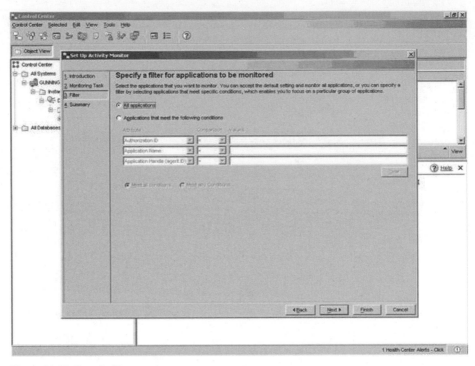

Figure 11.26: Specify filter panel

Click **Next** to review the summary panel (Figure 11.27), and then click
Finish to start monitoring.

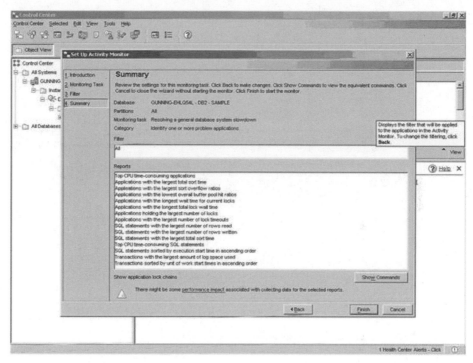

Figure 11.27: Activity Monitor setup summary

For more information about the Activity Monitor, visit the DB2 Information Center.

After setting up a monitoring task, you can use the Activity Monitor to help solve application and database performance problems. Figure 11.28 illustrates using the monitor to identify applications that are potentially causing a database slowdown.

Note: Be advised that the Activity Monitor activates snapshot monitor switches in the background.

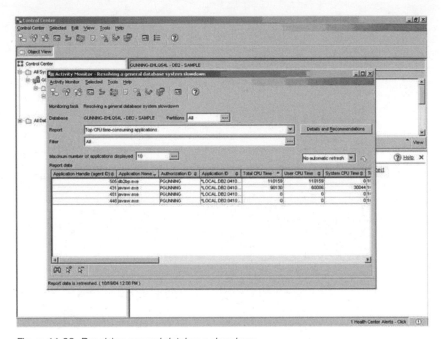

Figure 11.28: Resolving general database slowdown

In the figure, we've selected the "Top CPU time-consuming applications" report, specifying 10 as the maximum number of applications to display so that we'll see only the 10 applications consuming the most CPU time. With potentially hundreds of applications running, it's important to be able to focus on this group because the cause of our database slowdown is most likely to be one of the top 10 CPU resource consumers. The Activity Monitor displays the applications in descending order based on the value of the **Total CPU Time** column, making it easy to identify at a glance the application consuming the most CPU time.

Click the **Details and Recommendations** button to retrieve details about the report along with recommendations to help you resolve the problem being analyzed. Figure 11.29 shows the **Details** tab associated with the CPU-time report, and Figure 11.30 shows the **Recommendations** tab. You can use the Activity Monitor's recommendations to learn more about DB2 and to develop top-performing applications.

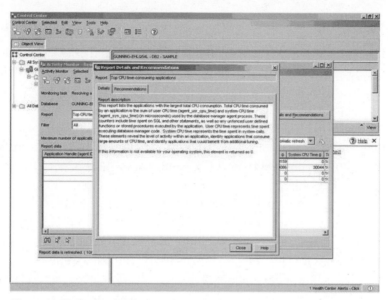

Figure 11.29: Report details

Figure 11.30: Report recommendations

db2pd Utility

DB2's db2pd utility is a command-line monitoring and troubleshooting tool with extensive capability. It is similar to the former Informix OnStat utility, which was the basis for the db2pd tool introduced in DB2 UDB V8.2 (formerly known as the Stinger release). Not all of the former OnStat features are included in the current tool, but IBM will probably continue to add functionality to db2pd in future releases or versions. In DB2 9, db2pd now provides information about Fast Communication Manager (FCM) buffer utilization.

The db2pd utility is an excellent tool for obtaining operating system information, discovering and resolving lock-contention problems, and identifying index usage, tables being scanned, and tables and indexes in need of reorganization. The utility is the only DB2 built-in monitoring facility that provides information about index activity. Best of all, db2pd doesn't use DB2 engine resources, and it places no overhead on the database manager. As such, it acquires no locks on DB2 resources but reads from DB2 memory sets. Because no locks are obtained, the data returned by db2pd may not be completely current; however, zero use of database engine resources is a good trade-off to make in exchange for the wealth of information db2pd provides.

It's important to become familiar with the capabilities that db2pd offers and use them to augment snapshot monitoring. Snapshot monitoring remains the best source of information for I/O activity at the database, buffer pool, and table space levels.

> **Note:** As of DB2 9, IBM has not yet incorporated db2pd output into other built-in DB2 monitoring facilities or tools. Some third-party vendors, however, are integrating db2pd data into their monitoring products.

> **Note:** Unlike snapshot table functions, db2pd provides no built-in mechanism for inserting its output directly into DB2 tables and making this data part of your historical performance database. For now, you'll have to do this via a script or manual procedure.

Utility db2pd provides information at the operating system, instance, and database levels. You can run the tool from a DB2 command line either by issuing the db2pd command followed by the desired option parameter or interactively by issuing the db2pd command and then issuing db2pd option parameters to the db2pd interactive shell. Standard db2pd command-line options include the following:

- -c (command): To read commands from an input file
- -r (repeat): To repeat db2pd execution after a specified number of seconds
- -i (interactive): To run db2pd interactively
- -file: To specify an output file

Running db2pd requires SYSADM authority. On UNIX/Linux, the user ID must be the instance owner. No connection or attachment is required. To retrieve database-level information, db2pd requires the database to be active.

To have db2pd default to a predefined command and option, you can set the db2pdopt environmental variable. Do so from a Windows command line as shown in Figure 11.31.

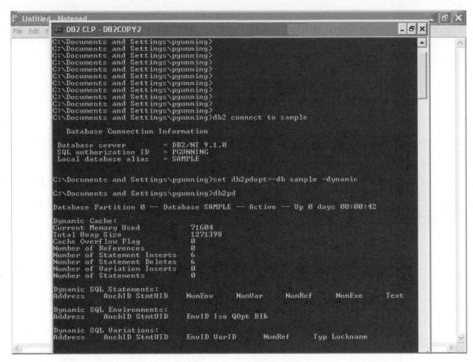

Figure 11.31: Setting and invoking db2pd using the **db2pdopt** *variable*

This example sets db2pdopt using the following command:

```
set db2pdopt=-db sample –dynamic
```

Then simply issue the command **db2pd** from a command line to execute
the utility using the settings in the environment variable. (Note that an active
database connection is required.) A similar tool, db2pdcfg, lets you set the
database system behavior for problem determination analysis. We cover
db2pdcfg in more detail in Chapter 14.

The db2pd utility uses operating system, instance, and database level scope
options to group its functionality. Table 11.2 lists the command options and
provides brief descriptions.

Table 11.2: db2pd command options

Option	Returns information about	Use to
Operating system scope options		
-osinfo	Number of configured and online CPUs, CPU load, hardware multithreading, CPU speed, total physical and virtual memory, free and available memory, message queues, semaphores, shared memory, disk, and file system	Gather information about operating system, CPU, and physical and virtual memory availability and usage and to obtain disk and file system information
Instance scope options		
-inst	All instance scope options	Gather information about an instance
-utilities	Utilities	Gather information about utilities, ID, and status
-fmp	Fenced processes	Gather information about fenced processes
-agents	Current, idle, active, and pooled agents	Monitor agent activity (you can specify an agent ID)
-fcm	Fast communication manager (FCM) buffers and channels	Monitor FCM resource usage and high water mark for buffers from the start of the instance
-memsets (both instance and database)	Instance-level memory set usage (reserved and committed)	Monitor instance-level memory usage
-mempools (both instance and database)	Instance memory pools and associated database manager configuration parameters	Monitor instance-level memory usage
-dbmcfg	Instance-level configuration parameters	Monitor in-memory and on-disk database manager configuration parameter settings.
-sysplex	List of servers associated with the database alias for all databases or a particular database	Gather information about gateways in the Sysplex

Table 11.2: db2pd command options (continued)		
Option	**Returns information about**	**Use to**
Database scope options		
-database	Physical and virtual memory and CPU configuration and speed	Obtain database information
-alldatabases	Memory sets for all databases	Obtain information for multiple databases; best used when redirected to a file for parsing with a script or for import to a historical performance database
-everything	All memory sets and all database scope options	H
-hadr	Database high-availability configuration and status	Obtain information about HADR connection, role, time, and status
-applications	Applications	Obtain application status and activity
-bufferpools	Buffer pools	Monitor buffer pool activity.
-catalogcache	Catalog cache	Monitor and tune catalog cache
-dbcfg	Settings of the database configuration parameters	Retrieve database configuration settings
-dynamic	Execution of dynamic SQL	Obtain SQL statements from dynamic SQL cache
-logs	Logs	Obtain information about log configuration, status, log head (the beginning of the log chain), and performance
-locks	Locks	Obtain information about database lock activity
-recovery	Recovery activity	Gather recovery activity information
-reopt	Cached SQL statements that were reoptimized using REOPT ONCE option applications	Obtain information about dynamic SQL using the REOPT option
-reorg	Table reorganization	Monitor REORG status
-static	Execution of static SQL and packages	Obtain information about static packages and static cache usage
-tablespaces	Table spaces	Obtain space usage information for table spaces

Table 11.2: db2pd command options (continued)		
Option	Returns information about	Use to
-tcbstats	Tables and indexes	Obtain information about index activity, table scans, tables in need of REORG
-transactions	Active transactions	Retrieve transaction information to resolve lock-contention issues
-version	Current DB2 version and level	Determine current version and fix pack
-pages	Buffer pool pages	Review types of buffer pool pages and usage patterns
-help	db2pd command help	Retrieve option and syntax for commands
-dbpartitionnum n or –dbp n	A specified database partition server	Obtain information about the specified partition
-alldbpartitionnums or -alldbp	All database partition servers in the instance	Obtain information about all partitions

db2pd Examples

Let's look at some examples now of the most commonly used db2pd options.

To obtain operating system information, issue the command with the –osinfo option:

```
db2pd –osinfo
```

Output from the –osinfo option, shown in Listing 11.13, includes information about the number of cores and hardware multithreading (HMT) capability, available virtual and physical memory, configured and used CPUs, and file system and disk information. (The –osinfo output will differ based on the operating system in use.) This option provides lots of valuable configuration information for DBAs, operations staff, and system administrators.

```
Operating System Information:
OSName:   WIN32_NT
NodeName: GTSTST1
Version:  5.2
Release:  Service Pack 1
Machine:  AMD64 Family 15, model 4, stepping 8
CPU Information:
TotalCPU    OnlineCPU    ConfigCPU    Speed(MHz)  HMTDegree  Cores/Socket
16          16           16           3003        4          2
Physical Memory and Swap (Megabytes):
TotalMem    FreeMem      AvailMem     TotalSwap   FreeSwap
8191        959          959          1606        5436
Virtual Memory (Megabytes):
Total       Reserved     Available    Free
9797        n/a          n/a          6395
```

Listing 11.13: -osinfo option output

To obtain database manager configuration information, issue this command:

```
db2pd –dbmcfg
```

The –dbmcfg option provides the current in-memory value of the database manager configuration parameters along with the on-disk value (highlighted in bold in Listing 11.14).

```
Database Partition 0 -- Active -- Up 0 days 00:55:52

Database Manager Configuration Settings:
Description                 Memory Value           Disk Value
RELEASE                     0xb00                  0xb00
CPUSPEED                    2.873427e-007          2.873427e-007
COMM_BANDWIDTH              1.000000e+002          1.000000e+002
NUMDB                       8                      8
FEDERATED                   NO                     NO
```

Listing 11.14: –dbmcfg option output (part 1of 4)

```
TP_MON_NAME
DFT_ACCOUNT_STR
JDK_PATH (memory)            C:\PROGRA~1\IBM\SQLLIB\java\jdk
JDK_PATH (disk)              C:\PROGRA~1\IBM\SQLLIB\java\jdk
DIAGLEVEL                    3                       3
NOTIFYLEVEL                  3                       3
DIAGPATH (memory)
DIAGPATH (disk)
DFT_MON_BUFPOOL             OFF                      ON
DFT_MON_LOCK               OFF                      ON
DFT_MON_SORT               OFF                      ON
DFT_MON_STMT               OFF                      ON
DFT_MON_TABLE             OFF                      ON
DFT_MON_TIMESTAMP         ON                       ON
DFT_MON_UOW              OFF                      ON
HEALTH_MON               ON                       ON
SYSADM_GROUP (memory)     DB2ADMNS
SYSADM_GROUP (disk)       DB2ADMNS
SYSCTRL_GROUP (memory)
SYSCTRL_GROUP (disk)
SYSMAINT_GROUP (memory)
SYSMAINT_GROUP (disk)
SYSMON_GROUP (memory)
SYSMON_GROUP (disk)
CLNT_PW_PLUGIN
CLNT_KRB_PLUGIN           IBMkrb5                  IBMkrb5
GROUP_PLUGIN
LOCAL_GSSPLUGIN
SRV_PLUGIN_MODE           UNFENCED                 UNFENCED
SRVCON_GSSPLUGIN_LIST
SRVCON_PW_PLUGIN
SRVCON_AUTH
AUTHENTICATION            SERVER                   SERVER
CATALOG_NOAUTH            NO                       NO
TRUST_ALLCLNTS            YES                      YES
TRUST_CLNTAUTH            CLIENT                   CLIENT
FED_NOAUTH               NO                       NO
```

Listing 11.14: –dbmcfg option output (part 2 of 4)

```
DFTDBPATH (memory)          C:
DFTDBPATH (disk)            C:
MON_HEAP_SZ (4KB)           66                  768
JAVA_HEAP_SZ (4KB)          512                 512
AUDIT_BUF_SZ (4KB)          0                   0
INSTANCE_MEMORY (4KB)       AUTOMATIC           AUTOMATIC
BACKBUFSZ (4KB)             1024                1024
RESTBUFSZ (4KB)             1024                1024
SHEAPTHRES (4KB)            0                   0
DIR_CACHE                   YES                 YES
ASLHEAPSZ (4KB)             15                  15
RQRIOBLK                    32767               32767
QUERY_HEAP_SZ (4KB)         1000                1000
UTIL_IMPACT_LIM             10                  30
AGENTPRI                    SYSTEM              SYSTEM
MAXAGENTS                   401                 400
NUM_POOLAGENTS              200                 Calculated
NUM_INITAGENTS              0                   0
MAX_COORDAGENTS             400                 400
MAXCAGENTS                  400                 400
MAX_CONNECTIONS             400                 400
KEEPFENCED                  YES                 YES
FENCED_POOL                 MAX_COORDAGENTS     MAX_COORDAGENTS
NUM_INITFENCED              0                   0
INDEXREC                    RESTART             RESTART
TM_DATABASE                 1ST_CONN            1ST_CONN
RESYNC_INTERVAL             180                 180
SPM_NAME                    GTSLAPTO            GTSLAPTO
SPM_LOG_FILE_SZ             256                 256
SPM_MAX_RESYNC              20                  20
SPM_LOG_PATH
SVCENAME                    db2c_DB2            db2c_DB2
DISCOVER                    SEARCH              SEARCH
DISCOVER_INST               ENABLE              ENABLE
MAX_QUERYDEGREE             ANY                 ANY
INTRA_PARALLEL              NO                  NO
FCM_NUM_BUFFERS (4KB)       4096                4096
```

Listing 11.14: –dbmcfg option output (part 3 of 4)

```
FCM_NUM_CHANNELS          2048                    2048
CONN_ELAPSE               10                      10
MAX_CONNRETRIES           5                       5
MAX_TIME_DIFF             60                      60
START_STOP_TIME           10                      10
```

Listing 11.14: –dbmcfg option output (4 of 4)

To obtain information about active transactions, issue this command:

```
db2pd –db db2mon –trans
```

The output from the –trans (–transactions) option includes the application handle, transaction ID, transaction state, and amount of log space used. This option lets you identify the state of transactions and locks held. Used in combination with the db2pd utility's –locks and –application options, –trans can help you identify potential performance problems. Listings 11.15A and 11.15B shows some sample –trans output.

```
Database Partition 0 -- Database DB2MON -- Active -- Up 1 days 04:27:09     /
                                                                           \
Transactions:                                                              /
Address      AppHandl [nod-index] TranHdl Locks State Tflag      Tflag2    \
0x027D1000   599      [000-00599] 99      0     READ  0x00000000 0x00000000 /
0x027D1A80   591      [000-00591] 100     0     READ  0x00000000 0x00000000 \
0x027D2500   589      [000-00589] 101     0     READ  0x00000000 0x00000000 /
0x027D2F80   588      [000-00588] 102     0     READ  0x00000000 0x00000000 \
0x027D3A00   9        [000-00009] 103     2     READ  0x00000000 0x00000000 /
0x027D4480   8        [000-00008] 104     0     READ  0x00000000 0x00000000 \
```

Listing 11.15A: –trans option output (left half)

```
/ FirstIsn        LastIsn          LogSpc SpaceRsrvd TID                AxRegCnt GXID
\ 0x000000000000 0x000000000000 0      0          0x000000009016 1            0
/ 0x000000000000 0x000000000000 0      0          0x000000008FF6 1            0
\ 0x000000000000 0x000000000000 0      0          0x000000008FFD 1            0
/ 0x000000000000 0x000000000000 0      0          0x000000009012 1            0
\ 0x000000000000 0x000000000000 0      0          0x0000000003FA 1            0
/ 0x000000000000 0x000000000000 0      0          0x000000009014 1            0
```

Listing 11.15B: –trans option output (right half)

Output from the –trans and –locks option can be mapped to the output from the –trans option to identify the activity of the lock owner. In Listings 11.16A and 11.16B, you can see that transaction 103 is holding two locks and that they have been granted.

```
Command: db2pd -db db2mon -locks
Database Partition 0 -- Database DB2MON -- Active -- Up 1 days 04:44:50     /
                                                                            \
Locks:                                                                      /
Address       TranHdl  Lockname                      Type     Mode  Sts     \
0x032DE790    103      4442324143434553BBCB10EC41    Internal P ..S  G       /
0x032DE740    103      53514C4445464C5428DD630641    Internal P ..S  G       \
                                                                            /
Snippet from previous –trans output:
0x027D3A00 9        [000-00009] 103    2    READ    0x00000000 0x00000000   /
0x027D4480 8        [000-00008] 104    0    READ    0x00000000 0x00000000   \
```

Listing 11.16A: Output from –trans and –locks options (left half)

```
Owner  Dur  HldCnt  Att       ReleaseFlg
\    103    1    0          0x0000   0x40000000
/    103    1    0          0x0000   0x40000000
\
/ 0x000000000000 0x000000000000 0      0          0x0000000003FA 1            0
\ 0x000000000000 0x000000000000 0      0          0x000000009014 1            0
```

Listing 11.16B: Output from –trans and –locks options (right half)

Identifying and resolving lock-contention problems is one of the main tasks DBAs perform in online realtime monitoring. Unlike the lock snapshot, the output from the –locks option presents lock activity in an easy-to-use format, letting you quickly identify lock holders and waiters. Listings 11.17A and 11.17B show an example of identifying lock holders and lock waiters.

```
Database Partition 0 -- Database SAMPLE -- Active -- Up 0 days 16:39:33      /
db2pd -db GTSTST1 -locks -file /tmp/lockc.txt                                \
Locks:                                                                       /
Address     TranHdl  Lockname                       Type      Mode   Sts    \
0x0459C510  2        53514C4332453036BD4A32C841      Internal  P .. S  G     /
0x0459CA10  3        53514C4332453036BD4A32C841      Internal  P .. S  G     \
0x0459CA60  3        0100000001000000001007B0056     Internal  V . S   G     /
0x0459C9E8  3        53514C4445464C5428DD630641      Internal  P . S   G     \
0x0459EF90  2        02000300270000000000000052      Row         . X   G     /
0x0459CAB0  3        02000300270000000000000052      Row        .NS     W     \
0x0459C8F8  2        02000300000000000000000054      Table      .IX    G     /
0x0459CA88  3        02000300000000000000000054      Table      .IS    G     \
```

Listing 11.17A: Output from –locks option (left half)

```
Owner   Dur   HldCnt   Att      ReleaseFlg
\   2     1      0        0x0000   0x40000000
/   3     1      0        0x0000   0x40000000
\   3     1      0        0x0000   0x40000000
/   3     1      0        0x0000   0x40000000
\   2     1      0        0x0008   0x40000002
/   2     1      0        0x0000   0x00000001
\   2     1      0        0x0000   0x40000002
/   3     1      0        0x0000   0x00000001
```

Listing 11.17B: Output from –locks option (right half)

As you can see in these results, TranHdl 2 has an X lock on one row at address 0x0459EF90. TranHdl 3 is waiting for an NS lock on the same row.

You can use this information to resolve lock-contention problems. And you can put it all together as shown in Listings 11.18A and 11.18B.

```
Locks:                                                                   /
Address     TranHdl Lockname                      Type    Mode  Sts      \
0x0485E3B0 3          0200030027000000000000052 Row     .NS   W         /
0x0485C998 2          0200030000000000000000054 Table   .IX   G         \
                                                                         /
Transactions:                                                            \
Address     AppHandl [nod-index] TranHdl Locks State Tflag      Tflag2   /
0x045B1580 236        [000-00236] 2        8     WRITE 0x00000000 0x00000000 \
0x045B2000 425        [000-00425] 3        5     READ  0x00000000 0x00000000 /
0x045B2A80 339        [000-00339] 4        0     READ  0x00000000 0x00000000 \
                                                                         /
Applications:                                                            \
Address     AppHandl [nod-index] NumAgents  CoorTid   Status            /
0x01B19950 425        [000-00425] 1          3652      Lock-wait         \
0x0090BE70 236        [000-00236] 1          2452      UOW-Waiting       /
                                                                         \
Dynamic SQL Statements:                                                  /
Address     AnchID StmtUID NumEnv NumVar NumRef NumExe Text              \
0x05E289C0 123     1       1      1      1      1      select * from staff /
0x05E26FB0 129     1       1      1      1      1      SELECT SCHEMA, NAME, \
    STATS_DETAIL, STATS_STATE, STATS_TIME FROM SYSTOOLS.HMON_ATM_INFO WHERE /
    (STATS_STATE = 2 OR STATS_STATE = 6) AND STATS_FLAG ='Y'              \
```

Listing 11.18A: Putting it all together (left half)

```
\ Locks(continued):
/ Owner      Dur HldCnt Att     ReleaseFlg
\ 2          1   0      0x0000 0x00000001
/ 2          1   0      0x0000 0x40000000
\
/ Transactions (continued):
\ FirstIsn        LastIsn        LogSpc SpaceRsrvd TID             AxRegCnt GXID
/ 0x000003A9800C 0x000003AA27B6 234    572        0x0000000014DD 1        0
\ 0x000000000000 0x000000000000 0      0          0x000000001716 1        0
```

Listing 11.18B: Putting it all together (right half) (part 1of 2)

```
/ 0x000000000000 0x000000000000 0       0          0x00000000168C 1         0
\
/ Applications (continued):
\ C-AnchID C-StmtUID  L-AnchID L-StmtUID  Appid
/ 123      1          0        0          *LOCAL.DB2.050920034220
\ 0        0          149      1          *LOCAL.DB2.050920021447
```

Listing 11.18B: Putting it all together (right half) (part 2 of 2)

To put all the output together, I like to start with the –locks option, then identify the application and transaction holding the lock, then associate the application with the SQL statement involved, and take action as necessary. Note that you can observe the current statement (C-AnchID) and the last statement (L-AnchID). In the preceding listings, you can see that TranHdl 3 with AppHandl 425 is in a lock-wait status and is running the SQL with AnchID 123.

The db2pd utility provides a powerful tool for resolving lock-contention problems, all without any overhead in the database manager. You should familiarize yourself with this tool and its numerous options and capabilities. For more information about the command, consult the *DB2 9 Command Reference*.

Memory Tracker

Memory Tracker is another utility in DB2's stable of built-in monitoring tools. You launch Memory Tracker from the command line to display information such as instance and database memory, memory pool high water marks, maximum heap value allocated, and amount of agent private memory being used per agent. Issue the following db2mtrk command to run Memory Tracker as indicated:

```
db2mtrk –i –p –m –v
```

Listing 11.19 shows sample output.

```
Tracking Memory on: 2006/03/24 at 15:08:29
Memory for instance
    Backup/Restore/Util Heap is of size 16384 bytes
    Package Cache is of size 2048000 bytes
    Catalog Cache Heap is of size 524288 bytes
    Buffer Pool Heap is of size 33177600 bytes
    Buffer Pool Heap is of size 105676800 bytes
    Buffer Pool Heap is of size 253329408 bytes
    Buffer Pool Heap is of size 1343488 bytes
    Buffer Pool Heap is of size 819200 bytes
    Buffer Pool Heap is of size 557056 bytes
    Buffer Pool Heap is of size 425984 bytes
    Buffer Pool Heap is of size 360448 bytes
    Lock Manager Heap is of size 8421376 bytes
    Database Heap is of size 3948544 bytes
    Database Monitor Heap is of size 180224 bytes
    Other Memory is of size 16777216 bytes
    Total: 427606016 bytes
Memory for agent 3520
    Application Heap is of size 147456 bytes
    Application Control Heap is of size 16384 bytes
    Total: 163840 bytes
Memory for agent 1564
    Application Heap is of size 147456 bytes
    Application Control Heap is of size 16384 bytes
    Total: 163840 bytes
Memory for agent 2248
    Application Heap is of size 147456 bytes
    Application Control Heap is of size 16384 bytes
    Total: 163840 bytes
Tracking Memory on: 2004/03/24 at 15:08:34
Memory for instance
    Backup/Restore/Util Heap is of size 16384 bytes
    Package Cache is of size 2048000 bytes
    Catalog Cache Heap is of size 524288 bytes
```

Listing 11.19: Sample Memory Tracker output (part 1 of 2)

```
    Buffer Pool Heap is of size 33177600 bytes
    Buffer Pool Heap is of size 105676800 bytes
    Buffer Pool Heap is of size 253329408 bytes
    Buffer Pool Heap is of size 1343488 bytes
    Buffer Pool Heap is of size 819200 bytes
    Buffer Pool Heap is of size 557056 bytes
    Buffer Pool Heap is of size 425984 bytes
    Buffer Pool Heap is of size 360448 bytes
    Lock Manager Heap is of size 8421376 bytes
    Database Heap is of size 3948544 bytes
    Database Monitor Heap is of size 180224 bytes
    Other Memory is of size 16777216 bytes
    Total: 427606016 bytes
Memory for agent 3520
    Application Heap is of size 147456 bytes
    Application Control Heap is of size 16384 bytes
    Total: 163840 bytes
```

Listing 11.19: Sample Memory Tracker output (part 2 of 2)

Memory Tracker displays different information depending on the platform on which DB2 is running. IBM has updated the tool in DB2 9 to permit the –d switch to return information about database memory on Windows platforms. You can use output from the db2mtrk command to monitor agent usage and identify the total amount of memory used by agents. This information is valuable when you're developing a summary of overall DB2 memory use and to identify agents that are using large amounts of memory; you can then target the agent activity for further analysis. For more details about Memory Tracker, see the *DB2 9 Command Reference*.

Event Monitoring

As you've seen, snapshot monitoring shows you performance data at a point in time. With snapshots, you may or may not capture the information of interest, depending on when you take the snapshot, whether the event you're trying to capture is running or has been completed, and how frequently snapshots are taken. Often, snapshot data provides enough information to identify and solve a problem. In rare instances, however, an *event monitor* is required to capture the complete picture. When snapshot data is inconclusive and you need further data capture, use event monitors.

> **Note:** Since DB2 UDB V8, event monitors can write output directly to event monitor tables. You use the db2evtbl tool to create and customize event monitor output and tables.

Event monitors capture and record data as events are completed. You can customize event monitors to capture events based on APPL_ID, AUTH_ID, and APPL_NAME event conditions. DB2 provides eight types of event monitors:

- *Database event monitors* record an event record when the last application disconnects from the database.
- *Table event monitors* record an event record for each active table when the last application disconnects from the database. An active table is a table that has changed since the first connection to the database.
- *Table space event monitors* record an event record for each active table space when the last application disconnects from the database.
- *Buffer pool event monitors* record an event record for buffer pools when the last application disconnects from the database.
- *Connection event monitors* record an event record for each database connection event when an application disconnects from the database.
- *Statement event monitors* record an event for every SQL statement issued by an application (for both dynamic and static SQL).
- *Transaction event monitors* record an event record for every transaction when it is completed (as indicated by a COMMIT or ROLLBACK statement).
- *Deadlock event monitors* record an event record for each deadlock event. When you create a deadlock event monitor using the WITH DETAILS option, the event monitor will generate a more complete deadlock connection event for each application involved. Additional details include the following:

» The statement text from the application that was executing when the deadlock occurred.

» The locks held by the application when the deadlock occurred. In a partitioned database environment, the locks are included only for the database partition in which the application was waiting for its lock when the deadlock occurred.

» Connection event information for the connections involved.

» Additional detail about held locks.

The database manager incurs additional overhead when you specify the WITH DETAILS option. Don't use this option unless you're specifically troubleshooting deadlock problems, and be sure to turn off the event monitor when you no longer need it.

Event Monitor Creation

You create an event monitor via the CLP or the DB2 Control Center as a database event object. Event monitors can write their event records to pipes, files, or tables; you indicate the desired type of output mechanism in the CREATE EVENT MONITOR SQL statement. Use the following criteria to determine which type of output mechanism you should use:

- Transaction volume
- Planned use for the event data
- Required throughput
- CPU capacity
- Available disk storage
- Use of third-party vendor tools

To create an event monitor, you must have either DBADM or SYSADM authority.

The following command creates a connection event monitor that uses default values and writes its output to tables:

```
CREATE EVENT MONITOR PGUNN
   FOR CONNECTIONS
   WRITE TO TABLE
```

You start and stop event monitors by setting the monitor's STATE to 1 or 0, respectively:

```
SET EVENT MONITOR <event monitor name> STATE = 1
SET EVENT MONITOR PGUN2 STATE = 0
```

CREATE EVENT MONITOR Command Options

Options on the CREATE EVENT MONITOR statement let you control the amount of information collected, determine how the event monitor stops and starts, and specify the location and size of output files or pipes, types and size of buffers, and scope (local or global) of the event monitor.

We've already discussed the various types of event monitors. We'll now focus on the major event monitor options and associated details.

Event Condition Options

You use the CREATE EVENT MONITOR statement's WHERE event condition clause to specify one of three possible event conditions. Specifying an APPL_ID event condition indicates that the event monitor should compare the application ID of each connection with a specified comparison string to determine whether the connection should generate CONNECTION, STATEMENT, or TRANSACTION events (if specified). You can also define an event condition by specifying specific AUTH_IDs or APPL_NAMEs. In each case, the comparison string is a character string that the event monitor compares with the APPL_ID, AUTH_ID, or APPL_NAME of each application that connects to the database. If the specific event condition is met, event data is captured.

Output Options

You use the WRITE TO option of the CREATE EVENT MONITOR statement to identify the target output mechanism that will hold the event monitor data. An event monitor can write to a pipe, file, or table. I'll briefly describe how DB2 event monitors write to pipes and files here and go into greater detail later about event monitors that use the WRITE TO TABLE capability that was added in DB2 UDB V8.

When writing event monitor data to a pipe, the event monitor writes the data in a single stream, as if the data were a single, infinitely long file. When writing data using this method, the event monitor does not perform blocked writes. This point is important because if no room exists in the pipe buffer, the event monitor will discard the data. To ensure no loss of data, the monitoring application that is using the pipe must read the data without delay.

Using a pipe to receive event monitor data is efficient and imposes the least overhead on the database. However, it's uncommon for DBAs to use pipes for event monitors because you need an application to read the data from a pipe, and the application must be started in advance of writing data to a pipe. ISVs, on the other hand, use pipes frequently because they provide an application as part of the tool to read the pipe and process the data.

When event monitor data is written to a file (or set of files), the event data streams to files that use the following naming convention (unless limited by the MAXFILES option):

00000000.evt, 00000001.evt, 00000002.evt . . . *nnnnnnn*.evt

Even though multiple files may be used, DB2 treats the data as one logical file.

Table Options

Table options on the CREATE EVENT MONITOR statement let you specify the logical-data-group data elements that are written to event monitor tables. By default, all data elements are written. You can use the evmGroupInfo and evmGroup options to customize and limit the amount of data written to target tables.

> **Note:** Event monitors separate the data stream into one or more logical data groups and insert each group into a separate table. Data for groups that have a target table is retained, whereas data is discarded for groups without tables. The event monitor maps each monitor element to a table column of the same name. Elements without corresponding table column are discarded.

Event Monitor Scope Options

Depending on the database configuration you use, an event monitor can have one of two scopes:

- GLOBAL: A global event monitor reports on all database partitions. As of DB2 UDB V8, only event monitors defined on DEADLOCKS and DEADLOCKS WITH DETAILS can be defined as GLOBAL.
- LOCAL: A local event monitor reports on only the database partition that is running, providing information about that particular partition.

Event Monitor Catalog Tables

Once you've created an event monitor, DB2 stores information in the following SYSCAT views:

- SYSCAT.EVENT MONITORS: Records event monitor definition
- SYSCAT.EVENT: Records event monitor events
- SYSCAT.EVENTTABLES: Records the names of the event monitor target tables when you use the WRITE TO TABLE option

You can query these tables to check the status of an event monitor or obtain event monitor definition data.

Write-to-Table Event Monitors

As I've noted, write-to-table event monitors debuted in DB2 UDB V8. The power of this capability lies in the ability of DB2 to capture and store event monitor data in a 24x7x365 environment. You can use the stored data to conduct performance analysis and retain it for historical and trending purposes. You can also create event monitors to run during off-hours in unattended mode, using a user-written script. This capability, which lets you analyze the data the next day, fills a void that existed in DB2 until Version 8.

By default, DB2 creates the following 13 event monitor tables when you create a write-to-table event monitor:

- BUFFERPOOL
- CONN
- CONNHEADER
- CONTROL
- DB
- DEADLOCK
- DLCONN
- DLLOCK
- STMT
- SUBSECTION
- TABLE
- TABLESPACE
- XACT

If your CREATE EVENT MONITOR statement specifies only a subset of events, DB2 creates only the tables needed for those events. When creating event monitor tables, DB2 uses the following naming convention:

schema-name.table-name_event-monitor-name

For example, assume a DBA with the user ID PRODDBA issues the following statement:

CREATE EVENT MONITOR PGUN2 FOR CONNECTIONS WRITE TO TABLE

DB2 will create the event monitor tables with a schema of PRODDBA and append the table suffix PGUN2 to each event monitor table name. The tables would be created as follows:

```
proddba.conn_pgun2
proddba.connheader_pgun2
proddba.control_pgun2
```

If you don't specify a table space, the tables will be created in table spaces as indicated by the IN *tablespaceName* clause. If specified, the table spaces must already exist; the CREATE EVENT MONITOR statement does not create table spaces.

General Considerations for Write-to-Table Event Monitors

If the creation of an event monitor target table fails for any reason, DB2 returns an error to the application program, and the create statement fails. During CREATE EVENT MONITOR processing, if a table already exists but is not defined for use by another event monitor, no table is created; processing continues, and DB2 returns a warning to the application program.

> **Note:** The LOCAL and GLOBAL keywords of the CREATE EVENT MONITOR statement are ignored for a write-to-table event monitor because an event monitor output process or thread is started on each database partition in the instance, and each of these processes reports data only for the database partition on which it is running.

Only one event monitor can use a target table. During CREATE EVENT MONITOR processing, if a target table is found to already have been defined for use by another event monitor, the CREATE EVENT MONITOR statement fails, and an error is returned to the application program. You can tell whether a table is already defined for use by another event monitor if the table name matches a value found in the SYSCAT.EVENTTABLES catalog view.

> **Note:** DB2 does not drop target tables as part of the DROP EVENT MONITOR statement.

While an event monitor is running, it inserts event records into target tables. If an insert fails, uncommitted changes are rolled back, a message is written to the administration notification log, and the event monitor is deactivated.

> **Note:** Make sure the table spaces being used for your event monitor target tables have enough space to handle your requirements. For database managed space (DMS) table spaces, you can use the CREATE EVENT MONITOR command's PCTDEACTIVATE option to specify, as a percentage, how full the table space can get before the event monitor is automatically deactivated.

DB2 Event Analyzer

To analyze event monitor data that has been written to tables using the write-to-table option, you can use the DB2 event analyzer tool, db2eva. You issue the db2eva command from the command line and can invoke the command with or without parameters. If you specify no parameters, the **Open Event Analyzer** dialog box is displayed, letting you choose the database and event monitor name from a drop-down list. Figure 11.32 shows sample output generated by the db2eva command.

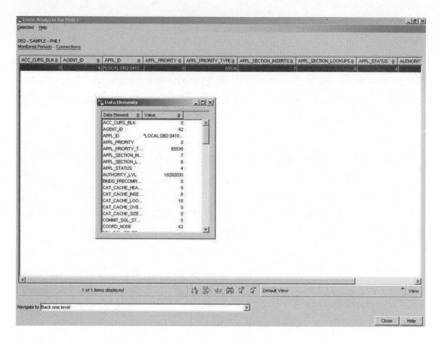

Figure 11.32: db2eva analyze connection events view

You can also use the event analyzer to analyze the data of an active event monitor; however, data captured after invocation of the analyzer might not be shown. To view event monitor data using the DB2 Control Center, simply select the event monitor from the list of event monitor objects.

Summary

This chapter introduced the two categories of monitoring performed for DB2—online monitoring and exception-based monitoring—and covered a variety of tools and utilities built into DB2 to help you perform these important tasks. You learned about the basics of snapshot monitoring, SQL administrative routines and convenience views, the DB2 Heath Center and Health Monitor tools, the Activity Monitor, and the versatile db2pd command. The importance of establishing and using a snapshot repository for current and historical monitoring purposes was emphasized.

We concluded with an overview of DB2 event monitoring, seeing how to create event monitors to capture and record data as events are completed. Based on the information covered in this chapter, you should be able to use DB2 monitoring facilities and tools to monitor and tune DB2 instances and databases.

12

Performance

In this chapter, we build on the information covered in Chapter 11, concentrating on evaluating and tuning DB2 instance and database configuration parameters based on output from the DB2 monitoring facilities. We'll use data from the following DB2 facilities and tools:

- Snapshot monitoring
- SQL administrative routines
- SQL convenience views
- Health Center and Health Monitor
- Memory Visualizer
- Activity Monitor
- db2pd utility
- Memory Tracker
- Event monitors

You'll learn how to use the output from these monitoring facilities, and I'll recommend which monitoring facilities to use for various performance problems. We'll also discuss how to arrive at specific tuning and performance recommendations, examine the new DB2 9 Self Tuning Memory Manager (STMM), and review some DB2 best practices.

DB2 Memory Model

DB2 allocates memory at three different levels: instance, database, and agent. Figure 12.1 depicts the memory areas that make up the DB2 Memory Model.

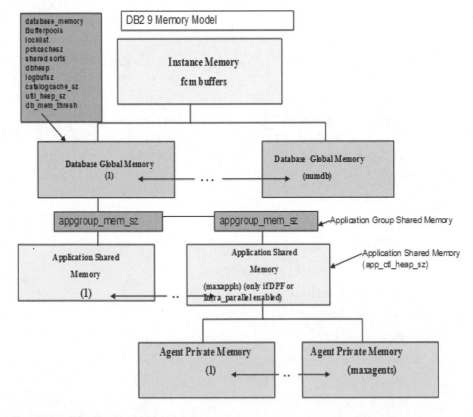

Figure 12.1: DB2 Memory Model

Instance Memory

Memory allocated at the instance level is shared across all databases in the instance. Instance-level memory consists of the memory heaps shown in Figure 12.2.

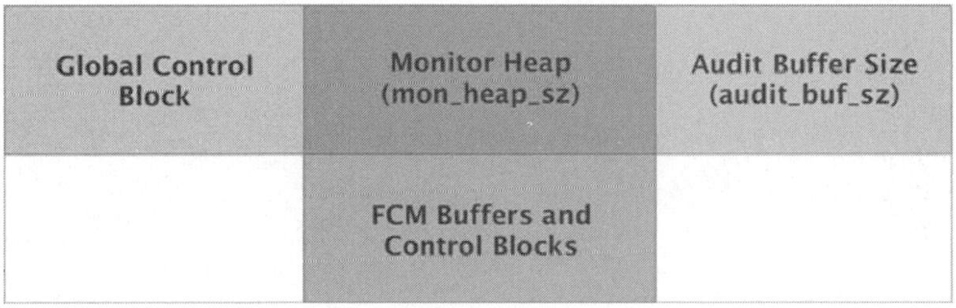

Global Control Block	Monitor Heap (mon_heap_sz)	Audit Buffer Size (audit_buf_sz)
	FCM Buffers and Control Blocks	

Figure 12.2: DB2 instance memory

Database Shared Memory

Memory at the database level is referred to as *database shared memory*. Memory allocated at this level is available to all agents operating within a database. Database shared memory consists of the memory heaps shown in Figure 12.3.

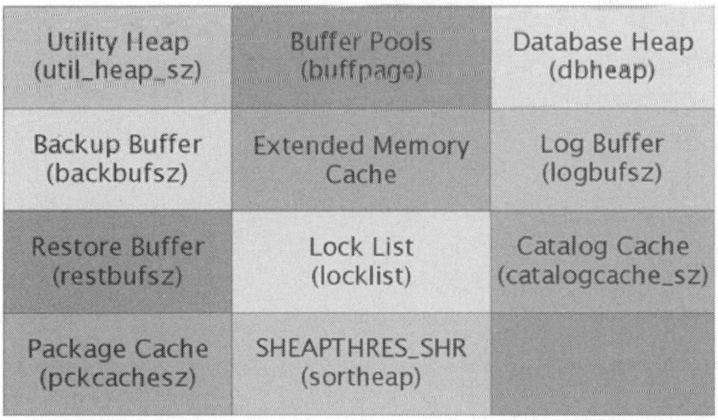

Utility Heap (util_heap_sz)	Buffer Pools (buffpage)	Database Heap (dbheap)
Backup Buffer (backbufsz)	Extended Memory Cache	Log Buffer (logbufsz)
Restore Buffer (restbufsz)	Lock List (locklist)	Catalog Cache (catalogcache_sz)
Package Cache (pckcachesz)	SHEAPTHRES_SHR (sortheap)	

Figure 12.3: Database shared memory

New in DB2 9, the db_mem_thresh database configuration parameter defines the maximum percentage of committed but currently unused database shared memory that the database manager will allow before releasing committed pages of memory back to the operating system (OS). When used with the DB2

9 Self Tuning Memory Manager, the default parameter value of 10 should be adequate in most cases. With this setting, the database manager will release database shared memory when more than 10 percent is currently unused.

You should monitor database and OS memory usage by taking database manager and database snapshots and by executing the db2pd, db2mtrk, vmstat, ps, and vmo commands and utilities. (I cover the vmstat command in Chapter 13. For information about ps and vmo in an AIX environment, consult the *AIX Command Reference*.)

Agent Private Memory

Agent private memory is allocated per agent and is used by each agent to accomplish work on behalf of an application. Agent private memory consists of the memory heaps shown in Figure 12.4.

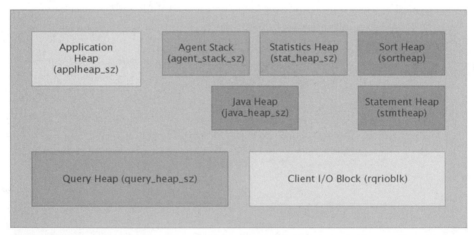

Figure 12.4: Agent private memory

DB2 Process Model

The DB2 Process Model uses a client-server structure that has the application and agent at its core. The model consists of clients running applications, with agents doing work on behalf of applications. Each agent is assigned agent private memory with which to accomplish this work. Prefetchers prefetch data into the buffer pool. As the buffer pool fills with dirty pages, I/O cleaners write dirty pages asynchronously to disk. The logger process writes undo/redo information to the log and commits it from the log buffer at commit time, when the log buffer is full, or when some other system event happens.

Figure 12.5 provides an overview of the DB2 Process Model.

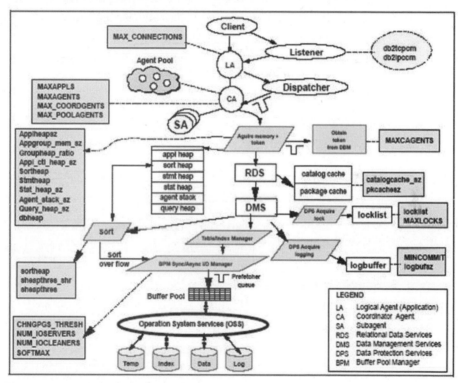

Figure courtesy of IBM, used with permission.

Figure 12.5: DB2 Process Model

The figure depicts agents accomplishing work on behalf of applications. As work is accomplished, various memory heaps and queues are used. The diagram shows the process flow, memory heaps, and associated configuration parameters. Memory heaps are used at the instance, database (database shared memory), and agent level.

The illustration represents a typical transaction flow with connection concentration enabled. The transaction flow is as follows:

1. A client application connects to the database via the listener process.

2. If the value of the max_connections database manager configuration parameter has not been reached, a connection is made. (The maxagents, max_coordagents, and max_appls values are also applied.)

3. Before performing work on behalf of the application, the agent must obtain a token from the database manager. The maxcagents database manager configuration parameter controls how many coordinating agents can be executing at once.

4. Agent memory—consisting of the memory heaps applheap, sortheap, stmt_heap, statistics_heap_sz, agent_stack_sz, and query_heap_sz— is allocated.

5. SQL is prepared (if not found in the package cache), and descriptors are read either from the catalog cache or from the DB2 catalog tables on disk.

6. The SQL statement is copied to agent private memory.

7. The statement is executed via Relational Data Services (RDS) and Database Management Services (DMS).

8. Locks are acquired (parameters locklist and maxlocks).

9. Indexes and/or tables are accessed.

10. Data Protection Services (DPS) ensures data integrity is maintained (via logging).

11. The Bufferpool Synchronous/Asynchronous I/O Manager processes asynchronous prefetch requests off a prefetch queue, or agents perform synchronous I/O via the Operating System Services (OSS) layer.

12. Buffer pool manager processes then conducts I/O cleaning (chngpgs_thresh, num_iocleaners, softmax).

As I noted, the figure depicts transaction flow with connection concentration enabled—that is, when parameter max_connections is set to a value greater than that of max_coordagents. With connection concentration, applications are assigned to logical agents from a pool of agents.

For Web or OLTP applications with many simultaneous user connections, the connection concentrator may improve performance by letting DB2 process many more client connections efficiently. The connection concentrator also reduces memory use for each connection and decreases the number of OS-level context switches. This feature is intended for short-running Web applications, not for long-running applications (e.g., the production of big reports).

When a client application connects to a database, an *application control block* is associated with it. The application is a logical representation of a client connection. Applications always belong to a particular *application group*, which is a logical representation of a set of resources that applications within the group share.

A *coordinator agent* is a physical agent process created by the server to perform a unit of work on behalf of an application/client connection. In general, a dispatcher process creates coordinator agents when it detects a request on a client connection and cannot find a suitable pooled coordinator agent to service the request. If a suitable pooled coordinator agent is found, it will be used, and no new coordinator agent process will be created.

After obtaining a coordinator agent process, the dispatcher passes the active client connection to the coordinator agent, which is then associated with that client connection and its application group. The agent process then serves requests on behalf of the application for the duration of a single transaction. The transaction ends when the client issues a commit or a rollback, at which point the coordinator agent passes the client connection back to the dispatcher process and disassociates itself from the application. The coordinator agent is then usually placed in a pool on the application's app-group for reuse by other applications performing work. When pooled, the coordinator agent remains associated with the application group in question to improve performance of subsequent transactions.

DB2 UDB V8.2 introduced a database-level *idle agent pool*, which consists of one or more pools for particular groups of applications. Initially, at system start-up, only one application group exists. As more connections are added, DB2 automatically and transparently creates additional application groups and defines an idle pool for each new group. There are typically 100 to 200 applications per application group. Application groups help spread out access to critical resources (e.g., shared SQL work space) across agents. This design can help reduce contention in very high user throughput environments with hundreds to thousands of users.

As we discuss tuning considerations, I'll describe how affected memory heap areas are used and provide tuning recommendations for optimizing the use of various memory heap areas.

DB2 Self-Tuning Memory Manager

The Self Tuning Memory Manager is new in DB2 9. This facility, which runs as a regular DB2 application, automates memory management and tuning, requiring no DBA intervention. STMM algorithms automatically sample and compute optimum memory settings for eligible shared memory heaps.

STMM dynamically allocates memory between database shared memory areas as the consumption of memory changes over time. STMM is an adaptive tuner and enables hands-off, automatic, online memory tuning without DBA involvement. STMM adapts quickly as workload shifts require the redistribution of memory—for example, as a workload transitions from OLTP to batch, from normal to month-end processing, or simply from peaks in regular demand. Within just one hour, STMM adapts tuning frequency based on the workload. When optimal memory configuration is reached, STMM stops tuning.

The following features are highlights of the STMM:

- STMM algorithms can evaluate and update memory requirements up to 60 times per hour.
- The facility optimizes memory based on the currently running workload.

- STMM can do in an hour what it would take a DBA weeks to do.
- STMM can optimize memory requirements in just one hour.
- Once STMM is enabled, no DBA interaction is required.
- STMM automatically stops tuning when optimal configuration is reached.

Particularly noteworthy is the fact that in little more than an hour, STMM can tune memory to a point that would take an experienced DBA several days or weeks to achieve.

Memory that can be managed by the STMM consists of memory areas allocated from database shared memory. Remember, database shared memory is allocated per database.

STMM is enabled by default in DB2 9 and is controlled by the self_tuning_ mem database configuration parameter. For databases migrated to DB2 9, this parameter will not be enabled. To determine whether self-tuning memory is enabled, issue the following command and review the output (this example uses the gtstst2 database):

```
db2 get db cfg for gtstst2 show detail
```

Listing 12.1 shows the output you'll see if the parameter is not enabled.

```
        Database Configuration for Database gtstst2

Description                 Parameter      Current Value  Delayed Value
 ------------------------------------------------------------------
...
Self tuning memory (SELF_TUNING_MEM) = OFF            OFF
...
```

Listing 12.1: Self-tuning memory database configuration parameter status

If self-tuning is enabled, self_tuning_mem will be set to ON or ON (INACTIVE). (I'll discuss the meaning of INACTIVE a bit later in the chapter.) You can configure this parameter online, and any changes take effect immediately.

In DB2 9, STMM tunes the database_memory database configuration parameter and eligible heaps by default. The setting of the self_tuning_mem database configuration parameter defaults to ON for newly created DB2 9 databases and, when combined with the default-enabled eligible heaps, enables complete automatic tuning for DB2 9 databases. The following eligible database shared memory heaps are enabled for memory tuning by default:

- Buffer pools (controlled by the CREATE BUFFERPOOL and ALTER BUFFERPOOL commands)
- Package cache (parameter pckcachesz)
- Locklist (parameters locklist and maxlocks)
- Shared sorts (parameters sheapthres_shr and sortheap)
- Database shared memory (parameter database_memory)

These database shared memory heaps are the only heaps currently eligible for automatic memory management by STMM.

> **Note:** Buffer pools that have been enabled for self-tuning will have an npages value of –z.

For newly created databases, STMM tuning of buffer pools is enabled by default. For databases migrated to DB2 9, you can enable buffer pools for STMM tuning by altering the buffer pool or by using the DB2 Control Center as shown in Figure 12.6.

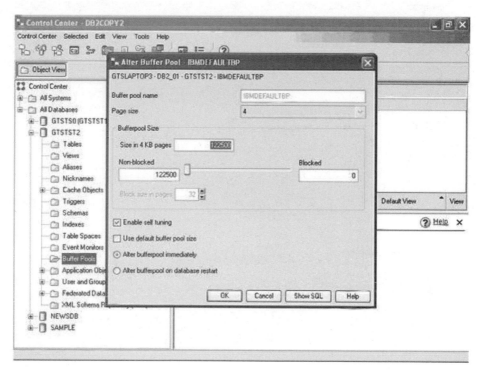

Figure 12.6: Enabling buffer pools for STMM

Once you've enabled STMM for the buffer pool of interest, the size (npages) will be set to –2, and the buffer pool will be reported as enabled for self-tuning as shown in Figure 12.7.

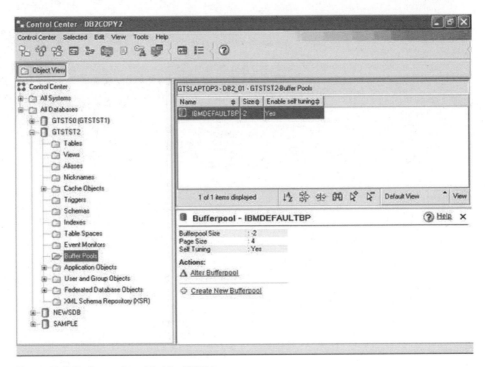

Figure 12.7: Buffer pool enabled for STMM

STMM Tuning Modes

STMM has two modes of operation:

- Tuning of the database_memory configuration parameter and eligible heaps
- No tuning of the database_memory parameter but tuning of eligible heaps

For database_memory tuning to occur, the database_memory parameter must be set to AUTOMATIC. This value is the default for newly created databases in DB2 9.

> **Note:** You cannot set parameter database_memory to AUTOMATIC on HP-UX, Linux, or Solaris because these operating systems don't support the shrinking of subsets of memory. With database_memory set to AUTOMATIC, STMM grows or shrinks the size of DB2 database shared memory by allocating or deallocating memory to or from the OS as necessary.

> **Note:** Use the default setting of 10 for the new DB2 9 db_mem_thresh database configuration parameter, which defines the maximum percentage of committed but currently unused database shared memory that the database manager will allow before releasing committed pages of memory back to the OS.

STMM dynamically allocates memory between database shared memory areas as the consumption of memory changes over time.

The second mode of operation is no database_memory parameter tuning but tuning between eligible heaps. With this mode, the memory used by the database remains constant; however, memory is allocated between eligible heaps, with STMM moving memory between the heaps as needed. For tuning between heaps to occur, at least two eligible heaps must be enabled for self-tuning (heap settings set to automatic). The STMM automatically determines the particular demand for a consumer of database shared memory and dynamically reallocates memory based on that need.

Use the following command to determine the status of STMM tuning:

```
db2 get db cfg for <dbname> show detail
```

A self_tuning_mem setting of ON (ACTIVE) means that STMM is actively tuning memory on this database. ON (INACTIVE) means that the database configuration parameter is enabled but memory self-tuning is not occurring because fewer than two database shared memory areas are enabled for self-tuning. At least two database shared memory areas must be enabled for self-tuning to occur. Note that self-tuning of the sort heap (sortheap) will occur regardless of whether other memory consumers are enabled for self-tuning.

> **Note:** When enabled, STMM runs automatically and samples database shared memory usage and eligible heaps every three minutes by default.

In environments that use the Database Partitioning Feature (those with more than one partition), parameter self_tuning_mem will show ON (ACTIVE) only for the database partition in which STMM is running. ON (INACTIVE) will appear for all other partitions.

You can view the status of STMM tuning by reviewing the contents of the STMM.log in the instance STMMLOG subdirectory. When the log reaches a predefined size threshold, DB2 will use the next log available.

> **Note:** By default, DB2 allocates five STMM logs of 10 MB each. When a log becomes full, the next available log is used. DB2 reuses the logs in a circular manner.

Changes made by STMM are also recorded in the db2diag.log file; these changes are prefixed with STMM CFG. Listing 12.2 shows portions of a sample STMM log (the actual log is many times larger than this excerpt).

```
2007-01-07-12.15.29.176000-300 A417625H400    LEVEL: Event
PID    : 2772              TID : 5196    PROC : db2syscs.exe
INSTANCE: DB2_01           NODE : 000    DB   : GTSTST2
APPHDL : 0-25              APPID: *LOCAL.DB2_01.070107170922
AUTHID : PGUNNING
FUNCTION: DB2 UDB, Self tuning memory manager, stmmMemoryTunerMain,
         probe:1387
MESSAGE : Starting New Interval
```

Listing 12.2: STMM log excerpt (part 1 of 11)

```
2007-01-07-12.15.29.186000-300 A418027H835   LEVEL: Event
PID     : 2772              TID  : 5196    PROC : db2syscs.exe
INSTANCE: DB2_01            NODE : 000      DB   : GTSTST2
APPHDL  : 0-25              APPID: *LOCAL.DB2_01.070107170922
AUTHID  : PGUNNING
FUNCTION: DB2 UDB, Self tuning memory manager, stmmLogRecord
          BeforeResizes,
          probe:496
DATA #1 : String, 433 bytes

***   stmmCostBenefitRecord ***
Type: LOCKLIST
PageSize: 4096
Benefit:
  -> Simulation size: 75
  -> Total seconds saved: 0 (+ 0 ns)
  -> Normalized seconds/page: 0
Cost:
  -> Simulation size: 75
  -> Total seconds saved: 0 (+ 0 ns)
  -> Normalized seconds/page: 0
Current Size: 2386
Minimum Size: 2304
Potential Increase Amount: 1216
Potential Increase Amount From OS: 1216
Potential Decrease Amount: 64
Pages Available For OS: 64

2007-01-07-12.15.29.186000-300 A418864H871   LEVEL: Event
PID     : 2772              TID  : 5196    PROC : db2syscs.exe
INSTANCE: DB2_01            NODE : 000      DB   : GTSTST2
APPHDL  : 0-25              APPID: *LOCAL.DB2_01.070107170922
AUTHID  : PGUNNING
FUNCTION: DB2 UDB, Self tuning memory manager, stmmLogRecord
          BeforeResizes,
          probe:496
DATA #1 : String, 467 bytes
```

Listing 12.2: STMM log excerpt (part 2 of 11)

```
***  stmmCostBenefitRecord ***
Type: SHEAPTHRES_SHR
PageSize: 4096
Benefit:
  -> Simulation size: 612
  -> Total seconds saved: 0 (+ 0 ns)
  -> Normalized seconds/page: 0
Cost:
  -> Simulation size: 1301
  -> Total seconds saved: 0 (+ 0 ns)
  -> Normalized seconds/page: 0
Current Size: 6502
Minimum Size: 250
Potential Increase Amount: 3264
Potential Increase Amount From OS: 3264
Potential Decrease Amount: 1280
Pages Available For OS: 1280
Interval Time: 495.811

2007-01-07-12.15.29.196000-300 A419737H864   LEVEL: Event
PID     : 2772                TID  : 5196    PROC : db2syscs.exe
INSTANCE: DB2_01              NODE : 000     DB   : GTSTST2
APPHDL  : 0-25                APPID: *LOCAL.DB2_01.070107170922
AUTHID  : PGUNNING
FUNCTION: DB2 UDB, Self tuning memory manager, stmmLogRecord
          BeforeResizes,
          probe:496
DATA #1 : String, 460 bytes

***  stmmCostBenefitRecord ***
Type: PCKCACHESZ
PageSize: 4096
Benefit:
  -> Simulation size: 7324
  -> Total seconds saved: 0 (+ 0 ns)
  -> Normalized seconds/page: 0
```

Listing 12.2: STMM log excerpt (part 3 of 11)

```
Cost:
  -> Simulation size: 7324
  -> Total seconds saved: 0 (+ 0 ns)
  -> Normalized seconds/page: 0
Current Size: 1245
Minimum Size: 320
Potential Increase Amount: 640
Potential Increase Amount From OS: 640
Potential Decrease Amount: 224
Pages Available For OS: 224
Interval Time: 496.221


2007-01-07-12.15.29.206000-300 A420603H906   LEVEL: Event
PID    : 2772           TID  : 5196      PROC : db2syscs.exe
INSTANCE: DB2_01        NODE : 000       DB   : GTSTST2
APPHDL  : 0-25          APPID: *LOCAL.DB2_01.070107170922
AUTHID  : PGUNNING
FUNCTION: DB2 UDB, Self tuning memory manager, stmmLogRecord
         BeforeResizes,
         probe:496
DATA #1 : String, 502 bytes

***  stmmCostBenefitRecord ***
Type: BUFFER POOL ( IBMDEFAULTBP )
PageSize: 4096
Saved Misses: 0
Benefit:
  -> Simulation size: 2048
  -> Total seconds saved: 0 (+ 0 ns)
  -> Normalized seconds/page: 0
Cost:
  -> Simulation size: 2048
  -> Total seconds saved: 0 (+ 0 ns)
  -> Normalized seconds/page: 0
Current Size: 20882
Minimum Size: 1000
Potential Increase Amount: 10464
```

Listing 12.2: STMM log excerpt (part 4 of 11)

```
Potential Increase Amount From OS: 10464
Potential Decrease Amount: 4160
Pages Available For OS: 4160
Interval Time: 495.983


2007-01-07-12.15.29.206000-300 A421511H791   LEVEL: Event
PID     : 2772              TID  : 5196      PROC : db2syscs.exe
INSTANCE: DB2_01            NODE : 000       DB   : GTSTST2
APPHDL  : 0-25              APPID: *LOCAL.DB2_01.070107170922
AUTHID  : PGUNNING
FUNCTION: DB2 UDB, Self tuning memory manager, stmmGetDBMem
          DataAutomatic,
          probe:2458
DATA #1 : String, 389 bytes
Configured memory on the system: 1592786944
Memory currently available: 466616320
Set's configured size: 228196352
Overflow left: 45613056
Uncommitted size: 99680256
Target consumer size: 149534484
Current consumer size: 182583296
Max growth: 0
Current overflow percent: 0.200000
Target overflow percent: 0.200000
Average benefit: 0
Global benefit: Instance: DB2_01 DB: GTSTST2  Benefit: 0


2007-01-07-12.15.29.236000-300 A422304H669   LEVEL: Event
PID     : 2772              TID  : 5196      PROC : db2syscs.exe
INSTANCE: DB2_01            NODE : 000       DB   : GTSTST2
APPHDL  : 0-25              APPID: *LOCAL.DB2_01.070107170922
AUTHID  : PGUNNING
FUNCTION: DB2 UDB, Self tuning memory manager, stmmLogRecord
          AfterResizes,
          probe:527
DATA #1 : String, 268 bytes
```

Listing 12.2: STMM log excerpt (part 5 of 11)

```
*** stmmCostBenefitRecord ***
Type: LOCKLIST
PageSize: 4096
Original Size: 2386
Desired New Size: 2322
Actual New Size: 2322
Minimum Size: 2304
Potential Increase Amount: 0
Potential Increase Amount From OS: 0
Potential Decrease Amount: 0
Pages Available For OS: 0


2007-01-07-12.15.29.256000-300 A422975H698   LEVEL: Event
PID     : 2772            TID  : 5196      PROC : db2syscs.exe
INSTANCE: DB2_01          NODE : 000       DB   : GTSTST2
APPHDL  : 0-25            APPID: *LOCAL.DB2_01.070107170922
AUTHID  : PGUNNING
FUNCTION: DB2 UDB, Self tuning memory manager, stmmLogRecord
          AfterResizes,
          probe:527
DATA #1 : String, 295 bytes

*** stmmCostBenefitRecord ***
Type: SHEAPTHRES_SIIR
PageSize: 4096
Original Size: 6502
Desired New Size: 5222
Actual New Size: 5222
Minimum Size: 250
Potential Increase Amount: 0
Potential Increase Amount From OS: 0
Potential Decrease Amount: 0
Pages Available For OS: 0
Interval Time: 495.811


2007-01-07-12.15.29.266000-300 A423675H694   LEVEL: Event
PID     : 2772            TID  : 5196      PROC : db2syscs.exe
INSTANCE: DB2_01          NODE : 000       DB   : GTSTST2
```

Listing 12.2: STMM log excerpt (part 6 of 11)

```
APPHDL  : 0-25                    APPID: *LOCAL.DB2_01.070107170922
AUTHID  : PGUNNING
FUNCTION: DB2 UDB, Self tuning memory manager, stmmLogRecord
          AfterResizes,
          probe:527
DATA #1 : String, 291 bytes

***  stmmCostBenefitRecord ***
Type: PCKCACHESZ
PageSize: 4096
Original Size: 1245
Desired New Size: 1021
Actual New Size: 1021
Minimum Size: 320
Potential Increase Amount: 0
Potential Increase Amount From OS: 0
Potential Decrease Amount: 0
Pages Available For OS: 0
Interval Time: 496.221

2007-01-07-12.15.29.296000-300 A424371H716   LEVEL: Event
PID     : 2772              TID  : 5196      PROC : db2syscs.exe
INSTANCE: DB2_01            NODE : 000       DB   : GTSTST2
APPHDL  : 0-25              APPID: *LOCAL.DB2_01.070107170922
AUTHID  : PGUNNING
FUNCTION: DB2 UDB, Self tuning memory manager, stmmLogRecord
          AfterResizes,
          probe:527
DATA #1 : String, 313 bytes

***  stmmCostBenefitRecord ***
Type: BUFFER POOL ( IBMDEFAULTBP )
PageSize: 4096
Original Size: 20882
Desired New Size: 16722
Actual New Size: 16722
Minimum Size: 1000
```

Listing 12.2: STMM log excerpt (part 7 of 11)

```
Potential Increase Amount: 0
Potential Increase Amount From OS: 0
Potential Decrease Amount: 0
Pages Available For OS: 0
Interval Time: 495.983


2007-01-07-12.15.29.306000-300 A425089H600   LEVEL: Event
PID    : 2772              TID  : 5196      PROC : db2syscs.exe
INSTANCE: DB2_01           NODE : 000       DB   : GTSTST2
APPHDL  : 0-25             APPID: *LOCAL.DB2_01.070107170922
AUTHID  : PGUNNING
FUNCTION: DB2 UDB, Self tuning memory manager, stmmLogRecord
         AfterResizes,
         probe:527
DATA #1 : String, 199 bytes

*** stmmCostBenefitRecord ***
Type: DATABASE_MEMORY
PageSize: 4096
Original Size: 55712
Desired New Size: 49984
Actual New Size: 49984
Potential Increase Amount: 0
Potential Decrease Amount: 2340


2007-01-07-12.15.29.316000-300 A425691H633   LEVEL: Event
PID    : 2772              TID  : 5196      PROC : db2syscs.exe
INSTANCE: DB2_01           NODE : 000       DB   : GTSTST2
APPHDL  : 0-25             APPID: *LOCAL.DB2_01.070107170922
AUTHID  : PGUNNING
FUNCTION: DB2 UDB, Self tuning memory manager, stmmMaintain
         OverflowSize,
         probe:3012
DATA #1 : String, 232 bytes
Original overflow size: 45613056
Target DBMem size: 186918105
Growth limit: 4090298368
```

Listing 12.2: STMM log excerpt (part 8 of 11)

```
Expected DBMem size: 198246400
Current DBMem size: 204603392
Current consumer size: 158597120
Overflow size: 40920678
Overflow percent: 0.200000


2007-01-07-12.15.29.326000-300 A426326H621   LEVEL: Event
PID    : 2772              TID  : 5196    PROC : db2syscs.exe
INSTANCE: DB2_01           NODE : 000     DB   : GTSTST2
APPHDL : 0-25              APPID: *LOCAL.DB2_01.070107170922
AUTHID : PGUNNING
FUNCTION: DB2 UDB, Self tuning memory manager, stmmCompute
         ValidatedSortHeap,
         probe:1238
DATA #1 : String, 216 bytes
SORTHEAP TUNING:
   Current Configuration:
      SORTHEAP=  326
      SHEAPTHRES_SHR= 5222
   Validation Values:
      RECOMMENDED= 262
      MIN= 29
      MAX= 1045
      REDUCED= 262
      VALIDATED= 262


2007-01-07-12.15.29.336000-300 A426949H539   LEVEL: Event
PID    : 2772              TID  : 5196    PROC : db2syscs.exe
INSTANCE: DB2_01           NODE : 000     DB   : GTSTST2
APPHDL : 0-25              APPID: *LOCAL.DB2_01.070107170922
AUTHID : PGUNNING
FUNCTION: DB2 UDB, Self tuning memory manager, stmmMemory
         TunerMain, probe:0
MESSAGE : ZRC=0x000005E2=1506
DATA #1 : String, 113 bytes
Going to sleep for 180000 milliseconds.
Interval = 3, State = 1, intervalsBeforeStateChange = 10,
lost4KPages = 0
```

Listing 12.2: STMM log excerpt (part 9 of 11)

```
        .
        .
        .
2007-01-07-13.28.13.942000-300 A447042H457   LEVEL: Event
PID    : 2772              TID  : 3128    PROC : db2syscs.exe
INSTANCE: DB2_01           NODE : 000      DB  : GTSTST2
APPHDL : 0-63              APPID: *LOCAL.DB2_01.070107182508
AUTHID : PGUNNING
FUNCTION: DB2 UDB, config/install, sqlfLogUpdateCfgParam, probe:2955
MESSAGE : STMM CFG DB GTSTST2: "Stmm_opt_buffpage" From: "0"
          <automatic>
          To: "13394" <automatic>


2007-01-07-13.28.14.122000-300 A447501H455   LEVEL: Event
PID    : 2772              TID  : 3128    PROC : db2syscs.exe
INSTANCE: DB2_01           NODE : 000      DB  : GTSTST2
APPHDL : 0-63              APPID: *LOCAL.DB2_01.070107182508
AUTHID : PGUNNING
FUNCTION: DB2 UDB, config/install, sqlfLogUpdateCfgParam, probe:2955
MESSAGE : STMM CFG DB GTSTST2: "Stmm_opt_sortheap" From: "0"
          <automatic>
          To: "227" <automatic>


2007-01-07-13.28.14.293000-300 A447958H456   LEVEL: Event
PID    : 2772              TID  : 3128    PROC : db2syscs.exe
INSTANCE: DB2_01           NODE : 000      DB  : GTSTST2
APPHDL : 0-63              APPID: *LOCAL.DB2_01.070107182508
AUTHID : PGUNNING
FUNCTION: DB2 UDB, config/install, sqlfLogUpdateCfgParam, probe:2955
MESSAGE : STMM CFG DB GTSTST2: "Stmm_opt_locklist" From: "0"
          <automatic>
          To: "4318" <automatic>


2007-01-07-13.28.14.473000-300 A448416H454   LEVEL: Event
PID    : 2772              TID  : 3128    PROC : db2syscs.exe
INSTANCE: DB2_01           NODE : 000      DB  : GTSTST2
APPHDL : 0-63              APPID: *LOCAL.DB2_01.070107182508
AUTHID : PGUNNING
```

Listing 12.2: STMM log excerpt (part 10 of 11)

```
FUNCTION: DB2 UDB, config/install, sqlfLogUpdateCfgParam, probe:2955
MESSAGE : STMM CFG DB GTSTST2: "Stmm_opt_maxlocks" From: "0"
          <automatic>
          To: "98" <automatic>


2007-01-07-13.28.14.583000-300 A448872H539   LEVEL: Event
PID    : 2772                 TID  : 3128    PROC : db2syscs.exe
INSTANCE: DB2_01              NODE : 000     DB   : GTSTST2
APPHDL  : 0-63                APPID: *LOCAL.DB2_01.070107182508
AUTHID  : PGUNNING
FUNCTION: DB2 UDB, Self tuning memory manager, stmmMemory
          TunerMain, probe:0
MESSAGE : ZRC=0x000005E2=1506
DATA #1 : String, 113 bytes
Going to sleep for 180000 milliseconds.
Interval = 2, State = 1, intervalsBeforeStateChange = 10,
lost4KPages = 0
  .
  .
  .
```

Listing 12.2: STMM log excerpt (part 11 of 11)

Using STMM in an HADR Configuration

In a High Availability Disaster Recovery (HADR) configuration, you can enable STMM on the primary database but must disable it on the standby database. Upon takeover by the standby, STMM can be switched to active on the former standby and back to inactive on the former primary.

When you're evaluating and tuning memory with a new database, enabling STMM and tuning with it is a good way to start. Use STMM to tune the workload over a one- to two-week period, and then disable the facility until you introduce a new workload, your processing requirements change significantly, or hardware is reconfigured. Experience has shown that most environments do not have database shared memory areas optimally set. Thus, most environments can reap performance improvement by using STMM to tune database memory and eligible heaps.

> **Note:** The db_mem_thresh database configuration value is ignored if any of the following registry variables are enabled: DB2_PINNED_BP, DB2_LARGE_PAGE_MEM, and DB2_MEMDISCLAIM.

Instance-Level Tuning Considerations

DB2 uses monitor heap (mon_heap_sz) instance memory to store snapshot data for retrieval via classic snapshots or SQL administrative functions. As you may remember from Chapter 11, instance-level memory is shared across all databases within an instance. Another important memory area is the memory reserved for instance-wide shared sorts. The sheapthres database manager configuration parameter has typically controlled the amount of memory available for shared sorts. However, as of DB2 9, if sheapthres is set to 0, the allocation and management of sort memory is controlled at the database level by the sheapthres_shr database configuration setting. By default, sheapthres_shr is now set to AUTOMATIC, which enables automatic tuning of sort memory at the database and agent (sortheap) levels. Shared sorts are used when any of the following conditions is true:

- Database manager configuration parameter intra_parallel is set to YES.
- Connection concentration is being used (max_connections is set higher than max_coordagents).
- The Database Partitioning Feature is being used.

In all other cases, DB2 uses only private sorts.

Now that you understand the difference between shared and private sorts, let's look at what happens when the value of instance parameter sheapthres is reached or exceeded.

Shared Sort Performance

Post threshold sorts occur when the sheapthres value is reached or exceeded. You can use the database manager snapshot to monitor these sorts. Listing 12.3 shows a sample snapshot.

```
            Database Manager Snapshot

Node name                                   =
Node type                                   = Enterprise
                                              Server Edition
                                              with
                                              local and
                                              remote clients
Instance name                               = DB2
Number of database partitions in DB2 instance = 1
Database manager status                     = Active

Private Sort heap allocated                 = 0
Private Sort heap high water mark           = 16
Post threshold sorts                        = 58
Piped sorts requested                       = 9863
Piped sorts accepted                        = 9850

Start Database Manager timestamp            = 11/07/2007
                                              14:36:31.000046
Last reset timestamp                        =
Snapshot timestamp                          = 11/08/2007
                                              13:51:53.244398


Remote connections to db manager            = 0
Remote connections executing in db manager  = 0
Local connections                           = 0
Local connections executing in db manager   = 0
Active local databases                      = 0

High water mark for agents registered       = 5
High water mark for agents waiting for a token = 0
Agents registered                           = 5
Agents waiting for a token                  = 0
Idle agents                                 = 4

Committed private Memory (Bytes)            = 14827520
```

Listing 12.3: Database manager snapshot – post threshold sorts (part 1 of 2)

```
Switch list for db partition number 0
Buffer Pool Activity Information  (BUFFERPOOL) = ON 11/08/2007
                                                13:44:16.354363
Lock Information                      (LOCK) = OFF
Sorting Information                   (SORT) = ON 11/07/2007
                                                19:45:09.852962
SQL Statement Information        (STATEMENT) = OFF
Table Activity Information           (TABLE) = OFF
Take Timestamp Information        (TIMESTAMP) = ON 11/07/2007
                                                14:36:31.000046
Unit of Work Information               (UOW) = OFF

Agents assigned from pool                    = 749
Agents created from empty pool               = 7
Agents stolen from another application       = 0
High water mark for coordinating agents      = 5
Max agents overflow                          = 0
Hash joins after heap threshold exceeded     = 0


Total number of gateway connections          = 0
Current number of gateway connections        = 0
Gateway connections waiting for host reply   = 0
Gateway connections waiting for client request = 0
Gateway connection pool agents stolen        = 0


Memory usage for database manager:
    Memory Pool Type                         = Database
                                               Monitor Heap
        Current size (bytes)                 = 98304
        High water mark (bytes)              = 180224
        Configured size (bytes)              = 278528

    Memory Pool Type                         = Other Memory
        Current size (bytes)                 = 7831552
        High water mark (bytes)              = 7880704
        Configured size (bytes)              = 1004535808
```

Listing 12.3: Database manager snapshot – post threshold sorts (part 2 of 2)

When sheapthres is exceeded for shared sorts, the agent requesting the sort will receive a negative SQL code, and the unit of work will be rolled back. When sheapthres is exceeded for private sorts, the amount of sortheap allocated will be less than the amount of sortheap defined to the database (as specified by the sortheap database configuration parameter). Recall that private sortheap is allocated out of agent private memory.

You can use the sheapthres_shr database configuration parameter to place a hard limit on the amount of shared sort memory used at the individual database level. If sheapthres_shr is not changed from its default (which sets it equal to the sheapthres database manager configuration parameter), the amount of database shared memory available for shared sorts defaults to that of the sheapthres value.

Piped and Non-Piped Sorts

A *piped sort* is a sort that completes in sortheap without the need for a temporary table. Piped sorts are always faster than non-piped sorts.

Non-piped sorts cannot complete in sortheap and require temporary tables that use the buffer pool and system temporary space. Thus, non-piped sorts are always slower than piped sorts.

Database manager snapshots record the following information about piped sorts:

- Piped sorts requested
- Piped sorts rejected

The number of piped sorts requested and the number of piped sorts rejected should be equal. If they are not, sort overflows or post threshold sorts are occurring. To see whether either circumstance is the case, review the database manager snapshot and the database snapshot, respectively.

Database-Level Tuning Considerations

Let's turn our attention now to tuning considerations at the database level. The primary source of monitoring information used for this purpose is the classic database snapshot. Recall that you can also take database snapshots using the SQL table function SNAPSHOT_DATABASE.

Database snapshots don't require you to enable specific monitoring switches, but if some switches aren't enabled, some data will be missing. When data isn't collected in this regard, the snapshot will contain the text "Not Collected" for the monitoring element.

Sort Performance

The DB2 optimizer determines how much sortheap a particular SQL statement will use either at compile time or at prepare time for dynamic SQL. The optimizer determines this number by analyzing the SQL statement and reviewing DB2 catalog statistics to estimate the number and width of rows to be sorted. When the statement is executed, sorting occurs in sortheap agent private memory for private sorts. If the entire sort can't be completed in the sortheap, the entire sort overflows to the buffer pool and system temporary space on disk. Thus, sort overflows are very costly in an OLTP environment, and you should avoid them whenever possible. The database snapshot records sort overflows at the database level. Listing 12.4 shows a sample snapshot.

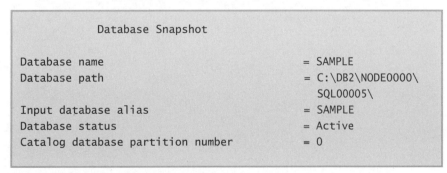

```
                    Database Snapshot

Database name                           = SAMPLE
Database path                           = C:\DB2\NODE0000\
                                          SQL00005\
Input database alias                    = SAMPLE
Database status                         = Active
Catalog database partition number       = 0
```

Listing 12.4: Database snapshot (part 1 of 5)

```
Catalog network node name                      =
Operating system running at database server = NT
Location of the database                       = Local
First database connect timestamp               = 07-18-2007
                                                 04:18:34.063360

Last reset timestamp                           =
Last backup timestamp                          = 07-18-2007
                                                 21:08:58.941289

Snapshot timestamp                             = 07-18-2007
                                                 12:05:42.025445


High water mark for connections                = 64
Application connects                           = 364
Secondary connects total                       = 0
Applications connected currently               = 62
Appls. executing in db manager currently       = 1
Agents associated with applications            = 62
Maximum agents associated with applications = 64
Maximum coordinating agents                    = 64


Locks held currently                           = 5
Lock waits                                      = 16
Time database waited on locks (ms)             = 647
Lock list memory in use (Bytes)                = 54480
Deadlocks detected                             = 0
Lock escalations                               = 0
Exclusive lock escalations                     = 0
Agents currently waiting on locks              = 0
Lock Timeouts                                   = 0
Number of indoubt transactions                 = 0


Total Private Sort heap allocated              = 86
Total Shared Sort heap allocated               = 0
Shared Sort heap high water mark               = 0
Total sorts                                     = 133507
Total sort time (ms)                            = 309525
Sort overflows                                  = 2538
Active sorts                                    = 2
```

Listing 12.4: Database snapshot (part 2 of 5)

```
Buffer pool data logical reads                  = 268585567
Buffer pool data physical reads                 = 40568061
Buffer pool temporary data logical reads        = 729534
Buffer pool temporary data physical reads       = 35038
Asynchronous pool data page reads               = 40078095
Buffer pool data writes                         = 71083
Asynchronous pool data page writes              = 71080
Buffer pool index logical reads                 = 2989423
Buffer pool index physical reads                = 94257
Buffer pool temporary index logical reads       = 0
Buffer pool temporary index physical reads      = 0
Asynchronous pool index page reads              = 58031
Buffer pool index writes                        = 2297
Asynchronous pool index page writes             = 2297
Total buffer pool read time (ms)                = 4925206
Total buffer pool write time (ms)               = 944594
Total elapsed asynchronous read time            = 4870965
Total elapsed asynchronous write time           = 944592
Asynchronous data read requests                 = 3657153
Asynchronous index read requests                = 5076
No victim buffers available                     = 13831
LSN Gap cleaner triggers                        = 0
Dirty page steal cleaner triggers               = 0
Dirty page threshold cleaner triggers           = 0
Time waited for prefetch (ms)                   = 293064
Unread prefetch pages                           = 5055916
Direct reads                                    = 76160
Direct writes                                   = 0
Direct read requests                            = 15139
Direct write requests                           = 0
Direct reads elapsed time (ms)                  = 1815
Direct write elapsed time (ms)                  = 0
Database files closed                           = 28
Data pages copied to extended storage           = 0
Index pages copied to extended storage          = 0
Data pages copied from extended storage         = 0
Index pages copied from extended storage        = 0
```

Listing 12.4: Database snapshot (part 3 of 5)

```
Host execution elapsed time                      = 0.045996

Commit statements attempted                      = 90191
Rollback statements attempted                    = 302
Dynamic statements attempted                     = 205787
Static statements attempted                      = 92255
Failed statement operations                      = 289
Select SQL statements executed                   = 91372
Update/Insert/Delete statements executed         = 8457
DDL statements executed                          = 107

Internal automatic rebinds                       = 0
Internal rows deleted                            = 0
Internal rows inserted                           = 1189
Internal rows updated                            = 1043
Internal commits                                 = 364
Internal rollbacks                               = 0
Internal rollbacks due to deadlock               = 0

Rows deleted                                     = 50
Rows inserted                                    = 6046
Rows updated                                     = 9366
Rows selected                                    = 229622
Rows read                                        = 549855688
Binds/precompiles attempted                      = 0
Log space available to the database (Bytes) = 20400000
Log space used by the database (Bytes)           = 0
Maximum secondary log space used (Bytes)         = 0
Maximum total log space used (Bytes)             = 0
Secondary logs allocated currently               = 0
Log pages read                                   = 0
Log read time (sec.ns)                           = 0.000000004
Log pages written                                = 0
Log write time (sec.ns)                          = 0.000000004
Number write log IOs                             = 0
Number read log IOs                              = 0
Number partial page log IOs                      = 0
```

Listing 12.4: Database snapshot (part 4 of 5)

```
Number log buffer full                      = 0
Log data found in buffer                    = 0
Appl id holding the oldest transaction      = 263
Log to be redone for recovery (Bytes)       = 0
Log accounted for by dirty pages (Bytes)    = 0


File number of first active log             = 0
File number of last active log              = 2
File number of current active log           = 0
File number of log being archived           = Not applicable


Package cache lookups                       = 99683
Package cache inserts                       = 7460
Package cache overflows                     = 1
Package cache high water mark (Bytes)       = 16073790
Application section lookups                 = 207549
Application section inserts                 = 20672


Catalog cache lookups                       = 33489
Catalog cache inserts                       = 89
Catalog cache overflows                     = 0
Catalog cache high water mark               = 0


Workspace Information
 Shared high water mark                     = 0
 Corresponding shared overflows             = 0
 Total shared section inserts               = 0
 Total shared section lookups               = 0
 Private high water mark                    = 14470317
 Corresponding private overflows            = 0
 Total private section inserts              = 20672
 Total private section lookups              = 98901


Number of hash joins                        = 291
Number of hash loops                        = 3
Number of hash join overflows               = 23
Number of small hash join overflows         = 10
```

Listing 12.4: Database snapshot (part 5 of 5)

You can also monitor the Health Center to determine whether sort overflows are occurring. Figure 12.8 shows a sort overflow warning captured by the Health Center. In this example, 40 percent of sorts overflowed during the one-minute monitoring interval.

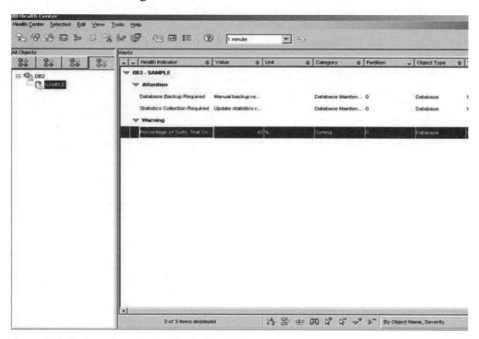

Figure 12.8: Sort overflow reported by the Health Center

Sort overflows should not occur in a pure OLTP environment. If you're experiencing sort overflows, you need to identify the SQL that is causing them and eliminate the sorts by tuning the SQL or redesigning indexes. You can use application snapshots, dynamic SQL snapshots, and event monitors to identify SQL statements causing sorts. Statements such as DISTINCT, ORDER BY, and GROUP BY cause rows to be returned in a specific order (or, in the case of DISTINCT, the elimination of duplicate rows). You can create indexes to eliminate sorts required by ORDER BY and GROUP BY statements. You can perform this task in conjunction with the Design Advisor. As of DB2 UDB V8.2, you can use statements in the package cache as input to Design Advisor. Another option is to take dynamic SQL snapshots and locate the snapshot output for the "Sort overflows" monitoring element. A non-zero value indicates SQL statements in need of tuning to eliminate sorts.

Hash Join Performance

Hash joins are enabled by default and provide significant performance improvements for most queries. The performance of hash joins is therefore important to the overall performance of the database. DB2 uses the sortheap as a work area while processing hash joins. Be sure to monitor and track the following database snapshot monitoring elements:

- *Number of small hash join overflows:* This element records the number of hash joins that overflowed sortheap when the amount of sortheap required was within 10 percent of the sortheap database configuration parameter setting. If the number of small hash join overflows is relatively high, consider increasing the sortheap value in small increments until small hash join overflows no longer occur or occur infrequently. This tuning is best done through a trial-and-error method.

- *Number of hash join overflows:* This element records the number of hash joins that overflow. If hash join overflows are occurring, first make sure you've undertaken an SQL tuning effort to eliminate sorts, thereby reducing the amount of sort activity. If you've tuned SQL, increase sortheap and then increase sheapthres if possible. Then evaluate your changes to see whether you've eliminated or reduced the number of hash join overflows. Don't increase sortheap to the point that swapping occurs, because that will offset the benefits of a larger sortheap. Again, use a trial-and-error process to perform this tuning.

- *Number of hash loops:* This element records the number of hash loops that have occurred. Hash loops occur when the inner table of a hash join has been written to a temporary table on disk and the matching rows of the outer table of a hash join are also written to a disk. You should avoid hash loops if at all possible. Take action as previously described for hash join overflows, but don't increase sortheap so as to reach the sheapthres value or to cause swapping.

Locking Performance

DB2 is designed to provide an efficient and reliable locking mechanism. Row-level locking is provided by default, offering a high degree of concurrency. Lock performance monitoring is provided via database, lock, and application snapshots along with SQL table functions and event monitoring.

Locklist High Water Mark

In addition to the database snapshot (classic snapshot or administrative routines), you can use the Health Monitor, Memory Tracker, and utility db2pd to monitor and track lock manager heap (locklist) usage at the database level. Listing 12.5 presents sample Memory Tracker output showing heap high water marks (HWMs).

```
db2mtrk -i -p -w
Tracking Memory on: 2007/11/12 at 14:04:25

Memory for instance

    Backup/Restore/Util Heap is of size 16384 bytes
    Package Cache is of size 22528000 bytes
    Catalog Cache Heap is of size 1572864 bytes
    Buffer Pool Heap is of size 33177600 bytes
    Buffer Pool Heap is of size 105676800 bytes
    Buffer Pool Heap is of size 211107840 bytes
    Buffer Pool Heap is of size 8912896 bytes
    Buffer Pool Heap is of size 819200 bytes
    Buffer Pool Heap is of size 557056 bytes
    Buffer Pool Heap is of size 425984 bytes
    Buffer Pool Heap is of size 360448 bytes
    Lock Manager Heap is of size 8421376 bytes
    Database Heap is of size 4718592 bytes
```

Listing 12.5: Memory Tracker output showing locklist HWM

The sample output indicates that more than 8 MB of locklist memory has been used and is the current HWM. You can also obtain the amount of used locklist memory by taking a database snapshot and reviewing the "Lock list memory in use" monitoring element. Make sure the amount of locklist memory used does not exceed 50 percent of the locklist as defined by the locklist database configuration parameter. When the locklist fills up, lock escalations occur until there is free locklist memory available. Lock escalations can happen quickly, and if enough available locklist isn't reserved for peak conditions, the locklist can fill up and lock escalations can occur, increasing database manager overhead and reducing concurrency until enough locklist memory is available. The db2mtrk utility is also useful for tracking agent memory usage.

Lock Escalations

The "Lock escalations" database monitoring element reports the number of times row-level locks have been escalated to table locks. Lock escalations can be caused by the locklist value being too small (the default of fifty 4 K pages is generally too low; see the formula in the *DB2 UDB Administration Guide: Performance* for use in setting locklist), parameter maxlocks set too low, or an application using an excessive number of locks. Before increasing locklist, review the applications to determine whether an application is causing the problem by not committing or perhaps is not committing frequently enough, is looping, or is responsible in some other way. The default maxlocks value of 22 percent for DB2 on Windows platforms is a good starting point but may be a bit low for many applications. Consider using a value of 30 percent instead. However, don't increase set maxlocks higher than 30 percent without ensuring that the application is committing frequently (say, every 1,000 to 2,000 updates) because increasing maxlocks unnecessarily can mask application design problems. Lock escalation is the mechanism DB2 uses to improve concurrency by freeing row locks and taking table locks instead.

Exclusive Lock Escalations

The "Exclusive lock escalations" database monitoring element reports either the number of times that several row locks have been escalated to one exclusive table lock or the number of times an exclusive lock on a row caused the table lock to become an exclusive lock. Other applications can't access data being held by an exclusive lock, so it's important to resolve exclusive lock escalations if they're occurring. Review the lock mode being used by the applications involved, and consider using shared locks if applicable.

Deadlocks Detected

The "Deadlocks detected" database monitoring element reports the number of times the DB2 deadlock detector has identified deadlocks. The deadlock detector checks for deadlocks based on the value defined for the dlchktime database configuration parameter. The default value of 10 seconds (expressed in milliseconds) is generally adequate. If deadlocks are occurring, review your application design and locking strategies.

If unnecessary lock escalations are occurring frequently, a locking-related problem is likely and should be investigated to determine the cause. Infrequent escalations (no more than a few an hour) are a natural database mechanism and shouldn't be cause for alarm. If unnecessary exclusive lock escalations and deadlocks are occurring at all, you should investigate your applications and application locking strategies.

Resolving Lock Contention Using the Activity Monitor

As I've noted, you can use the Activity Monitor to resolve realtime lock contention. Figure 12.9 shows an example of solving an application locking situation using the Activity Monitor.

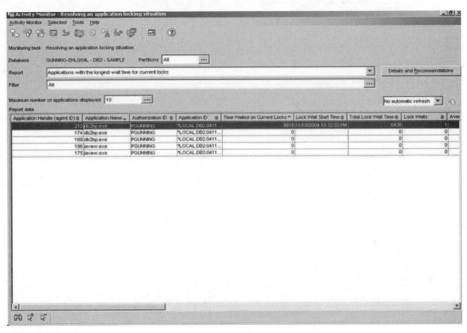

Figure 12.9: Resolving lock contention with the Activity Monitor

Here, we've selected the "Applications with the longest wait time for current locks" report and asked to see the top 10 applications. To review the lock chains for AGENTID 210, right-click on that application and select the **Show Lock Chains** option as shown in Figure 12.10.

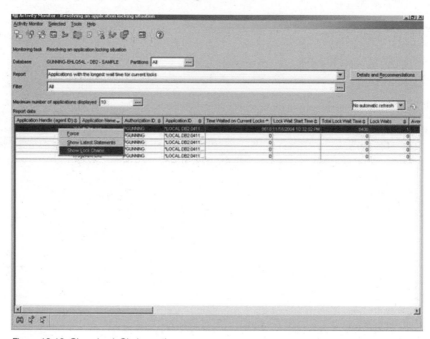

Figure 12.10: Show Lock Chains option

The lock chain for AGENT ID 210 is displayed as shown in Figure 12.11.

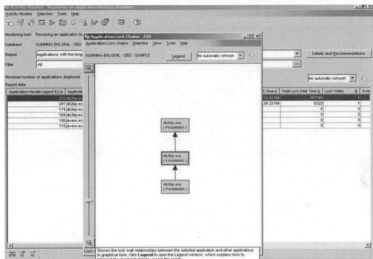

Figure 12.11: Lock chains

To review the lock details, right-click on the application in question and select **Show Lock Details** as shown in Figure 12.12.

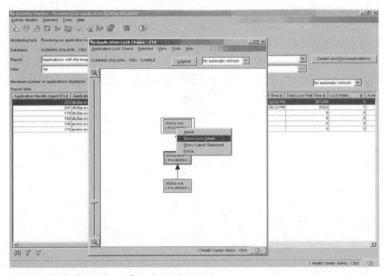

Figure 12.12: Show Lock Details option

The lock details, showing the lock holder and lock waiters, are displayed as shown in Figure 12.13.

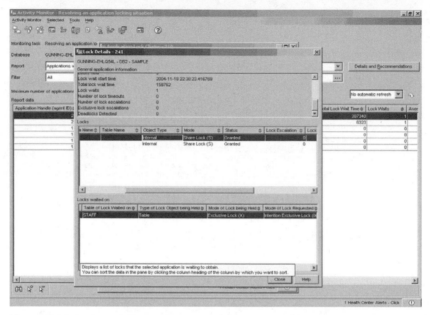

Figure 12.13: Lock resolution

From the displayed information, we can tell that the AGENTID 210 application (whose details appear in the lower part of the pane) was holding the lock (it had an exclusive lock on the STAFF table and had not released it, not shown) and that AGENTID 241 (upper part of the pane) was waiting for AGENTID 210 to release the lock on the STAFF table.

You can use the Activity Monitor to solve realtime locking problems on a routine basis.

Buffer Pool Performance

Properly configured buffer pools are one of the most important DB2 memory areas. Because data found in the buffer pool is accessed approximately

1,000 times faster than data accessed on disk, improperly configured buffer pools can have a significant negative impact on performance. With a 32-bit implementation on Windows, all DB2 buffer pools combined are limited to about 1.75 GB in size. With the Windows .INI /3GB switch enabled, this limit is increased to between 2 GB and 3 GB because the switch causes the Windows OS to make another 1 GB of virtual memory available to DB2. Of course, with 64-bit implementations, buffer pool size restrictions are almost unlimited (at least for the time being). Buffer pool and table space performance is best monitored by using buffer pool snapshots and table space snapshots, which provide similar data. Listing 12.6 shows a sample a buffer pool snapshot.

```
                   Bufferpool Snapshot

Bufferpool name                          = BP1
Database name                            = SAMPLE
Database path                            = C:\DB2\NODE0000\
                                           SQL00005\
Input database alias                     = SAMPLE
Snapshot timestamp                       = 07-17-2007
                                           15:31:04.824608


Buffer pool data logical reads           = 81892379
Buffer pool data physical reads          = 31015110
Buffer pool temporary data logical reads  - 1134648
Buffer pool temporary data physical reads = 25512
Buffer pool data writes                  = 62897
Buffer pool index logical reads          = 0
Buffer pool index physical reads         = 0
Buffer pool temporary index logical reads  = 0
Buffer pool temporary index physical reads = 0
Total buffer pool read time (ms)         = 4268665
Total buffer pool write time (ms)        = 770189
Asynchronous pool data page reads        = 30771234
Asynchronous pool data page writes       = 62893
Buffer pool index writes                 = 0
Asynchronous pool index page reads       = 0
```

Listing 12.6: Buffer pool snapshot (part 1 of 4)

```
Asynchronous pool index page writes      = 0
Total elapsed asynchronous read time     = 4232777
Total elapsed asynchronous write time    = 770189
Asynchronous data read requests          = 3622339
Asynchronous index read requests         = 0
No victim buffers available              = 16259
Direct reads                             = 0
Direct writes                            = 0
Direct read requests                     = 0
Direct write requests                    = 0
Direct reads elapsed time (ms)           = 0
Direct write elapsed time (ms)           = 0
Database files closed                    = 35
Data pages copied to extended storage    = 0
Index pages copied to extended storage   = 0
Data pages copied from extended storage  = 0
Index pages copied from extended storage = 0
Unread prefetch pages                    = 207985
Vectored IOs                             = 1344600
Pages from vectored IOs                  = 20323522
Block IOs                                = 0
Pages from block IOs                     = 0
Physical page maps                       = 0


Node number                              = 0
Tablespaces using bufferpool             = 11


Alter bufferpool information:
  Pages left to remove                   = 0
  Current size                           = 50000
  Post-alter size                        = 50000



              Bufferpool Snapshot


Bufferpool name                          = BP2
Database name                            = SAMPLE
```

Listing 12.6: Buffer pool snapshot (part 2 of 4)

```
Database path                                = C:\DB2\NODE0000\
                                               SQL00005\
Input database alias                         = SAMPLE
Snapshot timestamp                           = 07-17-2007
                                               15:31:04.824608


Buffer pool data logical reads               = 214
Buffer pool data physical reads              = 24
Buffer pool temporary data logical reads     = 0
Buffer pool temporary data physical reads    = 0
Buffer pool data writes                      = 13
Buffer pool index logical reads              = 3851902
Buffer pool index physical reads             = 69990
Buffer pool temporary index logical reads    = 0
Buffer pool temporary index physical reads   = 0
Total buffer pool read time (ms)             = 52124
Total buffer pool write time (ms)            = 9306
Asynchronous pool data page reads            = 0
Asynchronous pool data page writes           = 13
Buffer pool index writes                     = 6436
Asynchronous pool index page reads           = 44402
Asynchronous pool index page writes          = 6436
Total elapsed asynchronous read time         = 18330
Total elapsed asynchronous write time        = 9306
Asynchronous data read requests              = 0
Asynchronous index read requests             = 3680
No victim buffers available                  = 0
Direct reads                                 = 0
Direct writes                                = 0
Direct read requests                         = 0
Direct write requests                        = 0
Direct reads elapsed time (ms)               = 0
Direct write elapsed time (ms)               = 0
Database files closed                        = 3
Data pages copied to extended storage        = 0
Index pages copied to extended storage       = 0
Data pages copied from extended storage      = 0
```

Listing 12.6: Buffer pool snapshot (part 3 of 4)

```
Index pages copied from extended storage   = 0
Unread prefetch pages                      = 1573
Vectored IOs                               = 3680
Pages from vectored IOs                    = 44402
Block IOs                                  = 0
Pages from block IOs                       = 0
Physical page maps                         = 0

Node number                                = 0
Tablespaces using bufferpool               = 9

Alter bufferpool information:
 Pages left to remove                      = 0
 Current size                              = 25000
 Post-alter size                           = 25000
```

Listing 12.6: Buffer pool snapshot (part 4 of 4)

You can monitor and track table space performance using buffer pool and table space snapshots. These snapshots provide essentially the same data, but table space snapshots let you use all the performance metrics available to buffer pools to compute similar metrics for each table space. This capability is especially important because it enables you to review individual table space performance and target table spaces with suboptimal performance for tuning efforts. The monitoring elements listed in Table 12.1 apply to buffer pools and table spaces. These elements enable you to monitor, track, and tune buffer pools and table spaces to achieve business objectives.

Table 12.1: Buffer pool and table space monitoring elements	
Monitoring element	**Description**
Buffer pool data logical reads	The number of pages read from the buffer pool and physically read from disk. To determine the number of logical reads (pages found in the buffer pool), subtract "Buffer pool data physical reads" from "Buffer pool data logical reads."
Buffer pool data physical reads	The number of pages physically read from disk (i.e., not found in the buffer pool). In an OLTP environment, you should minimize the number of physical reads. In a BI/DW environment, where you typically have very large tables, this is not possible, and you should concentrate on tuning the I/O subsystem (table space layout, containers, number of physical disks, multiple containers for system temporary space).
Buffer pool temporary data logical reads	The total number of logical read requests that required I/O to get data pages into system temporary table space. This element was added in a DB2 UDB V8.1 fix pack.
Buffer pool temporary data physical reads	The number of physical disk reads required to get data pages from disk into the system temporary table space.
Buffer pool data writes	The number of times a buffer pool data page was written (a physical write) to disk.
Buffer pool index logical reads	The number of logical read requests for index pages that have been read from the buffer pool and from disk.
Buffer pool index physical reads	The number of times an index page was read from disk into the buffer pool.
Buffer pool temporary index logical reads	The number of logical read requests that required I/O to get index pages into the system temporary table space.
Buffer pool temporary index physical reads	The number of physical read requests that required I/O to get pages into the system temporary table space.
Total buffer pool read time (ms)	The total amount of elapsed time spent processing read requests that required index or data pages to be physically read from disk into the buffer pool. This element includes synchronous reads done by the agents and asynchronous writes done by the prefetchers.
Total buffer pool write time (ms)	The total amount of elapsed time spent physically writing index or data pages from the buffer pool to disk. This value includes data written by agents and page cleaners.
Asynchronous pool data page reads	The number of pages read asynchronously (by the prefetchers) into the buffer pool.

Table 12.1: Buffer pool and table space monitoring elements (continued)	
Monitoring element	**Description**
Asynchronous pool data page writes	The number of times a buffer pool page was physically written to disk by either an asynchronous page cleaner or a prefetcher. Prefetchers may write dirty pages to disk to make room for pages being prefetched into the buffer pool.
Buffer pool index writes	The number of times a buffer pool index page was physically written to disk. A buffer pool index page is written to disk either to free a page in the buffer pool so another page can be brought in or to flush the buffer pool.
Asynchronous pool index page reads	The number of index pages that were read into the buffer pool asynchronously by a prefetcher.
Asynchronous pool index page writes	The number of times an index page was physically written to disk. This could have been by an asynchronous page cleaner or a prefetcher. Remember, a prefetcher may write dirty index pages to disk to make room for pages being prefetched.
Total elapsed asynchronous read time	The total elapsed read time for prefetch requests.
Total elapsed asynchronous write time	The total elapsed time spent writing index or data pages from the buffer pool to disk by the page cleaners.
Asynchronous data read requests	The number of pages prefetched into the buffer pool (read asynchronously).
Asynchronous index read requests	The number of index pages prefetched into the buffer pool (read asynchronously).
No victim buffers available	The total number of times a victim buffer pool page was not available, which requires the agent to read the page into the buffer pool. See the additional description in the "Page-Cleaning Activity" section.
Direct reads	The number of direct read operations. Direct read operations do not use the buffer pool.
Direct writes	The number of direct write operations. Direct write operations do not use the buffer pool. Both direct reads and writes are performed in units, usually in 512-byte sectors. Direct reads and writes are used for reading or writing rows that contain the following data types: • LONG VARCHAR columns • Large object columns • Backup operations
Direct read requests	The number of requests to perform a direct read.

Table 12.1: Buffer pool and table space monitoring elements (continued)	
Monitoring element	**Description**
Direct write requests	The number of requests to perform a direct write.
Direct reads elapsed time (ms)	The total elapsed time in milliseconds to perform direct reads.
Direct write elapsed time (ms)	The total elapsed time in milliseconds to perform direct writes.
Database files closed	The total number of database files closed. This element is related to the setting of the database configuration parameter maxfilop. Files are open when data is required to be read into the buffer pool. Parameter maxfilop controls the maximum number of open files that an application may use. When this limit is exceeded, the element is incremented to report at the database level the number of database files closed. In OLTP environment, the number of database files should be 0 (zero) or close to 0. Monitor and adjust this parameter as necessary to achieve this goal.
Unread prefetch pages	The number of pages prefetched into the buffer pool but never used.
Vectored IOs	How often vectored I/O is conducted on those systems that support vectored I/O.
Pages from vectored IOs	The total number of pages read by vectored I/Os.
Block IOs	The number of block I/O requests requested. The value is an indicator of how often the system is performing block I/O. If this number is very high or very low, consider changing the block size. The extent size of the table spaces involved should match the block size defined on the block based buffer pool definition. If too many pages would be wasted using block I/O because of extent/block size mismatches, DB2 will revert to page based I/O.
Pages from block IOs	The total number of pages read by block I/O.
Tablespaces using bufferpool	The number of table spaces assigned to this buffer pool (that have been used).
Alter bufferpool information	Information provided after an alter has been performed on the table space.
Pages left to remove	The number of pages left to remove from the buffer pool to set the buffer pool to the specified size.
Current size	The size of the buffer pool in pages before an ALTER BUFFERPOOL command has been issued.
Post-alter size	The size of the buffer pool in pages after an alter operation has been completed

With that background on the monitoring elements provided by the buffer pool snapshot, let's turn our attention to some important buffer pool performance metrics that you should compute and track on a regular basis. These values will give you an accurate view of how buffer pools and table spaces are performing over time. As you learned in Chapter 11, both classic snapshots and SQL administrative routines are available for buffer pools and table spaces. Recall that SQL administrative routines enable you to insert snapshot data into DB2 tables, providing a historical snapshot repository for evaluating and tracking buffer pool and table space performance over time. The snapshot repository is an essential element in a good monitoring strategy. The performance metrics described in the following paragraphs were computed using the sample buffer pool snapshot (using buffer pools BP1 and BP2 where indicated) you saw in Listing 12.6.

Buffer Pool Combined Hit Ratio

The buffer pool *combined hit ratio (CBHR)* combines the index and data page hit rates so you can monitor overall buffer pool performance. You compute the CBHR as follows:

CBHR = 1 − ((*Buffer pool data physical reads + Buffer pool index physical reads / Buffer pool data logical reads +Buffer pool index logical reads*))

Plugging in the monitoring element values from Listing 12.6 yields the following result:

1 − ((1881286 + 253147) / (5998850 + 72112618))) = .9727

You can also compute the CBHR using the following SQL statement against the table containing the output from the SYSIBMADM.SNAPBP administrative view:

```
SELECT bp_name, 100 -
 COALESCE(DECIMAL(DECIMAL(100) *
 (pool_index_p_reads + pool_data_p_reads) /
  NULLIF((pool_index_l_reads + pool_data_l_reads),0)
                                  ,5,2)
                                  ,0)

AS overall_hit_ratio
FROM sysibmadm.snapbp
;
```

Buffer Pool Index Hit Ratio

The buffer pool *index hit ratio (IHR)* computes the number of times an index page was found in the buffer pool versus having to be retrieved from disk. You should monitor the index hit ratio over time. This metric is especially important when you haven't separated index table spaces and data table spaces into different buffer pools. You compute the IHR as follows:

IHR = 1 – (*B*uffer pool index physical reads / *B*uffer pool index logical reads)

Using the values from Listing 12.6:

1 – (253147 / 72112618) = .9965

You can also compute the IHR using the following SQL statement against the table containing the output from the SYSIBMADM.SNAPBP administrative view:

```
SELECT bp_name, 100 -
  COALESCE(DECIMAL(DECIMAL(100) * pool_index_p_reads /
   NULLIF(pool_index_l_reads,0)
                          ,5,2)
                          ,0)
AS index_hit_ratio
FROM sysibmadm.snapbp;
```

435

Buffer Pool Data Hit Ratio

The buffer pool *data hit ratio (DHR)* records the number of times a data page was found in the buffer pool versus having to be retrieved from disk. You should monitor the data hit ratio over time. This metric is especially important when you haven't separated index table spaces and data table spaces into different buffer pools. You compute the DHR as follows:

DHR = 1 − (*Buffer pool data physical reads / Buffer pool data logical reads*)

Using the values from Listing 12.6:

1 − (1881286 / 5998850) = .6864

As with previously shown commands, you can also obtain the DHR by computing it from the SYSIBMADM.SNAPBP administrative view.

Asynchronous Read Milliseconds

The *asynchronous read milliseconds (ARMS)* metric computes the average time it takes to complete an asynchronous I/O. You calculate the value as follows:

ARMS = (*Total elapsed asynchronous read time (ms)*) / (*Asynchronous pool data page reads* + *Asynchronous pool index page reads*)

Using the values from Listing 12.6 for buffer pool BP1:

4232777 / (30771234 + 0) = .1375 ms

You should compute and compare the ARMS value for all table spaces to identify table spaces with high read times.

Synchronous Read Milliseconds

The *synchronous read milliseconds (SRMS)* metric computes the average time to complete a synchronous read. You calculate the value as follows:

SRMS = (*Total bufferpool read time (ms) – Total elapsed asynchronous read time*) / ((*Bufferpool data physical reads + Bufferpool index physical reads*) *– (Asynchronous pool data page reads + Asynchronous pool index page reads*))

Using the values from Listing 12.6 for buffer pool BP2:

(52124 – 18330) / ((24 + 69990) – (0 + 44402)) = 1.39 ms

Again, monitor the value over time and compute it for all table spaces. Investigate table spaces with above-average SRMS values further to identify possible problems with container placement, too many containers per physical disk, or too few physical disks available.

Asynchronous Pages Read per Request

The *asynchronous pages read per request (APPR)* metric provides a measure of prefetch effectiveness. The table space prefetchsize parameter specifies how many pages are asynchronously prefetched into the buffer pool in anticipation of the application needing them. If the APPR value is less than prefetchsize for the table space, the buffer pool may be overheated or prefetchsize may be set too high. Possible solutions are to increase the size of the buffer pool, move the table space to a new buffer pool, or reduce the prefetchsize value. You compute the APPR as follows:

APPR = (*Asynchronous pool data page reads + Asynchronous pool index page reads*) / (*Asynchronous data read requests + Asynchronous index read requests*)

Using the values from Listing 12.6 for buffer pool BP1:

(30771234 + 0) / (3622339) = 8.49

Because 8.49 pages is less than the extentsize, you should conduct further analysis to determine the cause of the low APPR. Possible causes for a low APPR include too few configured page cleaners or an overheated (undersized) buffer pool.

Physical Pages Read per Minute

The *physical pages read per minute (PPRPM)* metric measures buffer pool effectiveness given a steady workload. You can use this value as a gauge to measure table space activity over time. By monitoring PPRPM, you can identify peak periods over time and various types of database activity (processing). DBAs can use PPRPM to rank table spaces based on physical I/O activity and then target table spaces with high PPRPM for potential buffer pool reassignment or enlargement of the existing buffer pool. To obtain the highest degree of I/O throughput, allocate multiple containers spread over multiple physical disks to table spaces with high PPRPM values.

You compute the PPRPM as follows:

PPRPM = (*Buffer pool data physical reads* + *Buffer pool index physical reads*) / (*Number of elapsed minutes since monitor switches activated or reset*)

Note that it is not uncommon for high-volume databases to read 100,000 physical pages per minute.

Asynchronous Write Milliseconds

Asynchronous write milliseconds (AWMS) computes the average time it takes to complete an asynchronous write. You compute the value as follows:

AWMS= *Total elapsed asynchronous write time(ms)* / (*Asynchronous pool data page writes* + *Asynchronous pool index page writes*)

Using the values from Listing 12.6 for buffer pool BP1:

770189 / (62893 + 0) = 12.24 ms

An AWMS value of 12.24 ms is on the high side. Well-tuned databases should experience AWMSs of around 1 ms. To detect possible asynchronous write problems, review the number of page cleaners, container numbers, and container placement.

Overall Read Milliseconds

The *overall read milliseconds (ORMS)* metric represents the overall read time (physical reads) for a table space. You should compute and compare this value for all table spaces. A high ORMS could be an indicator of table space containers on the same disk, containers of unequal size, or hot controllers or disks. Calculate the ORMS as follows (to determine the time agents spent waiting for data):

ORMS = (*Total bufferpool read time (ms)* / (*Bufferpool data physical reads* + *Bufferpool index physical reads*)

Using the values from Listing 12.6 for buffer pool BP1:

4268665 / (31015110 +0) = .1376 ms

Asynchronous Read Ratio

The *asynchronous read ratio (ARR)* computes the percentage of asynchronous read activity for the buffer pool or table space. In DW/BI environments, the ARR should be approximately 90 percent because these environments use more prefetching to bring data into the buffer pool due to the size of the tables. In a highly tuned OLTP environment, the ARR should be less than 10 percent because OLTP environments should use synchronous reads for index access. Calculate the ARR as follows:

ARR = ((*Asynchronous pool data page reads* + *Asynchronous pool index page reads*) / ((*Buffer pool index logical reads* + *Buffer pool data logical reads*)) * 100

Using the values from Listing 12.6 for buffer pool BP1:

((30771234 + 0) / (0 + 81892379)) * 100 = 37 percent

An ARR of 37 percent for a data table space buffer pool is on the low side. This value should be closer to 90 percent. The low ratio could be caused by a shortage of prefetchers or by table spaces having only one container defined. You can also use the SYSIBMADM.SNAPBP administrative view as follows:

```
select BP_NAME,
(INT(((FLOAT(pool_Async_Data_Reads + Pool_Async_Index_Reads)) /
(FLOAT(Pool_Index_L_Reads + Pool_Data_Reads))) * 100))
AS Asynch_Read_Ratio
FROM sysibmadm.snapbp;
```

Synchronous Write Milliseconds

Synchronous write milliseconds (SWMS) is an important metric to compute and track on a regular basis. SWMS represents the average time it takes for a synchronous write to be completed. You can compute the value at the database, buffer pool, and table space levels. Listing 12.7 shows part of a database snapshot used to computer the SWMS at the database level.

```
              Database Snapshot

Buffer pool data logical reads            = 5998850
Buffer pool data physical reads           = 1881286
Buffer pool temporary data logical reads  = 129322
Buffer pool temporary data physical reads = 8172
Asynchronous pool data page reads         = 1724737
```

Listing 12.7: Database snapshot excerpt (part 1 of 1)

```
Buffer pool data writes                       = 37515
Asynchronous pool data page writes            = 30079
Buffer pool index logical reads               = 72112618
Buffer pool index physical reads              = 253147
Buffer pool temporary index logical reads  = 0
Buffer pool temporary index physical reads = 0
Asynchronous pool index page reads            = 3887
Buffer pool index writes                      = 64425
Asynchronous pool index page writes           = 58041
Total buffer pool read time (ms)              = 1445756
Total buffer pool write time (ms)             = 7080754
Total elapsed asynchronous read time          = 1073958
Total elapsed asynchronous write time         = 6944166
Asynchronous data read requests               = 722698
Asynchronous index read requests              = 2006
No victim buffers available                   = 2052862
LSN Gap cleaner triggers                      = 0
Dirty page steal cleaner triggers             = 849
Dirty page threshold cleaner triggers         = 565
Time waited for prefetch (ms)                 = 354849
Unread prefetch pages                         = 178
Direct reads                                  = 16820
Direct writes                                 = 8576
Direct read requests                          = 3616
Direct write requests                         = 1751
Direct reads elapsed time (ms)                = 5137
Direct write elapsed time (ms)                = 2947
Database files closed                         = 1
Data pages copied to extended storage         = 0
Index pages copied to extended storage        = 0
Data pages copied from extended storage       = 0
Index pages copied from extended storage      = 0
```

Listing 12.7: Database snapshot excerpt (part 1 of 2)

Using the following equation and the sample data shown in the snapshot, we can compute SWMS as follows:

SWMS = (*Total buffer pool write time* – *Total elapsed asynchronous write time*)
/ ((*Bufferpool data writes* + *Buffer pool index writes*) – (*Asynchronous pool
data page writes* + *Asynchronous pool index page writes*))

(7080754 – 6944166) / ((37515 + 64425) – (30079 + 58041) = 9.88 ms

With good cache hits and depending on your environment, SWMS should
be less than 3 ms. Because our example yields an SWMS of 9.88 ms, the
I/O subsystem, container placement, number of containers per physical disk,
and number of physical disks available to the database should be reviewed to
identify causes of high SWMS. Table space snapshots can assist you in this
investigation by isolating the time to a specific table space.

Page-Cleaning Activity

DB2 uses page cleaners to write dirty buffer pool pages to disk. The database
configuration parameter num_iocleaners controls how many page cleaners
are available for a database. The threshold parameter chngpgs_thresh controls
when page cleaners are activated or awakened. The default threshold is 60
percent. In other words, if 60 percent of pages in the buffer pool are dirty, page
cleaners will write dirty pages to disk asynchronously so that agents don't have
to wait for dirty pages to be written when looking for pages in the buffer pool.

This behavior is good because we want page cleaning to occur asynchronously.
If the buffer pool fills up with dirty pages and no page cleaner is available, the
agent will have to cause the synchronous write to disk to occur, making applications wait until the write is completed. When agents wait, database users
experience longer response times, which generally is not good. Configure
the num_iocleaners parameter to the number of CPUs (include hardware
multithreading degree), and monitor and adjust its value as necessary
over time.

Dirty Page Steal Cleaner Triggers

The database snapshot's "Dirty page steal cleaner triggers" monitoring element records the number of times the page cleaners were triggered to write dirty pages to disk. Dirty pages are not written to disk as soon as they become dirty but when they are chosen as a victim, when the chngpgs_thresh is reached, when the softmax database configuration parameter is exceeded, or when a page contributes or is projected to contribute to an LSN gap. Dirty page steal cleaner triggers degrade performance because applications wait while this activity is occurring. Dirty page steal cleaner triggers are triggered when there are no victim pages available. This situation can be caused by the buffer pool being too small, the chngpgs_thresh not being reached, or too few page cleaners configured. If dirty page steal cleaner triggers are occurring frequently, consider lowering the chngpgs_thresh setting to a value of 20 percent to 30 percent for OLTP databases and increasing the size of the buffer pool if possible. Also consider enabling alternate page cleaning.

No Victim Buffers Available

The database snapshot's "No victim buffers available" monitoring element records the number of times an agent did not have a preselected victim buffer available. As pages are updated in the buffer pool, they become "dirty" pages until they are written to disk. After a changed page is written to disk, it becomes a clean page but remains in the buffer pool until its space is needed for new pages. Page cleaners normally write changed pages to disk asynchronously in the background. Clean pages that have been written to disk become eligible to be "victim" pages and are maintained on a victim list. Then, when an agent needs to add pages to the buffer pool, it searches the buffer pool for victim pages and uses them. However, if no victim buffers are available, the agent has to write changed page(s) to disk to make room for the new page(s). When this happens, the application waits. This situation can occur when not enough page cleaners are configured, the buffer pool is too small, or the chngpgs_thresh isn't being hit often enough. In these situations, consider using proactive page cleaning by enabling the DB2_USE_ALTERNATE_PAGE_CLEANING registry variable. When enabled, agents are informed of victim pages by means of a victim page list and can select preselected victim page(s) from the list instead of searching the entire buffer pool.

> **Note:** When the DB2 registry variable DB2_USE_ALTERNATE_PAGE_ CLEANING is enabled (set to ON), DB2 uses a new page-cleaning algorithm and does not use chngpgs_thresh. The new algorithm uses more even page cleaning so that I/O spikes don't occur. Consider setting this variable for high-volume OLTP databases.

Prefetching Performance

When an application uses sequential access, DB2 uses prefetchers to prefetch data into the buffer pool in advance of the application needing it. This prevents the application from waiting while data is retrieved from disk.

The num_ioservers database configuration parameter specifies how many prefetchers will be available to DB2. As agents request that pages be brought into the buffer pool, prefetch requests are placed on a common prefetch queue. Requests are processed from the queue in a first-in, first-out (FIFO) manner. At times, a prefetcher may not be available. In this case, the agent does the prefetch request, which causes the application to wait until the request is completed. This situation is usually undesirable because we don't want agents to wait. As a rule of thumb, configure as many prefetchers as the number of physical disks. DB2 tries to create a prefetcher for each container to obtain parallel I/O.

Logging Performance

The database snapshot extract in Listing 12.8 shows some new logging snapshot monitoring elements that have been added to the database snapshot (and associated SQL snapshot table function) to enable better monitoring and tuning of logging activity.

```
Log pages read                              = 0
Log read time (sec.ns)                      = 0.000000004
Log pages written                           = 9655347
Log write time (sec.ns)                     = 19733.000000004
Number write log IOs                        = 9215357
Number read log IOs                         = 0
Number partial page log IOs                 = 4125121
Number log buffer full                      = 0
Log data found in buffer                    = 0
Appl id holding the oldest transaction      = 760
Log to be redone for recovery (Bytes)       = 104095185
Log accounted for by dirty pages (Bytes)    = 103134227
```

Listing 12.8: Log-related monitoring elements in database snapshot

Table 12.2 defines the new logging performance snapshot elements and provides recommendations for their monitoring.

Table 12.2: New logging performance snapshot monitoring elements		
Monitoring element	**Description**	**Recommendations**
Log pages read	Number of log pages read from disk by the DB2 logger.	The logger could be reading log pages from disk due to rollbacks. Monitor this element over time to determine what is normal activity in your environment. Once you determine what is normal, monitor this element for excessive log pages read. Investigate application changes and review the db2diag log and administration notification log to diagnose problems.
Log read time (sec.ns)	Amount of time the logger has taken to read log pages from disk.	Compare this element's time with the average time to read a page from other disks to ensure that there is not a bottleneck reading the DB2 log from disk. Logs should be placed on the fastest disks in your system; therefore, the read times should be better than the average for other table spaces.

Table 12.2: New logging performance snapshot monitoring elements (continued)		
Monitoring element	**Description**	**Recommendations**
Log pages written	Number of log pages written to disk by the DB2 logger.	Because the last log page may not be full, the partial log page remains in the log buffer and additional records are written to the log page. The partial log page may be written to disk more than once. Therefore, you should not use this element to measure the number of log pages used by DB2.
Log write time (sec.ns)	Total elapsed time spent by the DB2 logger writing to disk.	Use this element with "Log pages written" to determine whether log writes are performing adequately. Average log writes should be less than a millisecond or no more than a few milliseconds at most. If log writes are higher, review disks assigned to the log to ensure that no other table spaces are conflicting with log writes and that the logs are on a fast disk.
Number log write IOs	Number of I/O requests issued by the DB2 logger for writing log data to disk.	
Number read log IOs	Number of I/O requests issued by the DB2 logger for reading log data from disk.	
Number partial page log IOs	Number of I/O requests issued by the DB2 logger for writing partial log data to disk.	
Number log buffer full	Number of times agents had to wait for log data to be written to disk while copying log records into the log buffer. This element is incremented per agent per incident.	If log buffer full occurs frequently, consider increasing the size of the log buffer (logbufsz database configuration parameter). My experience has shown that the logbufsz parameter is usually set too low; 512 or 1,024 4 K pages is a good range for this setting.

Table 12.2: New logging performance snapshot monitoring elements (continued)		
Monitoring element	**Description**	**Recommendations**
Log data found in buffer	Number of times an agent read log pages from the log buffer. It is preferable for an agent to read data from the log buffer rather than from disk.	
Log to be redone for recovery (bytes)	Amount of the log (in bytes) that will have to be redone for crash recovery. DB2 calculates this value at the time the snapshot is taken.	Monitor this element over time. If it appears to be excessive, check the logs accounted for by the dirty pages element to see whether page cleaning needs to be improved.
Log accounted for by dirty pages (bytes)	Amount of the log (in bytes) corresponding to the difference between the oldest dirty page in the database and the top of the active log. DB2 calculates this when the snapshot is taken.	You can use this element to determine the effectiveness of page cleaning. If page cleaning is effective, log_held_by_dirty_pages should be less than or approximately equal to the following: (softmax / 100) * logfilsiz * 4096 If this statement is not true, consider increasing the number of page cleaners. Note that you should monitor this element over time and make changes only after running a representative workload.

> **Note:** Because of the high amount of write activity to the logs, it is imperative that DB2 logs be placed on a dedicated array with sufficient physical disks. If not placed on a separate array, logging can become the bottleneck in your DB2. Use the newlogpath database configuration parameter to change the default logpath.

Summary

This chapter presented the memory and process models used by DB2 and discussed associated monitoring elements. You've seen how to use the output from various monitoring tools to measure and tune DB2 performance. The important instance and database monitoring elements were identified and tuning recommendations provided. STMM was highlighted and explained. Database, sort, lock and buffer pool tuning were highlighted using the Health Monitor, Activity Monitor, and buffer pool snapshots. Performance metrics were provided for tuning buffer pools and table spaces, and recommendations were provided for key DB2 configuration parameters.

13

OS Monitoring: Tips and Techniques

I t's not enough to monitor only DB2 database performance. You need to correlate database performance with operating system performance.

Too often on my consulting engagements I've found that clients were monitoring the DB2 database but not the OS. At sites where both DB2 and OS monitoring *were* taking place, the groups doing the monitoring weren't communicating with each other. Hence, OS- and disk-related configuration problems were hard to detect and correct. Disk performance is frequently the bottleneck, but the issue goes undetected. Worsening the situation is the fact that disk configuration and performance requirements are often poorly understood, in many cases due to a lack of disk subsystem documentation or of DB2 best practices for table space and disk layout configurations.

Previous chapters highlighted important DB2 performance metrics. In this chapter, I use some real examples to demonstrate the importance of a cohesive OS monitoring strategy, and I offer some tips and techniques you can use to achieve this strategy. These techniques have been time-tested over many consulting engagements and have proven to be very successful in helping to achieve and maintain good system performance.

Monitoring Methodology

To properly track DB2 and OS performance, you need to monitor the following areas on a continuous basis:

- Critical DB2 performance metrics (as outlined in Chapter 12)
  - » Database manager and database thresholds
  - » Top 10 SQL statements
  - » Read and write performance
  - » DB2 problems and diagnostic errors db2diag.log entries)
- Operating system performance
  - » CPU
  - » Memory
  - » I/O

If you monitor all these areas consistently, you can correlate DB2 problems with OS problems and vice versa. Although this advice seems quite simple, in reality it is rarely followed. As a consequence, DB2 and OS performance problems can be quite difficult to solve. However, use of this methodology has in every case led me to find the cause of DB2 or OS performance problems.

Scenario #1: High CPU and Disk Utilization

CPU is a critical system resource that you need to monitor continuously. Capture CPU utilization on a consistent basis, and use the information to assess system performance and capacity and in conducting troubleshooting and problem determination. If you track CPU utilization along with concomitant dynamic SQL and application snapshots (at a minimum), you can identify potential suboptimal SQL and applications and take corrective action. There are many ways to capture CPU performance. I'll discuss some of those as they pertain to AIX, Linux, and Windows.

Disk performance is another OS area to monitor and track on a consistent basis. Improperly configured table space containers, inadequate numbers of physical disks, and a general lack of understanding of disk architecture is prevalent throughout the industry. DBAs often lack access to information about the disks, and storage management personnel may or may not have this information. With disk densities ever-increasing, achieving good disk performance has never been more important to overall database performance. I'll use scenario #1 and a series of graphs from an actual consulting engagement to demonstrate how effective DB2 and OS monitoring can be.

Scenario #1 Description

We were contacted to conduct a performance and tuning engagement for a client running DB2 for Linux, UNIX, and Windows in a high-volume, OLTP, Web-based environment. The OS and hardware setup were as follows:

- Operating system: Windows 2003 Server, SP1, 64-bit
- CPUs: Two Xeon processors with two cores per socket, threading degree of four per core for a total of 16 CPUs
- Memory: 4 GB of RAM
- I/O subsystem: IBM DS4300 with fourteen 10 K RPM disks

The intent of this scenario is to show the importance of monitoring the OS, I/O (disk) subsystem, and DB2, so I'll cover the general DB2 monitoring steps involved but not delve into a lot of details because we've covered those in previous chapters.

Figures 13.1A through 13.1G show the performance metrics observed for the client's database, DB06.

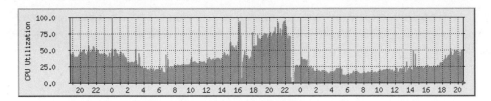

Figure 13.1A: DB06 total active CPU percent (before)

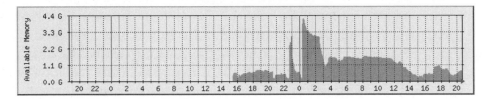

Figure 13.1B: DB06 available memory (before)

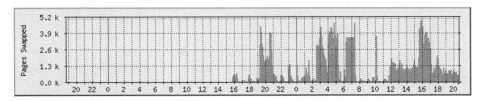

Figure 13.1C: DB06 pages swapped per second (before)

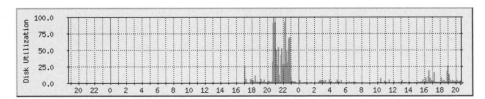

Figure 13.1D: DB06 active disk C percent (before)

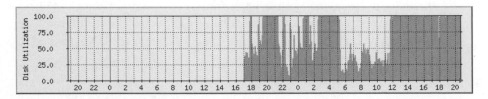

Figure 13.1E: DB06 active disk D percent (before)

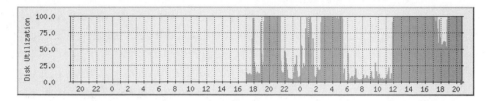

Figure 13.1F: DB06 active disk E percent (before)

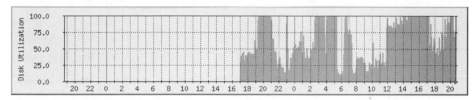

Figure 13.1G: DB06 active disk F percent (before)

Little (if any) DB2 or OS monitoring was being performed in this scenario. CPU utilization was the only metric the client was monitoring and graphing. After our initial first look, we recommended that disk I/O and memory usage be monitored, and this monitoring was added and data captured as shown in the graphs.

> **Note:** Note that the data used in this scenario was captured and displayed using the Multi Router Traffic Grapher (MRTG) by Tobi Oetiker, a free tool licensed under the Gnu GPL. MRTG is available for download at http://oss.oetiker.ch/mrtg.

Initial problems with the DB06 database were as indicated in the graphs, with high CPU and high disk utilization being the major problem, disks being close to 100 percent busy, system outages occurring due to 100 percent CPU utilization being reached, and subsequent slow response from the database or the database appearing to "hang."

Investigation revealed that in addition to high CPU, all three logical drives were close to 100 percent busy for extended time during peak periods. We took a database manager snapshot and found no problems with agents or post

453

threshold sorts. A database snapshot revealed sort overflows computed at 50 percent. Secondary logs were also being used, and dual logging was enabled (parameter MIRRORLOGPATH). The synchronous read milliseconds (SRMS) metric was computed at 96 ms. This means that, on average, it was taking 96 ms to read a page into the buffer pool. Asynchronous write milliseconds (AWMS) were computed at 9.6 ms. Both of these metrics indicated that serious I/O problems existed. To compute these DB2 metrics, we used the Metrics.2.sql script (available at *www.mc-store.com/5086.html*).

We took a table space snapshot and ran a list table space containers for <id> command for each table space contained in the snapshot. It was discovered that data and index DMS table spaces had been defined over the D, E, and F drives. However, the number of defined containers varied widely, with some table spaces having a few defined and others having six; there also were many containers of unequal size. Some containers were defined multiple times on the same logical drive. We also noticed that the primary LOGPATH was also using the D drive and that the MIRRORLOGPATH was using the E drive, along with the data and index table spaces. This situation explained the disk saturation seen in the graphs.

Additional investigation revealed that the entire database was running on a single RAID-5 array. The database size was 100 GB, and transactions per second were measured at 600 TPS. The best practice of 10 to 20 disks per CPU was not followed, with the configuration actually providing less than one disk per CPU.

Application and dynamic SQL snapshots revealed many suboptimal SQL statements and the fact that none of the 600-plus indexes on 150 tables had been created with the ALLOW REVERSE SCANS option, contributing to the over 50 percent figure for sort overflows. (To determine sort overflow percentage, we used the Metrics.2b.sql script, available at *www.mc-store.com/5086.html*).

OS paging was occurring and was a problem during peak periods. Available memory dipped to less than 500 MB during peak periods, and high OS paging and slow response were observed during the online backup, which ran from 6 a.m. to 8 a.m.

Corrective Actions

We initiated 24x7 snapshot monitoring using the scripts at *www.mc-store. com/5086.html* and tracked DB2 performance metrics. We turned off the MIRRORLOGPATH and moved the primary LOGPATH to the F drive, adding an additional physical disk to that drive. 4 GB of RAM was added, for a total of 8 GB. Overall performance was improved as demonstrated by the graphs shown in Figures 13.2A through 13.2G.

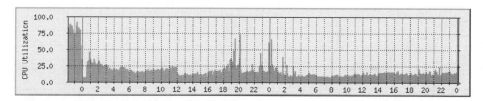

Figure 13.2A: DB06 CPU utilization (after initial tuning)

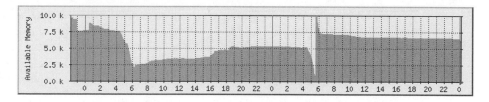

Figure 13.2B: DB06 available memory in megabytes (after initial tuning)

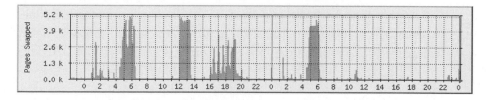

Figure 13.2C: DB06 pages swapped per second (after initial tuning)

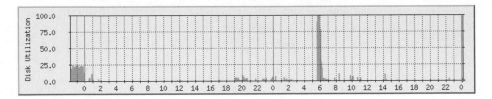

Figure 13.2D: DB06 active disk C percent (after initial tuning)

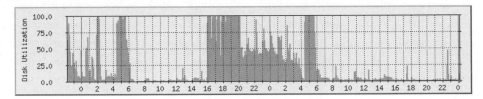

Figure 13.2E: DB06 active disk D percent (after initial tuning)

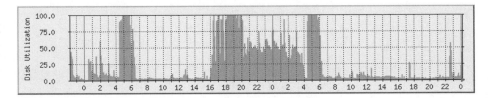

Figure 13.2F: DB06 active disk E percent (after initial tuning)

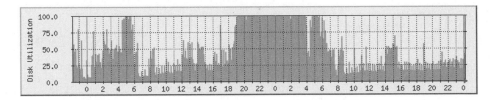

Figure 13.2G: DB06 active disk F percent (after initial tuning)

Although performance was improved, disk utilization remained high during peak periods, and users still were not totally happy with response time during peak periods (6 p.m. to midnight). The F drive, which holds the DB2 logs, was still driven to 100 percent busy during these time windows, adversely affecting the number of transactions per second that could be processed.

It was obvious that several additional steps were necessary. We took the following actions to improve performance:

- Captured and tuned the top 10 SQL statements
- Made 14 additional physical disks available
- Added a dedicated RAID-10 array for DB2 logs (H drive).
- Redid the table space container strategy:
  » Achieved better balance across D, E, and F drives
  » Reduced extent size from 64 to 32 for most tables
  » Set prefects set to 96
  » Enabled no file system caching for all user table spaces
- Added an additional 8 GB of RAM
- Increased buffer pools from 1.8 GB to 9 GB in size
- Altered buffer pools to use 35 percent block-based pages (because ARP was computed at 90 percent for most table spaces)
- Increased LOGFILSIZ from 10,000 pages to 50,000 pages and set LOGPRIMARY set to 20:
  » Set LOGSECOND to 60
- Set DB2_PARALLEL_IO to ON
- Dedicated the new H drive to DB2 logs

After these changes, we continued monitoring and captured data as indicated in the graphs shown in Figures 13.3A through 13.3E.

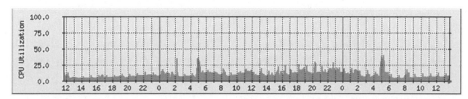

Figure 13.3A: DB06 total active CPU percent (after additional tuning)

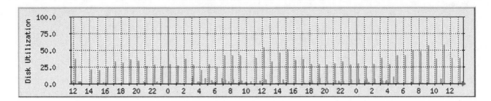

Figure 13.3B: DB06 active disk C percent (after additional tuning)

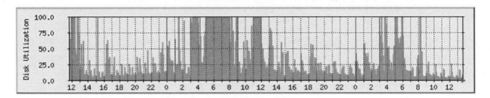

Figure 13.3C: DB06 active disk D percent (after additional tuning)

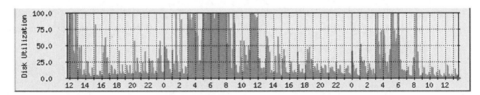

Figure 13.3D: DB06 active disk E percent (after additional tuning)

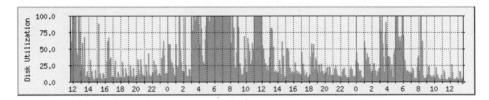

Figure 13.3E: DB06 active disk F percent (after additional tuning)

As a result of tuning, overall CPU utilization was reduced to less than 20 percent on average, and disk utilization was reduced to less than 10 percent on average. Resource utilization was much more consistent, which yielded steady performance.

Scenario #2: SQL Gone Wild

This next scenario demonstrates how you can detect an untested application change through OS monitoring alone and then confirm the change by capturing and analyzing which one of the top 10 running SQL statements is causing the problem. In this case, a problem was detected by regular review of the graphs. While doing routine monitoring, the client observed high disk utilization as illustrated in Figure 13.4.

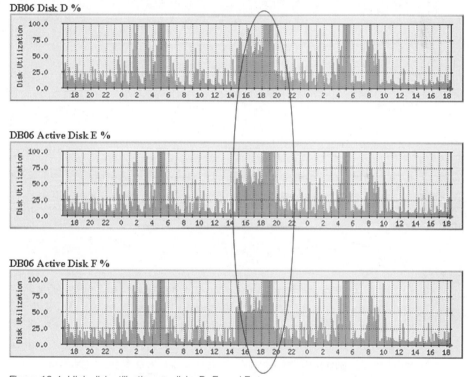

Figure 13.4: High disk utilization on disks D, E, and F

No database changes had been made, so the application development team was notified, and it was learned that a new application had been put into production just before the increase in disk utilization. When we captured the top 10 executing SQL statements using the Topit.sql script at *www.mc-store.com/5086.html*, the suboptimal SQL statement was easy to find. Figure 13.5 shows the output from the Topit.sql script.

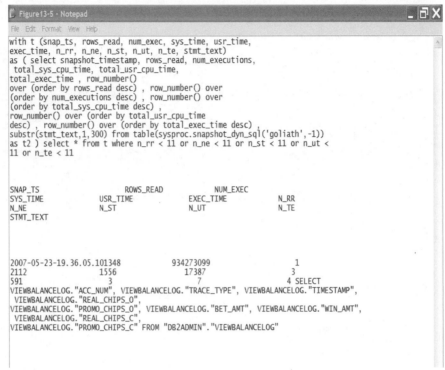

Figure 13.5: Top 10 SQL

Through conducting routine monitoring of this database over time, we had become familiar with the top 10 SQL and had tuned them several times as part of an iterative process. Based on the output shown in the figure, it was obvious to us that the Viewbalancelog SQL statement was new and that it had read more than 934 million rows during one execution. (Note that, in the interest of brevity, I've removed the other nine SQL statements from the figure.) When we brought this fact to the application team's attention, they indicated that although the application had been put into production, it should not have been running. The application was disabled. When we ran a Visual Explain, the results (shown in Figure 13.6) indicated that Viewbalancelog was a very high-cost statement with a suboptimal access plan.

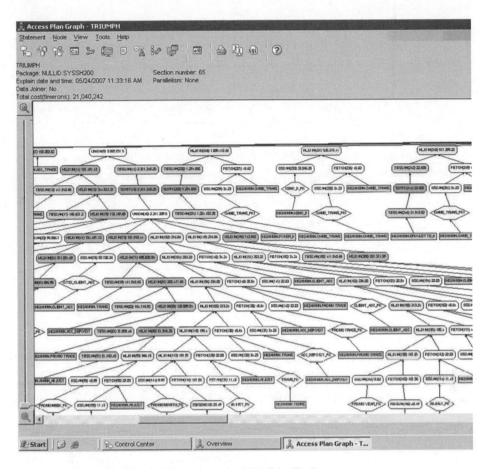

Figure 13.6: Visual Explain of statement causing high disk utilization

A subsequent check with the application development team revealed that the statement had inadvertently been promoted to production but was not yet ready. This fact was evident in the 21,040,242 timeron cost. Taking the statement out of production resolved the problem. Disk utilization during the period returned to normal as shown in Figure 13.7.

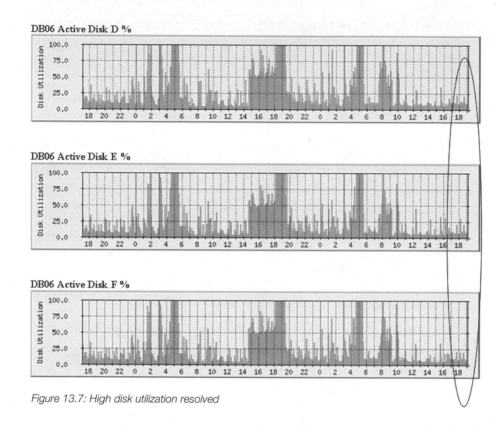

Figure 13.7: High disk utilization resolved

When you monitor disk utilization, percent busy isn't the only metric in need of monitoring, although it is one of the important indicators you need to watch on a continuous basis. The bottom line is that if we hadn't been monitoring disk activity, we wouldn't have been alerted to the fact that a new, suboptimal query had been introduced.

Continuing with scenario #2, we decided to add the average queue length (AQL) disk metric to our regular performance metric reporting. We also periodically gathered performance data from the disk subsystem; in this scenario, we were using an IBM DS4300. We took the performance specifications from the DS4300 documentation and from the IBM Redbook on the DS4300 and compared our DS4300 performance with the specifications and limitations from the DS4300 manuals. It's important to go through this exercise for the disk subsystem you're using because without it you really can't tell whether you're getting the expected performance from your disk setup. In large organizations, this task will require you to interact with the storage administration team. Figures 13.8A through 13.8D show the average queue length graphs.

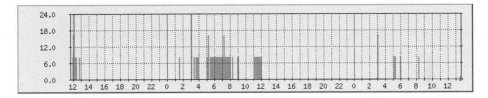

Figure 13.8A: DB06 average queue length for disk D

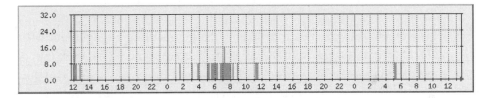

Figure 13.8B: DB06 average queue length for disk E

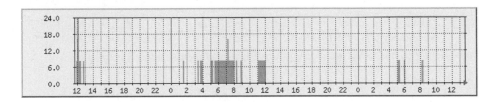

Figure 13.8C: DB06 average queue length for disk F

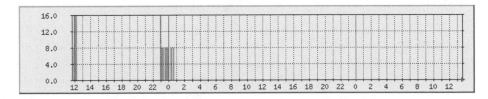

Figure 13.8D: DB06 average queue length for disk H

Each logical drive in this scenario is configured with one RAID-10 array with four physical disks. When evaluating average queue length, you need to take the number of disks in the array into c onsideration. Use the following formula:

AQL = Average number of entries in the queue / Number of physical disks in the array

In this scenario, the AQL is generally less than or equal to 2. In a Windows 2003 server environment, you want AQL to be no higher than 2. A value higher than 2 is indicative of a disk bottleneck. As the graphs illustrate, the system was exceeding this target during peak times, when average queue lengths of 6 or 8 were observed. These lengths indicate that more physical disks or possibly better table space balancing is needed to spread the I/O over more physical disks. Adapter utilization should also be monitored to ensure that the adapter isn't the bottleneck.

These examples were taken from an actual consulting engagement with DB2 on Windows in a high-volume OLTP environment. We took the metrics using a Simple Network Management Protocol (SNMP) agent, but we could have obtained them using Windows Performance Counters. Use caution when enabling performance counters, however, because some incur additional CPU overhead.

The techniques and methods we used also apply to DB2 on AIX or Linux; some of the tools used to gather the information just change.

Scenario #3: Monitoring DB2 on AIX and Linux

With AIX or Linux, you need to monitor the same resources (CPU, memory, and I/O) along with DB2 performance. In this next example, CPU utilization, memory usage, and disk performance were captured and reported using the vmstat command on AIX. Figure 13.9 shows the command's output. (Ignore the first line of this output; it contains accumulated values since the last boot.)

```
Untitled - Notepad
File  Edit  Format  View  Help
$ vmstat 5 5
kthr     memory              page                    faults         cpu
----- ----------- ------------------------ ------------ -----------
 r  b   avm    fre  re  pi  po  fr   sr  cy  in   sy  cs us sy id wa
 4  1 1638943   127   0  21  24 204    9   0 923 4654 2645  9 10 66 15
 4  2 1638984   127   0  26   0 1184 46291   0 3398 4308 4885 19  9 14 59
 3  2 1639026   127   0  15   0 883 16336   0 2519 3606 3696  3  6 18 72
 1  2 1639057   121   0  13   0 1120 15138   0 3071 3985 4540  3  8 18 71
 1  2 1639077   128   0  25   0 1298 22343   0 3541 4305 5099  5  9 15 71
```

Figure 13.9: VMSTAT output

The high values in the wa column indicate a high amount of I/O. This column reports the percentage of CPU wait across all CPUs on the server/LPAR that were waiting for I/Os to be completed during the last interval. A wa value of 20 (percent) or higher can indicate that the system is I/O-bound. Use vmstat to investigate memory and CPU problems. It is an excellent tool and incurs little overhead in the OS. To obtain more detailed information about I/O problems, the iostat command (covered later) is a better choice.

> **Note:** The vmstat command on Linux provides similar information and is normally included with the more well-known distributions.

You might want to use a graphical tool such as nmon to monitor your AIX or Linux system. This facility can provide more information than vmstat, and you can use it to generate data that can be displayed in a graphical form. You can run nmon from a command line as a standard UNIX command-line tool, and it can generate data to be used for graphing purposes. It is available via download for free at *http://www-941.haw.ibm.com/collaboration/wiki/display/WikiPtype/nmon*. Check the download page for specific distributions. You can also download the "nmon analyser," a tool for generating performance reports, from this site. IBM's Nigel Griffiths developed and maintains nmon, incorporating new enhancements about every six months. Figure 13.10 shows sample output that was produced using nmon.

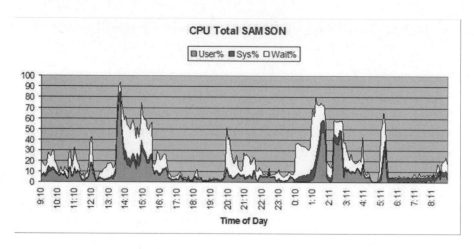

Figure 13.10: AIX CPU utilization

The graph in the figure is an example of similar monitoring conducted on an AIX OS in a mixed OLTP/DW environment. It's clear from the graph that I/O wait is a significant problem during peak processing times. Peak processing time in this example is during the early afternoon and from about midnight to 5:30 a.m. daily. The next step in this situation is to drill down deeper into the I/O wait problem by running iostat and graphing the output using nmon as shown in Figure 13.11.

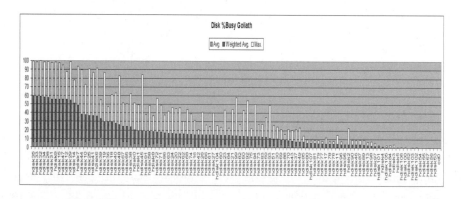

Figure 13.11: Disk busy and unbalanced I/O

As this graph indicates, I/O wait is a serious problem on this system. The graph also shows that I/O isn't balanced evenly across all available disks. As demonstrated in previous scenarios in this chapter, DB2 and OS performance data must be correlated. In this scenario, we captured the top SQL and took application and table space snapshots as summarized in Figure 13.12.

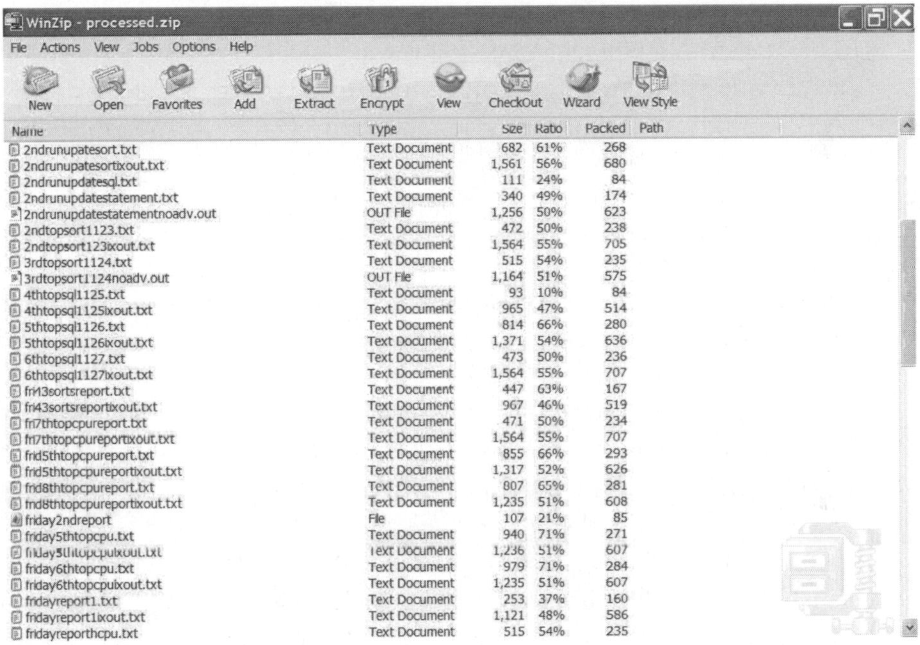

Figure 13.12: Partial list of top SQL and other DB2 snapshots captured

We captured a list of DB2 containers and file systems so we could relate DB2 activity to the physical/logical disks associated with the related UNIX file system and DB2 table space activity. In addition to these steps, you may need to coordinate with storage administrators so that physical-to-logical disk mapping can be accomplished. I've used these techniques many times to find out ultimately that many DB2 table space containers had been defined on the same logical disks!

You also need to identify the logical disk involved and determine the spec rate from the disk vendor's documentation. Review this information to determine whether the disk load is more than 70 percent of the spec rate. If it is, it may be that more physical disks are required. Also check the disk adapter to determine whether that is causing a bottleneck. If the disk array is performing as specified and the adapter isn't saturated, container placement or too few physical disks is likely to be the issue. In my consulting engagements, too few physical disks is one of the main performance problems. Remember, instead of asking for space for DB2, ask for spindles! And, as an aside, make sure you have enough space.

iostat

Depending on how the logical disks in your storage subsystem are presented to the AIX operating system, you may need to investigate the problem further with your storage or network administration team. You also need to identify the table space containers and file systems contained on the disk involved. Once this is done (by running the DB2 command list table space containers for <id> and using the output from this command with the UNIX/Linux DF OS command), you'll have enough information to identify the physical disk where the container is located. You can even take this further and identify the tables in the table space in question. You can then use DB2 snapshots or the db2pd utility to find SQL going against these tables. To drill down and investigate disk performance of the particular disk, use the iostat command.

> **Note:** On Linux, the iostat command is provided with Fedora Core 2 and SUSE (Novell) 9.1. It is available as part of the sysstat package at *http://perso.wanadoo.fr/sebastien.godard*.

Figure 13.13 shows the iostat output for our scenario.

```
tty:       tin          tout     avg-cpu:  % user    % sys    % idle    % iowait
           0.0          0.0                  34.0      8.5      13.7      43.9

Disks:         % tm_act     Kbps        tps     Kb_read    Kb_wrtn
hdisk0          0.4         2.4         0.6        12          0
hdisk1          7.2        32.8         8.2        60        104
hdisk34        33.6      1866.1       139.1      9300         40
hdisk35         0.0         0.0         0.0         0          0
hdisk36         0.0         0.0         0.0         0          0
hdisk37         0.0         0.0         0.0         0          0
hdisk26        32.4      1761.4       130.7      8756         60
hdisk27         0.0         0.0         0.0         0          0
hdisk28         0.0         0.0         0.0         0          0
hdisk29         0.0         0.0         0.0         0          0
hdisk30        29.6      1750.2       137.7      8732         28
hdisk31         0.0         0.0         0.0         0          0
hdisk32         0.0         0.0         0.0         0          0
hdisk33         0.0         0.0         0.0         0          0
hdisk22        30.8      2165.8       163.6     10808         32
hdisk23         0.0         0.0         0.0         0          0
hdisk24         0.0         0.0         0.0         0          0
hdisk25         0.0         0.0         0.0         0          0
hdisk2         29.0      2135.5       156.8     10668         20
hdisk3          0.0         0.8         0.2         4          0
hdisk4          0.0         0.0         0.0         0          0
hdisk5          0.0         0.0         0.0         0          0
hdisk6         30.6      2053.9       164.8     10248         32
hdisk7          0.0         0.0         0.0         0          0
hdisk8          0.0         0.0         0.0         0          0
hdisk9          0.2         0.8         0.0         4          0
cd0             0.0         0.0         0.0         0          0
```

Figure 13.13: IOSTAT output

As you can see in the figure, the iowait value in this scenario is 43.9 percent. We ran this command on a system experiencing DB2 performance problems. Indicative of this fact is the unbalanced I/O pattern you can glean from the output. Only a few disks are being used, while the others are almost idle. If DB2 table space containers were balanced across available disks, the I/O would be much more balanced and would engage many more disks when I/O was performed.

Summary

In this chapter, you saw some examples of how to monitor OS performance and correlate it with DB2 performance. To be successful in supporting production databases, you need to know how to identify DB2 problems from OS monitoring and vice versa. Monitoring only DB2 isn't good enough. DB2 may be fine, but one of the elements of the OS might not be tuned. Or, the OS may be fine, while DB2 isn't tuned properly. If you can't correlate DB2 performance with OS performance, you'll always have nagging problems that never get solved. In large organizations, it's difficult to pull all the necessary data together, but as a DBA or developer you must interact with system, network, and storage administrators to ensure you have a closed-loop monitoring system in place. If you're able to do this, you'll go a long way in helping your company to meet its business objectives.

14

Problem Determination

To be a successful DBA, you need good problem-determination skills. Even with continued improvements in DB2 and client applications, problems can still occur, so you must know how to identify, locate, and resolve issues quickly.

You should develop standard troubleshooting procedures for your environment. If you document and practice these procedures when investigating problems, you'll be able to routinely identify and solve problems in a short amount of time. This acquired skill will enable you to help your company maintain or improve its competitive advantage. Remember that downtime costs money and reflects negatively on your company.

Your primary source of DB2 9 and problem-determination information is IBM's DB2 9 Information Center. Here, you can also find links to DB2 9 tutorials and other useful information. You can find this resource on the Web at *http://publib.boulder.ibm.com/infocenter/db2luw/v9/index.jsp*.

The Information Center is the primary resource for finding problem-determination and troubleshooting information. By going to the home page and searching on a particular problem, you can quickly and easily go directly to content related to your problem or subject of interest. Links to related problems, DB2 9 manuals, and other DB2 sites are provided. Figure 14.1 shows a view of the DB2 9 Information Center home page.

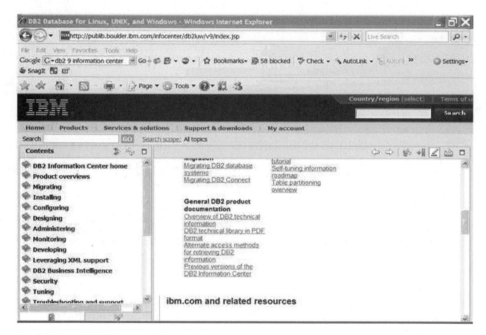

Figure 14.1: IBM DB2 9 Information Center

There are several categories we can use to classify problems:

- Connectivity problems
- Performance problems
- Application problems
- DB2 code problems

Connectivity Problems

Connectivity problems are by far the most common type of problems. They usually can be isolated to either the client or the server. Some of the most common connectivity problems result from the following issues:

- Client unable to connect to the database
- User ID and password problems
- Driver problems
- Intermittent connectivity problems
- Down database
- Down instance
- DB2COMM environmental variable not set properly
- DB2 TCP/IP service name (svcename) database manager configuration parameter not set
- Network issues

When investigating these types of problems, ask your users the following questions to help isolate the trouble:

- Is this the first time you've had this problem?
- Can anyone else using the same application connect to the database?
- Can you connect to or run the application from another PC?
- Are other people who are using the same applications able to connect, or are they experiencing the same problems?
- Does the problem happen all the time, or is it intermittent?
- Can you re-create the problem? If not, how frequently does it occur?
- Can the problem be re-created in a test environment?
- Can the problem be re-created from a command line?

After gathering answers to these questions, you should have enough information to isolate the problem to the client, application, or database. During your fact-finding effort, you can be testing connections to the database in question, verifying whether the instance is up, and making sure the database is available. If your quick tests don't reveal any problems, immediately check the db2diag.log and administration notification log on the server for errors.

If errors are found, investigate those errors using the Information Center and the messages and codes manual. If no errors are found, look at the db2diag. log on the client. You'll typically find errors on the client if you've eliminated the server as the problem. Look up the error messages in the Information Center or the messages and codes manual, and take action as indicated.

> **Note:** In the Internet age, a good way to look for answers can be to use Google. Many newsgroup messages and articles provide an interpretation that goes beyond what is available in the manuals, and they present the answer in simpler language.

If these steps don't point you to the problem, you'll need to run a CLI/ODBC/JDBC trace on the client. We'll look at a sample CLI trace later in the chapter.

Performance and Application Problems

Performance problems are the second most-reported type of problem. The most common performance problems are usually the result of some type of change to the application, lack of RUNSTATS, a database configuration change, or possibly an application that was never tuned in the first place. Additional typical problem areas are long-running SQL, sort overflows, OS paging, high I/O wait times, and undersized buffer pools. When investigating performance problems, ask the following questions:

- When did the problem occur?

- What is the nature of the problem?

- Can it be reproduced?

- How long did the query or script normally run in the past?

- Were any changes made to the application? If so, what were the changes?

- Was the query explained? If so, what access path is it using? Has it changed?

- Are catalog statistics current?

- Were any database configuration parameters changed?

- Were any OS changes made?

- Were disk or file system changes made?

To identify long-running or suboptimal SQL, use snapshots and event monitoring. (Refer to Chapter 11 for specific details about these facilities.) Once you identify the SQL, use the Design Advisor and Visual Explain to determine whether you can improve the access path through index changes, additional indexes, or changes to the SQL. By using these tools, you should be able to resolve all problems of these types. You can also use a combination of snapshot and event monitoring data to identify sort problems and provide buffer pool performance data. Often, sort problems can be eliminated by tuning SQL and by creating or modifying indexes.

To ensure you have current RUNSTATS for the objects involved, you can use the Control Center. This will let you review whether RUNSTATS are current and determine whether they've ever been run. You can execute the RUNSTATS utility from the Control Center, the Command Center, or the CLP.

DB2 Code (Defect) Problems

At times, you may experience any of the four categories of problems highlighted at the beginning of this chapter due to DB2 defects. These errors are relatively infrequent, but you should know where to look for information concerning your particular problem. DB2 Support maintains a DB2 product support page on the Internet at *http://www-306.ibm.com/software/data/db2/support/db2_9*. Figure 14.2 shows a view of what is contained on the DB2 Support site.

Figure 14.2: DB2 Support site

Errors that occur due to DB2 defects typically are written to the diagnostic log file db2diag.log. Take the problem string identified in db2diag.log, and use it to search the support site for a possible fix. If your search finds a fix for the defect you're experiencing, you can download the fix, test it in a test environment, and apply it to production during a maintenance window. Always test a fix pack in a test environment before putting it into production.

DB2 Problem-Determination Aids

As of DB2 UDB V8.1, diagnostic information is now written to two separate files: the db2diag.log file and the administration notification log. IBM split db2diag.log into two files because too much information was being written to the file, causing "information overload" because it contained a mix of informational and severe errors. As a result of this issue and customer feedback, DB2 Development decided to create a separate file to record application errors, administrative errors, and miscellaneous error information, leaving the db2diag.log file dedicated to only severe-level errors. This approach has been continued in DB2 9.

db2diag Tool

IBM introduced the db2diag tool in DB2 UDB for Linux, UNIX, and Windows V8.2. Before that release, you had to manually review the contents of the db2diag.log or write your own script to monitor entries into the log file.

In DB2 9, the db2diag tool enables you to search the contents of the db2diag.log for warnings and severe errors, and it offers numerous command parameters to enable you to find and format db2diag.log entries. The tool contains good help information, with sample commands and a built-in tutorial. You can use db2diag to do the following:

- Search for specific errors, process IDs, and DB2 9 components
- Format output using a format string
- Archive a copy of the db2diag.log
- Continuously display appended records as the file grows
- Display descriptions of DB2 internal ZRC or ECF return codes
- Count specific errors

477

Figure 14.3 lists the db2diag command parameters.

```
DB2 CLP - DB2COPY1                                                    _ ㅁ x
Command parameters:

filename             - one or more space-separated path names of diagnostic logs
-help    , -h , ?    - help information. To get help on help, try "db2diag -h h"
-filter , -g         - case-sensitive search for a list of field-pattern pairs
-gi                  - case-insensitive search for a list of field-pattern pairs
-gv                  - case-sensitive invert matching
-gvi     , -giv      - case-insensitive invert matching
-invert , -v         - invert the sense of matching for all filtering options
-exist               - record field must exist in order to be processed
-pid                 - find all records for a list of process IDs
-tid                 - find all records for a list of thread IDs
-node    , -n        - find all records for a list of nodes
-error  , -e         - find all records for a list of errors
-level  , -l         - find all records for a list of severity levels
-history, -H         - display the history of logged records for a time interval
-time   , -t         - display all the records within a particular time interval
-count  , -c         - display a count of matching records
-verbose, -V         - display all record fields whether they contain data or not
-strict              - display records using one "field: value" pair per line
-cbe                 - display records in the Common Base Event (CBE) format
-fmt                 - format tool's output using a format string
-output , -o         - save output into a file
-follow , -f         - continuously display appended records as the file grows
-archive, -A         - archive a diagnostic log file
-readfile            - read from a file ignoring terminal input (used in scripts)
-rc                  - display descriptions of DB2 error return codes, ZRC or ECF
-ecfid               - display function info extracted from the numeric ECF ID

"db2diag -h <option1[,option2[,option3...]]>" - displays additional help and
 usage examples for one or more options specified in the options list

"db2diag -h brief"    - displays help for all options without examples

"db2diag -h examples" - displays a few typical examples to get started
```

Figure 14.3: db2diag command parameters

You can invoke the db2diag command from the DB2 command line processor by issuing the command and desired parameters. To see examples of the command's use, issue the command as follows:

```
db2diag -h examples
```

Figure 14.4 shows the resulting output.

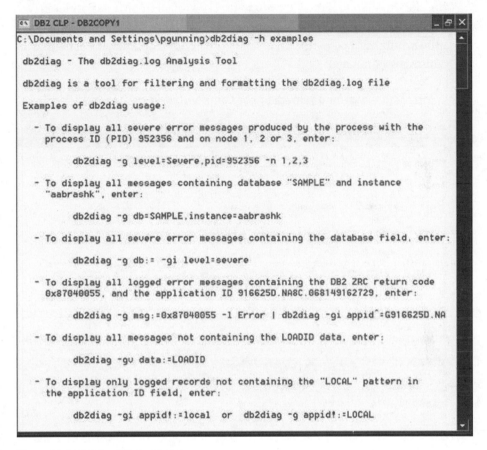

Figure 14.4: db2diag help examples

You can still browse the db2diag.log using Notepad as in previous releases, but the db2diag tool enables you to quickly focus in on a particular error or problem. Figure 14.5 illustrates using db2diag to search the db2diag.log for all warnings issued by the DB2 "data protection" component using the following command:

db2diag –l warning | db2diag –g "comp^=data prot"

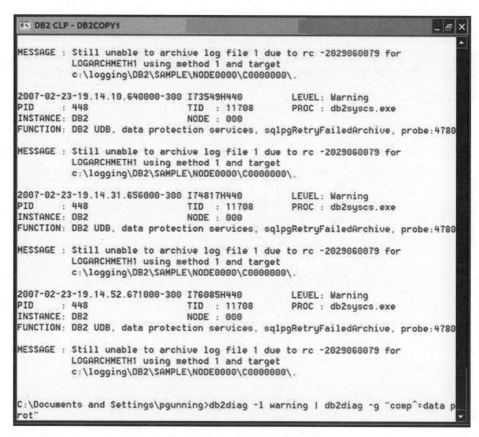

Figure 14.5: Show all warnings associated with a DB2 9 engine component

The db2diag.log File

The db2diag.log file is located in the SQLLIB directory. It is an ASCII file that you can view with a text editor or the db2diag tool. DB2 writes entries to this file when the following events occur:

- Severe errors
- DB2 internal errors

The database manager configuration parameter diaglevel controls the type of information written to the db2diag.log file. The default value for this parameter is 3; this setting ensures that DB2 records all severe errors that occur. I recommend that you use this setting, changing diaglevel to 4 only when you're trying to debug a particular problem that you haven't been able to identify through other means. As soon as you've captured the additional information, reset parameter diaglevel back to 3.

> **Note:** Upon receipt of a problem report, immediately check the last entry in the db2diag.log. Very often, the log will point you to a specific problem and save you precious time when trouble-shooting a production issue. If the problem is discovered after the fact, check the db2diag.log for entries made around the time that the problem occurred.

New entries written to the db2diag.log file are appended at the end of the file, so you should look at the end of the file when investigating current errors. As entries are written to the file, the file grows in size, and it will continue to do so it runs out of disk space or uses up all available space in the file system. Most DBAs copy the db2diag.log file nightly and then delete it. DB2 will automatically create a new file when needed. If you copy the log file nightly, you'll have a historical record for subsequent analysis if needed.

In DB2 9, you can use the db2diag tool with the –archive parameter to create an archive of the current db2diag.log file. Issue the command as follows:

```
db2diag –archive
```

DB2 will create the archive file with a date-timestamp suffix as shown in Figure 14.6.

```
C:\Documents and Settings\pgunning>db2diag -archive
db2diag: Moving "C:\PROGRA~1\IBM\SQLLIB\DB2\db2diag.log"
        to      "C:\PROGRA~1\IBM\SQLLIB\DB2\db2diag.log_2007-02-22-19.23.12"

C:\Documents and Settings\pgunning>
```

Figure 14.6: Using the db2diag tool to archive the db2diag.log

By creating an archive of the db2diag.log file on a regular basis, you can search specific date ranges (e.g., the current day and the previous day), thus reducing the amount of data to review and the time required for problem determination. If you have a copy of the db2diag.log file for each day, it can aid you in troubleshooting later.

Log Entry Format

DB2 uses a naming convention for naming its modules; see Table 14.1 for a key. The letter in the fourth position of the function name indicates which DB2 function was involved in the error. This information is helpful to know when searching for a fix or working with DB2 Support.

Table 14.1: DB2 component identification table	
Letter in fourth position	**Function involved**
B	Buffer pool management and manipulation
C	Communications between clients and servers
D	Data management
E	Database engine process
O	Operating system calls (privileged instructions)
P	Data protection
R	Relational database services
S	Sorting operations
X	Indexing operations

Entries written to the db2diag.log file are in First Failure Data Capture (FFDC) format. Figure 14.7 shows a sample db2diag.log FFDC entry.

```
1 2007-02-23-19.08.13.406000-300 I51167H383    2 LEVEL: Error
3 PID  : 448           4 TID : 11708   5 PROC : db2syscs.exe
6 INSTANCE: DB2         7 NODE : 000
8 FUNCTION: DB2 UDB, data protection services, 9 sqlpgArchiveLogDisk, 10 probe:2530
11 RETCODE : ZRC=0x870F0011=-2029060079=SQLO_PATH "an invalid path"
        12 DIA8514C An invalid file path, "", was specified.
```

Figure 14.7: db2diag.log entry format

Although the primary purpose of the log file is to record severe errors for problem-determination analysis by DB2 Development, if you learn how to interpret FFDC information you can use it to help solve problems that are within your capability. And if not, you'll at least be in a good position to provide information to DB2 Level II Support. We can break down the numbered data elements in Figure 14.7 as follows.

1. Message timestamp
2. Error severity
3. Process ID
4. Thread ID
5. Process or executable name
6. Name of instance
7. For a partitioned database, the database partition number of the partition generating the message
8. Identification of the DB2 component generating the message
9. The module reporting the error (using Table 14.1, we can identify the module as Data Protection because of the "p" in the fourth position of the module name)
10. The function ID (probe) within the module reporting the error; used by DB2 Support to locate the section of code that generated the error
11. The DB2 internal error code in hex
12. The diagnostic error code and message text

> **Note:** Depending on the type of db2diag.log entry, the application handle and application ID may be present. If the application is still running, you can use the commands db2 list applications and db2 get snapshot for application snapshot or utility db2pd to obtain additional information.

The key data elements you need to be concerned with in Figure 14.7 are the DB2 module reporting the error (element 9) and the DB2 internal return code (element 11). You can look up DB2 internal return codes (0x870F0011 in our example) on the Web using the Information Center. In this example, the error indicates that the path for the configuration parameter logarchmeth1 is not valid.

SQLCA Entries in File db2diag.log

DB2 uses the SQL Communications Area (SQLCA) to pass information from one program to another, to record the status of a call, and to return the status of results to the working application. DB2 may record the contents of an SQLCA associated with severe errors in the db2diag.log. For this reason, the log is very useful in helping you investigate application errors and other types of errors. Figure 14.8 shows an example of a db2diag.log SQLCA entry.

```
2006-08-08-23.31.37.307935 Instance:db2inst1 Node:000
PID:2640(asnapply) TID:8192 Appid:none
DRDA Application Requester sqljrDrdaArExecute Probe:90

DIA0001E An internal error occurred. Report the following error code :
"ZRC=0x8037006D".

1 PID:2640 2 TID:8192 3 Node:000 4 Title: SQLCA
5 sqlcaid : SQLCA sqlcabc: 136 6 sqlcode: -518 sqlerrml: 0
sqlerrmc:
7 sqlerrp : SQLRAGSN~
8 sqlerrd : (1) 0x8012007E (2) 0x00000000 (3) 0x00000000
(4) 0x00000000 (5) 0x00000000 (6) 0x00000000
sqlwarn : (1) (2) (3) (4) (5) (6)
(7) (8) (9) (10) (11)
9 sqlstate: 07003


2006-08-08-23.31.37.332392 Instance:db2inst1 Node:000
PID:2640(asnapply) TID:8192 Appid:none
oper system services sqlofica Probe:10
```

Figure 14.8: Sample SQLCA entry in db2diag.log

The SQLCA uses the standard FFDC format. SQLCA field definitions are as follows:

1. Process ID

2. Unique transaction ID

3. Node where the error occurred

4. Title

5. Eye catcher that identifies the beginning of the SQLCA data structure entries

6. SQL return code value

7. Reason codes, if provided

8. A hexadecimal value of up to six entries that caused the final SQL return code value generated (these codes are recorded in the sequence of events as they occurred)

9. SQLSTATE (the ANSI-standard SQLSTATE value)

485

In our example, we have a return code of 0x8012007E and an SQLCODE of -518. Using the DB2 Information Center, we can search on these codes and find that a -518 SQL code or a 07003 SQLSTATE means that "a statement named in the EXECUTE statement is not in a prepared state or is a SELECT or VALUES statement." You can use this information to help a developer solve an application problem.

DB2 Administration Notification Log

The administration notification log records errors of interest to DBAs and application developers. In a Windows environment, DB2 uses the Windows event log as the administration notification log, and you can view the log using the Windows Event Viewer tool.

> **Note:** The notifylevel database manager configuration parameter controls the level of administration notification messages written to the administration notification log. The default value is 3. This parameter must be set to a value of 2 or higher to enable the Health Monitor to send notifications to contacts defined in its configuration.

Figures 14.9 and 14.10 show typical administration notification log entries. As you can see in Figure 14.9, the initial entry record is shown using Event Viewer, which gives us a high level view of the problem.

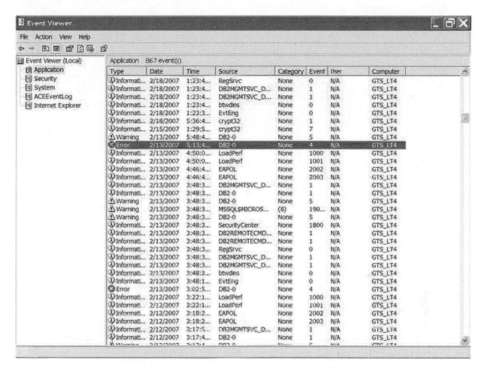

Figure 14.9: Windows Event Viewer entry overview

By double-clicking on an entry, we can view additional details as shown in Figure 14.10. The log provides a description of the problem and a recommended solution. In this example, the log has recorded a DB2 9 Health Monitor health indicator alarm threshold breach.

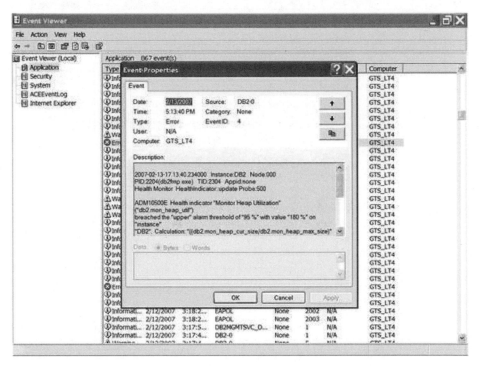

Figure 14.10: Event Viewer details

On non-Windows operating systems, the administration notification log is created as an ASCII file with a file name of the format *<instance_name.nfy>*. The file is located on the path specified by the diagpath database manager configuration parameter.

System Logs

System logs are another important source of problem-determination information. We've already discussed the Windows event log.

> **Note:** The database manager configuration parameter diagpath controls where FFDC information is recorded. This parameter is null by default. On Windows, the FFDC data is by default written to the db2diag.log on the following path: C:\Program Files\IBM\SQLLIB\DB2\db2diag.log. On UNIX, the FFDC data is by default written to the following path: $Home/sqllib/db2dump—for example, /prddb/sqllib/db2dump, where prddb is the name of the instance owner.

On UNIX, operating system logs are used to record severe DB2 errors and warning conditions. On AIX, use the errpt –a command to format the system log. You can view the contents of the system logs on other operating systems as follows:

- On Solaris: In the /var/adm/messages* directory
- On HP-UX: In the var/adm/syslog/syslog.log directory
- On Linux: In the /var/log/messages directory

On these operating systems, the system log can contain DB2 error information in the event of a DB2 crash. In some cases, DB2 may not have been able to write to the db2diag.log before it crashed. In that event, the system log will be an important source of information.

Errors are added to the system log based on priority and on which facility caused the error or warning condition. DB2 typically adds errors to the system log under the following conditions:

- Agents have been killed.
- The DB2 architecture has been compromised.
- I/O subsystem errors are causing DB2 to panic.

When conducting problem determination, cross-check the information from the db2diag.log, the administration notification log, and the system logs to correlate all failure data. On UNIX, you can use the dbx command to format core dumps. You can use this technique to determine whether a DB2 or OS event caused the dump. Dump files are used primarily by DB2 Support to investigate and solve problems.

CLI Trace

The output trace is typically what DB2 Support will want. A DB2 CLI/ODBC trace shows the calls received from the Open Database Connectivity (ODBC) Driver Manager, while an ODBC trace show the calls made by the application to the driver manager.

Enable the trace on the client by adding the following lines to the DB2CLI.INI file:

```
[COMMON]
TRACE = 1
TRACEFILENAME = C:\Traces\120202Prob.TXT
TRACEFLUSH = 1
```

Then restart the application. The added instructions will cause a trace record to be written to disk after each entry. If you're using Java Database Connectivity (JDBC), you can also use a JDBC or Java Call Control (JCC) trace used. The settings are similar; for additional information, see the Information Center.

DB2 Trace

IBM significantly improved the DB2 trace facility, db2trc, in DB2 UDB V8.1 and in DB2 9 added the ability to use trace masks to limit the trace points collected. However, you should use DB2 trace only in conjunction with DB2 Support. This facility records information about operations and formats it in to a readable form. On UNIX, you must have sysadm, sysctrl, or sysmaint authority to run a DB2 trace. On Windows, no authorization is required.

> **Note:** You can use db2trc to trace activity for an instance or for the DB2 administration server.

A connection to the database is not required. The db2trc command is useful when other FFDC facilities have failed to give you and DB2 Support enough information to identify and solve the problem being investigated. Tracing normally follows a three-step process:

1. Run the trace.
2. Dump the trace information.
3. Format the trace information.

The following is a sample db2trc command:

```
db2trc on -l 8m
```

This command enables tracing with an 8 MB buffer.

Use the following command to dump the trace information to a file:

```
db2trc dmp dbtrc.dmp
```

After you've dumped the trace to a file, you must stop the trace:

```
db2trc off
```

After turning off the trace, you can format it using the flw or fmt option:

```
db2trc flw dbtrc.dmp dbtrc.flw
db2trc fmt dbtrc.dmp dbtrc.fmt
```

Note that you must issue the db2trc command multiple times to gather the information and format it to a text file. You can also use db2trc used to capture DRDA data stream information when troubleshooting connectivity problems.

Dumps

DB2 creates dump files when it determines that internal information needs to be collected. DB2 creates two types of dumps:

- Type 1: Binary dump files
- Type 2: Locklist dump files

The format and naming conventions for these files are as follows.

- For Type 1 (binary dump) files:
  - » On UNIX: *pppppp.nn*, where *pppppp* is the process ID and *nnn* is the node where the problem occurred
    - » Example: 323646.000
  - » On Windows: *pppttt.nnn*, where *ppp* is the process ID, *ttt* is the thread ID, and nnn is the node where the problem occurred
    - » Example: 323646.000
- For Type 2 (locklist dump) files:
  - » On UNIX: 1*pppppp.nnn*, where *pppppp* is the process ID and *nnn* is the node where the problem occurred
    - » Example: 1323646.000
  - » On Windows: 1*pppttt.nnn*, where *ppp* is the process ID, *ttt* is the thread ID, and *nnn* is the node where the problem occurred
    - » Example: 1323646.000

Information written to dump files consist of internal DB2 control blocks and other diagnostic information. Each data item written to a dump file has a timestamp associated with it to aid in problem determination.

When a dump file is created or appended to, DB2 makes an entry in the db2diag.log file indicating the time and type of data written. The fully qualified path for the dump file is also recorded.

For UNIX systems, dump files might be created in core dump directories. These files are called *DB2 core files* and are specific to DB2.

> **Note:** The db2support tool collects these core files for further analysis.

DB2 core files are located in the path $HOME/db2dump/*core_directory*, where *core_directory* is the core path directory name. One directory exists for each process. Directory names start with the letter "c" followed by the process identifier (PID) number of the affected process. A name extension provides the partition for multi-partition databases.

These core files are intended for use by DB2 Support. You can use the db2support tool to develop a support bundle that can be sent to DB2 Support.

Dr. Watson

The Dr. Watson log on Windows (drwtsn32.log) contains a list of all exceptions that have occurred. This log is useful for developing a good picture of overall system stability and contains information about DB2 traps. The default path for the log is <installation_drive>:\Documents and Settings\All Users\Documents\DrWatson.

Traps

When certain severe errors are encountered, DB2 will issue a signal (on UNIX platforms) or an exception to itself. These events are known as *segment violations* or *traps*, depending on the operating system.

Signals or exceptions initiated by DB2 are reported in a trap file, which contains a function flow of the last steps that were executed before the system stopped. DB2 Support uses trap files to assist in resolving problems.

Trap files reside in the directory specified by the diagpath database manager configuration parameter and use the naming convention

```
t39336.000
t39338.006
```

where

- t identifies the file as a trap file
- 39336.000 is the name of the process with PID 39336
- 39338.006 is the name of the process with PID 39338.006, with 006 signifying the database partition on which the process was running

> **Note:** DB2 does not remove trap, dump, core, or trace files. After ensuring you no longer need the files for problem determination, you can delete them on a periodic basis.

db2xprt

You can use the db2xprt tool to format trap files on Windows. Invoked from the command line, db2xprt produces output in XML format, or you can redirect the output to a text file. Figure 14.11 shows an example of db2xprt options.

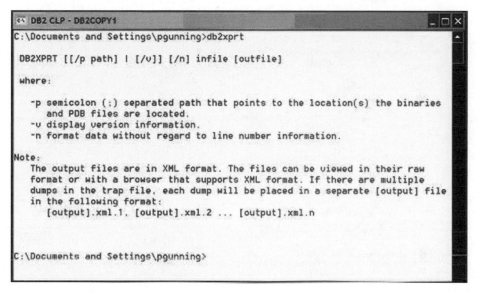

Figure 14.11: db2xprt command options

Figures 14.12 and Figure 14.13 present some sample db2xprt output. The output contains system-level information, environmental variable settings, current register values, and a pointer to the failing instruction (denoted by <<<< in Figure 14.13).

```
<?xml version="1.0" encoding="ISO-8859-1"?>
<?xml-stylesheet href="http://raspd.torolab.ibm.com/db2trapfile.xsl" type="text/xsl"?>
<DB2TrapFile version="1.0">
<Trap>
<Header>
DB2 build information: DB2 v9.1.0.356 s060629 (Release) SQL09010
timestamp: 2006-12-06-21.49.18.287000
uname: S:Windows
comment: NT32
process id: 228
thread id: 2208
</Header>
<SystemInformation>
Number of Processors: 1
Processor Type: x86 Family 6 Model 13 Stepping 6
OS Version: Microsoft Windows XP, Service Pack 2 (5.1)
Current Build: 2600
</SystemInformation>
<MemoryInformation>
<Usage>
Physical Memory:    1518 total,    1057 free.
Virtual Memory :    2047 total,    1991 free.
Paging File    :    3870 total,    3213 free.
Ext. Virtual   :       0 free.
</Usage>
</MemoryInformation>
<EnvironmentVariables>
<![CDATA[
[e] ALLUSERSPROFILE=C:\Documents and Settings\All Users
[e] CLASSPATH=.;C:\Program Files\IBM\SQLLIB\java\db2java.zip;C:\Program Files\IBM\SQLLIB\java\db2jcc
[e] CommonProgramFiles=C:\Program Files\Common Files
[e] COMPUTERNAME=GTSLAPTOP3
[e] ComSpec=C:\WINDOWS\system32\cmd.exe
```

Figure 14.12: db2xprt system-level output

```
<SignalDetails>
Exception C0000005 Occurred
Exception Address = 7C9106C3
Invalid linear address 0050005A
</SignalDetails>
<Registers>
GS  : 0000      FS  : 003B      ES  : 0023      DS  : 0023
EDI : 00500054 ESI : 0050005C EAX : 0050000C EBX : 00140000
ECX : 0000001C EDX : 3E030001
EBP : 0187D088 EIP : 7C9106C3 EFLG: 00010216 ESP : 0187CE68
CS  : 001B      SS  : 0023
</Registers>

<POFDisassembly>
<![CDATA[
Failing instruction at 7C9106C3
0x7C9106A3 ADD         BYTE PTR [EAX],AL
0x7C9106A5 PUSH        ESI
0x7C9106A6 CALL        7C9106FEH
0x7C9106AB MOV         ESI,EAX
0x7C9106AD MOV         DWORD PTR [EBP-30H],ESI
0x7C9106B0 TEST        ESI,ESI
0x7C9106B2 JZ          7C911606H
0x7C9106B8 LEA         EDI,DWORD PTR [ESI-8]
0x7C9106BB MOV         AL,BYTE PTR [EBP-24H]
0x7C9106BE MOV         ECX,DWORD PTR [EBP+10H]
0x7C9106C1 SUB         AL,CL
0x7C9106C3 MOV         BYTE PTR [EDI+6],AL                        <<<<
0x7C9106C6 MOV         EAX,EDI
0x7C9106C8 SHR         EAX,3

 0187CE68 :0020B1C0 0000000D 0020B1D0 FFFFFFFF  .. .......:....
 0187CE78 :7C910732 7C9106AB 7C9106EB 0187D110  2..|...|...|....
 0187CE88 :0020B1C0 00000000 0014E40C 00000014  .. .............
 0187CE98 :00000001 00000000 00000000 00000010  ...............
|
</Trap>
</DB2TrapFile>
The DB2XPRT command completed successfully.
```

Figure 14.13: db2xprt trap instruction and data output

db2pd

The db2pd command is an excellent problem-determination and monitoring tool that IBM introduced in DB2 UDB V8.2. DB2 Support may ask you to run db2pd with specific options as part of a problem management request (PMR) problem-determination effort. This tool has replaced the previous db2_call_stack command and is used with the db2cos callout script to collect problem-determination information.

You can use the command's –stack option with a specific process ID to capture the stacks for that ID, or you can use the plural –stacks option to dump the stacks for all processes. Figure 14.14 shows a sample command and its output.

```
c:\db2pd –stack 2632
Command response:
Attempting to dump stack trace for pid 2632.
See current DIAGPATH for trapfile.
```

Figure 14.14: db2pd stack trace command

Stack traces can be useful in providing DB2 Support with a detailed trace of internal DB2 functions in the order in which they were called.

db2pdcfg

The db2pdcfg tool configures the database for problem determination mode. This command should be used in conjunction with DB2 Support to collect or trap specific DB2 problems. You can use the command's –catch option to catch specific DB2 errors or warnings. You can specify this option to catch any SQLCODE, ZRC code, or ECF code and capture the information needed to help solve the problem. You can also use –catch with the db2cos script, which can be called to run any db2pd or OS command. For an example of how to set an error code catch flag to catch –911 SQLCODEs with reason code 68, see Figure 14.15.

```
•   Command: db2pdcfg –catch -911,68 db2cos
•   Output:
Error Catch #2
      Sqlcode:        -911
      ReasonCode:  68
      ZRC:            0
      ECF:            0
      Component ID:       0
      LockName:   Not Set
      LockType:   Not Set
      Current Count:      0
      Max Count:   255
      Bitmap:     0x261
      Action:     Error code catch flag enabled
      Action:     Execute sqllib/db2cos callout script
```

Figure 14.15: db2pdcfg –catch option

You can specify filters for a particular lock type or lock name. The captured data will be in the sqllib/db2dump/db2cos.rpt file. In addition to generating a report, db2pdcfg makes an entry in the db2diag.log file that records the status of the catch flag setting. Figure 14.16 shows a sample db2diag.log entry.

```
2006-09-01-17.49.59.065000-240 I2998718H296     LEVEL: Event
PID   : 220          TID  : 6024      PROC : db2syscs.exe
INSTANCE: DB2             NODE : 000
FUNCTION: DB2 UDB, RAS/PD component, pdErrorCatch, probe:30
START   : Error catch set for sqlCode -911 reasonCode 68
```

Figure 14.16: db2pdcfg –catch db2diag.log setting entry

Once you set an error or errors to catch, the setting remains in effect until it is cleared. You can reset the catch flags as follows:

```
db2pdcfg –catch clear all
```

Again, you generally should use the db2pdcfg command under the direction of DB2 Support.

db2cos

IBM ships the DB2 callout script, db2cos, with DB2. You'll find the script in the sqllib/bin directory on UNIX and Linux and in the $DB2PATH\bin directory on Windows. A default script and template are provided. The default script gives DB2 Support all the data needed to solve routine problems. However, it can be updated to include additional commands determined necessary by DB2 Support or to collect additional data as specified by the user.

The db2 callout script is called when the database manager cannot continue processing due to a panic, trap, segmentation violation, or exception. The script invokes db2pd commands to collect data. When the default script is invoked, it will collect data without using any latches (locks). In a Data Partitioning Feature (DPF) environment, db2cos will be invoked only on the partition encountering the trap. If you need information from other partitions, you can modify the default script to include the db2_all command or the–alldbpartitionnums option of the db2pd command. The types of signals trapped by the db2cos script are also configurable by the db2pdcfg –cos command. The default db2cos script runs when either a panic or a trap occurs. Generated signals will not launch the db2cos script by default.

When called, the db2cos script creates output files in the directory specified by the db2diag database manager configuration parameter setting. The files will be named using the following convention, where *xxx* is the process ID, *yyy* is the thread ID, and *zzz* is the database partition number:

db2cos.*xxxyyy.zzz*

If multiple threads trap, there will be a separate invocation of the db2cos script for each thread. Again, as with most advanced-problem determination output, db2cos output should go to DB2 Support for further analysis.

499

Sending Information to DB2 Support

Introduced in DB2 UDB V8.1, the Problem Analysis and Environment Collection tool, db2support, enables you to provide a "support bundle" to DB2 Support. You can run this command with or without prompting. Figure 14.17 shows a listing that displays the various db2support options.

```
DB2 CLP - DB2COPY1 - db2support -h                              _ 日 X

C:\Documents and Settings\pgunning>db2support -h

Syntax: db2support <output path>  [-f] [-a | -r]  [-d <db name> [-c]] [-m]
                                  [-g] [-h] [-l] [-n <pmr number>]
                                  [-p <password> [-u <user>]] [-q] [-s]
                                  [-v] [-x] [-o <filename>]
                                  [-st <"sql statment">] [-sf <filename>]
                                  [-se <filename>][-cl <level>][-td <delimiter>]

                                  [-cs <cur schema>][-ro] [-co]
                                  [-cd <cur degree>][-ol <opt level>]
                                  [-ra <refresh age>][-fp <func path>]
                                  [-op <opt profile>][-ot <opt tables>]
                                  [-il <isolation level>]

    -f  -flow         Turn off pausing.
    -a  -all_core     Capture all core files
    -c  -connect      Attempt to connect to specified DB (default is no)
    -d  -database     Specify the database name
    -g  -get_dump     Capture all files in dump directory (excluding core)
    -h  -help         Help on what this tool does (display usage info)
    -l  -logs         Capture active logs
    -m  -html         Generate system output in HTML format
    -n  -number       PMR number/identifier for current problem, if known
    -o  -output       Specify the output file name, archived in ZIP format
                      Default file name is db2support.zip
    -p  -password     Connection password to use with -c
    -q  -question_resp Interactive problem analysis mode
    -r  -recent_core  Capture most recent core file (default is no)
    -s  -system_detail Gather detailed hardware and OS info
    -u  -user         User ID to use with the -c option
    -v  -verbose      Verbose output while running
    -x  -xml_generate Produce XML with logic used during -q mode
```

Figure 14.17: db2support options help

To invoke the tool, issue the db2support command from the command line with the desired options specified. Table 14.1 further describes the options available for db2support.

Table 14.1: db2support options	
Option	**Description**
\<output path\>	Specifies the path where the archived library is to be created. This is the directory where user-created files must be placed for inclusion in the archive.
-a or -all_core	Specifies that all core files are to be captured.
–c or –connect	Specifies that an attempt be made to connect to the specified database.
-cd or –curdegree	Specifies the value of the current degree special register to use. The default is the value of the dft_degree database configuration parameter.
-cl or –collect	Specifies the level of performance information to be returned. Valid values are 0 = Collects only catalogs, db2look, dbcfg, dbmcfg, db2set 1 = Collects 0 plus exfmt 2 = Collects 1 plus .db2service (this is the default) 3 = Collects 2 plus db2batch
–co	Collects catalogs for all tables in the database. The default is to collect catalog information only for the tables used in a query that has a problem.
–cs or –curschema	Specifies the value of the current schema to use to qualify any unqualified table names in the statement. The default value is the authorization ID of the current session user.
–d *database-name* or –database *database-name*	Specifies the name of the database for which data is being collected.
-f or -flow	Ignores pauses when requests are made for the user to press the **Enter** key to continue. This option is useful when running or calling the db2support tool via a script or some other automated procedure for which unattended execution is desired.

Table 14.1: db2support options (continued)	
Option	**Description**
–fp or –funcpath	Specifies the value of the function path special register to be used to resolve unqualified user-defined functions and types. The default value is "SYSIBM", "SYSFUN", "SYSPROC", X, where X is the value of the USER special register delimited by double quotation marks.
–g or –get_dump	Specifies that all files in a dump directory, excluding core files, are to be captured.
–h or –help	Displays help information. When you use this option, all other options are ignored, and only the help information is displayed.
–il or –isolation	Specifies the isolation level to use to determine how data is locked and isolated from other processes while the data is being accessed. By default, the CURRENT ISOLATION special register is set to blanks.
–l or –logs	Specifies that active logs are to be captured.
–m or –html	Specifies that all system output is dumped into HTML formatted files. If this parameter is not used, all system-related information is dumped into flat text files.
–n or –number	Specifies the problem management (PMR) number or identifier for the current problem.
–ol or –optlevel	Specifies the value of the optimization profile special register to use. The default is the value of the dft_queryopt database configuration parameter.
–op or –optprofile	Specifies the value of the optimization profile special register to use. You need to specify this option only if an optimization profile was in effect when the statement was bound. The default is "" (an empty string).
-ot or –opttables	Specifies the value of the CURRENT MAINTAINED TABLE TYPES FOR OPTIMIZATION special register, which is used to identify the types of tables the optimizer can consider when optimizing the processing of dynamic SQL queries. "SYSTEM" is the initial value of the special register.

Table 14.1: db2support options (continued)	
Option	**Description**
–p *password* or –password *password*	Specifies the password for the user ID.
–q or –question_response	Specifies that interactive problem analysis mode is to be used.
–r or –recent_core	Specifies that the most recent core files are to be captured. This option is ignored if you specify the –a option.
-ra or –refreshage	Specifies the value of the refresh age special register. This option applies only materialized query tables (MQTs) reference tables in the statement. The default value of CURRENT REFRESH AGE is 0 (zero).
-ro or –reopt	Specifies whether to use EXPLAIN with REOPT ONCE when explaining the query. The default is to ignore the REOPT ONCE option.
–s or –system_detail	Specifies that detailed hardware and operating system information is to be gathered.
-se *embedded-SQL-file* or –sqlembed *embedded-SQL-file*	Specifies the path of the embedded SQL file containing the SQL statement for which data is being collected.
–sf *SQL-file* or –sqlfile *SQL-file*	Specifies the file path containing the SQL statement for which data is being collected.
–st *SQL-statement* or –sqlstmt *SQL-statement*	Specifies the SQL statement for which data is being collected.
–td or –delimiter	Specifies the statement termination character. This option works the same as the –td option of the db2 command. The default termination character is a semicolon (;).
–u *userid* or –user *userid*	Specifies the user ID to connect to the database.
–v or –verbose	Specifies that verbose output is to be used while the tool is running.
–x or –xml_generate	Specifies that an XML document containing the entire decision-tree logic used during the interactive problem analysis mode (–q mode) be generated.

Depending on the selected options, the db2support tool will build a support bundle in a compressed format consisting of the following files:

- Core files
- Database manager and database configuration files
- db2diag.log file
- Trap files
- Operating system environment information
- Buffer pool and table space information
- Active logs
- Recovery history file
- Log control file
- DB2CLI.INI file
- Database directory
- Node directory
- Node backup directory
- Archive log
- JDK level
- DB2 release information
- Table space history recovery file
- Disk, CPU, and memory configuration

Upon completion of running db2support, which can include the PMR number as an option, you can send the output to DB2 Support for analysis and further problem determination. The default output file is db2support.zip. You can provide your own file name by specifying the –o option with an output file name.

db2support Examples

You should familiarize yourself with db2support because this is the primary problem-determination tool you'll use to gather and send problem-determination data to DB2 Support. The following sample db2support commands illustrate use of this tool.

The first example contains command options for a common invocation of db2support that is usually sufficient to collect most of the information DB2 Support needs to debug a problem:

```
db2support <output path> -d <database name> -c
```

The next example shows how to collect optimizer data by using the –st option:

```
db2support –d sample –st "select * from staff"
```

To read an SQL statement in from a file:

```
db2support –d sample –sf badquery.sql
```

To read in embedded static SQL from a C program:

```
db2support –d sample –se badquery.sqc
```

Summary

This chapter focused on problem determination, highlighting troubleshooting methods and the associated problem-determination aids, files, and tools available to help you resolve DB2 problems. The Information Center is the primary resource to use when analyzing return codes and error messages.

We discussed various traces that can help you identify and solve problems, and you learned how to interpret the db2diag.log and administration notification log entries. The importance of monitoring db2diag.log was emphasized. I recommend keeping copies of your db2diag.log files to assist in problem determination and for historical trending analysis.

Before concluding, we examined some advanced problem-determination tools, such as db2xprt, db2pd, and db2pdcfg. Last, you learned how to use db2support, a command that is particularly useful for gathering all available diagnostic and environmental information into a format you can easily send to IBM DB2 Support for use when investigating a problem.

DB2 Information Sources on the Web

This appendix lists DB2 for Linux, UNIX, and Windows information sources that you may find helpful as you work with and support DB2 9 databases. It serves as a quick reference for new or existing DB2 developers and DBAs.

DB2 9 Home Page
ibm.com/software/data/db2/9

IBM Information Management Training (certification, training, retail books, offers, and more)
ibm.com/software/data/education

DB2 9 Information Center
publib.boulder.ibm.com/infocenter/db2luw/v9/index.jsp

DB2 9 Support Home Page
ibm.com/software/data/db2/support/db2_9

DB2 9 Manuals and Documentation
ibm.com/support/docview.wss?rs=71&uid=swg27009474

The DB2ZONE
gunningts.com/db2zone

Blog on DB2 LUW
blogs.ittoolbox.com/database/db2luw

International DB2 User's Group (IDUG)
idug.org

International DB2 Users Group (IDUG) DB2-L Listserver
idugdb2-l.org

IBM developerWorks
ibm.com/developerworks/db2
ibm.com/developerworks/rational
ibm.com/developerworks/webservices
ibm.com/developerworks/websphere/
ibm.com/developerworks/xml

LAZYDBA Listserver
lazydba.com

comp.databases.ibm-db2 Google Newsgroup
groups.google.ca/group/comp.databases.ibm-db2/about

IBM Redbooks
www.redbooks.ibm.com

Planet DB2 (a blog aggregator that combines DB2 blogs from around the world)
planetdb2.com

DB2 Magazine Online
db2mag.com

B

SQL and XQuery Limits

This appendix on DB2 limits contains a quick reference for information often sought after by DBAs and application developers alike on architectural limits in DB2. The appendix provides limit definitions in the following areas:

- Identifier length limits
- Numeric limits
- String limits
- XML limits
- Date/time limits
- Database manager limits
- Database manager page-size–specific limits

By developing applications within these limits, you will enable applications to be easily portable across the DB2 family.

The following limit information is taken from Appendix A of IBM's *DB2 9 SQL Reference, Volume 1*, and is used with permission.

Identifier Length Limits	
Description	**Limit (in bytes)**
Authorization name (can be single-byte characters only)	30
Constraint name	18
Correlation name	128
Cursor name	18
Data partition name	128
Data source name	128
External program name	8
Function mapping name	128
Host identifier[1]	255
Identifier for a data source user (*remote-authorization-name*)	30
Identifier in an SQL procedure (condition name, for loop identifier, label, result set locator, statement name, variable name)	128
Label name	128
Namespace uniform resource identifier (URI)	1000
Package version ID	64
Parameter name	128
Password to access a data source	32
Savepoint name	128
Security label component name	128
Security label name	128
Security policy name	128
Server (database alias) name	8
SQL condition name	128
SQL schema name[2]	30
SQL variable name	18
Statement name	18
Transform group name	18

Identifier Length Limits (continued)	
Description	**Limit (in bytes)**
Type mapping name	18
Unqualified alias name, function name, index name, method name, nickname, procedure name, sequence name, specific name, table name, or view name	128
Unqualified buffer pool name, database partition group name, table space name, trigger name, or type name	18
Unqualified column name	30
Unqualified data source column name	255
Unqualified data source index name	128
Unqualified data source table name (*remote-table-name*)	128
Unqualified package name	8
Wrapper name	128
XML element name, attribute name, or prefix name	1000
XML schema location URI	1000

Notes:

1. Individual host language compilers may impose a more restrictive limit on variable names.

2. The SQL schema name for a user-defined type is limited to 8 bytes.

Numeric Limits	
Description	**Limit**
Smallest SMALLINT value	–32 768
Largest SMALLINT value	+32 767
Smallest INTEGER value	–2 147 483 648
Largest INTEGER value	+2 147 483 647
Smallest BIGINT value	–9 223 372 036 854 775 808
Largest BIGINT value	+9 223 372 036 854 775 807
Largest decimal precision	31
Smallest DOUBLE value	–1.79769E+308

Numeric Limits (continued)	
Description	**Limit**
Largest DOUBLE value	+1.79769E+308
Smallest positive DOUBLE value	+2.225E-307
Largest negative DOUBLE value	−2.225E-307
Smallest REAL value	−3.402E+38
Largest REAL value	+3.402E+38
Smallest positive REAL value	+1.175E-37
Largest negative REAL value	−1.175E-37

String Limits	
Description	**Limit**
Maximum length of CHAR (in bytes)	254
Maximum length of VARCHAR (in bytes)	32 672
Maximum length of LONG VARCHAR (in bytes)	32 700
Maximum length of CLOB (in bytes)	2 147 483 647
Maximum length of serialized XML (in bytes)	2 147 483 647
Maximum length of GRAPHIC (in double-byte characters)	127
Maximum length of VARGRAPHIC (in double-byte characters)	16 336
Maximum length of LONG VARGRAPHIC (in double-byte characters)	16 350
Maximum length of DBCLOB (in double-byte characters)	1 073 741 823
Maximum length of BLOB (in bytes)	2 147 483 647
Maximum length of character constant	32 672
Maximum length of graphic constant	16 336
Maximum length of concatenated character string	2 147 483 647
Maximum length of concatenated graphic string	1 073 741 823
Maximum length of concatenated binary string	2 147 483 647
Maximum length of hexadecimal constant digits	32 672
Largest instance of a structured type column object at run time (in gigabytes)	1
Maximum size of a catalog comment (in bytes)	254

XML Limits	
Description	**Limit**
Maximum depth of an XML document (in levels)	125
Maximum size of an XML schema document (in bytes)	31 457 280

Date/Time Limits	
Description	**Limit**
Smallest DATE value	0001-01-01
Largest DATE value	9999-12-31
Smallest TIME value	00:00:00
Largest TIME value	24:00:00
Smallest TIMESTAMP value	0001-01-01-00.00.00.000000
Largest TIMESTAMP value	9999-12-31-24.00.00.000000

Database Manager Limits	
Description	**Limit**
Maximum number of columns in a table[7]	1012
Maximum number of columns in a view[1]	5000
Maximum number of columns in a data source table or view that is referenced by a nickname	5000
Maximum number of columns in a distribution key[5]	500
Maximum number of rows including all overhead[2, 7]	32 677
Maximum number of rows in a non-partitioned table, per database partition	128×10^{10}
Maximum number of rows in a data partition, per database partition	128×10^{10}
Maximum size of a table per database partition in a regular table space (in gigabytes)[3, 7]	512
Maximum size of a table per database partition in a large DMS table space (in gigabytes)[7]	16 384
Maximum number of data partitions for a single table	32 767
Maximum number of table partitioning columns	16

Database Manager Limits (continued)	
Constraints	
Maximum number of constraints on a table	Storage
Maximum number of columns in a UNIQUE constraint (supported through a UNIQUE index)	64
Maximum combined length of columns in a UNIQUE constraint (supported through a UNIQUE index, in bytes)[9]	8192
Maximum number of referencing columns in a foreign key	64
Maximum combined length of referencing columns in a foreign key (in bytes)[9]	8192
Maximum length of a check constraint specification (in bytes)	65 535
Triggers	
Maximum runtime depth of cascading triggers	16
User-defined types	
Maximum number of attributes in a structured type	4082
Indexes	
Maximum number of indexes on a table	32 767 or storage
Maximum number of columns in an index key	64
Maximum length of an index key including all overhead[7, 9]	*Indexpagesize*/4
Maximum length of a variable index key part (in bytes)[8]	1022 or storage
Maximum size of an index per database partition in an SMS table space (in gigabytes)[7]	16 384
Maximum size of an index per database partition in a regular DMS table space (in gigabytes)[7]	512
Maximum size of an index per database partition in a large DMS table space (in gigabytes)[7]	16 384
Maximum size of an index over XML data per database partition (in terabytes)	2
Maximum length of a variable index key part for an index over XML data (in bytes)[7]	*Pagesize*/4 − 207
SQL	
Maximum total length of an SQL statement (in bytes)	2 097 152
Maximum number of tables referenced in an SQL statement or a view	Storage

Database Manager Limits (continued)	
Maximum number of host variable references in an SQL statement	32 767
Maximum number of constants in a statement	Storage
Maximum number of elements in a select list[7]	1012
Maximum number of predicates in a WHERE or HAVING clause	Storage
Maximum number of columns in a GROUP BY clause	1012
Maximum total length of columns in a GROUP BY clause (in bytes)	32 677
Maximum number of columns in an ORDER BY clause	1012
Maximum total length of columns in an ORDER BY clause (in bytes)	32 677
Maximum level of subquery nesting	Storage
Maximum number of subqueries in a single statement	Storage
Maximum number of values in an insert operation	1012
Maximum number of SET clause in a single update operation	1012
Routines	
Maximum number of parameters in a procedure	32 767
Maximum number of parameters in a user-defined function	90
Maximum number of nested levels for routines	64
Applications	
Maximum number of host variable declarations in a precompiled program[3]	Storage
Maximum length of a host variable value (in bytes)	2 147 483 647
Maximum number of declared cursors in a program	Storage
Maximum number of rows changed in a unit of work	Storage
Maximum number of cursors opened at one time	Storage
Maximum number of connections per process within a DB2 client	512
Maximum number of simultaneously opened LOB locators in a transaction	32 100
Maximum size of an SQLDA (in bytes)	Storage
Maximum number of prepared statements	Storage
Concurrency	
Maximum number of concurrent users of a server[4]	64 000
Maximum number of concurrent uses per instance	64 000

Database Manager Limits (continued)	
Maximum number of concurrent applications per database	60 000
Maximum number of databases per instance concurrently in use	256
Monitoring	
Maximum number of simultaneously active event monitors	32
Security	
Maximum number of elements in a security label component of type set or tree	64
Maximum number of elements in a security label component of type array	65 535
Maximum number of security label components in a security policy	16
Databases	
Maximum database partition number	999
Table spaces	
Maximum number of table spaces in a database	32 768
Maximum number of tables in an SMS table space	65 534
Maximum size of a regular DMS table space (in gigabytes)[3]	512
Maximum size of a large DMS table space (in terabytes)[3, 7]	16
Maximum size of a temporary DMS table space (in terabytes)[3]	16
Maximum number of table objects in a DMS table space[6]	51 000
Maximum number of storage paths in an automatic storage database	128
Maximum length of a storage path that is associated with an automatic storage database (in bytes)	175
Buffer pools	
Maximum NPAGES in a buffer pool for 32-bit releases	1 048 576
Maximum NPAGES in a buffer pool for 64-bit releases	2 147 483 647
Maximum total size of all buffer pool slots (4K)	2 147 483 646

Notes:

1. This maximum can be achieved using a join in the CREATE VIEW statement. Selecting from such a view is subject to the limit of most elements in a select list.

2. This count does not include the actual data for BLOB, CLOB, LONG VARCHAR, DBCLOB, and LONG VARGRAPHIC columns. However, information about the location of that data does take up some space in the row.

3. The numbers shown are architectural limits and approximations. The practical limits may be less.

4. The actual value will be the value of the MAXAGENTS configuration parameter.

5. This limit is an architectural one. The limit on the most columns in an index key should be used as the practical limit.

6. Table objects include data, indexes, LONG VARCHAR or VARGRAPHIC columns, and LOB columns. Table objects that are in the same table space as the table data do not count extra toward the limit. However, each table object that is in a different table space from the table data does contribute one toward the limit for each table object type per table in the table space in which the table object resides.

7. For page-size–specific values, see the "Database Manager Page-Size–Specific Limits" table, below.

8. This length is limited only by the longest index key, including all overhead (in bytes). As the number of index key parts increases, the maximum length of each key part decreases.

9. The maximum may be less, depending on index options.

Database Manager Page-Size–Specific Limits				
Description	4K page size limit	8K page size limit	16K page size limit	32K page size limit
Maximum number of columns in a table	500	1012	1012	1012
Maximum length of a row including all overhead	4005	8101	16,293	32,677

Database Manager Page-Size–Specific Limits (continued)				
Description	4K page size limit	8K page size limit	16K page size limit	32K page size limit
Maximum size of a table per database partition in a regular table space (in gigabytes)	64	128	256	512
Maximum size of a table per database partition in a large DMS	2048	4096	8192	16,384
Maximum length of an index key including all overhead (in bytes)	1024	2048	4096	8192
Maximum size of an index per database partition in an SMS table space (in gigabytes)	2048	4096	8192	16,384
Maximum size of an index per database partition in a regular DMS table space (in gigabytes)	64	128	256	512
Maximum size of an index per database partition in a large DMS table space (in gigabytes)	2048	4096	8192	16,384
Maximum size of an index over XML data per databasepartition (in terabytes)	2	2	2	2
Maximum size of a regular DMS table space (in gigabytes)	64	128	256	512
Maximum size of a large DMS table space (in gigabytes)	2048	4096	8192	16,384

Database Manager Page-Size–Specific Limits (continued)				
Description	**4K page size limit**	**8K page size limit**	**16K page size limit**	**32K page size limit**
Maximum number of elements in a select list	500	1012	1012	1012
Maximum number of columns in a GROUP BY clause	500	1012	1012	1012
Maximum total length of columns in a GROUP BY clause (in bytes)	4005	8101	16,293	32,677
Maximum number of columns in an ORDER BY clause	500	1012	1012	1012
Maximum total length of columns in an ORDER BY clause (in bytes)	4005	8101	16,293	32,677
Maximum number of values in an insert operation	500	1012	1012	1012
Maximum number of SET clauses in a single update operation	500	1012	1012	1012

C

New Environment Variables in DB2 9

This appendix provides information about five environment variables that are new in DB2 9. For complete details about all the DB2 registry and environmental variables, refer to the IBM documentation at *http://publib.boulder.ibm.com/infocenter/db2luw/v9/index.jsp?topic=/com. ibm.db2.udb.admin.doc/doc/c0007340.htm.* You can use that information and the descriptions here (which are taken from that source) to ensure that the systems you support are optimally configured.

Four variables have been deprecated and discontinued in DB2 9:

- DB2_FORCE_FCM_BP (AIX)
- DB2_LGPAGE_BP
- DB2LINUXAIO
- DB2_SCATTERED_IO

In addition, the following variables have been changed in DB2 9 (refer to the online documentation for details):

- DB2_LARGE_PAGE_MEM
- DB2_MEM_TUNING_RANGE (AIX and Windows)
- DB2_PINNED_BP (AIX, HP-UX, Linux)

New DB2 9 Environmental Variables

The following five environment variables are new in DB2 9:

- DB2_COPY_NAME
- DB2RCMD_LEGACY-MODE
- DB2_OPT_MAX_TEMP_SIZE
- DB2_ENABLE_AUTOCONFIG_DEFAULT
- DB2_MAX-LOB_BLOCK_SIZE

DB2_COPY_NAME

DB2_COPY_NAME is a system environment variable on Windows operating systems. The variable stores the name of the copy of DB2 currently in use. If you have multiple DB2 copies installed on your machine, you cannot use DB2_COPY_NAME to switch to a different copy of DB2. To change the copy currently in use, you must run the following command:

```
[INSTALLPATH]\bin\db2envars.bat
```

The default value of DB2_COPY_NAME is the name of the default copy of DB2 installed on your machine.

DB2RCMD_LEGACY_MODE

DB2RCMD_LEGACY_MODE is a system environment variable on Windows operating systems. This variable lets users enable or disable the DB2 Remote Command Service's enhanced security.

To run the DB2 Remote Command Service in a secure manner, set DB2RCMD_LEGACY_MODE to NO, OFF, FALSE, 0, or null. (The secure mode is available only if your domain controller is running Windows 2000 or later.) To run in legacy mode (without enhanced security), set DB2RCMD_LEGACY_MODE to YES, ON, TRUE, or 1.

> **Note:** If DB2RCMD_LEGACY_MODE is set to NO, OFF, FALSE, or 0, you must have SYSADM authority to have the DB2 Remote Command Service execute commands on your behalf.

> **Note:** If DB2RCMD_LEGACY_MODE is set to YES, ON, TRUE, or 1, all requests sent to the DB2 Remote Command Service are processed under the context of the requestor. To facilitate this functionality, you must allow either or both the machine and service logon accounts to impersonate the client by enabling these accounts at the domain controller.

DB2_OPT_MAX_TEMP_SIZE

The query compiler variable DB2_OPT_MAX_TEMP_SIZE specifies the amount of space (in megabytes) that can be used by a query in all temporary table spaces. The default value is null.

Setting DB2_OPT_MAX_TEMP_SIZE can cause the optimizer to choose an access plan that uses less space in the temporary table spaces but is more expensive than what would normally be chosen. If you set this variable, be sure to balance your need to limit use of temporary table space against the efficiency of the plan that your setting causes to be chosen.

If you run a query that uses temporary table space in excess of the value set for DB2_OPT_MAX_TEMP_SIZE, the query does not fail, but you receive a warning that its performance may be suboptimal because not all resources may be available.

The following operations considered by the optimizer are affected by the limit set by DB2_OPT_MAX_TEMP_SIZE:

- Explicit sorts for operations such as ORDER BY, DISTINCT, GROUP BY, merge scan joins, and nested loop joins
- Explicit temporary tables
- Implicit temporary tables for hash joins and duplicate merge joins

DB2_ENABLE_AUTOCONFIG_DEFAULT

The DB2_ENABLE_AUTOCONFIG_DEFAULT variable controls whether the Configuration Advisor is run automatically at database creation. If DB2_ENABLE_AUTOCONFIG_DEFAULT is not set (i.e., is null, the default value), the effect is the same as if you set the variable to YES, and the Configuration Advisor is run at database creation. You don't need to restart the instance after setting this variable. The AUTOCONFIGURE command and the command CREATE DB AUTOCONFIGURE override the setting of DB2_ENABLE_AUTOCONFIG_DEFAULT.

DB2_MAX_LOB_BLOCK_SIZE

Variable DB2_MAX_LOB_BLOCK_SIZE sets the maximum amount of large object (LOB) or XML data to be returned in a block. This setting is not a hard maximum; if the value is reached on the server during data retrieval, the server finishes writing out the current row before generating a reply for the command (e.g., FETCH) to the client. Valid values are 0 to 21487483647; the default is 0 (no limit).

Index

NOTE: Boldface numbers indicate illustrations; italic t indicates a table

More DB2 Books from MC Press

DB2 9 Fundamentals Certification Study Guide
ISBN: 978-158347-072-5
Author: Roger E. Sanders
http://www.mc-store.com/5088

DB2 9 Linux, UNIX, and Windows Database Adminstrator Certification Study Guide
ISBN: 978-158347-077-8
Author: Roger E. Sanders
http://www.mc-store.com/5090

DB2 9 for z/OS Database Adminstrator Certification Study Guide
ISBN: 978-158347-074-9
Authors: Susan Lawson and Dan Luksetich
http://www.mc-store.com/5089
Available: November 2007

DB2 9 for Linux, UNIX, and Windows Advanced Database Administrator Certification Study Guide
ISBN: 978-158347-080-0
Authors: Roger Sanders and Dwaine Snow
http://www.mc-store.com/5093
Available: May 2008

DB2 9 for Developers
ISBN: 978-158347-071-8
Author: Philip K. Gunning
http://www.mc-store.com/5086
Available: January 2008

MC|PRESS*online*

YOUR SOURCE FOR EVERYTHING IT

- Technical and Thought-leadership Articles

- Daily/weekly/semi-monthly newsletters

- Industry-leadng columnists

- Forums

- Blogs

- Industry News

- Resource Directory

- Industry Event Calendar

- White Papers, Webcasts, Trial Software

- and more...

Visit us at *www.mcpressonline.com* today!

See Our Full Line of IT Books and Training Materials at mc-store.com

Choose from a wide variety of topics, including

- Security
- IT Management
- DB2
- IBM System i
- IBM WebSphere
- RPG
- Java and JavaScript
- SOA

...and many more.

MC PRESS

mcpressonline.com ~ mc-store.com